PENGUIN HANDE

The Penguin Guide to Me

Richard Barber lives near Woodbridge in Suffolk. He divides
his time between his own writing and managing a publishing
firm, Boydell and Brewer Ltd, which he helped to found in
1969. His books include three on the Arthurian legends, *Arthur
of Albion* (revised as *King Arthur in Legend and History*), *The
Figure of Arthur* and *The Arthurian Legends: An Illustrated
Anthology*. He has written on other subjects: *Henry Plantagenet,
The Knight and Chivalry* and *Edward Prince of Wales and
Aquitaine*, a biography of the Black Prince. He has also written
Samuel Pepys Esq (linked to the National Portrait Gallery's
1968 Pepys exhibition), *A Dictionary of Fabulous Beasts*, and
The Companion Guide to South West France, which covers the
scene of much of the Black Prince's career. He has written
three children's books: *A Strong Land and a Sturdy*, on Britain
in the Middle Ages, *Tournaments*, which won a *Times
Educational Supplement* Information Book Award, and *A
Companion to World Mythology*. He has edited *The Pastons: A
Family in the Wars of the Roses* for Penguin.

Richard Barber

The Penguin Guide to Medieval Europe

Penguin Books

PENGUIN BOOKS

Published by the Penguin Group
27 Wrights Lane, London w8 5tz, England
Viking Penguin Inc., 40 West 23rd Street, New York, New York 10010, USA
Penguin Books Australia Ltd, Ringwood, Victoria, Australia
Penguin Books Canada Ltd, 2801 John Street, Markham, Ontario, Canada L3R 1B4
Penguin Books (NZ) Ltd, 182–190 Wairau Road, Auckland 10, New Zealand

Penguin Books Ltd, Registered Offices: Harmondsworth, Middlesex, England

First published 1984
5 7 9 10 8 6 4

Copyright © Richard Barber, 1984
Maps copyright © Reg Piggott, 1984
Calligraphy copyright © Nancy Winters, 1984
All rights reserved

Made and printed in Great Britain by
Richard Clay Ltd, Bungay, Suffolk

Contents

PART TWO:
EMPIRE AND NATIONS

PART THREE:
LORDS, PRINCES AND VASSALS

PART FOUR:
THE WORLD OF LEARNING

List of Illustrations

Maps

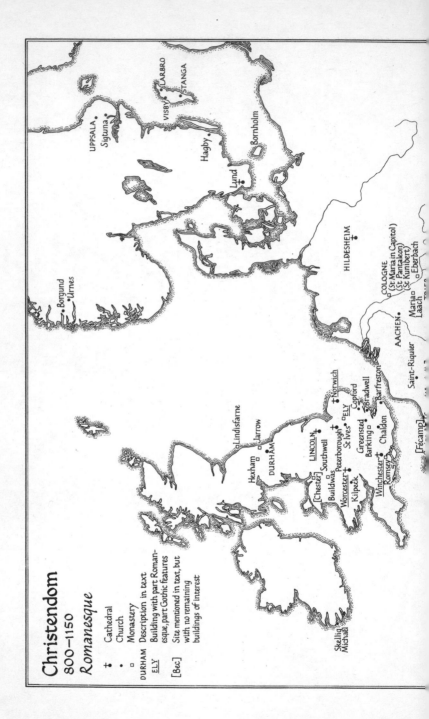

Christendom
800-1150
Romanesque

† Cathedral
• Church
□ Monastery

DURHAM Description in text
ELY Building with part Romanesque, part Gothic features
[Bec] Site mentioned in text, but
with no remaining
buildings of interest

UPPSALA
• Siguna

Borgund •
• Urnes

VISBY •LARBRO
• •STANGA
Hagby
• Bornholm
Lund †

HILDESHEIM †

COLOGNE
(St Maria in Capitol)
(St Pantaleon)
(St Kunibert)
Maria • • Eberbach
Laach
AACHEN

Saint-Riquier •

†Norwich
Copford
•Bradwell
•Barfreston
□ELY
Greensted • •Chaldon
St Ives• †
Barking □ •
Winchester † †Romsey
[Fécamp]

•Lindisfarne
Hexham □ •Jarrow
DURHAM •

LINCOLN †
[Chester] □ Southwell
Buildwas
Worcester † •Kilpeck
Peterborough †

Skellig
Michael

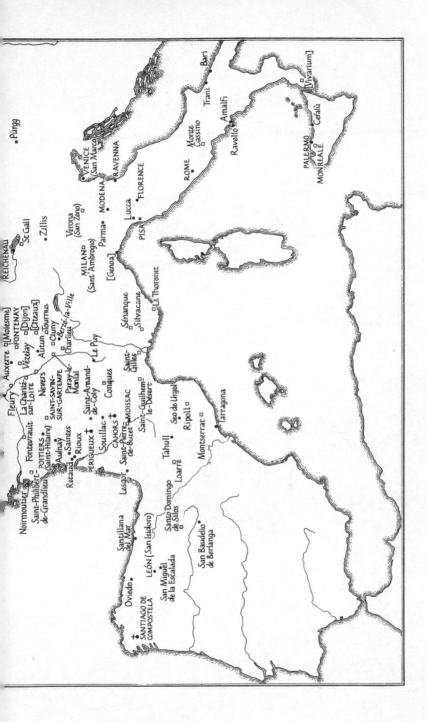

Pürgg

[REICHENAU]

St. Gall

Zillis

Bari

Trani

Amalfi

Monte Cassino

Ravello

Cefalù

PALERMO

MONREALE

ROME

VENICE (San Marco)

RAVENNA

Verona (San Zeno)

MODENA

Lucca

FLORENCE

Parma

PISA

MILAN (Sant'Ambrogio)

[Genoa]

Le Thoronet

Sénanque

Silvacane

[Molesme]

FONTENAY

Auxerre

Vézelay

[Dijon]

[Cîteaux]

Fleury

La Charité-sur-Loire

Autun

Tournus

Cluny

Berzé-la-Ville

Charlieu

Nevers

SAINT-SAVIN-SUR-GARTEMPE

Parayle-Monial

Le Puy

Saint-Amand-de-Coly

Conques

Saint-Gilles

Saint-Guilhem-le-Désert

Seo de Urgel

Ripoll

Tarragona

POITIERS (Saint-Hilaire)

Aulnay

Saintes

Rioux

Retaud

PÉRIGUEUX

Souillac

CAHORS

MOISSAC

Saint-Pierre-de-Buzet

Lescar

Tahull

Montserrat

Loarre

Fontevrault

Saint-Philibert-de-Grandlieu

Noirmoutier

Santillana del Mar

LEÓN (San Isidoro)

Santo Domingo de Silos

San Baudelio de Berlanga

Oviedo

San Miguel de la Escalada

SANTIAGO DE COMPOSTELA

[Vivarium]

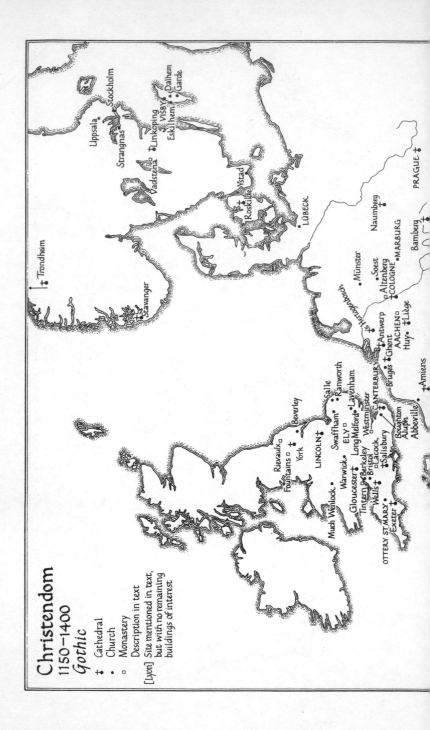

Christendom
1150–1400
Gothic

† Cathedral
• Church
▢ Monastery
[Lyon] Site mentioned in text,
  but with no remaining
  buildings of interest

Trondheim †

Stavanger •

Uppsala •
Stockholm •
Strangnas
Linköping †
Vadstena ▢
Eskilhem •
Visby •
Dalhem •
Garde •

Ystad •
Roskilde †

LÜBECK •

Naumberg •
Soest •
Münster •
Altenberg •
MARBURG •
COLOGNE †
Bamberg •
PRAGUE †

Hertogenbosch ▢
Antwerp •
AACHEN ▢
Huy • † Liège
Ghent †
Bruges •
Amiens †
Abbeville •

Rievaulx ▢
Fountains †
Beverley •
York •
LINCOLN †
Salle •
Ranworth •
Swaffham •
ELY ▢
Long Melford • Lavenham •
Warwick •
Much Wenlock •
Gloucester †
Tintern ▢
Berkeley •
Bristol •
Lacock ▢
Wells •
Salisbury †
OTTERY ST MARY •
Exeter †
Westminster †
CANTERBURY †
Boughton
Aluph •

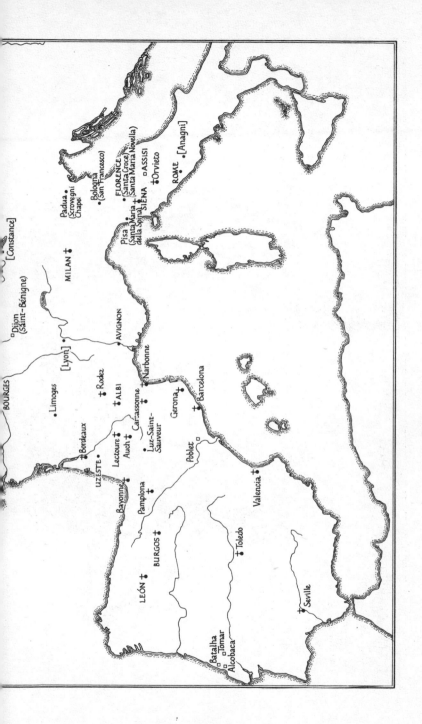

[Constance]

□ Dijon
(Saint-Bénigne)

BOURGES

• Limoges

[Lyon]

† Rodez

† ALBI

Narbonne

MILAN †

AVIGNON •

• Bordeaux

† UZESTE

† Lectoure
† Auch

Carcassonne †

Luz-Saint-
Sauveur

† Gerona

Barcelona •

Bayonne †

Pamplona †

Poblet □

BURGOS †

Valencia †

LEÓN †

† Toledo

Batalha □
□ Tomar
Alcobaça □

† Seville

Padua •
(Scrovegni
Chapel)

Bologna •
(San Francesco)

FLORENCE •
(Santa Croce)
(Santa Maria Novella)

Pisa •
(Santa Maria
della Spina)

□ ASSISI

SIENA †

□ Orvieto

ROME • [Anagni]

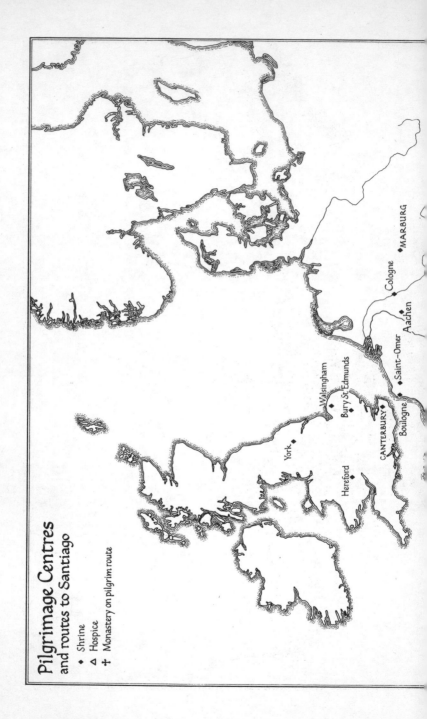

Pilgrimage Centres
and routes to Santiago

◆ Shrine
△ Hospice
✝ Monastery on pilgrim route

York ◆

Hereford ◆

Walsingham ◆

Bury St Edmunds ◆

CANTERBURY ◆

Boulogne ◆

Saint-Omer ◆

Aachen ◆

Cologne ◆

MARBURG ◆

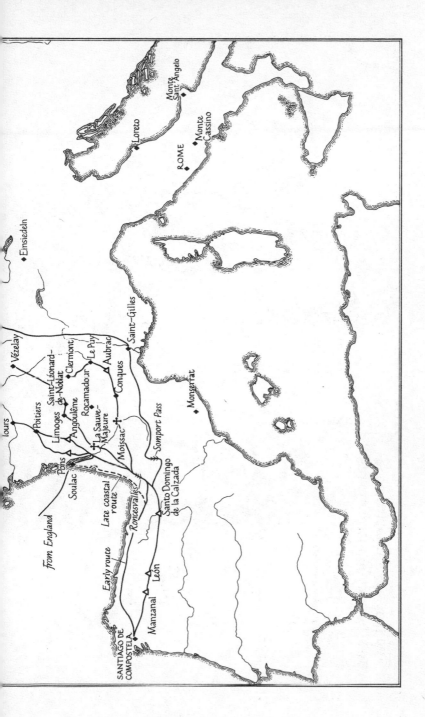

Einsiedeln

Monte
Sant'Angelo

Loreto

Monte
Cassino

ROME

Vézelay

Saint-Léonard-
de-Noblat

Clermont

Le Puy

Aubrac

Saint-Gilles

Poitiers

Limoges

Angoulême

Rocamadour

Conques

La Sauve-
Majeure

Monserrat

Tours

Pons

Moissac

Somport Pass

Soulac

Santo Domingo
de la Calzada

from England

Late coastal
route

Roncesvalles

Early route

León

Manzanal

SANTIAGO DE
COMPOSTELA

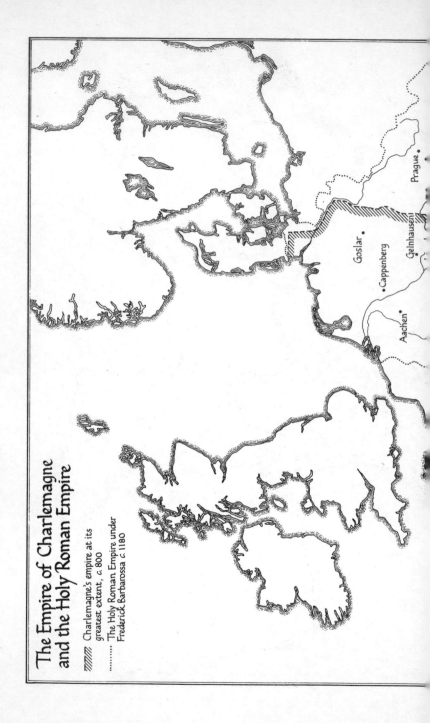

The Empire of Charlemagne and the Holy Roman Empire

///// Charlemagne's empire at its greatest extent, c. 800

.... The Holy Roman Empire under Frederick Barbarossa c. 1180

Goslar

•Cappenberg

•Gelnhausen

Prague•

Aachen•

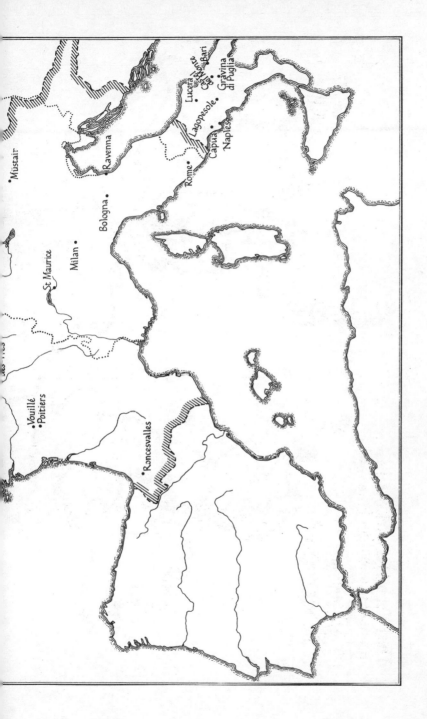

Müstair

Ravenna

Lucera · Bari
Lagopesole · Gravina di Puglia
Capua · Naples

Rome

Bologna ·

Milan ·

St Maurice

Vouillé ·
· Poitiers

Roncesvalles ·

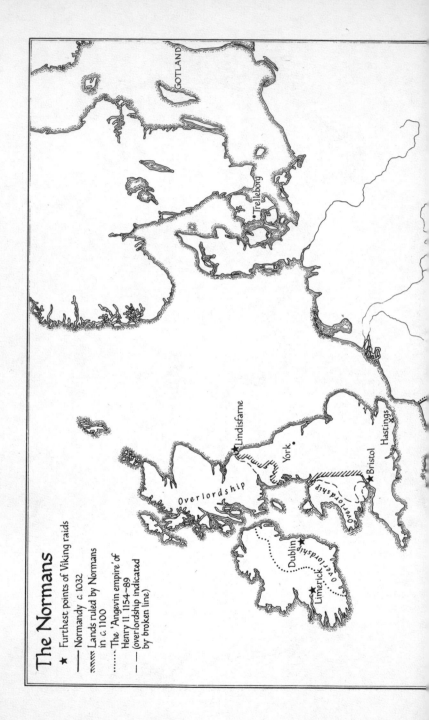

The Normans

★ Furthest points of Viking raids

Normandy c. 1032

〰〰〰 Lands ruled by Normans in c. 1100

.... The 'Angevin empire' of Henry II 1154–89

— — (overlordship indicated by broken line)

GOTLAND

•Trelleborg

Lindisfarne

York •

Overlordship

Overlordship

Bristol ★

Hastings

Dublin ★

Overlordship

Limerick ★

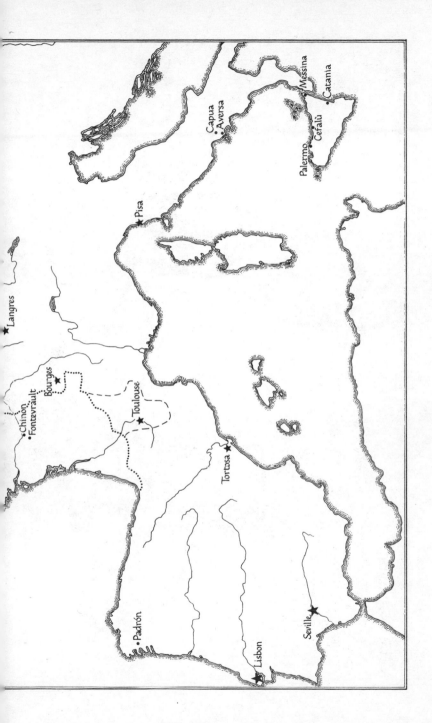

Castles

Marksburg

Ghent

Arques

Newcastle

Scarborough

Tattershall

Orford

Kirby Muxloe

London

Richmond

Rochester

Dover

Flint

Rhuddlan

Conwy

Beaumaris

Caernarvon

Harlech

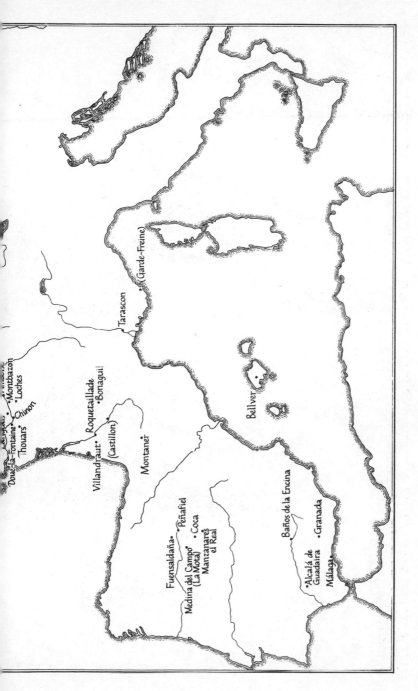

Doué-la-Fontaine •Montbazon
Thouars •Chinon •Loches

Villandraut• •Roquetaillade •Bonaguil
          (Castillon)

Montaner•

Tarascon

(Garde-Freine)

Bellver

Fuensaldaña• •Peñafiel
Medina del Campo• •Coca
   (La Mota) Manzanares
          el Real

Baños de la Encina

•Alcalá de
Guadaira •Granada
Málaga

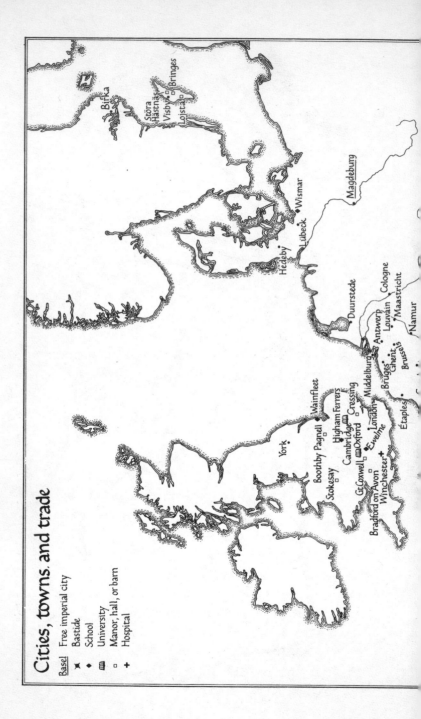

Cities, towns, and trade

<u>Basel</u>   Free imperial city
✖   Bastide
◆   School
🏛   University
□   Manor, hall, or barn
✝   Hospital

Birka

Stóra
Hastnäs

Visby □ □ Bringes
Lojsta □

Wismar

Magdeburg

Hedeby

Lübeck

Duurstede

Antwerp   Cologne
Louvain   Maastricht
Namur

Middelburg

Bruges • Ghent
Brussels

Étaples

Wainfleet

Boothby Pagnell □
Higham Ferrers
Cambridge 🏛 □ Cressing
Stokesay □ Oxford 🏛 □ London
Ewelme •
Gt Coxwell □ Winchester ✝
Bradford on Avon

York

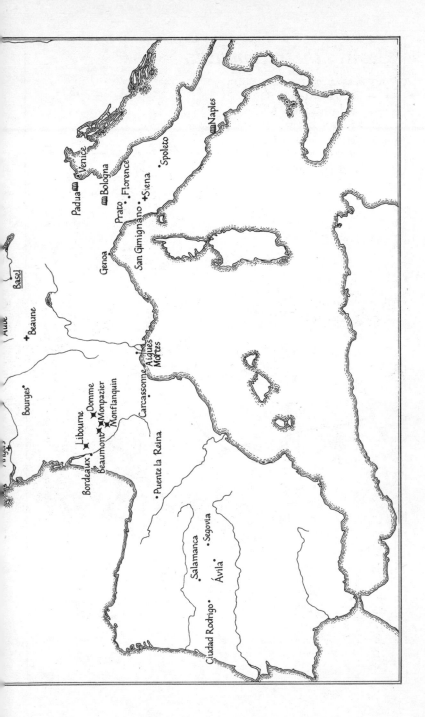

Aube

Basel

Beaune

Bourges

Genoa

Libourne

Bordeaux

Beaumont

Domme

Monpazier

Monflanquin

Carcassonne

Aigues Mortes

Puente la Reina

Ciudad Rodrigo

Salamanca

Segovia

Ávila

Padua

Venice

Bologna

Prato

Florence

Siena

San Gimignano

Spoleto

Naples

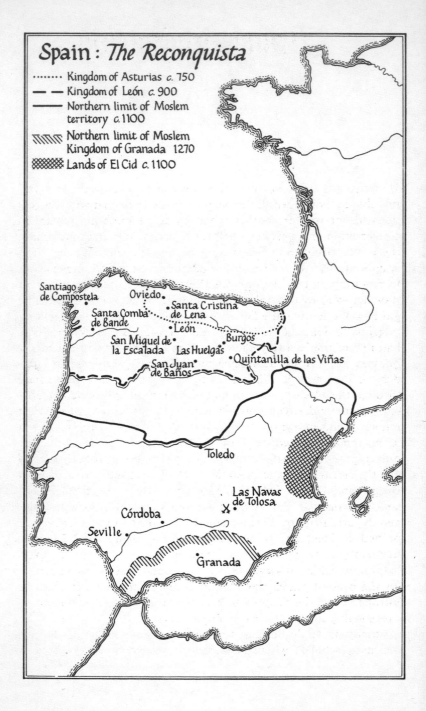

Spain : *The Reconquista*

- ┈┈┈┈ Kingdom of Asturias *c.* 750
- ─ ─ ─ Kingdom of León *c.* 900
- ──── Northern limit of Moslem
  territory *c.* 1100
- ▨▨▨ Northern limit of Moslem
  Kingdom of Granada 1270
- ▨▨▨ Lands of El Cid *c.* 1100

Santiago
de Compostela

Oviedo

Santa Cristina
de Lena

Santa Comba
de Bande

•León

Burgos

San Miguel de
la Escalada

Las Huelgas

Quintanilla de las Viñas

San Juan
de Baños

Toledo

Las Navas
de Tolosa

Córdoba

Seville

Granada

Acknowledgements

In writing a book such as this, over a long period, it is impossible to remember all the people who have helped with suggestions in one way or another, often by an illuminating remark in conversation or by giving a helpful reference. On the other hand, there is no problem in recognizing where my main debts lie. First and foremost, I must thank my companions on various expeditions to far-flung parts of Europe for their patience with an impatient traveller working to a tight schedule: Eric Elstob was an invaluable guide to Gotland, while Derek and Elisabeth Brewer were fellow-pilgrims to Santiago de Compostela on a journey which perforce had few of the leisurely characteristics of a medieval pilgrimage, but was none the less most rewarding. Secondly, I owe a particular debt to Professor R. Allen Brown, who spared the time to read through the whole typescript and made innumerable and valuable corrections and suggestions. Needless to say, any errors which remain – and in a book as wide-ranging as this there are bound to be some – are entirely my own responsibility. Thirdly, the purely practical business of travelling around Europe has been greatly assisted by the hospitality of Olau Lines on a visit to Bruges and Ghent, DFDS Lines on a visit to north Germany and Scandinavia, Townsend Thoresen Lines on a visit to Normandy, and Brittany Ferries, whose Plymouth–Santander service proved an ideal way of reaching northern Spain. Mrs Lucinda Barttelot of the Spanish Government Tourist Office was most helpful in making arrangements for the same visit, no small matter for the present guide, since Spain is one of the few countries in Europe where the visitor can stay in a medieval environment at a reasonable cost, in the excellent *paradors*.

Finally, it would be ungrateful not to acknowledge my debt to the many scholars whose books and monographs I have used. I have not included a bibliography; a selection would be misleading and invidious, while a full list of books used would run into dozens of pages. I must however acknowledge a particular debt to the relevant volumes of the Pelican History of Art series, while in terms of a preliminary visual survey, the volumes illustrated by Wim Swaan and published by Paul Elek on cathedrals, monasteries and castles were invaluable in the early stages of planning this book.

Preface

The Middle Ages are still physically very much in evidence in modern Europe. Even in these days of high-rise buildings, many towns are dominated by a medieval cathedral or castle, and many streets contain medieval buildings which have changed little since they were built. Less immediately obvious are the medieval town plans and road networks, the landscapes and field patterns created by medieval man, which only a trained eye can detect. This book is an attempt to go beyond a mere survey of the obvious physical presences, the tangible ghosts of the past, and to rediscover the spiritual, intellectual and political context in which such buildings were created, so that we can begin to look at Santiago through the eyes of a medieval pilgrim, at Bruges through the eyes of a medieval merchant. It aims to supply the missing dimension of a long-vanished and very different world from our own, a world which is so often absent from the guidebooks which load us energetically with 'real' facts and dates and yet bring us no closer to the true atmosphere of the past. Even so, because this book attempts to encompass a region both rich and vast, there must be crucial elements which cannot be included. Much of what follows is about abstract organizations – 'the church', 'the empire', the feudal 'system' – rather than about real people, though I have tried to place some characters in the context of this rich but lifeless scenery. For the confines of a single book can only suffice as a starting point for voyages of discovery into medieval art, literature and thought. If I have mapped the paths which link Dante's *Divine Comedy* to the ruins of an imperial palace in Germany, or the Bayeux tapestry to the splendours of a Sicilian palace, I will have achieved my purpose.

The book is therefore laid out, not geographically, but by themes. It is a guide to the intellectual and political history of

Europe in the Middle Ages as much as a handbook to some of its surviving physical relics. Limitations of space mean that there are inevitable problems of emphasis; for instance, Romanesque churches on the grand scale are much rarer than their Gothic counterparts, but I have chosen to give equal weight to the two periods at the expense of including some lesser Romanesque architecture in the place of undoubted Gothic masterpieces. Furthermore, the object of this book is not to offer a comprehensive list of the finest examples of, say, Romanesque parish churches or fourteenth-century castles. So please do not turn to the index and complain that this superb example of secular architecture or that great masterpiece of painting is missing. What follows is not intended as a catalogue, but as a portrait or sketch for a portrait, drawn from the surviving images of the medieval world. I have tried to use the painstaking work of historians of art and architecture as a basis for a broader picture of what that world was like, and to show the ways in which we may re-create imaginatively today the atmosphere of Europe in the Middle Ages.

Prologue:
The 'Middle Ages' and 'Europe'

What do we mean by 'Medieval Europe'? The term 'the Middle Ages' is first suggested by the fifteenth-century humanists, who saw a 'middle time' between the end of the Roman empire and their own revival of classical ideals; the phrase 'middle time' first appears in 1468, and 'Middle Ages' in 1518. *Medium aevum*, from which our word medieval derives, is first recorded in 1604, but became the standard phrase only in the late seventeenth century. The concept of a barbarian interval between the decline of classical civilization and its revival was central to the rationalist thinking of the eighteenth century, and the period was now precisely defined: Chambers' Encyclopaedia in 1753 equates the Middle Ages with the centuries between the reign of Constantine and the taking of Constantinople, and the accepted dates soon became from *c.*500 to *c.*1500 AD. 'Medieval', an invented word, is first found a century later. An invented word for an invented period? Most historians would agree. The 'fall' of the Roman empire took centuries; the Renaissance, the supposed rebirth of that same civilization, also took centuries. So for one arbitrary definition, I propose to substitute another, no better, and, I hope, no worse. This book deals with the period from the coronation of Charlemagne to the troubled time at the end of the fourteenth century when the whole of western Europe seemed subject to anarchy and sudden change, and which arguably represents the crucial moment of transition from the old idea of Europe and Christendom as an entity to the modern, narrower ideal of the nation-state. I shall step outside this period on occasion, but for those who like to fasten on to dates and the illusion of precision which they give, 800 AD to 1400 AD is the span of this book.

How then do we define 'Europe'? Here there is a double problem. My basic definition is that of Latin Christendom, the area where the pope's mandate was obeyed. But this takes us to some areas palpably outside Europe, such as Cyprus and the Holy Land, and so over this outline we must lay another, that of western Europe today. This is, after all, in part at least a book for the modern traveller, so I have therefore touched only briefly on the border-lands of medieval Europe, Poland, Hungary and Bohemia. Classic medieval European castles are to be found as far afield as Finland and Syria, but these belong to the history of medieval European colonialism and its *alter ego* the crusades, to the history of the German *Drang nach Osten* and to the French expansion in *Outremer*.

Instead of definitions, perhaps it is better to turn to imaginative visions of Europe. How did medieval writers conceive of Europe? In geographical terms they were perfectly aware that Europe was by no means the whole world. John of Trevisa, translating Bartholomew the Englishman's Latin encyclopaedia in the four-teenth century, says of Europe:

Europe is said to be a third of the whole world, and has its name from Europa, daughter of Agenor, the King of Libya. Jupiter ravished this Europa out of Africa, and brought her to Crete, and called most of the land after her Europa ... Europe begins at the river Tanay and stretches along the Northern Ocean to the end of Spain. The east and south part rises from the sea called Pontus [the Black Sea] and is all joined to the Great Sea [Mediterranean] and ends at the islands of Cadiz [Gibraltar] ... If this part of the world is smaller than Asia, yet it is its equal in number and nobility of men, for as Pliny says, it feeds men who are more huge in body, more strong in might and virtue, more bold of heart, more fair and handsome of shape than men of the countries and lands of Asia and Africa.

This account is based largely on received tradition, the works of classical geographers, rather than on actual travellers' reports. To the medieval mind, tradition carried more weight than observation, and so their image of 'Europe' was a formal, inherited concept only vaguely related to geographical or indeed political realities. It was a scholar's theory rather than an idea common among ordinary people.

Against this, let us set the vision of a modern poet deeply influenced by medieval thought. Charles Williams, in his Arthurian poems, sees Arthur's mission as the resurrection of Christian learning and civilization out of the ruin and waste created by the barbarians – a mission which was indeed accomplished, piecemeal and gradually, by Charlemagne and his successors. In his poem *The Vision of the Empire*, Charles Williams envisages Europe as the figure of a reclining woman: the head is in Britain; the breasts are in France, where Paris provides the milk of learning; in Rome are the hands, symbolized by the pope's gestures as he says mass, 'the heart-breaking manual acts'; in Byzantium – though he does not say so explicitly – the heart; and in Jerusalem, the womb. Beyond, in the unknown regions to east and south, the Antipodes, are the 'feet of clay', the home of chaos and evil.

The image is of course less literal and more complex than I have made it sound; but Williams conveys in it some essential truths. Medieval Europe did indeed see itself as an entity, as Christendom; it recognized an uneasy relationship, therefore, with Byzantium and Jerusalem, both of which were briefly occupied by its armies. But beyond these frontiers lay unknown lands, the *terra incognita* of the map-makers, home of savages and strange monsters. Europe was at the same time both the whole known world, outside which nothing mattered, and also a fortress besieged by half-fabulous hordes of heathen.

PART ONE

CHRISTENDOM

1
𝕲𝕳𝕖 𝕻𝕒𝕡𝕒𝕔𝕪

> And if a man consider the originall of this great Ecclesiasticall Dominion, he will perceive that the *Papacy*, is no other, than the *Ghost* of the Roman Empire, sitting crowned upon the grave thereof.
>
> Thomas Hobbes

It was Christianity that gave medieval Europe its identity and unity: from Iceland to Sicily, from Portugal to Finland, you could go into a church and attend a service in which the ritual and the language were largely the same. The organization of the church was correspondingly vast, an international bureaucracy which ran parallel to the secular government, with its own revenues and courts. It was hardly surprising if the spiritual world seemed remote from the everyday preoccupations of many of the clergy, and yet the church's authority was never seriously challenged during these centuries.

This vast network of power had grown up gradually and often by chance. Although Christianity had become the official religion of the Roman empire only under Theodosius I in 391, it was Christianity that came into much of the inheritance of the emperors. By the end of the fifth century, when the western empire was beginning to crumble before the barbarian onslaughts, Christianity was firmly established throughout Gaul, Spain and Italy; it was perhaps less secure in Britain, where there were some signs of a reversion to paganism. When the secular imperial administration collapsed, its shadow, the church hierarchy, often survived, preserving the old patterns and eventually providing the base for a renewal of government under the barbarian kings. For instance, in Gaul the bishoprics were based on the old Roman centres of administration, the cities; and although there are exceptions – two or three Roman *civitates* which did not become bishoprics, and half a dozen bishoprics centred on towns which had never been cities – the church continued the imperial pattern. Many medieval cathedrals are built on the site of great pagan temples; to take only two examples, the cathedral of Lectoure in south-west France was built on the place where a temple dedicated to Cybele had once stood, whose worshippers were initiated by being drenched in the blood of a slaughtered bull; at Uppsala in Sweden, the temple sacred to the Norse gods, with its grove where nine male victims of every species were sacrificed every ninth year, became the site of the archbishop's cathedral in the eleventh century.

At the centre, in Rome itself, the head of the church inherited imperial titles and ambitions. The pre-eminence of the bishop of Rome as father (*Papa*) of the church was largely brought about by the emperors. Rome, it is true, was the oldest bishopric in the west, tracing its origins back to St Peter. But other apostles had founded other sees in the east, which were of equal seniority: Antioch, which also claimed St Peter as its founder, and Alexandria, which was said to have been founded by Mark. Other churches with less wealth and authority could also lay claim to apostolic foundation: Corinth, Ephesus, Thessalonika, Smyrna, Philippi. But these were not politically influential. As early as the beginning of the third century AD, pope Calixtus I invoked the words of Our Lord to St Peter – 'on this rock I will build my church' – and tried to assert his authority over other churches. His efforts were in vain, and the church remained loosely organized, as a union of independent bodies, during the years of persecution which preceded the first edict of tolerance under Constantine in the early fourth century. Constantine, although he was baptized only on his death-bed and never made his personal position as a Christian clear until that moment, favoured the church and gave freely to it, as did his mother Helena. It was he who gave the Lateran Palace to the bishops of Rome as their official residence, and built the first church in Rome there, using as model the classical public building known as a basilica, a spacious hall with a wooden roof. His dealings with the church seem to have been part of a scheme to use it as a state religion which would bind together the empire: he interfered in matters of purely spiritual importance, condemning one heresy personally at a church council in 316 and attempting to resolve another by his own compromise formula in 325. Constantine wanted a unified church, obedient to the emperor. As part of that policy, he promoted the bishop of Rome's claim to be *Papa* or pope, final arbiter of disputes and ruler of a single church. For Constantine must at least be credited with political foresight: much of the turmoil of the later Roman empire was occasioned by violent theological controversy, over points of belief which were sometimes central and crucial, sometimes unbelievably obscure. These theological controversies spilled over into secular life: the Arian heresy, which Constantine tried to resolve in 325, almost gave rise to a separate and parallel church, at its zenith holding sway in Spain, north Africa and much of Italy, determining the allegiances of kings. Hence a spiritual authority was needed to ensure political harmony.

But Rome was not necessarily the place for that authority. The imperial capital was at Milan from 286 until 402, and the bishopric of that city, particularly under St Ambrose, enjoyed great influence. Constantinople became co-capital in 330, and the empire was formally divided in two halves in 395. In 402 the western capital was moved to Ravenna; in 410 the Goths sacked Rome. Rome, in the early fifth century, was therefore only a provincial city in the western empire. Furthermore, the emperors were trying to make Constantinople a see second only to Rome, and it was the appearance of this dangerous rival that spurred the bishops of Rome into their formal claim for control of the whole church. Their moment of opportunity came under Leo I, in the mid fifth century. With the west in chaos and the east divided by heresies, he boldly claimed the primacy, and the emperor Valentinian III decreed, in 455, that if 'any bishop summoned to trial before the bishop of Rome shall neglect to come', the imperial authorities – such as they were – were to compel him to come. Leo also succeeded in getting his views on church doctrine accepted by the council of Chalcedon in Asia Minor in 451, but the same council also dealt a blow to his ambitions by declaring that the bishop of Constantinople had the same rights in the east as the bishop of Rome in the west. The political division was to be reflected in the organization of the church as well. But in 476 the western empire came to an end, and the Roman Senate recognized the eastern emperor once again.

The reconquest of Italy for the eastern empire under Justinian in the sixth century altered the pope's standing once more. Italy was ruled by the imperial representative, or exarch, from Ravenna, and Justinian himself interfered brutally and directly in the church's affairs. Rome was reduced to a minor bishopric on the edge of the eastern empire; the popes were usually Greek or Syrian. The city was even isolated from Ravenna by the Lombards, who conquered much of northern and central Italy. As a result of this isolation, the pope became the temporal as well as the religious ruler of Rome, and under Gregory I at the end of the sixth century the papacy's lands were reorganized on the lines of a great prince's estate. Gregory also acted as ruler of Rome in the emperor's name, paying armies and making peace treaties with the Lombards. Furthermore, his temporal successes enabled him to lay down the pattern for a church hierarchy which was controlled from the centre, with a clear chain of authority: bishops were to be answerable to archbishops, and archbishops answerable to the pope.

For the next century and a half the uneasy relationship between pope and eastern emperor persisted; when the empire was weak, the papacy gained in independence, at the expense of Rome being exposed to attack. But such attacks grew less likely as the tide of Arianism retreated. By the end of the seventh century the rulers, if not the common people, had returned to Catholicism, and the Lombards in Italy had been converted. The empire, on the other hand, had to face the rise of Moslem power, and had lost Syria and Egypt. At this point the most violent of the many theological controversies of these centuries erupted, when Leo the Isaurian, first of a new dynasty of emperors, banned the worship of images in 726. Popes Gregory II and III both resisted the iconoclasts, or image-breakers, as they were called; and in 733 Leo removed the dioceses of southern Italy and what is now Yugoslavia from the jurisdiction of Rome and transferred them to the see of Constantinople. This was coupled with the confiscation of the pope's estates there, and Rome's spiritual power seemed to be on the verge of collapse.

But the imperial power in the west was also weak in the extreme, and renewed Lombard attacks led to the fall of Ravenna. Rome itself was threatened in 751 and it seemed that the papacy would soon fall under new Lombard masters, who were likely to be as harsh as the emperor. In this extremity, pope Stephen II, a Roman by birth, appealed to Pepin, the ruler of the Frankish kingdom. ntous meeting at Pepin's villa at Ponthion on 6 January igreed to intervene. Furthermore, he agreed to 'restore' extensive lands in Italy which would make the papacy an independent principality. The whole political pattern of the medieval papacy stems from this agreement. The popes became bound to the Frankish royal house, who became their protectors, and they also became lords in central Italy, with secular interests and ambitions there. In theory, none of this need have affected their spiritual standing; in practice, it undoubtedly did. Pepin had reason to favour the church, since he owed his royal title to Stephen's predecessor Zacharias. Pepin, ruler in all but name, had deposed the last of the hereditary Merovingian dynasty, Childeric III. Faced by the problem of legalizing his position he had appealed to the pope, who, drawing on the example of Samuel and David in the Old Testament, had arranged for St Boniface to anoint him as king. Now Pepin repaid the debt by leading his army into Italy in 754 and again in 756. The Lombards were defeated, but the pope did not get the lands he had hoped for. Pepin's son Charles, known to us as Charlemagne, went further and overthrew the Lombard kings, becoming king of the Lombards himself. We shall look at Charlemagne's conquests later; as far as the popes were concerned, they found that they had in him a new Justinian; God had made him 'ruler of the Christian people', and on him depended 'the whole salvation of Christ's Church'. Like Constantine and Justinian before him, he interfered imperiously in church matters; when the iconoclastic dispute was settled in 787 with the approval of pope Hadrian I, Charlemagne summoned a council at Frankfurt to reverse the decision. When, in 795, Hadrian died, a new pope was chosen who was less likely to confront the king. On Christmas Day 800, Charlemagne was crowned emperor by the pope in St Peter's, apparently against his will, though Leo probably intended the gesture as a compliment. For the previous year Leo had been accused of perjury and adultery, and the question of who should judge the pope was brought up. In the event Charlemagne had accepted that no one could judge the pope, and he was allowed to clear himself by swearing an oath. But whatever Leo's motives in crowning Charlemagne, the latter saw that, if he accepted without protest, it would mean that the pope could dispose of the empire as he wished. Hence, when Charlemagne wished to ensure the succession of his son Louis, he crowned Louis himself at Aachen in 813. With hindsight, we can see that the stage was set for one of the central conflicts of medieval Europe: that between the papacy and the empire. The popes, in their most extreme moments, claimed that the emperors were subordinate to them, had their office from them, and could be deposed by them; the emperors retorted that the popes had no secular authority and could only intervene in spiritual affairs.

As Charlemagne's empire dissolved, so the papacy regained its independence. Nicholas I, in the mid ninth century, formulated the ideas about the relationship of papacy and empire which Leo's action had implied, and his successors claimed the right to depose unjust monarchs and to watch over the political actions of the emperors. But these high claims contrasted with a worsening of the situation in Italy; by the end of the ninth century, the popes had become playthings of the local politicians, ruling for a year or two, or no more than a matter of months, before they died, or, in several cases, were murdered. Many were nobles from the ruling families of Rome, and in the early eleventh century the counts of Tusculum nearly succeeded in turning the papacy into a hereditary office; brother succeeded brother; nephew succeeded uncle. It was only when the descendants of Charlemagne, the German sovereigns who ruled over his eastern lands and called themselves Holy Roman emperors, were powerful enough to intervene that the urgently needed reform of the papacy became possible. It was not until 1049, with the appointment by Henry III of Leo IX, a German bishop of noble birth, that the pope was once again a man of moral stature, concerned with spiritual and international affairs rather than mere local feuds. He brought to Rome leaders of the reform movement which had sprung up in France and Germany over the previous century, but which had had no opportunity of influencing the papacy itself until now. And indeed Leo was able to effect his reforms only by keeping his distance from Rome, carrying out his work at gatherings in France and Germany well away from Roman politics. But as the reforms were carried out, so the pope's authority grew once more; and when Gregory VII became pope in 1073, the mood of the papal court had become noticeably more self-confident. The claims made by earlier popes were revived, and the reformers by and large encouraged them, because the empire grew noticeably weaker after Henry III's death and hence less reliable as a source of support for the new ideals. To carry out reforms which often encroached on the interests of secular princes the popes needed secular support; and the weakness of the emperors meant that they turned to the emperor's enemies, among them the

Normans, who had recently established themselves in southern Italy and Sicily. In 1059, the Norman leader swore to uphold a new electoral decree, which meant that in future popes would be elected by the cardinals alone, and the emperor could only veto or affirm such an election. Fourteen years later, when Gregory VII was elected pope, he did not even ask for the emperor's approval, but merely informed him of the decision. Furthermore, the general attitude of the church had now moved to an extreme position: secular interference in the choice of bishops or abbots was decreed to be worthy of excommunication in 1075. This may seem reasonable enough to modern eyes, but bishops and abbots were not merely church officials. By reason of the great estates which the faithful had given to the church, they were great landowners, and as such were responsible for providing men for the king's armies; and they were also important figures in the royal government, often holding high offices such as the chancellorship or head of the royal secretariat. So it was vital to the king's interests that men suitable not only to the church's purposes, but also to his own, were chosen. The involvement of high church dignitaries in secular business was anathema to the reformers; but when there was no other source of highly educated, literate and numerate officials, it was just as impossible to run the secular government without clerics as it would have been to run the church without secular landholdings.

In the end, after the dramatic clash of personalities between Gregory VII and the emperor Henry IV, when the two of them managed to make papal principles and politics seem diametrically opposed to those of the empire, a compromise was gradually reached. Put in its broadest terms, the church was to elect bishops and abbots, the king or emperor to confirm the election. It was not an ideal situation, and both kings and popes continued to interfere in church elections – and to complain about each other's activities – throughout the Middle Ages. But the papal claim to superiority over secular monarchs had been stated in unambiguous terms: in a private memorandum, the *Dictatus Papae*, written in 1075, Gregory had stated as his twelfth proposition on the nature and powers of the papacy that 'it is lawful for him (the pope) to depose emperors', a dictum he tried to enforce a year later. He failed to remove Henry IV; but the claim had been made. The claim to independence from the state was equally unsuccessful, leading only to the compromise of the concordat of Worms in 1122; but it too had been made, and the mere existence of these claims finally set the papacy apart in men's minds as a universal institution belonging to the divine order rather than the imperfect world of men. If it was so corrupt, it was the fault not of the institution but of its personnel, perhaps the papal officials and their hangers-on, perhaps the prelates, perhaps even the pope himself; but the concept was greater than any such human weaknesses.

For success in the harsh realities of twelfth-century Europe, more than ideals were needed. It was the achievement of Urban II, who became pope three years after Gregory's death, to give the papacy the formal organization it needed to enforce its powers. Taking as his model the royal administrative systems, Urban created a papal court which copied its secular contemporaries, with a chancery for the preparation and recording of documents and a financial organization to control and administer papal revenue. The cardinals, whose position had long been ambiguous, now became a kind of papal council, the pope's close advisers, just as the great barons might advise the king. Furthermore, the law of the church, canon law, was developed into a complete and coherent system running parallel to that of the king. In broad terms, clerks – men in any kind of holy orders – were held to be exempt from secular justice and could be tried only in a court of canon law. Canon law was to receive its most authoritative statement in Gratian of Bologna's *Decretum* (c.1140), and the whole system as expounded by him relied on the pope's supremacy over all other authorities, both secular and ecclesiastical.

Rome during the twelfth century was therefore the centre of a substantial organization with international interests, if we look at the papacy in purely secular terms. The pope enjoyed a prestige and power unknown before, and this was reflected in the wealth of churches and in the papal palace, the Lateran, given by Constantine to pope Miltiades in the fourth century. But medieval Rome has largely vanished, as a result of the energetic building activities of the sixteenth-century popes. Of the medieval Lateran, only the Scala Sancta and the chapel of St Laurence survive, though the nearby Tribune contains copies of the mosaics from the old banqueting hall of the old palace, the remains of a grandiose scheme of decorations glorifying the papacy. Among the lost mosaics was one which caused a diplomatic incident: in 1157 Frederick Barbarossa wrote to Hadrian IV asking him to paint out a scene showing a previous emperor, Lothair III, holding the pope's stirrup, an action implying that the emperor was the pope's vassal. The Scala Sancta is said to have been the staircase of Pilate's house in Jerusalem, which Christ descended after his trial, and which St Helena, mother of Constantine and a great collector of relics, brought to Rome. The Lateran Palace was the home of the popes until 1308–9, when in quick succession disastrous fires raged through both the palace and the adjoining basilica of St John Lateran, which was (and still is) the cathedral of Rome, and was the most impressive church in the city until the rebuilding of St Peter's in the sixteenth century. At the end of the thirteenth century Nicholas IV, a member of the noble Roman Colonna family, had spent large sums on embellishing it. It was rebuilt soon after the fire of 1309, but was burnt down again in 1360; very little of the medieval structure has survived the successive remodellings and rebuildings of the Renaissance and of the later centuries. St Peter's was entirely rebuilt; and it is fair to say that the majority of Rome's churches were either demolished and rebuilt, or very substantially altered, between 1450 and 1750. Even a pope like Clement XI, who promulgated a decree protecting antiquities and works of art in 1701, presided over the wholesale remodelling of medieval churches.

Among those vanished glories, a few traces of medieval Rome's splendours do survive. The best examples are San Clemente, Santa Maria Maggiore and Santa Maria in Aracoeli. San Paolo fuori le Mura, which preserves the original plan, was almost entirely rebuilt after a fire in 1823 and suffers from a nineteenth-century glossiness of finish. San Clemente and Santa Maria Maggiore (like San Paolo) are basilica churches, the traditional plan of early Roman Christianity which derived from the Lateran basilica: the aisles are divided from the nave by pillars and are of equal height. The same form is found elsewhere in Italy, particularly in the south (as at Trani), and occasionally in Gothic architecture, where it is known as a *Hallenkirche*, but it is the Romanesque version which brings out most strongly the continuity between the classical original and its medieval successor. Perhaps the finest of all basilica churches is the sixth-century Sant' Apollinare in Classe at Ravenna, but San Clemente, rebuilt from

1108 onwards after the earlier church had been destroyed in the
sack of Rome by the Normans in 1084, is a close competitor. It
has the original entrance plan (lacking at Sant'Apollinare) of a
cloister or *quadriporticus* in front of the main entrance. The interior
follows the patterns of early basilicas so faithfully that it was long
believed to be the original church, repaired rather than rebuilt;
but in 1857 the earlier church was shown to exist below the present
church, and was excavated soon afterwards. The upper church has
a fine 'cosmatesque' pavement, a kind of marble inlay found only
in and around Rome, named after two craftsmen called Cosmo
whose signature is to be found on several such works. It also has
original furniture, with an enclosure for the choir in the centre
of the nave, and twelfth-century mosaics, though the walls and
ceiling are encrusted with eighteenth-century ornamentation. The
excavated lower church has frescoes dating from the ninth to the
eleventh century, and even further down is a Mithraeum, or temple
of Mithras; but the site is supposed to be Christian in origin, as
it was traditionally the house of St Clement, afterwards confiscated
and dedicated to the cult of Mithras.

San Clemente is relatively small; Santa Maria Maggiore is one
of the four great basilicas of Rome, which, despite a new façade
and the rebuilding of the apse, preserves more of its original aspect
than the others. Parts of the church built by Sixtus III in
432–40 remain, including the 'impressionist' mosaics above the
nave arches and on the apse arch, and there is a twelfth-century
cosmatesque pavement. The main apse mosaics, carefully preserved in the rebuilding, are later thirteenth-century, representing
the Coronation of the Virgin, by Jacopo Torriti, whose work
deliberately draws on early Christian art in its symbolism. But it
is the distinctive layout and grand scale of the interior, with its
rows of great marble columns, that must have impressed the
medieval pilgrims; coming from the massive Romanesque architecture of the north or the exuberance of Gothic, this rich yet
restrained interior must have seemed to them a different world,
echoing the imperial monuments in the city outside.

The imperial echoes are even stronger at Santa Maria in
Aracoeli, which stands on the summit of Capitoline Hill, on the
site of Rome's ancient citadel and overlooking the forum. It is in
parts sixth-century, built with columns from pagan buildings; most
of it is thirteenth-century brick in the severe style favoured by the

Franciscans who rebuilt it. The paintings and sculptures largely belong to the early Renaissance, but there are two ambos, the pulpits from which the gospel and epistle were read, with inlays signed by the two Cosmos, and a tomb decorated in the same style. A shrine in the north transept, the 'temple of St Helena', is said to mark the spot which gives the church its name; for this is the *ara coeli* or altar of heaven, built by Augustus when one of the Roman Sibyls, or prophetesses, foretold the coming of Christianity – or so the medieval story ran: the church is first so named officially in the thirteenth century. This 'altar of the firstborn of God' ranked with Virgil's supposed prophecy in his fourth eclogue of the coming of the Messiah as one of the great examples of the premonitions of Christ's coming, granted not only to the Jews, but to Gentiles as well. The idea of continuity with the imperial past was precious, and these stories were the spiritual equivalent of Romanesque architecture, equally rooted in classical tradition.

However, men came to Rome in the Middle Ages not as tourists, idly curious about the past, but on pressing business, spiritual business of one kind or another. On the one hand, hordes of pilgrims made their way to this, the oldest Christian centre in the west, to worship at the 'seven churches'; on the other hand, lawyers and diplomats came to settle spiritual matters which only the pope or cardinals could judge. The pilgrims were heirs to an ancient tradition, stretching back before Christianity itself, when Greeks and Romans journeyed to the shrines of the Near East. (See Chapter 5 below for later pilgrimages.) Rome had attracted Christian pilgrims from at least the third century onwards, as graffiti near the tombs of the early popes show. In the fourth century, Prudentius describes the crowd of pilgrims around the tomb of Hippolytus. At the beginning of the eighth century, Benedict Biscop, who founded the great Northumbrian monasteries at Wearmouth and Jarrow, travelled widely on the continent. He brought from Rome not only a valuable library, but also the arch-cantor of St Peter's to teach the monks music and Roman rites. In all, Benedict made five visits to Rome; on his first visit, aged about twenty-five, he went as a pilgrim, returning twelve years later, still as a layman, one of the many Anglo-Saxon pilgrims for whom the Hospice of Santo Spirito was originally built and who are still remembered in the street name Lungotevere in Sassia, Sassia being the Saxon quarter. Soon after his second visit, Benedict became a monk, and his later visits were all on business. This mixture of pilgrimage and more mundane matters was typical of the more distinguished travellers to Rome throughout the Middle Ages, but thousands of humble men and women made their way there each year with no other thought than to visit the seven pilgrimage churches: the four great basilicas of the patriarchs, St John Lateran, St Peter's, San Paolo fuori le Mura, and Santa Maria Maggiore, and three lesser basilicas, San Sebastiano, Santa Croce and San Lorenzo fuori le Mura, built near the catacombs specifically to cater for pilgrims. More striking were the pilgrimages made by Anglo-Saxon kings; between 668 and 726, no less than four of them abdicated and went to Rome to die near the tomb of St Peter.

Pilgrimages to Rome were given an additional impetus in 1300 by the declaration of a jubilee year by Boniface VIII, under somewhat mysterious circumstances. According to a contemporary account a rumour was rife in Rome late in 1299 that anyone who visited St Peter's on 1 January 1300 would receive full absolution of their sins, according to ancient custom. A search was made in the archives for references to such a custom, but nothing could be found, and the only supporting testimony was that of an aged peasant, who remembered his father benefiting a century earlier. By this time, so many pilgrims had arrived that the pope issued a bull on 22 February proclaiming the year 1300 as a jubilee, from the Old Testament observation of every fiftieth year as a special year, and granting absolution to pilgrims who visited either St Peter's or St Paul's during that time. Originally the Christian jubilee was envisaged as occurring once every century, but the interval was reduced to fifty years in 1343, at the urgent request of the people of Rome, whose interest was primarily commercial, in that the pilgrims were an important source of income; but the request was supported by both St Bridget of Sweden and the Italian poet and humanist Petrarch. Soon afterwards the interval was reduced to thirty-three years, and finally to twenty-five years in 1470. The jubilee of 1500 was well attended, but in 1525 the disputes within the church at the time of the Reformation led to a drastic drop in pilgrims, and it was only in the nineteenth century that the old mass pilgrimages really returned. There were in fact only a bare half-dozen jubilees celebrated between 1300 and 1450, but they made a great impression, and did much to confirm the standing of pilgrimage as a spiritual exercise in an age when travel was, if not easier, at any rate more common than in the early Middle Ages.

Besides the pilgrims, lawyers and clerics came in large numbers to Rome. Rome was the ultimate court of appeal for all matters subject to canon law, and this covered a wide range of topics which we today would consider part of secular law. Marriage and divorce were possibly the commonest topics of business at Rome, but wills and a whole host of ecclesiastical property rights were fought out in the Roman courts as well. The curial system, however, did not develop fully until the papacy's exile at Avignon in the fourteenth century (see p. 51 below). Before then, many of the clerical visitors to Rome were on more harmonious business. By an edict inspired by St Boniface in the mid ninth century, it was decreed that all archbishops had to go to Rome to receive the *pallium* or woollen band which was their badge of office and which could only be conferred by the pope himself. Sometimes the unfortunate archbishop reached Rome to find that the pope had just died, as in the case of Robert Winchelsey, newly elected archbishop of Canterbury, who reached Rome on 17 May 1293 and did not leave until 5 October 1294, because the election which led to the choice of the hermit Peter Morone as Celestine V had been so difficult and protracted.

Yet among those who came to the 'new Rome' of papal politics and church business, there were still a number who also came in search of, or at least were conscious of, Rome's classical past. Few of the monuments and temples of classical Rome were deliberately destroyed when Christianity became the state religion; it was only where pagans clung stubbornly to their beliefs that their shrines were torn down, and in the cities there had been little resistance to the change. So, despite the slow decay of the centuries, Rome in the twelfth century had a wealth of classical architecture and sculpture to offer the visitor. Some, like Henry of Blois, bishop of Winchester and half-brother to king Stephen, bought statues and shipped them home; others, like Hildebert, archbishop of Tours, who also visited Rome in the early twelfth century, wrote elegiac lines on 'ruins of incomparable grandeur which mournfully proclaim her ancient greatness', though he went on to proclaim her new greatness as the centre of Christendom. Rome as the chief city of the world and centre of a great empire still haunted men's imaginations: when Geoffrey of Monmouth came to invent a fitting climax for his newly

invented account of Arthur's career it was an attempt to conquer
Rome itself, thwarted only by Mordred's treachery. Later writers
allowed Arthur to complete the conquest: the ultimate triumph for
the ultimate hero, perhaps, but there is also more than an echo of
Charlemagne's entry into Rome and coronation there in 800.

This imperial past was fairly widely appreciated by visitors, as
the contemporary guidebooks show. The eighth-century 'Einsiedeln itinerary' preserves the wording from a map of Rome showing
the eleven principal routes followed by the pilgrims visiting the
Roman shrines. This bare list of names, scarcely a thousand words
in all, evokes a city rich in shrines, but intersperses these with the
names of the great classical buildings that survived: *'Circus
flamineus, rotunda, thermae commodianae, forum traiani et columna
eius'*; and similar entries appear among the saints and martyrs. The
most popular guide, the *Mirabilia Urbis Romae*, or *Marvels of the
City of Rome*, was originally written about 1150–75 and continued
to appear in printed versions well into the sixteenth century. Its
three sections offered a list of places of interest, a collection of
stories about the ancient monuments, and a suggested tour of
the city. The earliest version gives a bare list of purely classical
remains such as triumphal arches, palaces and other monuments,
without any reference to their Christian connections, though the
author ends his places of note with an account of 'places where
the saints suffered'. The legends are part Christian, part pagan.
Some are garbled accounts of monuments which survive today,
such as the bronze equestrian statue of Marcus Aurelius on the
Capitol, known popularly then as the horse of Constantine (though
the author denies this, and tells a different story to account for
it). Others account for the transfer to Christianity of such sites
as Santa Maria in Aracoeli and the Pantheon, and describe the
foundation of the three great basilicas. The last part is almost
exclusively concerned with the relics of ancient Rome, and the
author concludes:

These and many more temples and palaces of emperors, consuls,
senators and prefects were in the time of the heathen within this Roman
city, even as we have read in old chronicles, and have seen with our eyes,
and have heard tell of ancient men. And, moreover, how great was their
beauty in gold, and silver, and brass, and ivory, and precious stones, we
have endeavoured thus in writing, as well as we could, to bring back to
the remembrance of mankind.

While other guides certainly existed before the *Mirabilia* which gave lists of the Christian and ecclesiastical sights, it says much for the strength of imperial Rome's hold over men's thoughts that the mainly pagan *Mirabilia*, which hardly mentions the papacy, should have been the most popular of such works.

Indeed, towards the end of the Middle Ages, Rome was to lose its connection with the papacy for nearly a hundred years. During the eleventh and twelfth centuries the popes had established their control over the church, and Rome had become the unchallenged centre of ecclesiastical affairs; but despite apparent victories, the popes had not achieved a similar political success. Their ambition was to be recognized as the ultimate arbiter in secular affairs, but they lacked the physical resources to carry out their judgements. Even excommunication or an interdict on all church worship contained no real physical threat, powerful though such weapons were in psychological terms. On the other hand, the church was inevitably involved in politics to a greater or lesser degree by virtue of its position as a great landowner and its great wealth, while the popes were also trying to insulate themselves from the uncertainties of Roman and central Italian politics by establishing their own secular state, free from external interference. As it was, few of the thirteenth-century popes lived for long in Rome because it was the scene of perpetual civil war between the great Roman families.

So the popes were slowly but surely drawn into the spiritually dangerous business of everyday politics. Under Innocent IV (1243–54), the papacy became merely one of the political powers of Europe, pursuing purely secular objectives. This in turn meant that the popes needed money, and while the financial pressure made the papal administration more efficient and centralized, it also brought the papacy as a whole into disrepute: Louis IX of France complained that the pope was doing 'new and unheard-of things', and the record of the church council held at Lyon in 1245 reads more like the minutes of a secular ruler's advisers, with its emphasis on political problems. Under Gregory X (1271–6) there were the beginnings of an attempt at reform, and we shall see elsewhere (p. 141) how the orders of friars were in some senses a direct reaction to the growing secularization of the papacy. But the corruption was too deep-seated to be eradicated. In any case, only the pope himself could reform the papacy, and he was chosen by the cardinals, many of whom had a vested interest in the continuation of existing policy and could not envisage any other kind of papal government. Even when the cardinals regretted their choice and reacted by electing a reformer the next time, they often picked ineffectual figures. The most extreme example of this was the hermit Peter Morone, who became Celestine V in 1294. Unable to handle the pressure of business, he resigned after a few weeks; and the cardinals swung to the other extreme, by electing Boniface VIII, a lawyer and arch-politician, who was reputed to have speeded Celestine's resignation by fixing a speaking-tube in his bedroom and whispering 'angelic' messages down it urging him to give up the papacy and return to his hermitage. Boniface's political activities were more extreme than those of any of his predecessors. He was faced by the increasingly efficient and nationalist royal administrations in France and England, and the point of conflict was the old and troubled area of secular authority over the clergy, in particular whether the king could tax and arrest the clergy in the same way as his other subjects. Innocent I V had managed to win his argument with the German emperors by virtually destroying the empire; but Boniface's opponent, Philip the Fair, was ruler of a unified kingdom, and the pope could not count on the support of great magnates who were princes in their own right, as in the empire. He faced instead a people who looked to the king for leadership, and a king who well understood the use of propaganda. Short of raising a vast political alliance to invade France and destroy Philip – which Boniface indeed threatened to do – he had no means of attacking him.

Instead it was Philip who counter-attacked. Boniface claimed in 1302 that 'In this Church, there are two swords, the spiritual and temporal, as we are told by the evangelists ... it is necessary that the one sword be under the other, and that temporal authority be subject to spiritual authority ... and the spiritual authority is bound to judge it when it errs'. Philip replied that the pope was merely the head of the church by the consent of the church as a whole, and that a general council of the church was a higher authority than the pope himself. He denounced Boniface as a heretic, demanded his trial by such a council, and then overstepped the limit by trying to arrest Boniface physically at Anagni in September 1303. Boniface was rescued by the townspeople, but died a month later.

Two years later, after the brief pontificate of Benedict XI, the cardinals chose as pope the archbishop of Bordeaux, who was not a member of the papal court, but was known to be on good terms with both Philip of France and Edward I of England. It was hoped that he would settle the quarrel between the two kings over Aquitaine and the quarrel between Philip and the church. When he was elected, he was making a visitation of his diocese and was near Poitiers. Rather than delay his coronation until he reached Rome, he decided that it should be held at Vienne on the Rhône, on the border of France and the Holy Roman Empire. In the end, the ceremony took place at Lyon, just in French territory. But Clement did not continue his journey to Rome, partly because of renewed civil war there and partly because he wished to negotiate a settlement of the dispute over his native Aquitaine. So he settled first at Bordeaux, and then, after an uncomfortable incident at Poitiers in 1308, when Philip put pressure on him by filling the town with French troops, he moved south, stopping near the only papal lands north of the Alps, and took up temporary residence at Avignon. Avignon itself belonged to the kings of Sicily, who were papal vassals, and Clement hoped that he might thus escape direct involvement with Philip. He was wrong: when it seemed likely that the council of Vienne in 1312 would not fall in with Philip's wishes and condemn the order of Knights Templars as heretics, Philip had no hesitation in arriving at the head of an armed force to see that he got what he wanted. To the rest of the world, it looked as if the papacy was in 'Babylonish captivity', and had become the pawn of the French king.

This was not entirely true. The next pope, John XXII, a former bishop of Avignon, did indeed establish the papacy on a more definite basis at Avignon, and after 1334 the arrangement became permanent for the next eighty years. But the 'Avignon popes' were as varied as their predecessors, and far from being exclusively the creatures of the French court. Indeed, a much more important influence under Clement V and John XXII was nepotism: Clement created over a dozen Gascon cardinals, while John XXII was equally liberal to his kinsmen from Cahors. The papal court, long dominated by Italians and Germans, had become primarily French. None the less, John XXII was determined to return to Rome, but only when order had been restored there; in 1319 he actually sent a cardinal to lead a military expedition into northern Italy, and for the next fourteen years a papal army was active there, with varying success, until John dreamt up a scheme for creating a new kingdom in the Po valley to be ruled by a Bohemian prince under his auspices. The reaction this provoked led to an alliance of the Italian towns which drove the papal forces out of Italy in 1333, the year before John's death. John had also quarrelled with the Holy Roman emperor, Louis of Bavaria, whom he refused to recognize, and Louis had briefly set up an anti-pope in Rome. If John's politics were disastrous, his administrative reforms were on the whole successful, though they once again reinforced the idea that the papacy was primarily concerned with collecting taxes. Dante, who fiercely opposed the interference by popes in temporal affairs, roundly condemned both Clement and John at the end of his *Divine Comedy*, written about 1320. The speaker is St Peter himself:

> Never by our intention was it willed
> That Christendom should sit on either hand
> Of those who after us our office held
>
> Nor that the keys bequeathed to me should stand
> As emblem on a banner waging war
> Against the baptized in a Christian land;
>
> Nor that a signet which my features bore
> Should seal the lying privileges sold,
> Whence, coruscating, I blush the more.
>
> Rapacious wolves in shepherd's garb behold
> In every pasture! Lord, why dost thou think
> Such slaughter of the lambs within thy fold?
>
> Gascons and Cahorsins prepare to drink
> Our blood . . .

John XXII's successor, Benedict XII, undid some of the worst excesses of the former's rule; and he managed to stem the rising tide of bureaucracy which threatened to engulf the church. He also reformed the great monastic orders, which had grown lax in their observance, and he abandoned the projected return to Rome when he was unable to come to terms with the emperor, Louis of Bavaria. His weakness was that he lacked practical skills: his reforms were theoretical, and bore fruit only in the hands of men who were prepared to carry out the day-to-day business involved.

Under John XXII, the palace of the bishops of Avignon had become the papal residence, with some extensions to provide the extra space the papal curia required. Benedict XII bought the palace, provided the bishop with a new home (the 'Petit Palais' of today), and in 1335 began a major rebuilding programme, designed to provide permanent and suitable accommodation for the pope himself but mainly for the administration of the church as an international body. He employed a Gascon master-mason, who produced buildings in keeping with the tone of Benedict's pontificate: austere, undecorated and practical, as befitted a pope who had at one time been a Cistercian monk. The ceilings were of wood, the floors of glazed earthenware tiles. These buildings (the 'Vieux Palais') form the northern half of the papal palace as we know it today. Their austerity and their striking site high on the great rocky outcrop on which Avignon is built make them look more like a castle than an ecclesiastical palace, but defensive considerations were part of the original plans – the memory of the attack at Anagni was still vivid. The Vieux Palais follows the plan of the original bishop's palace and consists of a two-storey building around a central cloister, with the pope's apartments taking up most of the space. The striking 'Tour des Anges', 150 feet high on the south-east corner, contains the treasury, the pope's private chamber and his library. The pope's chamber is painted with an elaborate pattern of vines and oak branches in which birds and squirrels hide; these paintings may possibly belong to the original scheme of decoration, but, knowing Benedict's tastes, it seems more likely that they date from Clement VI's reign.

The rooms around the cloister itself are primarily administrative, providing space for the consistory, or assembly of cardinals, which was the highest council of the church, for the conclave, when the cardinals met to elect a new pope, and for the pope's household. The consistory rooms, which, like the majority of the palace, have lost the rich decoration added in the 1340s, are none the less impressive, particularly the Grand Tinel, or banqueting hall, where the original wooden barrel-vault roof is now being rebuilt. Finally, there were Benedict XII's chapel, now used as an archive room, and the four towers, of which the Tour de la Campane, standing on the highest point of the rock, is the most complete and impressive.

Clement VI, Benedict's successor, who became pope in 1342, continued the building operations, but in a very different manner. Clement was no monk, but a career administrator from the French court, secular in outlook, and determined to rule as a prince rather than as a pope. In sharp contrast to the disasters which overwhelmed the west under his reign – the collapse of the Florentine banks from 1342 onwards, the first battles of the Hundred Years' War, the Black Death – Clement turned Avignon into a luxurious, profligate, even debauched court, which paid lip-service to religious forms, but which, as he himself freely acknowledged, behaved in a way intended to impress other princes. He had no intention of returning to Rome, where Cola di Rienzi had tried to revive the idea of the Roman people as leaders of the western world and had declared himself tribune in 1347: Rome was far too unsafe. So in 1348 he bought Avignon from the queen of Sicily, and persuaded the emperor-elect to renounce any claim to sovereignty over the city. He was now master in his own house.

Clement's building programme reflected this change in outlook. The palace created by Benedict XII was virtually doubled in size by a series of state apartments on a much grander scale. The new façade, which provided the main entrance to the palace, is still fortress-like; Froissart was to describe the completed palace as 'the most beautiful and the strongest house in the world, and the easiest to defend'. But there are elegant pinnacles on the staircase towers which flank the entrance gate, and the courtyard around where the new buildings are grouped has traceried Gothic windows, the most prominent being the 'Indulgence window' at which the pope appeared on state occasions. The south wing contains the great audience chamber and, above it, the chapel. The great audience chamber was, like much of the rest of the palace, decorated by Matteo Giovanetti, who worked in Avignon from 1343 onwards. A group of figures of prophets is all that survives of his work in this room, though there are traces of a Crucifixion on the east wall. The capitals are purely secular in tone, with amusing subjects drawn from the bestiaries. From the audience chamber, a large well-lit staircase – itself an innovation for the period – leads up to the chapel, a spacious but relatively simple Gothic room of ample size, which was usually hung with tapestries. The altar has been recently restored, but the chapel is now unnaturally empty and gives little impression of its medieval appearance.

It is a room just off the eastern end of the chapel, connecting the old and new palaces, which gives the most vivid idea of Avignon under Clement VI. This is the so-called *Chambre du Cerf*, which was Clement VI's study. Here the elaborate frescoes, probably though not certainly by Matteo Giovanetti, have survived almost intact; they are not religious, but entirely secular, and are devoted to the pleasures of hunting, hawking and fishing. Very few examples of such rooms have come down to us; though we know that similar works were commissioned by the French and Bohemian kings, and by Italian connoisseurs, it is ironic that one of the finest should be here, where by rights profane topics should be excluded. On the east wall, an aristocratic falconer, dressed in the latest fashion, is about to fly his hawk at an unseen quarry, while his hounds nose about in the elaborate flowery field which is the background of all the frescoes and which derives from tapestry designs. To the south, there is a bathing scene and a delightful vignette of a ferret pursuing a rabbit, watched by a richly-attired hunter. There follows a stag-hunt and finally a pastoral fishing expedition on one of the papal fishponds, showing the different methods used – including, remarkably, a bow and arrow. On either side there are boys birds-nesting and a man luring game with a decoy call. Much of the decoration elsewhere in the palace was in similar vein. Clement VI once said, 'My predecessors did not know how to be popes,' but what he really meant was that they did not know how to be *princes*. He did his best to remedy this; liberal with his gifts in an age when a ruler's greatness was often measured by his extravagance, he exhausted the papal treasure not only in building this royal palace, but in filling it with an equally royal collection of *objets d'art*, jewels, metalwork and even a zoo, containing among other animals bears, camels and stags. On a more serious level, Clement VI laid the foundations of the papal library.

This taste for luxury extended beyond the papal palace. Though there are few traces of the flourishing culture of Avignon as a whole at this period, we must avoid seeing the palace in isolation. It was one of the cardinals who brought the great Italian painter Simone Martini to Avignon; his masterpiece, *Our Lady of Humility*, is now shown in the palace. There were lesser palaces and summer residences decorated in the same lavish style, as fragments in the museum in the Petit Palais bear witness. But Avignon's cultural flowering was brief, and it is for this reason that so little has survived.

For Clement VI was at once the most luxurious and the most powerful of the fourteenth-century popes. His successors were hemmed in not only by enormous political problems but also by the assertion that the cardinals as a body, the 'Sacred College', were superior to the pope, a claim which was made before his successor, Innocent VI, was elected. Although Innocent annulled this declaration, it was a pointer to the future. On the political front, the war between England and France and the lawlessness that followed resulted in Avignon itself being attacked in 1357 and 1360, and the pope had to order the construction of walls and battlements. Urban V, elected in 1362, managed to return briefly to Rome in 1367–70, but the administration of the church remained at Avignon. Urban died at Avignon, but his successor, Gregory XI, died at Rome in 1378, and for the first time for a century the conclave was held in Rome. The Romans urgently wanted an Italian or preferably Roman pope, who would keep the papacy at Rome; and an Italian, Urban VI, was duly elected, under considerable pressure from the mob. The circumstances of his election and his behaviour afterwards led the French cardinals to disown him, and the only result of the return to Rome was to produce a new schism: for the next twenty-five years there was to be one pope in Rome and a rival, backed by the French, in Avignon. Clement VI turned Avignon into a secular court; he did his best to advance his cause by diplomacy and political intrigue, but on his death Charles VI of France, weary of the schism, tried to prevent the election of another anti-pope. His message was ignored, and Benedict XIII was chosen. Within five years, he had lost the support of the French and was besieged by a mercenary captain employed by Charles VI. The siege was only lifted in return for Benedict's indefinite imprisonment in the palace, but in 1403 he escaped and fled to Provence.

Meanwhile, the Roman popes had proved scarcely more popular, and a general desire for church reform, expressed in the early 'protestant' movements of John Wycliffe and John Hus, finally ended in the general council of Constance: the church as a whole was now set above the pope, just as the cardinals had once tried to set themselves above the pope. The council lasted from 1414 to 1418, but it made little progress towards reform, and its one achievement was to secure the resignation of Gregory XII, the Roman pope. Benedict XIII refused to resign. He was therefore deposed, and died in obscurity in Spain in 1422, still protesting that he was pope. In 1417, a new pope was elected – Martin V, who was universally recognized and who returned to Rome. The papacy's exile in Avignon was over, and the stage was set for the political and material splendours of the Renaissance papacy.

2
Cathedrals

As the Christian church established itself within the Roman empire and turned from its missionary activity and the idea that the Second Coming was imminent, it began to develop a settled organization. The apostles had been missionaries; their successors, the bishops, were leaders of local churches, based on areas that often corresponded to the divisions of the empire. 'Diocese', which we use today to indicate the area under a bishop's control, meant originally a group of imperial provinces. At first, the bishop moved around his diocese, which could be very large, encouraging his flock; and this semi-missionary activity in a huge see can be found as late as the seventh and eighth century, in the work of St Willibrord and St Boniface in Germany. Saxon bishops in England were also more likely to move around, since the old Roman cities had fallen into decay long before the church was established. But where there was continuity between empire and church, the bishop's *cathedra* (a Greek word meaning seat) was usually established in a Roman city, and one of the early decrees of the church stipulated that this should be the rule: it was not fitting that a bishop should live in a village.

The bishop's church, which would in any case have been larger and grander simply because it stood in a city and served a larger congregation, soon acquired a distinctive character. By the sixth century it was called *ecclesia cathedralis*, the church where the bishop's *cathedra* was, or simply *ecclesia major*, the great church. Simpler folk called it the house of God, *Domus Dei*, and this became *duomo* in Italian and *Dom* in German.

The bishop was assisted by a group of clergy, attached to the cathedral church, who had no parishes but helped to administer the diocese as a whole. The number and standing of these clergy varied widely according to local circumstances, and although attempts were made to give them a formal rule of life as early as the 750s, it was not until the eleventh century that any general principles evolved. By 1100, the cathedral communities had become either monasteries attached to the cathedral or colleges, with specific statutes or 'canons', a name which was eventually transferred to the clergy themselves. Canons took no special vows – they were merely priests who belonged to a community. In the Middle Ages, a very large number of cathedral communities were in fact monastic, and it was only after the Reformation and the Protestant attack on the monastic orders that canons became the normal clergy of a cathedral, both in the reformed churches and in the Roman Catholic church.

The presence of this group of clergy affected the design of the church itself. In a parish church there would usually be a single officiating priest and two or three helpers, and the east end, where the altar was placed from a very early date, did not need to be particularly large. In a cathedral, the bishop and his attendant clergy needed much more space. The problem had been resolved in the Roman basilicas by providing stone seats round the walls of the apse, but later developments made the basilica impractical. The growth of the cult of relics meant that individual small chapels were needed for the exhibition of reliquaries; the increasing numbers of ordained priests among the cathedral clergy meant that more altars were required for them to celebrate mass; and all these chapels had to face eastward. So the east end became a cluster of chapels grouped round the main altar. At first the arrangement was awkward and haphazard, but a solution was soon found. It first appears in the crypts of Saint-Germain at Auxerre and of Chartres, where a circular passage surrounds the resting place of the relics, with chapels radiating off it. At Chartres, the passage wall is pierced, so that the whole becomes one open area, but in the tenth century the pilgrimage church of Saint-Martin at Tours was rebuilt using this plan for the end of the nave. This sophisticated solution was the basis for the majority of later medieval cathedrals. Further developments were the increasing importance given to the use of music in church services from the twelfth century onwards, which meant that the choir were given a separate and distinctive place between the body of the nave and the altar, while at the west end an impressive twin-towered façade marked the main doorway; this 'westwork' is first found in the great monastic church at Saint-Riquier, near Abbeville, built by abbot Angilbert in the 790s but now, alas, destroyed.

These, then, are the general features of the cathedral church; but there were over five hundred cathedrals in medieval Europe, and they vary immensely in age, size and status. So it is easy to find exceptions and local modifications to this scheme. For the same reason, it is impossible to cover in a brief space anything more than a random handful of the surviving cathedrals. Unlike most medieval buildings, only a very small proportion of medieval cathedrals have actually been destroyed in the succeeding centuries. They may have been drastically restored, encased in Baroque façades and otherwise made unrecognizable, but until the advent of modern high-rise buildings in the last fifty years the skyline of most cities was still dominated by a medieval cathedral. And the cathedral often remains as a focal point of civic pride, an inheritance from those earlier citizens by whose efforts it was built, in a way that the great monastic churches never do. In the early Middle Ages, a cathedral was often built on a scale that would allow the entire community to crowd within its walls. This idea is most vividly illustrated by the stark unfinished façade of the incomplete colossus of a new cathedral at Siena, where the existing church was to become the mere transept of its successor, until the Black Death swept through the town and removed both the need for the new building and the human resources by which it could be accomplished. The cathedral was often an indicator of the prosperity of a city; it could also become the symbol of a rivalry with other cities, and numerous over-ambitious schemes came to grief without the intervention of catastrophes such as plague, simply because they were beyond the means of the citizens. Equally, it was far from unusual for a cathedral to take centuries to complete: Cologne (p. 89 below) is perhaps the most extreme case.

So when we look at a cathedral today, we need to try to see it on a different scale: as the highest and greatest building in the city, built over centuries rather than months, and as incomparably the richest, both in artistic and in purely mercenary terms, filled with paintings, sculptures and masterpieces of the goldsmith's skill. Cologne has something of this feeling, with its great shrine of the Magi, rich treasury and fine paintings (though for a treasure-house of true magnificence we need to go to the Cámara Santa at Oviedo, with its extraordinary relics of the eighth-century Christian kingdom of the Asturias); but again our modern comparisons will play us false, when far greater religious paintings of the period are to be found in art galleries and the artifice of modern jewellers makes the work of their medieval forebears seem sober and restrained.

The building of a cathedral could take centuries, and during that time fashions in architecture changed. Even where building was completed to a unified plan, there was always the temptation to rebuild in a new style. The austere, elegant Romanesque cathedrals of Germany only survive because Germany was a troubled and impoverished country in the centuries when Gothic was at its height, and they escaped the almost wholesale rebuilding in the Gothic style that took place elsewhere. We shall find the equation of poverty and survival of archaic buildings again, especially at the level of country churches; it is not the only reason for such survivals, but by and large medieval citizens were just as conscious of the latest architectural fashions as large companies are today; for three hundred years possession of a Gothic cathedral was the great status symbol for a city, and the calm, dark severity of an existing Romanesque church was despised as old-fashioned. Again, we have to envisage the cathedral not as the static, completed monument we see today, but as an evolving structure, to be altered, added to, torn down and laboriously rebuilt, a dynamic centre for a dynamic religion.

Romanesque Cathedrals

Durham

The years following the Norman conquest saw a remarkable burst of church building in England. The most spectacular work was partly the result of the Norman reorganization of the English church; unlike their continental counterparts, the English bishops had often had their cathedrals in relatively rural areas, and indeed there was no very sharp distinction between a large Anglo-Saxon minster, which might serve a large area of countryside, and the cathedral proper. The Normans moved rural sees such as Dorchester in Oxfordshire and Elmham in Norfolk to larger centres, Lincoln and Norwich; and some of the towns lost their sees as well, Sherborne being moved to Old Sarum (later Salisbury). Yet where new cathedrals were not actually a necessity, the bishops of the established sees set about the rebuilding on a grand scale, and only two major churches were not reconstructed. Of the cathedrals built or renewed at this period, Winchester and Worcester retain some eleventh-century work, but it is Norwich and Durham that are least altered. Norwich, with its huge sweep of nave, fourteen bays in length, is typical of the confident later Romanesque style, relying on sheer size to produce powerful effects. The nave at Ely, only forty miles away, is in the same manner. But the most interesting of the Norman cathedrals is Durham, both technically and artistically a masterpiece.

Durham was an outpost of Norman rule, close to the Scottish border; when William of St Calais arrived as bishop in 1080, his predecessor had been murdered and there was general lawlessness in the countryside. William had made his career in the king's service, and it seems likely that he was sent to Durham both to care for the church and to enforce royal authority. But in 1088, when the northerners rose against William Rufus, he failed to supply the king with the expected number of troops from the lands of the bishopric and as a result spent three years in exile in Normandy. When he returned, in 1091, he set about building a new cathedral, reforming it as a cathedral priory of Benedictine monks, and work actually began in 1093. His exile seems to have been profitable in an artistic sense, for Durham was technically far ahead of its time. It was planned from the beginning to be vaulted in stone throughout, whereas most contemporary buildings were at least partially roofed in wood; only the great new abbey of Cluny seems to have preceded it in this respect. But the vaulting at Durham is also remarkable in that it is ribbed vaulting, the forerunner of Gothic vaulting, carried out in carefully dressed stone. Ribbed vaulting eventually made possible the marvellous lightness of Gothic; here it is still experimental and therefore massive, since the builders, exploring the potential of their new technique, relied on solidity and mass to ensure that the construction was safe. Even so, the vault over the choir had to be replaced later because the workmanship was not equal to the demands made by the new design.

The original plan of Durham provided for a choir roughly half the length of the nave, presumably to accommodate the monks of the newly founded priory. The effect of this division, giving an impression of great length, has been slightly disturbed by the introduction of a Gothic east end in the thirteenth century. Instead of the relative darkness of the Romanesque sanctuary, with its three apses corresponding to nave and aisles, lit by small windows, the east end is now flooded with light from a rose window. But the nave retains its original aspect: massive cylindrical pillars incised with geometric patterns alternate with grouped piers, in a very carefully proportioned composition. The gallery uses very simple forms, echoing the piers below, while the vaults are pierced by the clerestory windows to give a remarkable interplay of massiveness and light, complex patterning and simple proportions. All this was created in the space of forty years, an unusually short time in cathedral-building terms, and all the more unexpected in that this was not a rich city set in a peaceful and prosperous countryside, but a frontier post under threat of attack.

The setting of the cathedral, high above the river Wear, heightens the cliff-like aspect of the west front, with its massive four-square towers, completed in the thirteenth century, the west window being of the same period. The cathedral tower was heightened in the fifteenth century, but apart from the elaborate details of these later works, the overall outline of the cathedral is much as it was originally conceived. Its massiveness and strength go well with the almost royal authority wielded by the bishops in their palatinate county.

Beside the cathedral, the monastic buildings retain their Romanesque ground plan, although they were rebuilt in the Gothic style. The bishop was not only titular abbot of the monastery, but also the keeper of Durham castle (now part of the university), which stands side by side with the cathedral above the river gorge. The present building is the result of work over several centuries, from the Norman chapel and undercroft of the Great Hall, to the seventeenth-century embellishments of Nathaniel, Lord Crewe, who was bishop from 1674 to 1721.

Hildesheim

Hildesheim owes its existence as a town to its cathedral. Following Charlemagne's conquest and conversion of the Saxons, in the late eighth century, his son Louis the Pious chose Hildesheim as the 'forward base' for future missionary endeavours, founding a bishopric here in about 815. The first stone cathedral was consecrated in 872 but burnt down in 1013. The present building stems in plan and outline from the cathedral consecrated in 1061, a cruciform basilica with a nave and side aisles. Both the Romanesque crossing tower and the original west end had to be taken down for safety reasons in the eighteenth and nineteenth centuries, but it was the devastating air raids of March 1945 that led to the almost complete disappearance of the eleventh-century building. The reconstruction, completed in 1960, is an impressive modern re-creation of the Romanesque cathedral, whose greatest glories are the surviving pieces of Romanesque and medieval metalwork from the old cathedral.

The earliest of these masterpieces was created just after the fire in 1013. Bernward, then bishop of Hildesheim, had been to Rome and had probably seen there the doors of the church of Santa Sabina. On his return he commissioned for St Michael's church the huge bronze doors now in the western portal of the cathedral, two single castings each weighing two tons. The sheer technical achievement is remarkable enough; and the images produced, which show the whole cycle of the Bible story in sixteen panels, are striking in the strong movement of the figures, which are in high relief against ornate backgrounds of buildings in low relief. The panels read down the left-hand door, from the creation of Adam to Cain slaying Abel, and up the right-hand door, which begins with the Annunciation and ends with the Resurrection. The scenes are carefully balanced against each other, suggesting the divine remedy for each of mankind's lapses from grace.

Even more remarkable is the next surviving work commissioned by Bernward, the bronze pillar, based on Roman triumphal pillars such as those of Trajan or Marcus Aurelius. This is a hollow casting, in three pieces; the detail is even more striking than that of the doors. A spiral band shows twenty-four of the acts of Jesus, from his baptism to his entry into Jerusalem. The imperial achievements of the models for the pillar are replaced by Christ's divine progress, but otherwise the link between the art of the classical past and that of the new empire of the west is close. This is one of the most clearly 'Romanesque' works to survive, in the sense of deriving directly from Roman models.

Below the crossing hangs the earliest of the three great chandeliers which survive from eleventh-century Germany, commissioned by bishop Hezilo in the decade which saw the consecration of the rebuilt cathedral. As at Aachen, the 'crown of lights' represents the heavenly Jerusalem, and each of the towers and gates bears the name of an apostle or prophet; but it is much richer in detail than Frederick Barbarossa's chandelier, its gilded brass worked into intricate low relief patterns, and the architecture of its portals more elaborately represented.

Another bishop is commemorated by a splendid mid-twelfth-century reliquary chest in the crypt. St Godehard's intense, bowed figure peers out at us from one end of the casket, between the pope and another bishop. At the other end is Christ in Majesty, while the twelve apostles are ranged along the sides. A contemporary chest, also in the crypt, containing the relics of St Epiphanius, one of the patron saints of the church, is another reminder of the remarkable skill in metalwork of the craftsmen of the empire under the Salians.

The last of the wealth of masterpieces here is the font, a huge bronze basin supported on four figures, all on bended knee, representing the four rivers of paradise, and with a massive cover. The handling of both the supporters and the figures on the font itself is freer and more lifelike; yet the overall planning of the design is still formal, divided by borders with explanatory lettering and interrupted by medallions of prophets and virtues, emphasizing that the programme of the reliefs is more important than the artistic content.

Beyond the east end of the cathedral is a cloister, the walls of which are lined with memorials to clerics from the ninth century onwards. In the centre is a pleasing Gothic chapel, but the most famous sight is the legendary 'thousand-year-old' rose tree, said to be the tree associated with the foundation of Hildesheim. Louis the Pious's chaplain once absentmindedly left the relics from the emperor's private chapel hanging in a tree in the forest, after he had celebrated mass in the open air when Louis was on his travels. Some days later, he realized they were missing and rode back posthaste to the spot, only to find that he could not remove them from the tree and that a spring of pure water had appeared below them. The emperor, summoned to witness the miracle, decided to build his new cathedral on the spot. In the sixteenth or seventeenth century, the wild rose growing on the cathedral apse was identified with the tree of the miracle; and after the bombing of the cathedral in 1945, although apparently burnt beyond hope of recovery, it put out new shoots the following spring.

Bishop Bernward was also responsible for the building of the other great Romanesque church in Hildesheim, St Michael's. This was to be the church of a new monastery and its foundation stone was laid in 1001. It was dedicated in 1022. Bishop Bernward himself was buried here later that year. His remarkable career had included, besides building activities, travels in Italy and involvement in imperial politics, a successful defence of the town against the Vikings in 995. His tombstone can be seen in the crypt. Like the cathedral, St Michael's suffered from a fire in the twelfth century and from bombing in the Second World War. Its interior is largely a reconstruction, apart from the 'Angel Choir' of the twelfth century, with its delightful decorative arcades. However, the brilliantly painted roof, built after the twelfth-century fire, was carefully dismantled and stored in 1943 and is once again in place. In bold reds, blues and greens, it depicts the descent of Christ from Adam, through Jesse, David, Solomon, Hezekiah and Josiah; the last four are shown as crowned kings, and they are followed by the Virgin and a modern version of Christ in Majesty. Prophets bearing scrolls foretelling Christ's coming flank the central panels, and St Michael stands at Christ's right hand. The four evangelists and the four rivers of paradise also appear – the latter is an unusual motif, possibly due to some local relic or tradition. The outer border completes Christ's genealogy. Miniatures from this period are relatively common, but only a handful of painted works on this scale survive. There is a fine, almost contemporary, ceiling at Zillis in Switzerland, but St Michael's ceiling is on a far grander design and scale, a reminder that architecture was not the only medium in which a medieval artist could carry out a monumental scheme; a reminder, too, that colour and ornament were predominant in medieval churches and that today we all too often see only the bare bones.

Venice

French and German architects in the tenth and eleventh century worked in a tradition which stemmed from the 'classical revival' of Charlemagne's reign, the style we know as Carolingian Romanesque, which derived from Charlemagne's claim to be the heir to the Roman empire in the west. In the south of Europe, however, the Byzantine empire was a far stronger influence. In the early eleventh century it still held most of the Adriatic, apart from the north-western shore, and Byzantium was the most important commercial centre in the Mediterranean. It was natural, therefore, that a trading city like Venice, while keeping a wary eye on the activities of the German emperors, should be in many ways more closely linked to Byzantium, to which it had originally been subject, than to the western cities. A magnificent marriage alliance in 1062 between the son of the ruling doge and the niece of the co-emperor of Byzantium marks the political apogee of this relationship, though the Venetians were to become effective masters of Byzantium itself after the Fourth Crusade, which they succeeded in diverting from its proper goal in the Holy Land to sacking the capital of the eastern empire instead.

This Byzantine influence is nowhere clearer than in early Venetian architecture, and particularly in San Marco. San Marco was not designed as a cathedral (it was originally built as the doge's chapel, and became a cathedral only in 1807), but its scale and setting within the city are such that it cannot be classed with ordinary churches. The original basilica was begun in 825, when some enterprising Venetian merchants abducted a body said to be that of St Mark from Alexandria. The doge immediately ordered a chapel to be built to house the relic; it is possible that this was a large-scale building on a similar plan to the present church, though Venice was hardly wealthy enough in the ninth century to embark suddenly on such a great enterprise. It is more likely that either the rebuilding after the fire of 976 or the second rebuilding in 1063 took as its model the church of the Holy Apostles at Byzantium, built in the sixth century by the emperor Justinian, which had five domes arranged in a cruciform plan. The new building, begun by doge Contarini, was far enough advanced in 1095 for it to be dedicated, but work on the marble veneer and the mosaics – both typically Byzantine decorations – continued well into the twelfth century, to be resumed in the thirteenth century when the spoils from the capture of Byzantium itself by the Fourth Crusade made Venice immensely wealthy.

The façade as we see it today is basically that depicted on the mosaic above the left-hand doorway of the façade, carried out in about 1260–70, which shows the translation of St Mark's body to the new basilica. But the simplicity of the original outline has been obscured by the Gothic and later decoration of pinnacles, spires and statues around the arcade; the plain west window was inserted in 1419 in place of a smaller arcaded window. The four bronze horses, however, have been in their present position since the mid thirteenth century (except for a brief interlude when Napoleon carried them off to Paris). They are the only surviving Roman triumphal group of this type and came originally from Chios to the Hippodrome at Byzantium; they were seized in the course of the Fourth Crusade, and reached Venice soon after 1204.

The impressive width of the façade is due to the unusual arrangement of the west end, the whole of the nave being surrounded by an atrium, the right-hand branch of which contains the baptistery. The actual width of the church itself corresponds to the three central doorways. The upper part of the façade forms a magnificent terrace, used on state occasions by the rulers of Venice to watch festivals and tournaments held in the piazza below. To the right of the façade, the tower containing the treasury faces the Doge's Palace; it is possibly part of the original ninth-century palace of which San Marco was the chapel, and has fine tracery screen panels as part of its covering.

The atrium forms an exceptionally spacious porch to the body of the church. In an age when it was not uncommon for all kinds of business to be transacted in or around a church, the size of the atrium may reflect Venice's commercial importance. Here are to be found an exceptional series of mosaics, the finest in the building, showing scenes from the Old Testament. Their construction occupied almost the whole of the thirteenth century, and they have survived with relatively little restoration. The long period of work meant that the style gradually changed from static late Romanesque to a more fluid forerunner of Gothic art. The vast programme of subjects covered means that the mosaics are a series of vignettes, ranging from the naïve to the stately, with entertaining touches such as the selection of animals and birds which Noah takes into the ark. They are related to the early pictorial Bibles of the sixth and seventh centuries, such as the Cotton Genesis in the British Library, the miniatures of which were executed in a manner which was easily adapted to the very different medium of mosaic.

The interior of San Marco is one of the few buildings which retain the aura of splendour and mystery at which Romanesque architects seem to have aimed. It is a world away from the light and air of Gothic at its most refined, emphasizing instead awe and reverence, and the splendour which must surround the holy places. From the shadows there glow rich marbles and mosaics and the great jewelled shrine of the saint himself. There is no one focal point, but the impression of a vast and mysterious treasure-house, in both the spiritual and material sense. Part of every successive Venetian triumph in war or commerce went to enrich San Marco, not by any formal arrangement, but by gradual accretions, until it rivalled and even outshone anything in the city from which its artists and architects had drawn their inspiration, Byzantium itself. It is an extraordinary building in that it seems to be made up of the hoardings of centuries, apparently combined at random, and yet it manages to retain its unity. Many pieces are in many cases Roman or Greek in origin: the holy water stoup is a porphyry bowl from the second century AD; some of the pillars date from the third century, while others are sixth-century Byzantine work; the carved and pierced panels of the parapets are likewise plunder from the imperial past, made up with local copies in the eleventh century.

Succeeding centuries have also made their contributions: the rood screen is fourteenth-century and there is much work by Jacopo Sansovino, who not only carried out sensitive restorations from 1529 onwards, but also provided statues and sketches for mosaics, and the great bronze sacristy doors. The great gold altar screen typifies this process. Ordered in Byzantium about 976, it was enriched in 1105; in 1209 some of the spoils of the Fourth Crusade, in the form of Byzantine enamels, were added, and the whole screen was refashioned again, and more enamels added, in 1345. The enamels were not even exclusively religious, as there is a fine series of eighteen tenth-century secular scenes towards the foot of the screen. Perhaps the most spectacular piece of booty is the Virgin of Victory, 'Nicopoeia', which the Byzantine emperor used to carry at the head of his army when he set out on campaign and which was worshipped in turn as the protectress of Venice.

Besides the wealth of marvellous objects – and a full catalogue would run into volumes – the interior of San Marco has a succession of mosaics as resplendent, if not as coherent, as those in the atrium. They fall into two series: an early cycle begun before the building itself was complete, and a second cycle on which work began in the twelfth century and continued into the fourteenth. The mosaic workshop attached to San Marco has continued both to repair and to create new mosaics down to the present day, though its work now is almost exclusively conservation. The scheme of the mosaics is on a suitably grandiose scale. The subjects, by contrast with the atrium, are drawn from the New Testament, with a second series depicting the life of St Mark and the history of the church itself. The early set of mosaics are strongly Byzantine in character, with icon-like figures on a gold background. The figure of Christ as ruler appears in the traditional position in the apse, and the scenes are carefully laid out so that the most important episodes from the New Testament appear in and around the central cupola. The scenes of the Passion on the west arch below the cupola are especially powerful, for here the static Byzantine attitudes give way to the anguished attitudes typical of late Romanesque art. Many medieval churches must have had equally elaborate decorative programmes – that at Saint-Savin-sur-Gartempe, near Poitiers, is an example – but they were usually in fresco, and have therefore decayed or perished, whereas the mosaics here have survived almost unscathed.

The resplendent furnishings and decoration of San Marco were once matched by an even more spectacular treasury, but most of the treasure was melted down in the early days of the Napoleonic republic; what remains is none the less an impressive and varied collection, particularly of rare Byzantine pieces.

San Marco is unique; it stands apart from the rest of medieval European architecture, but it also reminds us that beyond western Christendom lay another, richer Christian civilization, which astonished and enchanted those from the distant west who saw it, just as San Marco astonishes and enchants us today.*

Périgueux

Only one church in the west seems to have been modelled on San Marco, the cathedral of Saint-Front at Périgueux. The link is not immediately obvious, but if we remember that when Saint-Front was designed, San Marco was still for the most part bare brickwork rather than glittering marble and mosaics, the immediate difference vanishes, and the similarities of plan stand out.

Its startling white silhouette dominates the old city as you

* See Sicily (pp. 204–9) for the other great link between Europe and the east.

approach Périgueux from the north. If Saint-Front looks remarkable today, it has had an even more remarkable history. The first
church to be built there, the ruins of which can be traced to the
west of the present building, was put up in honour of the saint
who brought Christianity to the Périgord region and whose relics
belonged to a monastery on this site. They were preserved in a
most unusual round tomb below the high altar. Probably as the
result of a fire which destroyed much of the monastery and
the old church in 1120, a new church was begun to the east of the
existing one, centring on the same high altar and therefore facing
west. A pilgrim entering the church would have passed under the
impressive bell-tower above the porch and would have been faced
immediately by the great shrine of Saint-Front. The bell-tower
is one of the few surviving original parts, though the detail and
the cone which crowns it were reworked during the restorations
of the last century. Otherwise, the ravages of the Protestants in
1575 (when the tomb of Saint-Front was destroyed), of the rebels
of the Fronde in 1652 under the Prince de Condé, and a succession
of makeshift attempts to repair the fabric had all left the cathedral
in a perilous state. In 1852 the architect Paul Abadie was called
in. His enthusiasm for Romanesque architecture was considerable;
but the knowledge and techniques needed for a proper restoration
were not to hand. Instead he virtually rebuilt the whole edifice.
The result may break the purist's heart, but the new church has
a strong character of its own. The exterior, with its multiple spires,
pinnacles and domes, is a forerunner of Sacré-Cœur at Montmartre,
but it has individual touches, such as the use of *lauzes*, flat stone
tiles heaped up to form the pyramidal roofs, and the pillared
supports below them, which are rooted in the local style of medieval
building. And no one can deny the force of its silhouette when
seen from across the river.

The interior is less successful. The proportions may be elegant,
but the greyish-white stone and regularity of the work make it
monotonous, and the church has now been 'turned round' so that
the altar is traditionally placed, to the east. The west end incorporates parts of the earliest church, including two curious cells,
called 'confessionals', to north and south. The cloister to the
south is in sharp contrast to the church. Little restored, it is lined
by square columns and a small formal garden has been made in

the centre; here the original top of the bell-tower is preserved. A staircase leads up to a terrace with views to the south, across the river; and for the adventurous there is a walk round Abadie's forest of spires, a fascinating tour – though only for the reasonably agile – with glimpses of the red and grey roofs of the old town with little balustraded verandas on some of the top storeys.

Pisa

By the end of the eleventh century, the Italian ports were among the most prosperous towns in the country. In addition to Venice and Bari on the east coast, the western ports had seen a dramatic rise in their fortunes. In 1001 and 1011, Pisa had been plundered by Moslem raiders: by 1034, with the decline of Arab naval power, it was Pisa which was plundering North Africa. The conquest of Arab Sicily by the Normans (see p. 204 below) was a further blow to Arab power and opened up a huge new market to the merchants of Pisa, Genoa and Venice. But there was also considerable rivalry between the ports, particularly those on the west: in 1135 Pisa destroyed Amalfi, but soon afterwards she ruined herself by remaining loyal to the imperial cause, while her neighbours were staunch supporters of the pope. Genoa became Pisa's main rival; what was at stake was the trade with Sardinia and Sicily, which the Genoese saw as a natural extension of their control of trade along the Mediterranean coast from Barcelona eastwards to Portovenere. Pisa's fortunes fluctuated with those of her imperial patrons, and, not long after the virtual collapse of imperial power in the interregnum of 1250–73, the Genoese overwhelmed the Pisan fleet at Meloria in 1284, and the city, hitherto fiercely independent, became the subject first of local lords, then of Milan, and finally of Florence.

The cathedral at Pisa and its associated buildings stand isolated in an open space to the north-west of the town, an unusual setting for an Italian church, and one which in itself is a reminder that Pisa has shrunk in size since her heyday in the twelfth century. Fortunately this freedom from surrounding buildings is ideally suited to the cathedral, as it allows the simplicity and regularity of the design to stand out. It is in fact a basilica church built in Romanesque style, modified from the plans of the original architect, Buschetus, who began work in 1063, by his twelfth-century successor Rainaldus. But it has highly original features. What is at first sight a simple basilica interior proves to be three basilicas, two of which, set face to face, make up the transepts. Each part is treated as a unit; the nave gallery is carried across the ends of the transepts, forming a miniature façade to the transept basilicas, and each terminates in a rounded apse, the width of the central part. The galleries continue round the transepts, again emphasizing their role as independent entities. The proportions of the three component parts are kept in balance by giving the nave double aisles. The basilican character of the main nave is further emphasized by the use of purely classical columns, and even the stripes of dark stone and white marble from nearby Carrara have precedents in classical architecture. The nave also retains an open timber roof, rebuilt in the early seventeenth century after a serious fire in 1595. A notable school of local sculptors worked on the building: the original pulpit, by Guglielmo of Pisa, is now in the cathedral at Cagliari in Sardinia, but the bronze doors by Bonanno of Pisa, made in the late twelfth century for the south door, are still in position: a series of original images in the manner of Byzantine icons illustrate the life of Christ in panels bordered by rosettes, while at the foot a row of saints between palm trees add an oriental touch. In the early fourteenth century, Giovanni Pisano created a new pulpit in the Gothic style, highly elaborate and vivid in its depiction of the Last Judgement, while his father Nicola carved the even finer pulpit in the baptistery in 1260. The fine tomb of the emperor Henry VII by Tino da Camaino is a reminder of Pisa's role as a supporter of the empire. Henry died suddenly near Siena in August 1313, ending hopes that he might be able to restore some kind of imperial authority in Italy. Dante, writing the *Divine Comedy* when he heard of his death, has a vision of the throne reserved for him in the highest part of heaven, and regards him as one of the greatest of the Holy Roman emperors. The tomb has Gothic figures but a suitably classical pedestal.

The outside of the cathedral is clad in marble, with narrow bands of darker stone: the overall effect, on a bright spring day, is of dazzling whiteness against blue sky and green grass. The elaborate pillared arcades on the façade break up its otherwise sheer and four-square lines, giving depth of light and shade. This façade is the latest part of the work, and is more emphatic than the rather subtle pilaster work around the rest of the exterior, which serves to emphasize the careful composition of the whole rather than to distract the eye with detail.

As elsewhere in Italy, there is a detached campanile. It has acquired such notoriety as the Leaning Tower of Pisa that it is hard to consider it as a bell-tower and as an integral part of the cathedral group. It was started in 1173, to a design which derives from cylindrical belfries at Ravenna, but which was adapted to match the cathedral by surrounding it by tiers of marble arcading. The tower was only thirty-five feet high when lack of adequate foundations caused it to tilt, but work continued none the less; the architect tried to compensate by loading the higher side of the tower and by curving the line of the tower as it rose. The tower was completed in the mid fourteenth century, with a bell-cage in a slightly more decorated style. It has continued to subside until the present day, and recent operations have succeeded only in slowing the rate of subsidence: it is now nearly fourteen feet out of true on a total height of 179 feet.

The baptistery, designed by an architect named Diotisalvi and begun in 1153, is a rotunda based on the church of the Holy Sepulchre in Jerusalem: Pisa had strong links with Palestine through the crusades, pilgrims and trade. The details hark back to classical architecture, but the present outline is due to Gothic remodelling, first in 1260–90 and then in the fourteenth century, when the original conical roof was turned into a dome, with the cone projecting as a kind of finial. The upper stages were given Gothic arcading at the same time, and the cone, originally open at the centre, was roofed over.

The survival of campanile and baptistery as well as the cathedral, all virtually in their original form, would be enough to make Pisa remarkable; the same group can be found in rare instances elsewhere, but never with such unity of style, nor in a setting which so emphasizes the coherence of the buildings. Even more unusual is the presence of a fourth building at Pisa, the Campo Santo, or medieval cemetery. It is a mainly Gothic building, much damaged in the Second World War and since restored, and the details are entirely Gothic. But the plan is that of a classical atrium, like that attached to basilica churches in Rome and Milan. Here the plan is retained, but the atrium has become detached. It retains a Romanesque aspect in the treatment of the pilaster work, which echoes that on the lower storeys of the cathedral. Inside, the famous frescoes, of which engravings were first published in 1812 and which may have influenced the English Pre-Raphaelites, have been deteriorating ever since they were first recognized as masterpieces; the bombardment of 1944 merely gave the *coup de grâce* to many of them. The earth within the Campo Santo is traditionally said to have been brought from the Holy Land by Pisan ships trading there in the twelfth century. In medieval times the poor were buried in the centre and the rich under the arcades. Many Roman sarcophagi remain, some of which were re-used in the Middle Ages.

The impression made by the cathedral at Pisa when it was first built can be judged by the number of churches in the region for which it served as model. Lucca has a cathedral whose façade is a variation on that at Pisa, made more dramatic by rising out of a closely packed townscape, and covered with exotic detail that enriches the pillars and arcades. Even parts of the cathedral at Genoa, Pisa's great rival, reflect the glory of the Pisan building. Ironically, it was Genoa's triumph and Pisa's consequent decline that has preserved the original in all its white splendour for us to marvel at today.

Modena

The sources of north Italian Romanesque architecture are more diverse than the rather restrained style of German Romanesque. There are traces not only of the original severity of Roman military engineering, but of experimental vaults from Armenia and decorative patterns from the churches of Syria, so that buildings with relatively simple plans are much more complex in finished detail. There was also a much greater weight of tradition in north Italy, and the nearby basilica churches of Rome and Ravenna could not be lightly disregarded, whereas north of the Alps there were very few such examples. The church sites were often ancient and influenced new building; at Sant'Ambrogio, in Milan, there is a huge forecourt, built in the Romanesque style but using the ground plan of an earlier basilica. Other sites in Italy were already hemmed in by buildings in the centre of a town, whereas north of the Alps the town often grew up around the cathedral.

The churches of Lombardy, an area disputed between partisans of pope and emperor during the eleventh and twelfth centuries, form a homogeneous group, whose particular characteristics are fine detached campaniles or bell-towers and the absence of western towers in favour of sheer screen-façades, elaborately detailed with arcading, contrasting with the broken silhouette of apses and transepts at the eastern end. The cathedral at Parma, rebuilt after an earthquake in 1117, shows how a variety of such forms – there are apses at the transept ends and characteristically Italian square roofs to transepts and choir – could become an impressive composition; the most striking touch is the octagonal central lantern, forerunner of the Renaissance dome of Florence cathedral.

At Modena cathedral, begun some twenty years before Parma (in 1099), we know the architect's name, Lanfranco. It is an individual building, with a remarkable triforium arcade which runs right round the exterior of the building. The façade is no longer a massive screen, but is stepped to correspond with the structure of nave and aisles. The rose window was enlarged in the late twelfth century, but otherwise the original plans were faithfully carried out over a period of more than a century. The façade has a projecting central loggia, with columns resting on a pair of lions, a theme which was to be a commonplace in Italian architecture and is to be found much further afield. The upper part of the loggia is part of the triforium, as if some great procession were meant to culminate with the appearance of a bishop or prince to a crowd in the cathedral square – but the detail is decorative and not meant for any real purpose.

The original Romanesque roof of openwork timbers was replaced by vaults in the fifteenth century, but the interior is otherwise unchanged. The architectural detail inside is much more restrained, though the layout is unusual to our eyes. The altar is raised on a tribune, which gives access to the crypt below; note the lions supporting the tribune pillars yet again. This raised altar was a not infrequent arrangement in pilgrimage churches, though later modifications either levelled the east end and destroyed the crypt, as at Angoulême, or screened it from view with staircases or other additions. Here the altar is approached by stairs from the aisles.

Modena has not only a striking architectural character, but also an important series of early Romanesque sculptures. We know the name of one artist, Wiligelmo, who worked on the main eastern porch between 1099 and 1106. The figures placed in an arcade which echoes the triforium above represent scenes from Genesis and are carried out with a minimum of external decoration: leaves suggest paradise, waves are drawn as lines on the background. There is no clear division of scenes, to avoid breaking the rhythm of the arcades, which are similar to those found on sarcophagi from classical times. Other talented sculptors worked on the south and north façades, and there is evidence that they drew on a much wider range of material, both in style and subject. It is possible to see echoes of the work of Gislebertus at Autun, and, on the frieze on the tribune, with scenes from the Passion and a formal Last Supper, Provençal influence. On the Porta della Pescheria, there is a sculpture which poses all kinds of cultural questions. It represents an episode from Arthurian romance, and it is generally agreed that it was carried out about 1120–30, that is, some thirty years before the earliest *written* version of the romance in question. Nor is Italy renowned as a home for Arthurian romance. How did the story get to Italy? Why should it have been chosen for the archivolt of a cathedral doorway? It is possible that the story came with the Bretons who accompanied duke Robert of Normandy on the First Crusade and who were in Modena just as the cathedral was being built; perhaps some local lord who had contributed to the costs asked for it to be placed there. It is a salutary reminder of how little we know about vast areas of medieval life, and how a whole network of traditional links represented by an unwritten, oral culture has almost entirely vanished from the records.

The Gothic Cathedrals

It is hard to believe today, when Gothic art is regarded as the supreme achievement of the Middle Ages, that it was once despised and labelled barbarous. Yet that is how the men of the Renaissance viewed the great works of their ancestors: looking back to classical antiquity as the only yardstick for artistic qualities, they condemned medieval art as a whole as the work of the Goths who had destroyed the Roman empire. The idea originated in Italy, where French medieval architecture and art had left relatively few traces, and so it also had nationalistic overtones: Goths began north of the Alps. It was a wholesale condemnation: the often highly classical work of Romanesque artists was included. Only in the nineteenth century did the term Gothic come to have its present meaning of thirteenth- and fourteenth-century art, deriving from styles first seen in France in the late twelfth century, whose hallmark is the replacement of the rounded arch by the pointed arch, and in which sculpture and painting lose their formal, hieratic appearance and become more vivid and three-dimensional, with an emphasis on movement and curving lines. A Romanesque artist tried to instil awe and respect; the new style appealed to the emotions instead.

These are of course broad generalizations, compass points rather than precise directions. In architecture, there are other factors at work, factors which we can often deduce only from the buildings themselves, because we have no treatises on architecture for this period. Firstly, there were enormous advances in civil engineering, and this is nowhere more obvious than in the great cathedrals. The Romanesque buildings rely on known, tried and trusted principles; where in doubt, the architect built more massively than he needed to. Because his prime concern was to impress, this did not concern him unduly. The Gothic cathedral, on the other hand, tended towards light, soaring lines and huge spaces, so that while greater and greater heights were demanded, the walls could not be proportionally heavier to achieve this; quite the reverse, because whereas Romanesque windows were small, the builders of the Gothic period were trying to insert huge areas of glass into the walls. The means to these various ends – pointed arches, ribbed vaults, flying buttresses – had been discovered by the mid twelfth century, and the Gothic architects refined the techniques until they transformed the outward appearance of the buildings.

The new buildings were immensely expensive. Few monasteries could afford such a church, and, as we have seen, many towns which had fallen on evil days were also unable to rebuild their existing cathedrals. The great Gothic churches are primarily civic monuments, funded by the new-found riches of the towns that had sprung up across Europe in the twelfth and thirteenth centuries. Indeed, the Gothic style is so universal for cathedrals that it is not uncommon, even in recent books on the latter, to find the cathedral being treated as synonymous with a Gothic building and their Romanesque predecessors being almost totally ignored. If the generalization that all medieval cathedrals are Gothic is patently untrue, we should also beware of linking the building of the cathedrals entirely with civic wealth and pride. Some of the greatest buildings are in relatively small towns, whose ecclesiastical importance is quite out of proportion to their population or resources. Canterbury is one such example: here the cathedral was rebuilt after a fire in 1174, out of the offerings made at the shrine of the newly martyred archbishop, Thomas Becket. Chartres is another, where money came not only from the town, but from the lords of the countryside around and from the king himself. Elsewhere, the great merchants, used to planning bold enterprises, widely travelled, and well able to contribute, might set the building of a cathedral in motion, but everyone in the community would contribute, either in cash or, for humbler folk, in kind – a day spent carting timber or hauling stone.

The finished cathedral was the focal point of a town. Its spire was a landmark for the approaching traveller: it stood in the very heart of a city, and the great festivals of the year were celebrated there. Its imposing bulk rose sheer out of the houses huddled around it (the cathedral square is usually an improvement of the nineteenth century) and everyday activities overflowed into the cathedral itself. Old St Paul's in London was perhaps exceptional – 'one of the most desecrated churches in Christendom' – but the activities recorded there at different times give an idea of how much secular life went on in a cathedral. Merchants would be found there, doing business; but they were merely talking, unlike the wine-sellers at Chartres or the stall-holders at fair-time in Exeter cathedral. Pedlars sold trinkets, prostitutes plied their trade and pickpockets worked among the crowds. Lawyers and city officials were to be found there. Beggars and penniless debtors haunted the area called 'Duke Humphrey's Walk', and the phrases 'to dine with duke Humphrey', meaning to go without dinner, came from these cathedral loiterers. In the crypt the London booksellers stored their stock.

All this took place in the outer parts of the cathedral, or possibly in the nave, which was bare of chairs or pews. The choir and altar were forbidden to ordinary laymen, and in the later Middle Ages this area became an isolated inner sanctum, protected from the hubbub of the nave by huge stone screens and elaborate choir-stalls. We are used to seeing the interiors of cathedrals as replanned in the eighteenth century, when the emphasis was on openness and the participation of the congregation in all services. In Protestant cathedrals the great rood-screens disappeared even earlier, at the Reformation, and we have to go to Auch or Albi in southern France to find an example of the 'closed' stone-walled inner sanctum in which the clergy isolated themselves to carry out their devotions, often in some comfort. Besides the main services of the cathedral itself, there would be innumerable chantry priests saying masses for the souls of the dead: Old St Paul's had over fifty such chapels. We tend to imagine cathedrals as empty buildings, used only on special occasions, and to bewail their invasion by crowds of eager tourists, but these crowds are only the latter-day equivalent of the secular use that medieval men made of cathedrals.

The new style of architecture replaced the solid outer walls of Romanesque buildings with walls that came to consist predominantly of pillars and windows. There was no room for the great fresco cycles that had once ornamented great churches, and Gothic frescoes are almost a contradiction in terms: few traces of elaborate wall-painting from this period survive. Instead, the stories of the Old and New Testament and the deeds of the saints appear in stained glass. This art form first appears in the building which was the prototype for Gothic architecture, the abbey of Saint-Denis at Paris, created by abbot Suger in the 1140s and 1150s. Sculpture, already important on Romanesque buildings, was used to depict more and more elaborate programmes, until – as on the west front of Wells – the entire west end became a vast gallery of figures, figures which, unlike their Romanesque predecessors, were no longer reliefs but detached, three-dimensional and very vivid. Wells originally possessed 400 such figures on the west front; Milan, at the very end of the Gothic tradition, has no less than 2,245 in all.

Such immense collections of sculpture underline the complex nature of the Gothic cathedral as a whole. We have the names of one or two Romanesque architects, chiefly in Italy; in the Gothic period, partly because records are fuller, partly because the master-mason was a much more important figure, we know a good deal about them. The master-mason co-ordinated the whole work as he would today, offering designs to his clients, consulting with scholars over the programme of sculptures; but he also acted as the contractor, supervising the workmen, though the actual hiring was usually done by a clerk of the works employed by the cathedral chapter. The names of these master-masons, whom we would call architects today, were recorded in the building itself, in prominent positions; and they were men of substance, paid at considerably higher rates than the ordinary masons, from whose ranks they had risen. A tombstone at Saint-Nicaise in Reims, destroyed in 1789, showed Hugues Libergier, the architect of the church, holding a church and with square and compasses beside him, in much the same style as a knight or a wealthy merchant. Nearby in the cathedral, a great labyrinth pattern inlaid in the floor listed the successive 'masters of the works'. By the fifteenth century, we hear of a Spanish architect being sent to study different cathedrals before he embarked on the construction of a new bell-tower at Valencia.

Most of the architect's work would be actual technical drawings, incised on a special plaster floor, traces of which survive at Wells and York. These drawings would derive from master-plans made on parchments. The most famous examples are those for the towers at Ulm and Cologne, rediscovered in the nineteenth century and used for their completion. The elevations were laid out with the help of complex geometrical rules, which have survived in sixteenth-century treatises, while details were similarly built up from geometrical patterns. John Harvey has pointed out that the great development of Gothic, which requires detailed geometrical knowledge, appears to follow the re-introduction of Euclid's geometry to the west, translated from the Arabic by Adelard of Bath in about 1125. We can see an architect at work in the famous sketchbook which Villard de Honnecourt compiled between 1220 and 1235. Many of the drawings are for sculpture, others are simply doodles or notes 'from the life'; but the most interesting for our purpose are ground plans of churches, using the same conventions as we would employ today, with the vaulting patterns indicated. There are drawings, too, for rose windows, flying buttresses and other details of church building, together with methods of measurement and sketches of the mechanical aids available to thirteenth-century builders. It reflects a world of high technical achievement, practical, yet with a sound theoretical grounding.

Because Gothic architecture is so much more technical than Romanesque, it is all too easy to see the new techniques as dictating the form of the buildings. But this is to put the cart before the horse: the techniques which made Gothic cathedrals possible came into being because men wanted to create buildings of a certain type, to move away from the massive and powerful lines of Romanesque towards elegance and light. Parallels can be found in the new philosophy of the twelfth century, the 'twelfth-century renaissance', with its emphasis on order and clarity and its search for simple and all-embracing definitions. Gothic buildings are more frequently designed as a unity than Romanesque ones; but it is dangerous to argue that unity distinguishes Gothic from Romanesque if we consider the ground plans of buildings such as Pisa or Speyer. A more reasonable explanation is that Romanesque patrons rarely had sufficient funds to plan and complete a building in one campaign, whereas the new disposable wealth available in the twelfth century enabled total rebuilding to be carried out. Furthermore, there was far less partial rebuilding of Gothic cathedrals (however unfashionable they may have been) by later architects than there was of Romanesque cathedrals in the Gothic age, when a new east end or tower or other detail was frequently added. So as we see them today, Gothic cathedrals are more unified than Romanesque, but this is not always due to a different approach on the part of their architects.

Proportion and order are also quoted as characteristic of Gothic; yet Romanesque is also deeply rooted in both these principles, if at a simpler level. I would define Gothic as an architecture in which technical mastery is used to transcend the nature of the materials, an apt parallel to the Christian preaching that man should transcend his material being. In a Gothic cathedral, the strong vertical lines make the building seem higher and more spacious than it is, the walls are apparently made of glass, the stone roof seems insubstantial, the stone statues are full of movement and are three-dimensional. There is a strong element of illusion, of things being other than they are, which contrasts with the sharp reality of Romanesque, its reassuring and protective solidity and its suggestion of God's presence in the recesses of the sanctuary. Romanesque architecture reassures us that God is with us here on earth; Gothic offers us a gateway to heaven.

Chartres

Chartres cathedral is dedicated to the Virgin Mary, and from the ninth century onwards was a great centre of pilgrimage. Its two most precious relics were an ancient image known as the 'Virgin about to bring forth' and the sacred tunic which she was said to have worn at the birth of Christ. With the rising tide of enthusiasm for the cult of the Virgin in the eleventh and twelfth centuries, the cathedral prospered and also became the centre of a famous school. The ninth-century church was opulently rebuilt by bishop Fulbert, one of the most famous teachers at the school of Chartres, after a fire in 1020, and in the mid twelfth century a new western façade with twin towers was begun. This had only just been completed when a second fire, on 10 June 1194, destroyed the east end and nave, leaving only the west towers and narthex standing. The precious relics were also thought to have been destroyed, but a massive crypt had been built below the east end, where the ground fell away; a day or two after the fire, it was discovered that some priests had taken refuge there with the relics and had survived unscathed. This was hailed as a miracle; indeed, the story comes straight from the pages of one of the collections of Miracles of the Virgin which were just becoming popular at the time, a collection devoted to the miracles wrought by the Virgin at Chartres.

Such a miracle aroused an enthusiastic response when an appeal for the rebuilding of the cathedral was made. The inhabitants of Chartres, of course, had economic reasons for wanting the cathedral rebuilt as soon as possible, because the pilgrims and the four great fairs on the feast days of the Virgin were their major source of income. But emissaries from Chartres were welcomed throughout France and were given permission to travel freely about England in search of donations. The response was immediate, and within twenty-five years the new cathedral was erected, though it was not until 1260 that all the glass and sculpture was in position.

The designer of Chartres had a major problem to overcome: the presence of the existing crypt and west façade, which were to be incorporated in the new structure. This meant that he was faced not only by a very wide vault to be spanned in stone instead of wood, but also by a complex base at the east end. He not only solved these problems and succeeded in imposing a very regular plan, but used the newly discovered principle of flying buttresses to support the vault. Until now, the weight of the vault had been taken up by walls with interior galleries; at Notre-Dame in Paris and here, the walls now rose sheer from the nave, and only the structural element of the galleries was retained, as a skeleton of stonework outside the church itself. At Chartres, for the first time, the nave walls are divided into three tiers instead of four, and the tribune gallery disappears entirely. Hence the clerestory windows become much deeper and the vertical lines more emphatic than ever. The area of glass is much greater; but it is not used simply to lighten the interior. Rather, the stained glass replaces the paintings which would have adorned an earlier church; they are a kind of illuminated fresco, brought to life by the light.

Stained glass is another of the innovations of the Gothic period, and the great masterpieces are to be found in and around Paris: at Saint-Denis, at Chartres, at the Sainte-Chapelle. The use of coloured glass can be traced back to fifth-century Byzantium, but the possibilities of the medium became apparent only when lead framing within the window was invented, in the tenth century. However, such a frame provided little strength, and in the following century iron bars were set across the window spaces to hold the glass in place. The windows at Chartres are therefore examples of the very latest techniques. Unlike many later windows, where miniature scenes appear in places where they could scarcely be read, at Chartres the great clerestory windows have figures on an appropriate scale, while the windows that tell the story of the Old and New Testaments (and other matters, such as the *Chanson de Roland*, as well) are placed at ground level, in the aisles and ambulatory. On a bright day, coming into the cathedral, the immediate effect is of darkness, until the windows gradually begin to glow with colour; for the glass is deliberately jewel-like, with bright but strong tones. There is relatively little white glass, and the backgrounds are dark blue and dark red. This is due to the limited technical resources available. Six or eight colours could be made easily and reliably by mixing certain chemicals with the glass sand: cobalt for blue, copper oxide for red and so on. The black details were painted on afterwards with a special pigment, and it is this that usually deteriorates first. The craftsmen had to overcome formidable difficulties to produce glass – for example, it had to be blown in cylinders, which were cut and flattened while still malleable; and some of the methods they devised to solve their problems cannot be reproduced today. The very unevenness of the resulting glass is turned to advantage, in that the light is reflected and refracted on it in a way that smoothly machined glass can never imitate. Yet all this skill would be in vain without the artistic power of the designs; to take just one example, 'Notre Dame de la belle verrière', erected in 1218 in memory of a local count, is one of the great masterpieces of early Gothic art.

Chartres is equally rich in sculpture, and presents on the west façade some of the few surviving works from the very end of the Romanesque period. The figures are placed in a typically Roman-esque layout, and the central characters are portrayed in the traditional statuesque attitudes, so much so that the statues on either side of the doorway are transformed into pillars, with stylized and elongated bodies. It is the portrayal of the faces which breaks away from the norms of Romanesque art: the heads become three-dimensional, with lively expressions and strong characterizations.* But, except for the figures of the apostles below Christ's feet, the effect is static. Compare the guardians of the west doorway with their counterparts to the north and south and the change over sixty years becomes apparent. Here work was begun about 1210 and continued until 1260. The figures are still elongated, but they move and look around, so much so that they have to be provided with canopied niches to integrate them with the architecture. They are less mannered than some of the early thirteenth-century sculpture elsewhere in northern France, which at its most extreme attains a Baroque violence of movement.

Chartres is particularly rich in sculpture because the west façade survived the fire, and the architect therefore introduced major south and north doorways, almost façades themselves and complete with rose windows, to demonstrate the riches of the new style. He also threw out deep porches, so that the statues are protected from the elements. All this makes Chartres outstanding among medieval cathedrals, and it is again exceptional in that very little alteration has been made since it was completed in 1260, the only major loss being that of the screen separating the choir from the nave; the spire on the north tower is flamboyant Gothic of the early sixteenth century. But otherwise Chartres is the most perfect example of a High Gothic cathedral that we possess today.

---

* Although the Chartres statues appear as an isolated phenomenon today, one wonders if they always were: so many heads on Romanesque sculpture have been damaged by iconoclasts that we cannot tell whether such lively portraits are typical of the period or not.

Reims

In 496, Clovis, king of the Franks, was baptized at Reims by the local bishop, Remigius. He was the most powerful ruler in northern France as a result of his victory over the Alemanni at Soissons ten years earlier, and his conversion was a milestone in the history of the church. Indeed, the account of it given by Gregory of Tours in his *History of the Franks* has clear overtones of the conversion of Constantine: like Constantine, Clovis prays to the Christian god for victory in the crucial battle, and his triumph leads to acceptance of the new religion. Gregory evokes a colourful picture of the baptismal ceremony:

The public squares were draped with coloured cloths, the churches were adorned with white hangings, the baptistery was prepared, sticks of incense gave off clouds of perfume, sweet-smelling candles gleamed bright and the holy place of baptism was filled with divine fragrance. God filled the hearts of all present with such grace that they imagined themselves to have been transported to some perfumed paradise.

Later legends recorded how a dove had descended from heaven bearing an ampulla of holy oil with which Clovis was baptized; this sacred phial, kept at the abbey of Saint-Remi, played a central part in the coronation of the kings of France from the end of the tenth century onwards, and the archbishop of Reims usually officiated at the ceremony, which was held in his cathedral. In October 1131 pope Innocent II crowned Louis VII at Reims; his son Philip Augustus, aged fourteen, was anointed there in November 1179 as his father lay dying, in order to secure his succession to the throne.

In 1210, the old cathedral was destroyed in a fire which swept through the town. Its special place in French history meant that the rebuilding was planned on an exceptional scale. The choir was completed in 1241, but the west façade was not finished until the middle of the fourteenth century; the nave had to be extended to accommodate the crowds who attended the coronations. The final stages of the work were held up by the troubles of the mid fourteenth century; the virtual collapse of French government after the battle of Poitiers in 1356 and the '*Jacquerie*', or peasants' rising, which followed were compounded by the siege of Reims in 1359–60 by Edward III, who hoped to make good his claim to the throne of France by capturing the town and having himself crowned by the archbishop, who was said to favour the English cause. The last stages of the work dragged on until 1481, when a fire destroyed the roof and central spire; as a result the hundred-foot-high spires designed to crown the western towers were never constructed.

But despite the extended period over which the cathedral was built, the original plans were followed, and the result is entirely in one style, the only variations being in the sculpture and some minor details. The plans were probably the work of Jean d'Orbais, recorded as master-mason until 1231, and are based on those of Chartres, though the truncation of the towers on the transepts after the fire of 1481 means that there is less emphasis on the north and south doorways. The major innovation at Reims is the use of a new and higher construction for the windows; just as the buttresses had been reduced to mere skeletons with the invention of the flying buttress, so only the structural lines of the window-walls are left with the introduction of bar-tracery. The wall-space becomes entirely window, framed by arches. This effect is seen at its best in the marvellous double rose of the west end and is exaggerated by the great west screen which conceals the remainder of the stonework, creating the illusion that there is nothing except glass in the outer wall.

The west front at Reims is immensely elaborate and original, and the decor hides the otherwise elegant proportions. But it is justly famous, and highly dramatic. The three great doorways, crowded with statues and full of movement, are steeply gabled and contain windows in the place of stone tympanums. They lead the eye up to the apex of the central gable, past the great rose window, to the monumental statues of kings, over fourteen feet high, which form a frieze around the roof-line, a feature paralleled at Saint-Denis and Notre-Dame in Paris, but carried out here in a way which proclaims Reims' title as the place of coronation: it is the kings of France – not of Israel as elsewhere – who are portrayed, and the baptism of Clovis is shown in the centre. The north and south sides exploit the fact that the cathedral was rebuilt without any of the restraints imposed by the need to re-use existing foundations; they are designed with absolute regularity, a feature noticeably absent at Chartres, where variety is the keynote. The interior, too, relies on scale and regularity to make its effect. It is one of the first of the sweeping Gothic naves which rely on the receding march of strongly marked vertical pillars to lead the eye onward and upward. The dramatic power of the west façade is repeated here, but using much simpler means, one of which is the sheer height of the vaults (125 feet). Only Amiens and Beauvais exceed this, and Beauvais represents the *ne plus ultra*: the choir was over 150 feet high, but had to be reinforced within twelve years of being built.

The sculpture at Reims is not only abundant, but of outstanding quality. It is much less restrained than that at Chartres. The first sculptors who worked here seem to have had contact with antique statues, possibly through the great metalworkers of the Meuse valley; the stiff folds of the drapery at Chartres are replaced by a revival of so-called 'damp-fold' drapery, particularly in the statues of the apostles on the north doorway. This rather elaborate rendering, with heavily bearded and highly characterized faces, is found in a simpler and more restrained style on the west portal; the latter is the most attractive phase of the Reims sculptors. As a result, the west portal contains figures as diverse as the purely classical head of the Virgin of the Visitation, the calm and radiant Virgin of the Presentation in the Temple and the precious and rather unattractive St Joseph, who comes from the last, mannered, phase of the mid thirteenth century, where graceful poses are spoilt by simpering, over-dainty heads; the same is true, to my mind, of the famous 'Smiling Angel' on the north doorway of the façade.

The natural grace of the torsoes in this last phase is matched by the equally lifelike foliage carved on the nave capitals, which was to set a fashion copied throughout Europe. The best English examples are at Southwell Minster, and bolder patterning of the same kind is to be found at Naumburg in Germany. A similar 'realism' is to be found on the west screen, where, in addition to rich foliage, a draped cloth is carved on the dado, down to the pins tacking it to the wall. The figures on the screen are again of outstanding quality. Abraham appears in the guise of a contemporary knight receiving communion, while the man next to him wears classical armour. They are set in deep niches, the final solution to the problem set by the evolution of the sculptures at Reims from elements in the architecture into independent works of art which, having no direct relation to their surroundings, require a specific architectural context to make them an integral part of the building. But in this, as in so much else, Reims points the way forward to the later Gothic cathedrals, where the embellishments – windows, statues, tracery – seem to take over and engulf the exterior. At Reims the different elements have not yet run riot, but are held in balance in this monumental meeting-place of king, church and people.

Cologne

Cologne's name comes from the Roman *colonia*, a settlement for ex-soldiers; here, on the Rhine, such a town acted both as a way of providing a living for them and as a reserve of troops for the frontier with the German tribes. It survived the barbarian invasions, and there is little break in the record of its ecclesiastical and economic life. From the fourth century AD it was an important bishopric, and in 785 Charlemagne made it an archbishopric. This was one of the bases of Cologne's medieval wealth. In the eleventh century the archbishops became *ex-officio* chancellors of the imperial lands in Italy; in 1180 they were given the duchy of Westphalia, to the east of the city; and in 1356, Charles IV, in the famous 'Golden Bull' which set out a constitution for the empire, made the archbishop of Cologne one of the seven magnates who elected the emperor. The most famous of the medieval archbishops was Rainald von Dassel, Frederick Barbarossa's chancellor. Politician rather than priest, he was as concerned as his master to uphold 'the honour of the empire'. He became chancellor in 1156 and until his death in 1167 was Frederick's closest adviser in his struggle against Alexander III. Much of his time was spent on campaign in Italy, where he directed operations against Milan and Rome, leading his troops to victory at Tusculum in 1167. His career is what Henry II might have hoped Thomas Becket's would be when Becket became archbishop of Canterbury: the state first, the church second. Rainald did not forget the church, however: Cologne owes its most precious relic, the bones of the Three Magi, to him, because Frederick gave them to him after the capture of Milan. They lie now in the great golden shrine made for them at the end of the twelfth century, which stands behind the high altar of the cathedral. They made Cologne the focus of popular pilgrimages in the Middle Ages; kings and princes as well as common folk came 'to the church of Cologne, where the Kings lie entombed'. The shrine, begun by the famous goldsmith

Nicholas of Verdun in 1191, is in the form of a Romanesque church, and recent work has restored it to its ancient splendour.

The cathedral in which it is housed is, by contrast, one of the great works of Gothic architecture. Begun on a grandiose scale in 1248, it was based on northern French Gothic designs and used the most advanced techniques of the time, including a full array of flying buttresses. It was an ambitious plan and the choir alone took seventy-four years to complete.

After the consecration in 1322, the choir was walled off from the nave, and work continued on the latter and on the transepts. In the meantime, work was started on the west front, under the direction of one of the Parler family, the famous south German architects. By 1473, the southern tower was completed up to the level of the belfry, but it lacked its spire, and the northern tower remained a mere set of foundations when all work came to an end in 1560 in the aftermath of the Reformation. Surmounted by the giant crane used to lift the building materials, the cathedral remained a kind of fossilized building site for the next two hundred and fifty years. Early in the nineteenth century, the plans drawn up by Michael Parler were rediscovered, and, fuelled both by the revival of interest in Gothic architecture and by German nationalist pride, work was begun again in 1842. Modern techniques meant that work was rapidly completed: in 1863 the fourteenth-century choir wall was demolished and the nave opened up, and in 1880 the entire cathedral, including the northern tower, was finished. Today, after a century of smoke from the railway has blackened the stone, old and new work are scarcely distinguishable. Equally, because the original plans were scrupulously followed, what we see today is in effect a purely medieval cathedral, the largest in northern Europe, as conceived in the mid fourteenth century. Its underlying plan is that of Master Gerhard, the architect of 1248: his successors elaborated details and redesigned the west façade, but the interior is faithful to Gerhard's design. Looking at the ground plan, the most striking feature is its absolute regularity and harmony, a regularity which is at once apparent in the building itself. The result could have been merely mechanical, like much nineteenth-century Gothic; but in the words of Paul Franke, Cologne is not cold or academic: 'this cathedral is not dead: it is solemn, festive, and sublime, *fascinans* and *tremendum* at the same time, as clear as mathematics and as irrational as life itself'.

The nave is on a gigantic scale, with vaults surpassed only by the ill-fated venture at Beauvais in northern France; but it is the choir which attracts attention, because of its fine original furnishings, including the early fourteenth-century choir-stalls with frescoes above, the statues in canopied niches on the pillars, the high altar of the same date in French Gothic manner, and of course the shrine of the Magi itself. Elsewhere in the transepts and chapel are the superb effigy of archbishop Conrad von Hochstaden, who undertook the rebuilding of the cathedral, shown as an idealized prince at the age of thirty-three, the age at which, according to medieval legend, men would be reborn at the Second Coming. The cathedral treasury is also full of riches, including a gospel book from Reichenau which shows the church there as it was in Carolingian times, and other early manuscripts.

Until 1944, the twin towers of the cathedral soared out of a mass of tiny narrow streets, which constituted one of the largest surviving medieval town centres in Europe. All this disappeared, devastated by Allied bombs, and of the famous 365 churches of medieval 'holy Cologne' only fragments remain, either as much restored replicas or as parts of modern buildings. The most notable are St Maria in Capitol, of the mid eleventh century, with its trefoil apse and a marvellous pair of wooden doors which echo the ivory carvings of Charlemagne's court; the church of the Apostles, late twelfth century, with an elaborate arrangement of colonnades, pediments and towers over the outside of its trefoil apse, reminiscent of Speyer cathedral; and St Pantaleon, one of the few surviving examples of tenth-century architecture in Germany. This outward display of holiness was matched in the thirteenth century by a reputation as an intellectual centre; although there was no formal university at Cologne then, Albertus Magnus, one of the greatest of medieval philosophers, taught here from 1248 until his death in 1280, and his pupil Thomas Aquinas worked with him in the early years. Duns Scotus, the 'subtle doctor', who elaborated on Aquinas's thought, was at Cologne in 1307–8 and is buried in the cathedral. But without the formal framework of a university, no permanent school of philosophy was established.

Apart from the cathedral and the three churches already mentioned, the best evocation of 'holy Cologne' is to be found in the Schnütgen Museum, housed in the church of St Cecilia. This collection, formed in the late nineteenth century, contains a wealth of church treasures, gathered in an age when such things were little regarded: one bronze reliquary was said to be a mousetrap! Carolingian ivory plaques and ritual combs, elaborate gold and silver bookcovers, Limoges enamels (including a reliquary depicting the death of Becket), represent Romanesque decorative arts, while the sculpture of the same period includes a remarkable plaque of a musician. For the Gothic period, sculpture predominates, and there is a fine collection of textiles. There are, however, no paintings in the Schnütgen Museum; for these, and in particular for the work of the greatest painter of the fifteenth-century Cologne school, we must go to the Wallraf-Richartz Museum and back to the cathedral. The surviving panel paintings from Cologne date from 1400 onwards. The early ones are conservative, in the French and English High Gothic tradition, but in the 1440s an individual master of international standing appears: Stefan Lochner. His *Madonna in the Rose Garden* and the *Adoration of the Magi* in the cathedral bring an element of realism into the formal works of Gothic art. The *Madonna* is a tender and intimate work, foreshadowing the great Netherlands masters.

The other aspect of medieval Cologne, its greatness as a trading centre, has survived far less well. A few pieces in the town museum are a pale echo of its teeming activity, and the old merchants' houses have vanished. A little of the early history of Cologne's trade can be seen in the fine Römisch-Germanisches Museum, where sixth- and seventh-century objects from as far afield as southern Russia are displayed. In the heyday of the Cologne merchants, Cologne was predominant in the Hanseatic League (see p. 305 below), even though it stood apart from the rest of the Hanse in that it was not a seaport. It also had its own trade links apart from the east–west trade of the Hanse, lying on the Rhine route which linked Italy, Germany and England. The only secular memorial of this prosperity is the Gothic part of the Rathaus; but it was out of this trading wealth that the ambitious plans for the cathedral were financed, from the merchants that the gold and precious stones of the great shrine were bought, and for the wealthy patrons of the town that Stefan Lochner worked, so that even in the predominantly religious survivals we can still detect the vigorous economic life of medieval Cologne.

Burgos and León

Burgos lies on the north-eastern edge of the vast central plateau of Spain, and was the capital of Castile from its foundation in the tenth century until the end of the Middle Ages. Castile was in the forefront of the *reconquista*, the recapture of Spain from the Moors (see p. 219 below); and as a royal city it was an international centre, with links with France and Germany. So when the bishop of Burgos commissioned a new cathedral in 1221, he looked to the latest creations of the architects of northern France, which may have been his home country. The site he chose was unusual, close to a hillside, a feature which was skilfully exploited by the master-masons, Maestro Ricardo and Maestro Enrique, who were responsible for building the main body of the church between 1221 and 1260. The hill behind the cathedral was dominated by a royal castle, now ruined; a century later a redoubtable defensive gateway was built to the south, which still guards the bridge over the river. Even by medieval standards, the cathedral was more than usually hemmed in; and today, even though squares have been created on three sides, the impression one has is of a series of close-ups and of a carefully contrived series of perspectives from different levels.

The main body of the cathedral is fairly orthodox French Gothic, less ornamented with statues and with more plain walling than its French counterparts. This forms a sharp contrast to the upper parts, which are very late Gothic of the fifteenth century, with a sixteenth-century lantern. The most important of the carvings are those on the south doorway, a traditional layout with statues on the jambs and in the arch, where the musicians of heaven play a variety of instruments, and a bold tympanum of Christ in Glory flanked by the evangelists, each busily writing at his desk; Matthew and John work at a double desk, set on a cloud held aloft by angels. The figures are stiff, in the early French Gothic manner, and are akin to those at Amiens; but the placing of the gallery of kings on the west end, and the shape of the rose window, seem to owe something to Reims.

It is the work of the fifteenth-century architects, brought back in 1442 by a bishop of Burgos who had travelled in Germany, that gives Burgos its distinctive character. For nearly a century Hans von Köln and his family worked on the cathedral; his son, Simon, became Simon de Colonia, and his grandson bore the Spanish name

Francisco. So though the roots of their architecture are late German Gothic, their style evolved into something quite independent, which was to lead to the fantastic 'Plateresque' of the Spanish Renaissance. The towers, spires and balustrading of the west front are Hans von Köln's work, openwork with the words '*pulcra est et decora*' (It is beautiful and fair) worked into the balustrading. The façade thus develops from the earthbound plainness of the doorways, getting progressively lighter as it rises, to the ethereal fantasy of the spires, which seem to dissolve into the sky. Hans's central tower collapsed in 1539 and was replaced by one designed by his grandson, even more fantastic than the spires. The north doorway has French Gothic sculpture on the main portal but sixteenth-century Plateresque on the east door beside it.

The same contrasts continue inside the cathedral, which has an exceptionally large central choir, beginning halfway down the nave, broken under the crossing (where a black marble slab marks the tomb of 'El Cid', the legendary hero of the Castilian *reconquista* whose real name was Rodrigo Díaz, and who fought both for and against the Moslems as the mood took him). Above his tomb rises the glorious interior of the central lantern, ending in a traceried star which echoes the wooden ceilings of the Moorish south as well as the fantasies in stone of English Tudor Gothic. At the east end is another warrior's monument, the chapel founded by Hernandez de Velasco, constable of Castile in 1482. Here the detail is early Renaissance within a Gothic shell: we are into the self-confident world of the humanists, and the great effigy of the constable and his wife is – appropriately – of Carrara marble imported from Italy.

Burgos shows how very varied influences from different parts of Europe – northern France, the Rhine, Andalucia and finally Italy – could shape one building over the centuries. **León**, a hundred miles to the west, is rather the reverse. It was almost certainly built by the architect who planned Burgos, its nearest neighbour, in the thirteenth century; but here he experimented with new ideas within the same basic framework to such an extent that he overstepped the technical limits of his art. He built a very high nave with a glazed triforium, an idea accomplished in the choir at Amiens about the same time. But this made the building so unstable that windows had to be blocked, and only a virtual rebuilding between 1859 and 1901 saved it from collapse. Yet the glass, which was intended to be the glory of the church from the outset and which is the finest in Spain, has survived largely intact. It lacks the boldness of design of Chartres, and the innumerable small panels are often placed too high for them to be clearly visible. The apse windows and the west rose is an exception; here the scale is well-judged and the design succeeds. Interestingly, these are the earliest parts of the glass.

The sculpture at León also has affinities with Reims, but is generally less accomplished. The main doorway has a splendidly secular vision of paradise, with a gay and sensual crowd making its leisurely way through the fields of heaven. From the cloisters, the tympanum on the north doorway, with its original paintwork, can be seen by the dim light of the entrance, a rare reminder of the multi-coloured appearance of much medieval sculpture; it is an unfamiliar experience, and one to which it is difficult to respond favourably, conditioned as we are to look for beauty of form and line in sculpture, rather than admiring colour and realism.

Ely

Ely is unusual in many respects, not least in that it was planned as a monastic church, but became a cathedral well before the building had been finished. The abbey of Ely, an ancient foundation dating back to the seventh century, was destroyed in a Viking raid in 870 and refounded a century later in the great revival of monasticism in the tenth century. It became a centre of Saxon resistance after the Norman conquest. Lying in the fenland, its remote and inaccessible site enabled the English to hold out for five years, and when the Normans finally seized the island the monastery was sacked. But a decade later, William appointed his own kinsman, Simeon, the eighty-seven-year-old prior of Winchester, in a move to revive the monastery; and despite his great age, Simeon embarked on the construction of a great new church. This was designed on a traditional Romanesque plan, with a semi-circular apse and large transepts. His successors adapted this, partly to give more space behind the altar for the shrine of St Etheldreda, foundress and patron saint, and partly to reflect the new status of the church, which became a cathedral in 1109. A magnificent and well-proportioned nave (the three tiers of arcades are in the ratio 6 : 5 : 4) and an impressive 'westwork' was added to the original plain cruciform plan. The west front was altered in the early

thirteenth century by the addition of a 'Galilee' porch; and although
the east end was rebuilt and extended in the Gothic style by 1252,
Ely might have survived as a primarily Romanesque building had
it not been for the collapse of the central tower at the crossing in
1322, due to the lack of solid foundations and the poor quality of
some of the masonry.

The rebuilding of the central part of the church was one of the
greatest engineering feats of the fourteenth century, as original in
its way as the 'crazy' vaulting of the choir at Lincoln, but on a
far greater scale. Instead of replacing the tower, it was decided,
probably at the suggestion of the sacrist, Alan of Walsingham, to
retain the open space created by the fall of the tower, which was
the full width of the church, instead of merely the width of the
nave. Even to bring the stone for the new piers, bridges, quays
and roads had to be repaired and strengthened; and the building
of a vault over seventy feet across in stone was out of the
question. The solution was found in a timber roof, but nothing
of this size had ever been built previously. A great crane was
erected, and in 1323 an unnamed master arrived from London to
supervise the work. By 1334, the stonework was ready for the roof
to be built; and by this time the monks had decided to go to one
of the greatest experts in carpentry that they could find, William
Hurley, who became master-carpenter to the king in 1336, but continued to supervise work at Ely. Although there is no specific
evidence, it is generally assumed that he designed the timberwork
of the octagon, a radical solution to an unusual problem. The vault
is timber from the head of the piers upwards; the stonework ends
at the head of the arches linking the piers. The structure of the
lantern works on the general principle of the hammerbeam roof,
but the whole upper part projects above what would normally be
the apex of the roof: the eight great corner posts weigh over ten
tons each, and are sixty-three feet long by three feet square. How
they were raised into position ninety feet above the ground with
the primitive engineering methods of the time is something of a
mystery. The beautiful geometrical patterns produced by the
vaulting were enriched by elaborate painting, carving and glass,
of which only John of Burwell's great central boss of Christ in
Majesty has survived intact; the rest is a nineteenth-century re-
creation by Sir George Gilbert Scott. The glass is unexciting, but
the painting has something of the right feeling, and Scott did re-

work the architecture of the lantern to the original designs, after its mutilation in the eighteenth century.

Not content with their ambitious undertaking in the centre of the church, the monks also built at the same period the Lady Chapel, a special chapel devoted to the cult of the Virgin. This was planned on an ambitious scale with a very wide stone vault. It survives as a bare ruin of its former splendour: the sculpture has gone, the windows are filled with plain glass, and almost all traces of painting have disappeared. What was once an immensely rich building, glowing with colour and alive with statues, has become a mere skeleton. Only the coloured roof-bosses and the decorative sculpture of the arcades remind us of its former glories, and the elaborate window tracery is as starkly outlined as in a ruin.

On either side of the east end, behind the high altar, are two chantry chapels, where priests would have said mass for the souls of the founders of the chapels. These were established by two early sixteenth-century bishops of Ely and were completed in 1500 and 1534 respectively. Together with the tomb of bishop Redman, who died in 1505, these represent the last and most elaborate stage of Gothic tracery and sculpture. The local hard chalk or clunch is very easy to carve into fantastical patterns, and the result is theatrical and overloaded with detail, particularly in the canopies on the outside of bishop Alcock's chantry; the once admired virtue of *mesura*, restraint, has been entirely cast aside, and despite the sheer spectacle the results are, at least to me, unsatisfying. But tastes and fashions in architecture change. Thirty years ago, a much respected writer could say of the Romanesque nave at Ely and of twelfth-century arcades in general that 'monotonous repetition has a grandeur of its own, if it is heavy and inert, lacking in both inspiration and imagination', whereas today there must be many, myself included, who would regard the sweep of the great pillars and the subtlety of the surviving south-west transept as the finest thing at Ely, excepting only the octagon itself; and who would not lament the loss in the eighteenth century of the Norman pulpitum or rood-screen as much as the loss of the decor and glass in the Lady Chapel. Equally, the late-twelfth-century south doorway, with a superbly vigorous Christ in Majesty and pillars decorated with spirals of foliage and vignettes of human and animal life, is far more moving than the Gothic stonework elsewhere in the cathedral. But, like the medieval wheel of Fortune, the wheel of modern taste moves inexorably on, and this view will doubtless seem out of date in due time.

With the disappearance of the Norman screen, the choir was moved in the nineteenth century from below the octagon to the east end. The layout of the cathedral after the building of the octagon, beginning from the west, was therefore: Galilee porch, nave, rood-screen, choir, sanctuary with the shrine of St Etheldreda. The present 'vista', broken only by Sir George Gilbert Scott's wrought-iron choir-screen, is entirely a modern invention. Yet much of Ely's interest derives from precisely this often harmonious adaptation of the structure by different generations: admirers of Romanesque, Gothic or Victorian architecture can all find something to please them here, and there is a sense of continuity with the distant past often lacking where rebuilding or restoration have imposed a uniform style on a church.

Lincoln

Lincoln became the seat of a bishopric only after the Norman conquest, when the loosely organized Anglo-Saxon church was re-modelled in line with the new and more efficient continental ideas; for William I knew that the ecclesiastical hierarchy could be a valuable support for the civilian government. So when Remigius was brought from the Norman abbey of Fécamp to become bishop of Dorchester-on-Thames, a small town near Oxford, and found that his huge diocese lay almost entirely to the north and east, he transferred the see to Lincoln. Remigius had been a clerk in William's household, his appointment being a reward for political services, and the choice of Lincoln was not entirely logical in terms of geography, since it was well to the north of the diocese; one suspects political reasons as well. Lincoln had a royal castle; its site on the edge of a plateau was not only easily defended, but also provided a dramatic setting for the new cathedral, which was almost complete at Remigius's death in 1092.

The building survived a great fire in 1141, only to succumb to an earthquake forty years later, on Palm Sunday 1185. Only the west front and the twin towers behind it escaped. The task of re-building fell to the new bishop of Lincoln, appointed by Henry II in the following year, Hugh of Avalon. Hugh had been invited to England by the king to become prior of the Carthusian house at Witham in Somerset, which Henry had founded as part of his expiation for his involvement in the murder of Thomas Becket. Hugh was a remarkable character, determined, ascetic and yet with a sense of humour which could disarm the king's Angevin rages. Once, summoned to the royal presence to answer for something that had offended the king, he caught up with Henry and his incessantly journeying court as they rested in a forest clearing. Henry was sewing up a leather bandage on his finger, while the courtiers awaited Hugh's arrival in silence, aware of the king's anger. Hugh sat down and watched Henry for a while: then he remarked, 'How like your cousins of Falaise you are!', referring to the mother of William I, who had been a tanner's daughter. Henry burst out laughing, and Hugh was quickly able to make his peace.

The plan for the rebuilding of the cathedral initiated by Hugh was carried through faithfully by his successors, except for the re-modelling of the east end, and was completed in about 1280. The only subsequent changes were the rebuilding of the central tower and the end wall of the south transept, and the addition of the choir-screen. So Lincoln today is close to the original concept of Hugh and his architects eight hundred years ago. The plan is typically English Gothic in that it is drawn in terms of straight lines; indeed, only the chapels in the eastern transepts have rounded apses. Behind the Norman west front, extended to make an even more imposing triumphal entrance by the addition of arcading above it and to each side, a nave of impressive length and height was built, with details which are almost entirely English in origin and with lavish use of Purbeck marble, brought from Dorset by sea and by river. The dark green of this stone contrasts well with the local yellowish-brown limestone, and the design of the arcading throughout the cathedral is exceptional, particularly in the double arcading in the choir aisles, and that in the transepts and in the triforium of the nave. Much of the original effect of Lincoln was due to careful attention to detail within a restrained and elegant overall design, qualities which it is not too fanciful to associate with Hugh himself, as a member of the austere Carthusian order who was none the less an excellent judge of artistic merit. Henry once gave him the great Bible which the monks of Winchester had prepared for their own use and which is one of the surviving glories of English illumination of the period; but

Hugh learnt how the king had 'requested' it and returned it to its rightful owners, almost certainly aware that it was no ordinary manuscript.

The early Gothic work at Lincoln is notable for the absence of figures; the capitals are foliate, and the other details are entirely patterning. By the mid thirteenth century, some figurative work appears, but it is not until the building of the 'Angel Choir' after 1256 that sculpture plays an important part. Hugh of Avalon was canonized after his death, and his shrine became one of the most popular pilgrimage sites in the Midlands. To cope with the increasing crowds, the cathedral chapter decided to copy the solution adopted at Ely and to rebuild the eastern end of the cathedral behind the high altar to provide a suitably spacious setting for the shrine. Hugh's three-sided apse was demolished, and the line of the nave was extended by over a hundred feet, to form a spacious rectangular area behind the choir. A splendid jewelled shrine was erected to hold the saint's remains, and, although the proportions of the architecture were necessarily the same as the nave, the detail was vastly richer; thirty angel-musicians decorate the spandrels of the triforium, many of them individual masterpieces of harmonious line and form; there are elaborate roof-bosses in the aisles, and outside there is a suitably imposing entrance, the judgement porch, with striking portraits said to be of Edward I and his two queens, the first of whom, Eleanor of Castile, is commemorated by an effigy within the choir. There are other famous figures from the court of Edward III: bishop Burghersh, who baptized the Black Prince, and his brother Sir Bartholomew Burghersh, the prince's mentor; and Katherine Swynford, John of Gaunt's mistress and later his third wife, mother of Henry Beaufort, bishop of Lincoln. Here too is the tomb of Robert Grosseteste, one of England's greatest scholars, bishop of Lincoln in the mid thirteenth century. A more sombre monument is the tomb of 'Little St Hugh', a child alleged to have been ritually murdered by Jews in the mid thirteenth century as a prelude to an attack on the latter, a bitter reminder that racial hatred is no new thing.

After 1280, no major structural changes were made to the cathedral. The fourteenth century saw the decoration of the main choir with the immensely rich choir-stalls and stone screen. The stalls are justly famous not only for their Gothic traceried canopies, but also for the series of misericords on the underneath of the seats, while the screen, although it has lost its original colouring and gilding, is in the same vein: hardly a square inch of the surface is left without ornament. The same century saw the completion of the towers, though not the silhouette familiar today. All three towers had wooden spires; the central one is said to have risen to over 500 feet and to have been visible from forty miles away.

Lincoln has a good claim to be considered 'the finest of the English cathedrals', and it is impossible to do it justice in a short space. The great rose windows, the early thirteenth-century ten-sided chapter house, the sheer wealth of detail (down to the famous grotesque figure known as the 'Lincoln imp' in the Angel Choir) all claim attention. The surrounding streets, too, are rich in medieval survivals, notably the 'Jew's house', 'Jew's court' and 'Aaron's house' on the steep hillside, the latter claimed to be the oldest continuously inhabited house in England. Elsewhere there is the ruined Guildhall of St Mary, and the old city gates survive in varying degrees of completeness, the best being the Exchequer gate.

Prague and Vienna

In the western half of Europe, cathedral building was primarily inspired by local pride and carried out from the resources of the cathedral town. In eastern Europe, however, political considerations predominated. The two great cathedrals at Prague and Vienna belong less to urban history than to the history of the Holy Roman Empire. At Prague, Charles IV of Luxemburg, who had been brought up at the French court, deliberately set out to create a new capital when he chose it as his residence in 1333; and he supported the bishop of Prague's attempts to become an archbishop, independent of the see of Mainz, a claim which became reality in 1344. Two years later Charles was elected emperor, and the archbishopric was provided with a suitably imperial cathedral, designed by the second of a remarkable dynasty of architects, Peter Parler, whom Charles had brought to Prague at the age of twenty-three. Peter Parler seems to have learnt his trade from his father Heinrich, who may have worked on Cologne cathedral. He took over from the Frenchman Matthias of Arras as architect of the cathedral in 1353, when only the chapels of the apse had been built, and at once set about a series of technical innovations which seem to draw on English work. Here, at the extremity of western Christendom, is one of the most international of Gothic cathedrals: on the porch of the Wenceslas chapel is an Italian mosaic, and the interior is adorned with semi-precious stones, possibly in imitation of the description of the imaginary Temple of the Holy Grail in a contemporary romance.

A parallel on a lesser scale to Charles IV's work at Prague can be found at Vienna, capital of the Habsburg dukes who were eventually to succeed him as emperors. Charles's son-in-law Rudolf IV imitated him in creating a new university and in building a new cathedral, though Rudolf's project was limited by Vienna's existing status as an archbishopric and the fact that the cathedral already possessed a Gothic choir. The Romanesque west end of c.1258 was also retained, and a new nave with twin transept towers was planned. The work continued well into the fifteenth century, and much of it was influenced by Peter Parler's work at Prague; the architect at Vienna in 1415 bought a vineyard from Peter Parler's son, so the links may have been close. But the original plan was not carried out, and only the spectacular tower was completed. Looking at the cathedral today, it is easy to say that the asymmetrical result is more effective; but it is doubtful whether a Gothic architect would have appreciated the striking contrast between the elaborate, almost detached tower with its strong vertical emphasis and the horizontal line of the roof of the nave and choir. The south tower – like that at Ulm, also designed by a pupil of the Parler family – fulfils the characteristic late-Gothic ambition of creating a structure which fades into nothingness: the elaborate ornament blurs the line between stone and sky, and the spire seems to soar to an infinite height. The main roof, with its polychrome tiles and huge area, is equally striking in a very different way: the tile patterns, including a huge Habsburg eagle over the chancel, are curious rather than beautiful, but the gable ends, copied from the single fifteenth-century gable which was completed, are delightful, with the same blurring of boundaries to be seen in the spire; here the tracery conceals a blank, solid wall, part of the structure needed to support the vast roof, and the gable ends transform what would otherwise have been obtrusive triangles of stone into a fanciful and delicate pattern, the main gable being echoed by three miniature gables at the foot.

We are reminded that this is the cathedral of the Habsburgs' centre of power by the statues on the west front and on the tower, and by the late-fourteenth-century stained glass in the Ducal Chapel. The sculptures from the west front are now in the Historisches Museum, safe from the weather. They include figures of Rudolf IV, Catherine of Bohemia, and Blanche of Valois, wife of Charles IV of Luxemburg, all dressed in the latest fashion of tight-fitting tunics with a low-slung belt; the ladies are shown with elaborate hairstyles. This secular element is also to be found in the stained-glass portraits of Habsburg rulers; unusually, they are shown as monumental figures in their own right, not as donors worshipping at the feet of Christ or the saints.

From the very last decades of Gothic, there is a highly convoluted pulpit by Anton Pilgrim, with striking 'portraits' of the fathers of the church. Around them, the Gothic tracery has become soft and curving, as if it were decaying back into the foliage patterns which once inspired it. It is a virtuoso piece; but looking at it one can see why soon afterwards men turned to the hard classical lines of Renaissance art. The Habsburgs outgrew their provincial origins, and St Stephen's was left as a memorial of the past, untouched even when the emperors at last returned to Vienna.

Siena

In the thirteenth century, Siena was the great rival of its neighbour, Florence. Both were trading cities, whose bankers lent money throughout Europe; the Sienese were bankers to the papacy, just as the Florentines became bankers to Edward I. The Sienese rivalry with Florence, however, led to their invoking the aid of the imperial party, and after 1260 Siena went over to the enemies of the papacy, only to be defeated by Florence in 1269. Thereafter Siena was unable to challenge Florentine supremacy except for brief intervals, and her prosperity depended on peace with her neighbour, while her position was weakened by interminable quarrels among her citizens over the form of government within the city. Yet despite her political troubles, Siena was one of the wealthiest of medieval Italian cities, and her cathedral reflects the continuing vitality of her commerce. As at Florence, the cathedral was the responsibility of the office of works of the cathedral, which was run by the officers of the commune rather than by the cathedral chapter: the patronage of the arts arising from the work on the cathedral was closely associated with the ideals of the Sienese themselves.

The present cathedral was begun in 1226. It was purely Romanesque in style, as Italy was essentially traditional at this period, and Gothic made little headway here until the latter part of the thirteenth century. The design was unusual, if not eccentric: a hall-church, with nave and aisles of equal height, with a hexagonal tower and hexagonal east end. The horizontal banding of the walls in black and white marble is the most striking feature of the whole building; relatively light in the early parts, it becomes fiercely insistent in the central hexagon and in the nave, where it dominates all other impressions of the architecture. A further unusual feature was the presence of the baptistery below the eastern end, which led to plans for an eastern façade (for which a fourteenth-century drawing in High Gothic style survives) which were never executed.

This drawing, however, may be connected with the even more radical plan, adopted in 1339, at a moment when Siena's star seemed to be in the ascendant. This was no less an undertaking than the transformation of the present cathedral into the mere transept of a huge new building on a north–south axis: the east façade would then have been the equivalent of a south transept entrance. The new building, designed by Lando di Pietro, was put in hand, and the eastern aisle was completed; but the problems of building on a steeply sloping site, which made buttressing difficult, and perhaps a lack of understanding of the mechanics of Gothic architecture, resulted in an unstable structure, which began to show signs of becoming dangerous not long after the first vaults were completed. These difficulties were by no means unknown, and could have been overcome had it not been for a rapid decline in Siena's fortunes: the Black Death struck with particular violence here, and in 1348 over 80,000 of her inhabitants are said to have perished. Nine years later, the projected new cathedral was abandoned, and only arches of the nave and the outer wall of the nave were preserved, a gigantic arcade along one side of the cathedral square. The western façade of the cathedral, which had progressed no further than the level of the gables, was now finished in a Gothic version of Giovanni Pisano's original Romanesque plan. Pisano's façade, modelled on that of the cathedral in his native city, would have had a smaller central window and an arcade; the Gothic version enlarged the central window (though it remained a plain window, without stone tracery) and broke the solid outline of the Romanesque front by elaborate spires and crockets along the skyline. The result is a delightful if somewhat muddled piece of architecture, with a variety of decorative motifs rarely found elsewhere: statues as finials for the gables, a rigidly four-square central panel surmounted by an equally regular triangular pediment with a huge (modern) mosaic, framed in Gothic details of the freest kind.

The interior, dominated by the horizontal banding we have already noted, would be austere but for its later decor, which includes a huge Renaissance high altar and Baroque side chapels. The other striking feature is the inlaid marble pavement; unfortunately, this has to be protected from wear, and the earliest parts are usually on display only from 15 August for a month. The pulpit is an echo of that in the baptistery at Pisa, slightly later in date and more lively in its treatment of figures; Nicola Pisano and his pupils worked on it from 1266 to 1268, and their work here is much less formal and classical, and nearer to northern Gothic art. It is still very restrained, however, when compared to Giovanni Pisano's pulpit of 1302–10 in Pisa cathedral itself. (Giovanni was in fact Master of the Works at Siena from 1287 to 1296.) These pulpits were turned into a specialized vehicle for elaborate sculpture by the Pisano family; rather as in a French cathedral, the west façade would carry the most ambitious sculpture, but this was already complete, so they concentrated their artistic endeavours on the pulpit. There are parallels elsewhere, such as the ambo at Ravello near Amalfi, but it is here and at Pisa that the decorated pulpit reaches its climax.

The original altar screen of the cathedral consisted of Duccio di Buoninsegna's *Virgin and Child with Saints, Prophets and Patriarchs (La Maestà)* which is now in the cathedral museum in the arcades of the unfinished cathedral. The altar was almost in the centre of the cathedral, and the altar painting was therefore two-sided. The front contained as main panel the Virgin and Child, the Virgin being the protectress of Siena and nominal head of the Sienese government. On the back, the Crucifixion formed the central panel, and the smaller panels portrayed Christ's life and ministry. The *Maestà* is well documented. Far more was paid for it than for the pulpit by Nicola Pisano, and when it was completed in 1311 it was carried in solemn procession from Duccio's house at 89 Via Stalloreggi to the cathedral, accompanied by the pealing of the cathedral bells and a rejoicing crowd. Yet Duccio himself is a shadowy figure, whose relationship with northern Gothic is uncertain and whose influence on his great successor, Simone Martini, is not definitely recorded, though the latter is generally accepted as his pupil. If this is the case, Duccio's *Maestà* is one of the seminal works of Italian painting, moving away from Giotto's monumental frescoes to a more human scale. Simone Martini's masterpiece, *The Annunciation*, was also painted for Siena's cathedral in 1333, though it is now in the Uffizi in Florence. Here the still statuesque lines of Duccio's art become flowing and urgent, as the angel kneels before the timid Virgin, who cowers away from this resplendent messenger. Later Sienese artists in particular developed the art of 'predella' panels below an altarpiece into a delightful miniature art-form in its own right, and the Pinacoteca at Siena has many engaging examples. It is an art which corresponds to the city's populist traditions, just as the cathedral reflects the city's fortunes, its ambitions and disasters.

3
Parish Churches

The parish church is the most familiar surviving monument from
the Middle Ages. Even today, it would be hard to travel more than
a few miles anywhere in Europe without coming across a church
which was in part medieval; and superb and almost intact
churches from the eleventh century onwards can be reckoned in
hundreds for each European country. Indeed, the choice is so rich
that the few examples which follow are chosen almost at random
– for each one described, there are a score of other candidates for
inclusion of equal quality and similar date. But before we look at
the buildings themselves, we must turn to the way in which the
church was organized, and its place in the everyday life of towns
and villages, of which these churches are the memorial. And, first
of all, we need to enter a warning to the unwary: many of the great
parish churches which we see today as parish churches were not
in fact built as such, but were adopted for parish use following
the demise of a non-parochial institution, usually an abbey or
priory. More rarely, cathedrals have been demoted to parish use;
even Cologne cathedral was briefly reduced to this status in the
early nineteenth century. The imperial chapel at Aachen (see p. 177
below) is now technically a parish church.

So we are concerned with churches which in medieval times
served a parish. The system of dividing responsibility for the care
of souls into territorial areas dates, like the bishoprics, from the
end of the Roman empire; it evolved gradually over a period of
centuries rather than years.

A parish (*parochia*) was originally the name for the organized
Christian community within a Roman city, and its leader was the
bishop, who was assisted by other clergy. However, the latter were
unable to carry out any important duties in the church except as
his deputies, even though the community might have a number

of churches. In Rome itself, as late as the fourth century AD, the pope, as bishop of Rome, carried out all baptisms and celebrated all masses. But with the spread of Christianity to the countryside in the later fourth and fifth centuries, churches began to be built outside the cities. These too were called parishes or dioceses, and only later did the modern usage appear: a parish became a unit within the diocese. The early country churches were few and far between, even by the end of the sixth century, to be numbered in dozens rather than hundreds in each diocese. But it was obviously impossible for a bishop to carry out all his traditional functions in a large area of countryside, and so the administration of the sacraments was delegated to priests in charge of individual churches. Because there were not many such churches, great landowners might build private chapels on their estates; these were originally independent of the system of parishes, but gradually became absorbed into it.

The great development of the parochial system took place under Charlemagne, whose object was to ensure that Christianity was more than a merely official religion, and that Christians should have the means of frequent worship. This meant that a church was needed in every large village. But the bishops, who had previously borne the expenses of church building, were unable to undertake such a huge task, and, for a complex variety of reasons of which the simplest was that they were the leaders of the local community, it was the lords who in most cases organized the building of village churches. Because they had paid for them, the churches became their property; and a tension similar to that between pope and emperor over the investiture of bishops arose. The lord owned the church and the right to appoint the priest; only the bishop could confirm the appointment. The parish was now given precise boundaries, and Christians were forbidden to worship in parishes other than their own. The continuing expenses of the church were met by endowments of land, and, much more important, a levy of one-tenth (or a tithe) on all produce within the parish, payable to the parish priest. The parish thus became a self-financing organization.

This system gradually supplanted the older network of 'mission churches' throughout Europe. The last strongholds of such churches were in the regions which had once been on the frontier of Christianity, in Scandinavia and in England; the English 'old minsters' survived until the eleventh century as the basis for church organization in some areas, but, as their name suggests, the future lay with the village churches. The process of founding such village churches was well advanced by the time of the Norman conquest and was virtually complete by the end of the eleventh century.

The geography of church life was therefore a pattern of small churches, whose clergy served individual communities, which were controlled by the bishop, whose seat was a cathedral church. The ownership of the parish churches, however, remained in the hands of the local lords. The lord defended his property rights in the same way as the great rulers tried to protect their political power when faced with the demands of reforming churchmen. But in this case, part of the property was bricks and mortar, the fabric of the church itself, and it was this that eventually weakened the lord's control, combined with the feeling fostered by the reformers of the eleventh century that it was wrong for a secular lord to make a profit out of owning a church. So the lord, faced with costly repairs to a crumbling fabric and unable to collect rent for the church, eventually made over his rights in the church itself to the community, to the bishop or to a monastery. What he usually retained was the patronage, the right to nominate the priest, and this right survives even today in the Church of England. He would also retain a strong interest in the church founded by his ancestors, but only as *primus inter pares*; it was rarely the lord who paid for the rebuilding or beautifying of a church after 1100. Other factors conspired to remove both the ownership and care of the parish from the local community: after 1100, it became increasingly common for the property rights in parishes to be given to monasteries, an apparently spiritual solution which often led to the total neglect of the parish and the use of the revenue to enrich the monastery. The priests themselves began to employ curates, paying them only a small proportion of the revenue of the parish, while they lived elsewhere and kept the bulk of the income.

Yet the parish church remained a place where the individual could make a permanent mark, unlike the vast and anonymous efforts needed for the building or rebuilding of a cathedral. Wealthy members of the community were often personally responsible for rebuilding, restoring or extending churches, while memorials in parish churches are often much more vivid than the great state tombs in cathedrals. From Orm son of Gamal, who bought St Gregory's minster at Kirkdale in Yorkshire in the 1060s when it was all broken and fallen down and caused it to be rebuilt from the ground up, we can trace English benefactors of churches to the end of the Middle Ages, to men like John Chapman, the pedlar of Swaffham, who with his wife Catherine built the north aisle of Swaffham church and gave £120 towards the steeple, and whose wealth, like that of Dick Whittington, made him a hero of folktale. Such benefactions would be remembered in the prayers of the parishioners, and the benefactors' names would be entered on the parish bede-roll, a list which was read out at certain festival services. Indeed, such an entry was sometimes made a condition of a gift.

An equally potent reason for building activity within parish churches was the desire for commemorative services or chantries, which would help the soul of the departed to pass through the rigours of purgatory more quickly. The concern for the fate of the soul in purgatory, and the idea that spending or bequeathing great sums of money here on earth could influence the divine sentence, was something that the Reformation largely swept away, though the underlying doctrine remains part of Roman Catholic and Orthodox teaching. Both the chantry movement and the sale of indulgences (documents which granted a reduction of so many days or years in purgatory in return for mere payments in money) were essentially late-medieval phenomena. Chantry chapels (chapels set aside for the saying of chantry masses) are first found in the years after the Black Death, and the majority are fifteenth-century in origin. Even more impressive were the collegiate foundations. Nowadays the word 'college' has acquired an educational overtone, but it originated in the institution of groups of clergy living in a community, whether as canons of a cathedral or priests of a chantry foundation, bound by rules (from the Latin *colligere*, to bind together). Many parish churches became chantry colleges, because some famous or important man had wished to be remembered in his birthplace, or had wished to create a suitable monument for himself. In architectural terms, such collegiate churches often stand out as quite disproportionate in size to the community which they serve, as at the little town of Uzeste on the edge of the Landes in south-west France, where the Gascon pope Clement V founded a college at the place where he was to be buried and built a splendid Gothic church on a scale which competes with the local cathedral at Bazas. Obviously such foundations were beyond the means of all but the very richest and most powerful: members of a royal house, bishops and occasionally great merchants. Chantry colleges could also be the basis for hospitals, almshouses and indeed educational establishments.

Other types of collegiate churches within parishes have a much longer history. We have already noted the early 'minster' churches serving wide areas which preceded the parish churches; these, like cathedrals, were often staffed by a group of priests organized as a college, and where the minster itself was wealthy the collegiate system often survived its reduction to the status of a parish church, as at Beverley minster and Southwell minster. Other colleges might be founded as a means of providing local schools; this seems to have been the intention behind Bishop Grandisson's foundation at Ottery St Mary in Devon, where among the forty members of the college was a master of grammar. The church, adorned with the Grandisson arms and containing the tombs of Grandisson's younger brother Sir Otho and his wife Beatrix, is also a memorial to the Grandisson family; with forty resident clergy, it was built on a generous scale, the most unusual feature being twin towers over the transepts. The chancel is actually slightly larger than the nave, a feature which would in itself betray a collegiate origin. The founder is portrayed on the central boss of the crossing, one of a series of fine bosses which are matched by other stonework of a high standard.

Such a church is a far cry from the simple buildings which originally served as parish churches and which survive in modified form in thousands of parishes. The most primitive type of church was a simple oblong building, with no distinction between nave and sanctuary; the same lack of distinction is to be found in the plan of the great Roman basilicas, and is as much the result of the religious attitudes of the early church as of the need for simplicity of construction. A good example is St Peter-on-the-Wall at Bradwell in Essex, a seventh-century church which survived owing to its isolated position and to its use as a barn for many years. The interior is indeed 'barnlike', but all traces of ornament have long since disappeared, and the simplicity is perhaps deceptive. But the basic model for the medieval parish church is the 'two-cell' arrangement, in which the nave has a smaller and narrower sanctuary at the east end, reached through an arch cut in the east wall. This plan is to be found in varying degrees of sophistication throughout Europe: even the church at Gardar in Greenland followed this basic plan. A single example, to show the elegance with which this plan outline can be treated, might be the late-eleventh-century church of Saint-Pierre-de-Buzet, in the Garonne valley near Agen in south-west France. The original wooden roof has been replaced by a brick vault, the plaster has been painted to look like stone, and there are two small additions to the south, a porch and vestry; but otherwise the form of the building is unchanged. The sanctuary would often be without ornament, but here an elegant arcade surrounds the altar. The more complex pattern of later medieval churches usually arises out of total or partial rebuilding of the basic plan. The most common alterations are the rebuilding of the choir in the latest current style, the addition of north and south aisles, and the building of a tower at the west end. It is relatively common, in other words, to find the original nave embedded in a structure whose outward appearance would indicate a much later date. Such basic changes reflect changes in the fortunes of the community as a whole: a new choir or tower means that the village or town has become prosperous, a new aisle or aisles that its population has increased. In areas which were less fortunate in the later Middle Ages we shall find a higher proportion of Romanesque survival. This is true of southern France, which was wealthy in the twelfth century. The same is true of Catalonia; whereas in Picardy, Flanders and England Gothic predominates, because these were wealthy areas in the fourteenth and fifteenth century.

With such a vast number of surviving churches, it would be invidious to describe only two or three particular examples. All that can be done is to give a rapid survey of the kind of riches that wait to be discovered, and the best way of doing this is to look at specific features in turn. In purely architectural terms, the parish church is dwarfed by the monastery or cathedral, though there are a number of churches which come near to rivalling the lesser cathedrals in size. In some cases these are the old minster churches, designed to serve a larger area than a parish, as at Beverley and Southwell, which are indeed on a cathedral-like scale. Others are the churches of wealthy towns which aspired to cathedral status but never attained it; and here there are endless examples, some

of which we shall look at in the context of the town as a whole –
the Marienkirche at Visby, the church of the same name at
Lübeck, the Sebalduskirche at Nuremberg, Saint-Pierre and Saint-
Nicholas at Caen, Saint-Urbain at Troyes, Notre-Dame at Alençon,
St Mary Redcliffe at Bristol. These great town churches, however, are all Gothic, from the severe brick Gothic of the north
German towns to the flamboyant stonework of France. In the
Italian towns, where one might expect to find similar parish
churches, they are absent for two reasons: the Italian dioceses were
smaller, and the major town church is almost always a cathedral,
while the lesser churches are very often Franciscan foundations,
as at Santa Croce in Florence and San Francesco in Siena.
Spectacular churches can also be found outside the great towns,
in places which may today be no more than small villages. The
outstanding examples are the wool churches of East Anglia, such
as Lavenham and Long Melford, though the now isolated church
at Salle in south Norfolk is perhaps the most poignant reminder of
vanished prosperity. Again, the wealth of fifteenth-century Somerset is reflected in its outstanding churches, as is that of twelfth-
century Poitou and Saintonge or ninth-century Asturias.

On a humbler scale, the parish churches show the considerable
regional differences in architectural styles. The great churches,
patronized by bishops, princes and merchants, could never be
isolated from the latest international ideas; but in rural areas,
distinctive styles developed, influenced by the availability of building materials or supply by local tradition. The twelfth-century
churches around Périgord in south-west France are often built with
a series of domes forming the nave roof; Norfolk churches of the
same period have round towers; and neither feature is commonly
found elsewhere. In both cases, building requirements dictated the
form: domes are much more stable than tunnel vaults, and it is
impossible to build a square flint tower without using substantial
quantities of stone for the corners. Other local variants, such as
the Bavarian 'hall-church', with nave and aisles of equal height,
which extends across the frontier of Romanesque and Gothic
(examples can be found from the eleventh to the fifteenth century),
are less easily explained. Even more distinctive as a regional group
are the Norwegian stave-churches, survivors of a type which was
once the norm throughout much of northern Europe, of which
Greensted in Essex is the only English example. About twenty

of the Norwegian churches survive, of which Borgund, with its spectacular tiered roof, is the best preserved. The architecture here derives from earlier pagan halls and possibly even temples: at nearby Urnes, the great wooden doorway has the vigorous intertwining animal and foliage patterns common in both pagan and Christian art.

Churches can also be found adapted to a dual role. The church would normally be used as a communal meeting place and for a variety of purposes which we would now regard as unsuitable. Perhaps the most curious example of this is the warehouse in the roof of the Marienkirche at Visby (p. 303 below). A much more practical second use was as a place of defence, and many churches were specifically adapted for this purpose. They can be found throughout Europe, but obviously are most frequent in regions which were particularly unsettled. The east coast of Sweden has 'keep-churches', circular in form, with massive walls and arrow-slits, as at Hagby. On the Danish island of Bornholm there are found round churches which may be based on the church of the Holy Sepulchre at Jerusalem, but which are also equipped for defence. Other examples of fortified churches are to be found in south-west France, at remote villages in the Landes like Lesgor, near Dax, with a defensive chamber in the roof, or, more spectacular, at Saint-Amand-de-Coly near Périgueux, where the defence system determines the whole appearance of the church. Set on a hillside, it has a massive western tower designed like a keep, with three points from which attackers at the foot of the tower could be bombarded. There is an upper walkway from which archers could defend the church from outside; and even if the enemy succeeded in entering the church, there are vantage points inside for archers and others to shoot down on them.

Even the simplest of churches contained some form of decoration. Sculpture has survived better than either wall-paintings or glass. Some areas are relatively poor in suitable stone, and other expedients are used, such as the patterned flint flushwork of the great East Anglian churches. Romanesque sculpture is seen at its best in the smaller churches: the more ambitious programmes on cathedrals have rarely survived, and its emphasis on pattern is best seen in the doorways and capitals of the eleventh and twelfth centuries, where the hieratic and rigid style of pre-Romanesque gives way to a more fluid and human style. Parish churches with an elaborate scheme of sculpture were always exceptional and usually owed their decoration to a wealthy patron. Yet relatively humble churches could have rich statuary and carving, such as the tiny Kentish church of Barfreston, with its magnificent south doorway, or Kilpeck in Herefordshire. On Gotland, the church at Stånga has the remains of a monumental cycle of the stations of the cross set in the south wall beside an elegant, half-Romanesque, half-Gothic doorway with a poly-lobed arch. The greatest riches of all are perhaps to be found in Saintonge, where minute churches, half-lost in the fields, are like jewel-caskets, covered in exquisite patterns: Rioux and Rétaud, south of Saintes, come particularly to mind. The church at Aulnay, on the borders of Poitou and Saintonge, is one of the most ambitious examples of these ornamented churches. The relatively simple interior has a fine set of figured capitals, but it is the exterior that is alive with sculpture. A triple arcade on the west front gives space for two tympana and a centre doorway with four shallow bands of sculpture around the arch. The south façade is even more ornate, with an upper arcade above a deeply recessed sculptured doorway. Both here and on the east end figures and foliage are used alternately to form dense patterns.

Other churches depart from the traditional oblong plan, either because of some special requirement, or from sheer artistic invention. Saint-Germigny-des-Prés, on the upper reaches of the Loire, is a much restored example of the private oratory which was the forerunner of the parish church. The plan is a square with apses on all four sides, and the interior is an arched hall. It is related to similar survivors from an early period in Spain, such as San Miguel de la Escalada, near León, by the use of horseshoe arches as a decorative feature inside the building. San Miguel, however, was a monastic church, and is therefore on a more spacious basilica plan. A better, though much later, parallel is the eleventh-century hermitage of San Baudelio de Berlanga, south of Burgos, where the arcading and vaults spring from a single central pillar. This remarkable interior also contains a small raised oratory on horseshoe arches and a shrine formed in the central pillar, as well as the remains of rich frescoes.

But we have strayed from purely parish churches. The form of San Baudelio is due to its very purpose, but it is a reminder of the existence of places of worship even smaller than the parish church, the individual chapels founded for the use of way-farers or pilgrims, often as a result of a vow in time of danger. Such chapels were to be found on prominent coastal sites, on bridges or on mountain passes. Surviving examples are rare, because of the difficulty of maintaining such isolated buildings, and bridge chapels usually disappeared when the bridges were rebuilt. There are only four examples in England, including that at St Ives near Huntingdon. The chapel on the ruined twelfth-century bridge at Avignon has survived.

Returning to churches proper, examples of an unusual plan can be found at all periods. A consistent variation is the Greek cross plan, as at the Liebfrauenkirche at Trier (p. 292), but it is commoner in large Romanesque buildings and very rare in Gothic architecture, with its emphasis on length and height rather than mass. Another church of extremely unusual plan, the church of the Holy Ghost at Visby, is circular with two storeys and a choir extending east-wards (see p. 304). It has been argued from the plan that it is per-haps one of the churches built by the military orders; Templar churches were given a circular plan, on the model of the church of the Holy Sepulchre at Jerusalem, and with the dissolution of the order in the early fourteenth century some of these became parish churches before the end of the Middle Ages; but they were not designed as such.

Stained glass of really high quality was always a luxury item by comparison with sculpture, which needs no special resources other than those available in any area where building in stone was common. Glassmaking was a highly technical process and relied on a supply of specific chemicals and ingredients; and the basic glass for much of Europe was made in a dozen centres and supplied to the local glaziers in sheets; they would make up the windows and add the overpainting, fusing it to the base by re-heating the glass in a small kiln, so although the great country churches of the fifteenth century contain fine stained glass, the most spectacular examples are usually in cathedrals or town churches. Where there was a particularly active local centre for glassmaking, the churches in the area benefited: this was the case with York and Norwich and with Somerset as a whole in the fifteenth century. Otherwise important stained glass generally goes hand in hand with imposing architecture, and in many cases is to be found in the churches already mentioned, for example Notre-

Dame at Alençon, the Sebalduskirche and St Lorenz at Nuremberg.

These are Gothic examples; Romanesque glass is exceptionally rare, though isolated examples can be found, one of the earliest being the tenth-century window at Château Landon, east of Paris; in Germany, two cycles of windows survive in Romanesque apses, at St Kunibert in Cologne and at Bücken on the Weser near Minden, which date from the early thirteenth century, at the transition between Romanesque and Gothic.

The wholesale destruction of stained glass in certain areas at the Reformation was tempered only by the cost of replacing, even in plain glass, the huge areas of window involved; whereas decorative or non-sacred subjects in sculpture were often acceptable to the reformers, the condemnation of painted glass was wholesale, in the quest for an austere and plain interior. Furthermore, glass was much easier to destroy than sculpture, which, unless it was free-standing, had to be chiselled off laboriously.

The commonest form of decoration in the medieval parish church was wall-painting. Wall-paintings ranged from the crudest of daubs by an amateur hand to the glories of the Italian artists who were precursors of the Renaissance. Fortunately, a number of the lesser works have been preserved because the most common method of disposing of this unwanted decoration was by simply whitewashing the walls, and many relatively humble churches can therefore boast medieval wall-paintings. Most of these are didactic in pur-pose, illustrations to a sermon text, though the vivid red-ochre doom at the little church at Chaldon in Surrey needs no preacher to point its moral. Folk-art of this kind can be seen elsewhere, and often includes figures of St Christopher and the mysterious figure once called the 'Christ of the Trades', in which Christ appears surrounded by the implements of various craftsmen. The Chaldon doom is probably twelfth-century, but the tradition of doom paintings continued throughout the Middle Ages, and even in the years just before the Reformation a much more sophisticated doom was painted at Wenhaston in Suffolk.

A number of churches contained extensive cycles of paintings of the story of the Old and New Testaments, and the lives of the saints, miniature versions of the mosaics at San Marco in Venice. But even traces of complete cycles are rare: only the shadows remain at churches such as Wissington in Suffolk. Many churches possessed only paintings of the most important scenes in biblical history, usually those of the life of Christ, as at the little chapel at Pürgg, east of Hallstatt, in Austria, where the rather Byzantine frescoes were painted about the middle of the twelfth century, or the leper chapel at Petit-Quevilly in Normandy, founded by Henry I I, where the scenes are medallions in a sophisticated framework in the vault of the choir. One particular type of decoration is a humbler form of the ornamentation of the Byzantine churches, and has a long history in Christian art. This is the apse painting of Christ in Majesty. It can be found in Sicily, at Ravenna, in Catalonia, and in England, at Copford in Essex, where the paintings are as sophisticated as those at Petit-Quevilly. However, it is a group of Catalan churches which are the most striking. Sadly, the most important examples have had to be torn from their context and put into the safe-keeping of museums, such as the Museo de Arte at Barcelona, which contains the apses of Seo de Urgel, Santa María de Tahull and a dozen others. Here Christ is shown as the divine judge of the Apocalypse, echoing the popularity of works on the Apocalypse in Spanish monasteries. The apse of San Clemente has a superb example of this theme: the figure of Christ in a mandorla takes up two-thirds of the space, and his head projects forward on the curve of the vault, to give him a presence at once imposing and challenging. At Santa María, it is the Virgin who has pride of place because of the church's dedication, and the scene chosen is the Adoration of the Magi. The remaining wall-space was often taken up with an array of saints, stiff in their hieratic robes, rather than with narrative scenes. Painted altar-frontals were also common in this area, again with a Christ in Majesty or Virgin and Child. In the same Catalan context, the frescoes at San Miguel de Pedralbes, done by Ferrer Bassa in 1343, deserve a mention; but they are an isolated example of Gothic in this region.

Another once prosperous country area which (like Catalonia) became impoverished in the later Middle Ages was Gotland, and here too there are fine wall-paintings in many of the churches, including Hejdeby and Vamlingbo, medallion paintings in a foliage frame at Eskilhem and a famous though over-restored set of murals (and some thirteenth-century stained glass) at Dalhem. By contrast with the latter, there are unrestored figures in the tower at Garde which take us back to eighth-century Byzantium.

The wooden roofs common in early medieval churches were another opportunity for decoration, as at St Michael's, Hildesheim. Wooden churches obviously lent themselves to painting just as much as plaster interiors, but the result was less likely to flake off: where wooden structures have survived, they are very often painted.

Perhaps the most striking example is the Romanesque ceiling at Zillis in Graubunden in Switzerland, which is made up of 153 panels, each about three feet square, painted in a style which is obviously based on a knowledge of manuscript miniatures and of current fashions in Germany, but which is bold and naïve in other respects, particularly in its use of outline drawing. The Norwegian stave-churches contain a number of Gothic wall-paintings.

Frescoes from the Gothic period as a whole are much rarer – the emphasis on glass and the vastly increased size of the windows left little wall-space to be decorated. It is only in Italy, where Gothic made less of an impression, that wall-paintings remain an important element in the thirteenth and fourteenth centuries. In view of the esteem and the high fees that painters commanded, for example Duccio at Siena (p. 105), it is only the great churches that possess frescoes, and the general tendency among art-historians has been to place these cycles among the forerunners of the Renaissance rather than with Gothic art. However, there is a case for looking at a work like Giotto's frescoes at the Scrovegni chapel in Padua in its medieval context. The paintings were done in the first decade or so of the fourteenth century, and belong to a tradition which can be traced through the paintings at Assisi (p. 142) and work at Rome in the 1290s. Giotto's work is undoubtedly avant-garde, the preserve of wealthy patrons with taste; the Scrovegni chapel was a private oratory, and his frescoes are a huge departure even from the traditions we have quoted. It is above all his handling of spaces and volumes which is original, though he also conveys individual character and gesture in a way which distinguishes him from medieval art in general. His subsequent career was to take him to the great churches of Florence, where he again worked on private chapels, and I do not think it is too fanciful to see a link between this private patronage of an original artist and the new individuality and intimacy of the resulting masterpieces.

Private patronage, and private chapels within churches, are

increasingly common features in the fourteenth and fifteenth centuries. We have already touched on the chantries in connection with collegiate churches; in the later Middle Ages, however, the commonest individual or family contributions to the parish church were special chapels for chantry foundations and elaborate tombs. We have already noticed some examples of these in cathedrals, such as the chantry chapels at Ely, but the effect of such building on parish churches was much more radical. In an extreme case, as at Boughton Aluph in Kent, the chantry chapel is parallel to, and as large as, the chancel. But very often the chantry chapel stood within the church, as with the stone 'cages' of some late Gothic chapels, where an unglazed screen forms a freestanding square enclosure. In parish churches, such a screen might well be wooden, and these have usually disappeared, as have the majority of the chapels formed by blocking off an aisle or part of an aisle. Sometimes chantry chapels were built as an extra aisle to the church, as was the magnificent fan-vaulted Dorset chapel of c.1520 at Ottery St Mary. Elsewhere, chantries were merely annexed to the church: at Berkeley church, in the shadow of Berkeley castle, the family chapel is entered by a separate external door. At the other extreme, a tomb-slab could serve as a chantry altar, as did Chaucer's monument in Westminster Abbey.

Memorials, both inside the church and outside in the churchyard, form one of the richest areas of medieval art, and it is difficult to do more than outline their development here. At the beginning of the medieval period, we find the individual standing stone, either a *stele*, which derived from Roman memorials, or the Celtic standing stone with a debased Latin inscription. The latter merge into the beautiful Celtic crosses of Ireland, which culminate in the 'wheel-headed' crosses of the ninth and tenth century, a purely local development of the early Christian 'slab' crosses. Some are entirely patterned with ornamental designs, as are those found along the river Barrow, while a later group have figures and narrative scenes, as at Clonmacnoise. These lead in turn to the great Anglo-Saxon crosses, with their affinity to Norse art, of which the supreme example is the Ruthwell cross. After this, the tradition of memorial crosses dies out, though there are exceptions, such as the crosses erected to commemorate the last journey of St Louis or those raised by the grief-stricken Edward I to mark the places where the body of Eleanor of Castile had rested on its journey from Lincoln to Westminster, the last of the series being Charing Cross.

If we follow Eleanor to her final resting-place at Westminster, we come face to face with one of the finest tomb-effigies of the Middle Ages, made by the London goldsmith William Torel. It is a tender, idealized portrait of the queen, who is shown in a natural, easy pose rather than with her hands formally clasped in prayer. Tomb-effigies, like crosses, have a long history reaching back to Roman times; but, even allowing for the disappearance of many monuments, the idea of a tomb-effigy seems to have been a product of the twelfth century, when burials began to take place inside the church. A unique survivor of a different class of memorials is the enamel plaque at Le Mans depicting Geoffrey Plantagenet, Henry II's father; but the earliest royal effigies are later than this. The first of the German emperors at Speyer to have an effigy is Rudolf of Habsburg in the late thirteenth century; the series of royal tombs at Saint-Denis begins with St Louis, who ordered effigies of his ancestors to be made; and the first English royal effigy is that of Henry II at Fontevrault, dating from the early thirteenth century. The fashion probably derives from the commemorative stones of abbots found in monasteries such as Moissac, where there is a striking portrait of abbot Durand, erected about 1120. Once tomb effigies were used to commemorate secular rulers, they were soon adopted by lords and knights: a widespread group of wooden effigies from thirteenth-century England bears testimony to the ambitions of the latter as a newly wealthy group who could not afford or perhaps obtain the more expensive stone effigy. Like chantries, tomb sculptures reach their zenith at the end of the Middle Ages; in England alone the products of the Purbeck marble sculptors (including king John's effigy at Worcester) and the Nottingham alabaster workers, as in the Yorkshire effigies, have been the subject of monographs. Metalworkers, too, produced superb effigies, but these were restricted to the very wealthy and are almost all to be found in cathedrals.

Much tomb sculpture survived the Reformation, which leads to a disproportionate view of the place of figure sculpture in the churches of Protestant countries, particularly in the parish churches, where the figures from rood-screens and altars have long since vanished. The screens themselves do survive, ranging from the stone and metalwork screens to be found in cathedrals to the wooden screens, often with painted panels, which were an English speciality, particularly in the West Country and in East Anglia. Even the finest of these English screens, however, such as that at Ranworth in Norfolk, lack the original 'rood' or Crucifixion which surmounted it. Many of the detached statues now in museums come from the stripping of such screens, and other altar-figures and crucifixes have also found their way into collections. A visit to collections such as those in the Victoria and Albert Museum or the Schnütgen Museum at Cologne helps to redress the balance.

Finally, the site of a parish church can often tell us something of the place which it serves. Sometimes the church is a dramatic memorial to a vanished community, standing in isolation amid the fields; others lie close to the manor and vicarage, in the heart of a still thriving village. Town churches often bear witness to a movement in the urban community: a derelict area of slums will sometimes cluster round a superb medieval church. Elsewhere, the siting of a church can mark the centre of a community, planned or otherwise: the bastides of south-west France (p. 281) usually have the churches overlooking the market square, and in many urban parishes an open space in front of the church has become the market place, a link with the medieval use of the church and its surroundings as a place of business.

Above all, the parish churches and cathedrals of the Middle Ages are our greatest direct link with that past. They were founded by members of that same community which still uses them today, despite all vicissitudes and changes of creed and dogma, for the purpose for which they were originally built; and in this way they provide a degree of continuity which no other part of our medieval heritage can match.

4

Monasteries

The origins of the monasteries of medieval Europe can be traced back to the holy men of eastern religion who withdrew from the world in order to lead a contemplative life, a practice adopted by the early Christians, particularly in Egypt. Such hermits, however, often attracted followers, who would settle nearby and would live according to the guidance of their 'abbas' or spiritual father. These informal congregations were still to be found in medieval Europe; when in the early twelfth century the great teacher Peter Abelard left the monastery of Saint-Denis and built himself a hermitage near Nogent-sur-Seine, his disciples followed him and settled in huts around him. The early fathers in the Egyptian desert found, like Abelard, that some kind of order and physical discipline had to be imposed, though this was often little more than attendance at a communal daily service and the shaping of communal tasks. This loose association of men who had vowed – formally or otherwise – to abandon secular life was typical of the monasteries of the remoter parts of medieval Europe, particularly those of the Celtic world. The Irish monks lived in individual stone or wattle cells grouped round a central chapel; and like their Egyptian predecessors, they sought out deserted places for their habitations. The settlements on Skellig Michael, eight miles off the coast of Co. Kerry, survive as impressive evidence of their determination, while on the mainland the stone-built Gallarus oratory near Kilmalkedar and the monastic cell at Aranmore in Co. Galway show us what such communities looked like in the sixth and seventh centuries.

But the mainstream of monastic life in western Europe developed in a different direction. The implications of isolation in the very word 'monastic', which derives from the Greek 'monos', alone, were abandoned in favour of the idea of an isolated community, living apart from the world. This was partly a reaction against the excesses of some of the desert saints; partly due to a feeling, powerfully expressed by St Basil, that 'the solitary life has one aim, the service of the needs of the individual' and was inherently selfish; and partly due to physical circumstances in the west, where a monastic community might often settle in what had once been a Roman villa on a great estate. The result was that in the European monastic communities, almost from the beginning, there was a much stronger emphasis on community, an emphasis to be found in the Near East and in the Greek Orthodox monasteries using the rule of St Basil, but which was to reach its highest development in medieval Europe. The monastery was seen as an integrated unit, under the absolute control of the abbot, who was not merely a guide or director, but had complete authority over the least detail of the monks' lives. The first attempt to give a formal framework to this new institution was made about the year 500, in central Italy, by an unknown writer; his work is generally known as the *Rule of the Master*, and it was edited and subtly reshaped some thirty years later by St Benedict as the opening chapters of his rule. The Benedictine rule is the basis for the organization of all western monasteries, and later reformers did little more than urge a return to the true principles which it contained. St Benedict saw the ideal monastery not merely as a place of spiritual retreat from the world, but as a community independent of the rest of the world, with its own means of subsistence, very much as the great Roman estates had become independent economic units as the central power weakened and trading links were disrupted. It was not to be a community of the elite, but a refuge for all who wanted to share this kind of life, from the learned to the labourer, from children to men who had finished their career in the world outside. This insistence that there was a place for everyone was another contrast with the eastern monasteries, and was a potential source of weakness. Even if everyone took part in the communal services, the degree of involvement could vary widely; but the great strength of the Benedictine rule was its breadth of vision and tolerance, its assumption that everyone had something to offer. St Benedict foresees the possibility of failures and envisages practical steps to deal with them. This practical yet deeply religious approach was the reason for the great success of his work. It is not an easy rule: to the materialist of today it seems impossibly hard in many of its demands. Complete and unquestioning obedience to the abbot and superiors, the surrender of all possessions and total chastity are the three central obligations; and the existence offered in return is harsh and unexciting, with long periods of obligatory silence varied by physical labour and by worship. Much depends on the abbot, who has almost tyrannical powers; but Benedict is quick to remind those set in high office that they are not there to rule, but to guide, and that their ideals must be the highest of all.

St Benedict's rule gained ground only gradually; in the disturbed times of the sixth and seventh centuries, many varieties of monasticism flourished. But it was soon adopted as the church's norm for monastic life, and Gregory the Great, before he became pope in 590, may have lived as a monk under the rule. He was certainly familiar with it, and through him many of its concepts became part of church doctrine. Yet it was in no sense imposed from above on the existing monasteries, but became their accepted basis over a period of centuries. The rule-book of any given monastery was frequently an anthology of various rules, depending on local custom. In the isolation and troubles of the eighth and ninth centuries it was the local group of monasteries which was more important than any central authority.

Two other elements in monastic life must be mentioned before we turn to the great monasteries themselves. Benedict envisaged a relatively small and simple community; but even in his day some monastic institutions were becoming large and wealthy, and far from isolated. The members of the monasteries in Rome were nearer to the cathedral clergy of today: their preoccupation was with the great ceremonial services held in the basilicas of Rome, and this in turn meant that the daily round of eight simple services of Benedict's rule became a multitude of complex liturgical practices. Other monasteries, such as that at Vivarium in central Italy, became refuges for scholars and acquired a reputation for learning, something which was not part of Benedict's original intentions, but which came to play a very important part in monastic life. Monasteries such as those in Rome had insufficient land for all the monks to work in turn on the monastery's estates, as Benedict had envisaged. So the purely manual labour for the support of the monastic house became other forms of labour useful in a more general sense to the community as a whole – the copying of manuscripts and teaching, to which care of pilgrims and of the sick were later added. In David Knowles's words: 'It cannot be too often repeated that in St Benedict's conception a monastery existed for the service of God and spiritual welfare of its inmates, and for no other reason.' The history of the monasteries in the Middle Ages was to be a continual falling away from, and intermittent return to, this ideal.

The Italian monasteries were the leading examples of monastic life in the sixth century; and throughout the Middle Ages, particular groups of monasteries exercised an influence quite out of proportion to their size or wealth. It was a world where individuals could make an outstanding contribution as abbots, scholars, founders or reformers. The first such group to emerge was that of the Northumbrian monasteries in the eighth century. We have already met Benedict Biscop, their founder, on his journeys to Rome. He founded the monastery at Wearmouth after his second journey there, in 674, and that at Jarrow eight years later. We know a great deal about both him and his monasteries because the lives of the abbots were written by his distinguished pupil, Bede, who had entered the monastery at Wearmouth as a child and had been one of the first monks at Jarrow. Benedict brought back from Gaul masons and glaziers to build in stone instead of the traditional English wood; he brought books, including one in Greek, and he himself taught theology and astronomy. He furnished the churches in the latest Roman style and brought back Roman teachers to instruct his monks in the Roman art of singing. Learning and the liturgy dominated the life of the monasteries, reflecting Benedict Biscop's liking for the way of life he found in the great monasteries at Rome. Two incidents from Bede's own life underline this. In his last days, he was able to go to the church only with great difficulty, and his fellow-monks tried to dissuade him. But he refused to be put off, saying: 'I know that the angels are present at the canonical hours, and what if they do not find me among the brethren when they assemble? Will they not say, where is Bede? Why does he not attend the appointed devotions with his brethren?' Elsewhere, Bede tells how from the age of thirty 'until my fifty-ninth year, I have worked ... to compile extracts from the work of the venerable Fathers on Holy Scripture, and to make commentaries on their meaning and interpretation'. At the same time he wrote his great history of the church in England, and works on astronomy and chronology as well. Yet while Bede exercised his special talents as a scholar, other monks looked after the mundane affairs of the monastery, and no distinction was made between learning and labour: abbot Easterwin 'remained so humble that he loved to thresh and winnow, milk the cows and ewes, and "occupied himself obediently in the bakery, garden, kitchen and all the work of the monastery"', exactly as the rule of St Benedict prescribed.

Benedict Biscop's monasteries were a showplace for the whole of northern England; we hear of the Celtic abbot Adamnan of Iona adopting the Roman style of worship after a visit to Jarrow. At the same time, men from these and other English monasteries set out as missionaries to their kinsmen across the North Sea, the greatest being St Boniface, the apostle of the Germans. And in many ways it was on the continent that the Anglo-Saxon monastic traditions and learning were to survive, for the Northumbrian monasteries were among the first to succumb to the Viking raids of the late eighth century. Lindisfarne, the monastery of St Cuthbert, which bridged the Saxon and Celtic worlds, was the first to be attacked, in 793; Jarrow was raided the following year. There followed a lull of thirty years; and then the storm broke. By 880 there was scarcely a monastery left in all England. As a result, there is little to be seen of the original buildings at Jarrow and Wearmouth, though the walls and lower part of the tower at the latter are probably seventh-century work, and a panel decorated in half-Roman, half-Norse style survives in the porch. What is striking is the small scale of the churches in these famous foundations. Equally, little has come down to us of the Roman element in Benedict Biscop's work: the artistic survivals from the golden age of Northumbria – the Lindisfarne Gospels in the British Library, the great cross at Ruthwell – are primarily Celtic in origin. Only at Hexham Abbey, built by St Wilfrid, a prince-prelate 'in the mould which afterwards produced Becket and Wolsey', does the crypt give some feeling of a wealthy and peaceful society ready to lavish money on new churches, which was an important characteristic of Northumbria.

The monuments of the next new impulse in monastic life, that of St Benedict of Aniane under the direction of Charlemagne, are equally few and far between. Charlemagne, in his efforts to re-create an empire where everything was regulated and ordered by a central authority, carried out extensive reforms in the church;

and the monasteries naturally attracted his attention. Benedict of Aniane won his reputation as the abbot of Saint-Guilhem-le-Désert, a small monastery in the hills of the Hérault in southern France, where the rule of St Benedict was observed with great zeal. In later years, as adviser to Charlemagne's son Louis the Pious, he presided over a conference of abbots at Aachen in 817 where a revised version of the rule was issued, which had the force of law and was binding on monks throughout Charlemagne's empire. The most important changes were that agricultural work now became exceptional, rather than the rule; the monks were only to teach oblates, men who wished to become monks, as other education was assigned by Charlemagne to secular clergy; and additional duties of prayer and worship were imposed. The vital element in this reform was the establishment of the original rule of St Benedict as the standard rule, rather than the best of many; and this innovation survived the decay of the monasteries in the late ninth and early tenth centuries in the face of Viking and Saracen raids. Rich and defenceless, they were easy prey for raiders, and the monks were driven further inland by successive attacks. The quest for deserted places had led to many monasteries being founded by the sea; now these solitudes became the front line of a one-sided war. The travels of the relics of saints in these years vividly illustrate the horrors of the time. Those of St Philibert were taken from the monastery on the island of Noirmoutier on the west coast of France in the face of the Viking threat in 836 to Saint-Philibert-de-Grand-Lieu on the mainland. Twenty years later, the monks retreated further inland to Cunault, in Anjou; four years later they moved south to Poitou, finally reaching Tournus in Burgundy in 875, only to have their new home sacked by the Hungarians in 937. On their journeys, the monks of Noirmoutier helped to create two outstanding early Romanesque churches, at Saint-Philibert-de-Grand-Lieu and at Tournus. Both survive in part, though much restored. Only at secluded sites such as the island of Reichenau on Lake Constance and at nearby St Gall did monastic life continue without disturbance. The abbey on Reichenau can still be seen today. The chapel of St Georg at Oberzell contains a fine sequence of Carolingian wall-paintings, derived perhaps from Byzantine sources and depicting the miracles of Christ; a similar series can be found at the chapel of St Sylvester at Goldtach near Überlingen on the north shore of the lake, but it is the com-

pleteness and unity of St Georg which is impressive. Elsewhere, the abbey was much enlarged in the eleventh century, and
the Münster at Mittelzell is now an example of a major eleventh-
century abbey church, far grander than that of the modest establishment which cherished the ideals of monasticism in the dark days
of the ninth century.

It was in Burgundy, in the heart of Europe and in the region
which had suffered least from the raiders, that the greatest
stimulus to the revival of monastic life started. Duke William of
Aquitaine, wishing to found a monastery, sought out the strictest
abbot he knew, Bertho of Baume, near Besançon. Bertho
promptly demanded the duke's favourite hunting lodge at Cluny
as the site of the new monastery, and obtained not only that, but
also a charter which gave the monks the right to elect their own
abbot without interference from the dukes of Aquitaine, and exemption from the jurisdiction of the local bishop. Under the second
abbot, Odo, who had been a monk at Baume, Cluny became the
centre of reform, sending emissaries to other houses at the request
of their patrons and founding daughter-houses or priories which
owed obedience to the abbot of Cluny. At Fleury, where St
Benedict's relics had been brought from Monte Cassino, the
Cluniac reforms were accepted, but, like many other houses at this
period, Fleury did not become one of Cluny's priories. Many
houses accepted Cluniac advice on reforms, ranging from the
thoroughgoing visitation which abbot Odo carried out at Fleury –
to the extent that the local bishop feared that the monks would kill
him – to the presence of a Cluniac monk as a temporary or permanent member of the community. Cluny was fortunate in her abbots,
for in the eleventh century she was ruled by two exceptional men,
St Odilo and St Hugh, whose combined abbacies stretched from
994 to 1109. St Odilo, while retaining the strictness of observance,
encouraged the beautifying of the church, and 'marvellously
adorned the cloisters with columns and marble brought from the
farthest parts of the province'. It was under Hugh that the system
of priories was developed, and Cluny's influence, hitherto indirect
or localized, spread throughout Europe in a formal network.

Cluny was not the only house to build up a network of associated
or dependent houses in this way; many other monasteries, often
influenced by Cluny in their early days, did so. In Italy the labours
of St William of Volpiano produced not only the renewal of the

Lombard monasteries but, following William's appointment as abbot of Saint-Bénigne at Dijon, the reforms there and later in Normandy. In Spain, Ripoll became the leading light of a group of monasteries, including that at the pilgrimage shrine of Montserrat. The German monasteries stood somewhat apart, because the political element in the appointment of abbots was strong; as with parish churches everywhere, so in the German monasteries the founder's family often remained patrons and retained a say in the choice of the head of the community. The political separation of Germany and France meant that German patrons rarely, if ever, chose abbots from France. But a reform movement appeared at much the same time, the leading houses being Gorze in the tenth century and Hirsau in the eleventh. England, standing apart from both France and the empire in the tenth century, drew on the traditions of both when St Dunstan began his reforms in the 960s.

This bare list of names cannot do justice to the extraordinary and unprecedented expansion of the monasteries in the tenth century. This expansion was to have profound effects on the future of European culture, because in many cases the activities of the re-founded monasteries preserved the inheritance of classical literature which had been severely threatened by the disturbances of the ninth century, and the scholarship of the later Middle Ages rests on the texts copied in the monastic writing rooms or *scriptoria* in this period. In the same way, much of Romanesque art results from the knowledge of classical antiquity kept alive by the monasteries. Furthermore, in the case of Cluny, whose abbots were responsible only to the pope, there were close links with Rome, reflected in the early twelfth-century wall-paintings at the priory of Berzé-la-Ville a few miles south of Cluny itself, which seem to emphasize St Peter and other Roman saints such as St Lawrence, as well as deriving their style from Roman work of the period.

In architecture, it was Cluny which had by far the greatest influence. Scholars no longer believe that each new house was built from precise master-plans drawn up at Cluny, but the Cluniac foundations are remarkably coherent as an architectural group, and there may well have been an archive of plans at Cluny. The abbey church at Cluny was itself rebuilt twice, but it was the first rebuilding which was most widely used as an exemplar: in the customs of the monastery of Farfa in Italy, a detailed measured description of the church at Cluny was recorded. Even today, the Cluniac predominance remains: 325 of their establishments survive, usually as ruins – by far the largest related group of medieval buildings. The general characteristics of their architecture are a liking for impressive, stone-vaulted churches; their love of vaulting has been attributed to the search for a suitable acoustic for the famous chant which was the standard feature of their services. In these monasteries, however austere the monks' life might be, the worship of God was to be carried out with all possible solemnity and splendour. Naturally, the most magnificent church of all was that at Cluny itself, and abbot Hugh set about its rebuilding in 1085. It was designed by one of the monks, who used the principles set out by the Roman architect Vitruvius, whose treatise he found in the abbey library; the construction was supervised by another monk, an expert mathematician, and it was completed by 1130. It was one of the great churches of Europe; Mabillon, the Benedictine scholar, said of it in the seventeenth century: 'If you see its majesty a hundred times, you are overwhelmed on each occasion.' Conceived on an almost unprecedented scale, the church was originally 600 feet in length, and was later extended to the west; the vault was over 100 feet above the nave floor, exceptionally high for a Romanesque building; and the sanctuary, with its elaborate pattern of chapels radiating off it, was ringed by classical columns. Alas, only fragments remain of this earthly version of the Heavenly City: the monastery, closed in 1790 after the French Revolution, was not even deliberately destroyed as a symbol of the hated *vieux régime*, but was sold off for demolition, and only fragments of the buildings remain. And the same is all too often the story of Cluny's daughter-houses, to the extent that in all three hundred survivors it is difficult to point to an outstanding complete example of a Cluniac monastery. Vézelay is probably the finest, but it stands somewhat apart from the mainstream, being a pilgrimage church belonging to a monastery which was only briefly Cluniac. We can point to survivals from different monasteries which are typically Cluniac, such as La-Charité-sur-Loire, Saint-Étienne at Nevers, Charlieu, which is modelled closely on the second church at Cluny itself, and above all Paray-le-Monial, a scaled-down version of the third church at Cluny, dating from *c.*1110.

Apart from architecture, the Cluniac love of sculpture is everywhere in evidence. Vézelay and Moissac are two names to conjure with in terms of Romanesque sculpture; but even the humblest priory tried to adorn its buildings with capitals (depicting everything from biblical scenes to exotic monsters) or impressive doorways and façades such as that at Saint-Gilles-du-Gard in Provence, with its antique columns and low profile reminiscent of Roman architecture and friezes and statues in the same vein. However, we cannot expect to find related Cluniac sculpture throughout their far-flung network of houses in the same way as we can trace architectural parallels: the work was carried out by local or itinerant artists. What is important is the attitude of the Cluniacs to the arts: sculpture and painting and rich architecture were there to be used to the glory of God.

Two of the most spectacular examples of Cluniac art are the cloisters at Santo Domingo de Silos near Burgos, and at Moissac, near Cahors. Both are relatively remote; both were fairly modest establishments, Santo Domingo having some forty monks, while Moissac was virtually in ruins in the mid eleventh century. In both cases, they were reformed through the patronage of princes.

Ferdinand I of Castile was responsible for appointing Santo Domingo as abbot of Silos, while Durand de Bredon, the first Cluniac abbot at Moissac, was appointed at the request of the count of Toulouse. This accounts in some degree for the appearance of outstanding works of art in otherwise remote places; but it was above all the Cluniac attitude to artistic endeavour that made both possible.

Santo Domingo de Silos was unusual in that it seems to have employed not only sculptors but also goldsmiths, jewellers and enamellers. Its illuminated manuscripts from the eleventh and twelfth centuries are justifiably famous and include a number of copies of commentaries on the Apocalypse, a text which gave free rein to artists with a dramatic imagination. The library, which contained 105 manuscripts in the thirteenth century, is now scattered; the Romanesque church was rebuilt in a severe neoclassical style in the eighteenth century; but the cloister with its elegant two-storeyed arcades remains. The upper cloister is twelfth-century, and the capitals are formal, mainly foliage. The masterpieces are all in the lower cloister, where an unknown but strikingly individual sculptor worked around the end of the eleventh century. His work has strong echoes of that at Moissac and at Souillac on the Dordogne – we shall see how the pilgrim roads could be the link between these groups of carvings.

At Silos the carvings occur on the flat surfaces in the four corners of the cloister arcade, and the same artist was probably also responsible for the capitals on the north and east sides, although these are in a quite distinct style. Elaborate networks and patterns surround familiar and unfamiliar animals, which themselves often form a secondary pattern; the richly ornamental effect has echoes of the Moorish love of tracery and intertwining lines. The animals and birds are drawn from biblical allegory and from the medieval books of beasts, which in turn hark back to creatures of classical myth such as the harpies. The reliefs are in a much simpler and more majestic style, with a strong sense of highly formal pattern. They show the main scenes of the gospel after the crucifixions, and in three of them all twelve disciples appear (Paul being shown as one of the twelve). This imposes severe restrictions on the sculptor, but varying the gestures of each figure and giving them a curving, almost swaying, line brings them to life. Perhaps the most appealing tableau is that of the disciples on the road to Emmaus: Christ, dressed as a pilgrim, towers over the other two figures, leading them firmly on in response to their hesitant and imploring gestures. The later masters who worked here in the twelfth century produced a fine series of figured capitals showing the events attending the birth of Christ, and another set depicting the events of Holy Week. Almost the last work was another masterpiece, an Annunciation almost Baroque in its sweetness, related to the early French Gothic with its classical echoes, but with a swirling drapery which contrasts with the severity of the faces. A few pieces of jewellery and copies of manuscripts from the heyday of Silos are to be seen in the museum, as a reminder that the sculpture in the cloister is not the result of a chance visit by a single genius, but part of the bequest of a flourishing centre of the arts.

At **Moissac**, the most spectacular feature is the south doorway of 1140–80, with its overpowering tympanum of Christ in Majesty from Chapter 4 of the Book of Revelations: note once again the apocalyptic theme. The sculpture is sophisticated and often very bold in its use of forms, as on the central pillar of the doorway with its pattern of lions standing on each other and the figures of Jeremiah and St Paul on the interior of the arch. There is a strong use of pattern, too: the outer edges of the doorways are boldly scalloped, and the lintel is a brilliant series of circular flowers. The capitals in the cloister also show this same freedom of treatment, but the results are less successful within the confines of the small space that a capital contains. The figure sculptures are cruder and bolder than at Silos. The most striking is the great memorial plaque to abbot Durand on one of the square corner pillars. This can be related to manuscripts produced here in the eleventh century, as can other details of the cloister capitals; once again, we are looking at the work of a school of artists, rather than of an individual. Among the capitals is one (near the centre of the east gallery) with a topical note: it portrays the crusaders at Jerusalem in 1099.

Our last example is not perhaps strictly Cluniac, in that we know almost nothing of the history of the abbey of **Saint-Savin-sur-Gartempe** in Poitou during the eleventh century, except that the church was rebuilt during this period, and, probably in the early twelfth century, an ambitious scheme of paintings was carried out. The painters probably drew on contemporary manuscripts, and some of the features of their style can be traced back to the art of Charlemagne's day. Once again, the Apocalypse figures prominently, in the decoration of the porch at the west end of the church; despite extensive restoration work, these frescoes have suffered badly, as have those in the tribune above, which depict New Testament schemes. It is the scenes from the Old Testament, which run the length of the nave roof, which are the most striking. Richly but soberly coloured and boldly drawn against a white background, the figures move energetically and use expressive gestures. The order is somewhat confusing, as the painting seems to have begun before the nave was complete: the events of Genesis occupy three bays on both tiers, whereas the concluding part, the story of Moses, occupies the lower tier only across six bays. The paintings are thus part of the original plan of the church; and one of the beauties of Saint-Savin is that its interior, with the carefully restored marbling on the pillars, is almost exactly as it was when first built; this is the pure Romanesque art and architecture of a great twelfth-century abbey church.

The reform movement based on Cluny was exceptional in scale and influence, and it is easy to overlook the many smaller-scale efforts that went on at the same period outside Cluny's direct influence. As one example of many, let us look at the Norman monasteries. In common with other coastal areas of Europe, the monasteries were devastated in the ninth century. In the course of time the descendants of the raiders who had plundered them became the dukes of Normandy and established themselves as Christian rulers in the late tenth century; but by then hardly a single monastery survived anywhere in the duchy.

Yet this devastation heralded an equally remarkable revival. It began with duke Richard I's refounding of Fontanelle (or Saint-Wandrille) about 960 and of Mont-Saint-Michel a few years later. Richard I asked for monks to be sent from Cluny to help to found a monastery at Fécamp (where the vast, much rebuilt monastery church survives as the cathedral), but it was only under his successor, Richard II, that his appeal was answered, and William, abbot of Dijon, who had been a monk at Cluny, arrived to become head of the community at Fécamp.

During the following fifty years, with the encouragement and patronage of the Norman dukes, the ancient religious houses of the region were revived. Among the most important of these were Jumièges, Bernay and Cerisy-la-Forêt. At Jumièges, on the bank of the Seine below Rouen, after several indecisive attempts to re-establish the monastery, abbot Robert began a successful campaign to rebuild it. He himself became bishop of London and then archbishop of Canterbury in 1051, the first Norman to hold the see; but his tenure was brief, for he was expelled in 1052 and returned to Jumièges as a simple monk.

All that remains of **Jumièges**, apart from some minor conventual buildings, is the old church of Saint-Pierre, belonging to the period before abbot Robert, and the new church of Notre-Dame. Saint-Pierre, the oldest surviving post-Viking church in Normandy, has some very interesting early Romanesque features, particularly on the inner side of the west façade. It is dwarfed, however, both artistically and physically, by its neighbour. Notre-Dame has two magnificent towers, which survive almost intact; they modulate gracefully from massive plain square bases to simple blind arcades and then to arcaded windows before the final octagonal storeys, one of which is almost round. The nave, with its succession of alternate round and compound pillars, has lost much of the detail from its upper storeys, and is roofless. It once had an ancient wooden ceiling: it was never vaulted. Towards the east end, the church becomes progressively more ruinous: the Gothic choir was systematically demolished between 1802 and 1824, and the central tower must have disappeared at the same period. The over-all effect is one of extreme architectural restraint, typical of Norman Romanesque, though Jumièges was never actually as austere as it now seems, since there is evidence of sculptured capitals and con-siderable decoration.

In its heyday, Jumièges was both a spiritual and a political centre, with rich lands on both sides of the Channel, but as a force in Norman and English politics it was overshadowed by **Bec** (or Le Bec-Hellouin, to give it its full modern title). Together with the two great abbeys at Caen (see p. 202 below), Bec was one of the rare new foundations of the period; but whereas the Caen abbeys were created by the duke and duchess, Bec was unusual in that it owed its origin to a private individual of relatively slender means, a knight named Herluin. Having tried monastic life in existing abbeys, he rejected it as not being sufficiently spiritual and retired to his estates with a few like-minded companions. By 1041, they had moved to Le Bec-Hellouin and had built a church. The fol-lowing year, a well-known Italian monk and teacher who had been at Avranches, Lanfranc, entered the community, seeking, like Herluin, a life of contemplation and retirement. His reputation was too great, however, and pupils soon flocked to him at Bec; he him-self went on to become archbishop of Canterbury, as did his greatest disciple, Anselm (famous as a theologian); with such personalities as these, and an important school, Bec became the leading light of Norman monasticism, and its members played a central part in the relations between church and state in the Anglo-Norman realm. Although there is once more a monastic com-munity at Bec, little now remains of the medieval abbey.

Bec's importance, however, was due as much to its status in the monastic world as to its influence in the world of politics. It is a prime example of how a monastery founded with the highest religious intentions, and producing men of saintly calibre, could be inexorably drawn into the secular world; the abbots might defy the neighbouring landowners and prelates and preserve their independence on a local scale, but it was impossible for them to ignore the commands of the duke of Normandy and king of Eng-land. Anselm proved to be a thorn in the side of the king who brought him to Canterbury, but it was not in his temperament to see monasticism as a way of life totally divorced from the world; and lesser abbots yielded all the more easily to the temptations of worldly splendour.

At the same time, the reformers of the eleventh century attempted to bring within the monastic scheme of things many of the clergy whose work was in fact in the world outside, the clerics attached to cathedrals. These we would call today Augustinian canons, because they followed the rule attributed to St Augustine rather than that of St Benedict; it was a less formal set of directions, and better adapted for men whose duties did not always lend themselves to the keeping of restrictive vows of silence or precise observance of the liturgy. Augustinian houses were much more varied than the Benedictine monasteries, ranging from cells in remote sites to royal abbeys such as Jedburgh in Scotland or wealthy town establishments like St Bartholomew's in London.

All this meant that there was a tendency to draw 'regular' clergy – clerics living according to a rule – back into the worldly ways which they were supposed to have abandoned. The Cluniac reformers had been primarily concerned with the revival, in almost physical terms, of monastic life, at a time when smallness of numbers and insecurity were as much of a danger as laxity of observance. Now that monastic life was assured of its place as part of Christian society, the zealous and pious turned their attention to the quality of that life and found that the purity of St Benedict's intentions had been sullied. Ascetics and hermits, like Herluin of Bec, set up an ideal of severity and solitude in opposition to the wealth and outwardness of the existing Benedictine houses. They valued learning, prayer and contemplation rather than the elaborate succession of services which occupied the monks of Cluny. The two great orders which exemplify the new direction of monasticism are the Cistercians and the Carthusians. The Carthusians were in fact groups of hermits, each living in individual cells, but sharing a communal church (like the desert fathers and the early Celtic monks); they chose remote sites, imitating their founders, who had settled in the hills of Savoy. The original foundation there, La Grande Chartreuse, is still, after many changes of fortune, the mother house of the order, though the medieval buildings have disappeared. The order has always been very close-knit, and indeed daughter-houses were founded only with some reluctance. The austerity of the life, the small scale of the organization and the stern attitude towards would-be recruits have meant that it is the one monastic order which has never had to be reformed: *nunquam reformata quia nunquam deformata*.

The Carthusians withdrew almost entirely from the world; the Cistercians set out to reform it, or so it seems when we come to their most spectacular figure, St Bernard of Clairvaux. The Cistercian ideal began with an attempt to return to the life of the desert fathers, but without the insistence on a hermit life: the community was based first at Molesme and then, in 1097–8, at Cîteaux, south of Dijon, but each time its reputation for austerity grew, it attracted donations from pious admirers and began to resemble the very monasteries it was trying to replace. The founder, St Robert, was a contradictory and uncertain character – or so it would seem from the vague stories about him – and it was only under the second abbot of Cîteaux, Stephen Harding, that the impetus of his ideas was given the form and shape necessary to success. The original members of the house at Cîteaux, as David Knowles puts it, 'felt a deep conscientious conviction that life under conditions governed by the customs traditional in monasteries of their province was a constant transgression of the monastic profession as defined by the rule of St Benedict; they therefore desired a life at once more severe and more retired'. They abjured all pomp and ceremony in their worship, rejected all kinds of small personal comforts, and refused to draw income from feudal rights or rights in church property or dues. Their only source of income was to be their own estates, to be worked by lay brothers of the order. The religious brethren were to spend their time in prayer and reading rather than worship. All this was embodied in the customs of Cîteaux, drawn up under Alberic, the first abbot; much of it echoed previous attempts at reform, but the master-stroke was a second document, the 'Charter of Charity', under 2,000 words in length, which established a constitution for the order which was to prove capable of dealing with an expansion beyond the wildest dreams of the men who drafted it. Its basic tenet was uniformity: the customs were to be mandatory for all future houses, identical service books were to be used and every house was to be visited once a year by the abbot of the house which had founded it. The order was to be ruled, not by a single head or house, but by a general council of abbots meeting annually at Cîteaux.

By the time the 'Charter of Charity' was written in 1118–19, under Stephen Harding's rule, Cîteaux already possessed four daughter-houses; within forty years, there were almost three hundred. This explosion of activity on the part of the 'white monks' (so called because they wore a habit of plain wool, in contrast to the Benedictine black habit) was led by one man, St Bernard of Clairvaux, who came to Cîteaux in 1112 and spent only three years there before becoming abbot of the new foundation at Clairvaux, which was to be the most influential of the daughter-houses. St Bernard himself, while insistent that a monk's place was in the cloister, played a great part in the politics of western Europe between 1120 and his death in 1153. Some of the success of the Cistercians was undoubtedly due to Bernard's influence with the popes and kings of his day and his unremitting criticism of the Cluniac monks. Bernard was no stranger to controversy: it was he who led the attack on Peter Abelard's philosophy, and one of his chief debates was with Peter the Venerable, the abbot of Cluny. He condemned the laxity of Cluniac houses in admitting novices too readily, in eating luxuriously and in refraining from any kind of physical labour. In a letter to another abbot, Guillaume de Saint-Thierry, written in 1124, Bernard attacks Cluniac art, denouncing

the immense height of their churches, their immoderate length and their superfluous breadth, costly polishing, and the curious carvings which attract the worshipper's gaze and hinder his devotion – wheresoever more abundant wealth is seen, there do men offer more freely. Their eyes are feasted with relics cased in gold, and their purse-strings are loosed – the church is resplendent in her walls, beggarly in her poor: She clothes her storeys in gold, and leaves her sons naked. Why lavish bright hues upon that which must needs be trodden underfoot? – And in the cloister what profit is there in those ridiculous monsters of deformed comeliness and comely deformity? To what purpose are those unclean apes, those fierce lions, those monstrous centaurs, those half-men, those striped tigers, those fighting knights, those hunters winding their horns? Here is a four-footed beast with a serpent's tail; there a fish with a beast's head – In short, so many and so various are the shapes on every hand that we are more tempted to read in the stonework than in books.

The Cistercian constitution, the 'Charter of Charity', had already forbidden most of these vagaries in the order's churches: no carvings, stained glass or wall-paintings were permitted, and even the crucifixes were to be painted wood rather than gold or silver, standing on a plain linen cloth. No more than five lamps were allowed in a church, and only two bells; and no stone towers 'of an excessive height' were to be built. These regulations were strictly enforced, and they give Cistercian art its particular qualities, its simplicity, severity and elegance.

Neither Cîteaux nor Clairvaux survive as more than ruins, but it is possible to recapture something of the feeling of the original foundations at **Fontenay** (between Auxerre and Dijon), begun by St Bernard in 1118. The buildings here are deserted but intact, save for the refectory; the church, completed in 1147, is a perfect example of the harmony and proportion by which Cistercian architects achieved their best effects. Only the presence of four chapels round the sanctuary departs a little from the original precepts of the order. The chapter house, library, scriptorium and dormitory are all more or less in their original state; the severity of the cloister, which is almost a perfect square, is in sharp contrast to those of Moissac or Santo Domingo, but even here the capitals and pillars are subtly shaped and placed: beauty of form replaces beauty of decoration. The site is a secluded one, and this too is one of the great characteristics of the Cistercian abbeys. Other examples, with similarly intact buildings, are at Le Thoronet, Sénanque and Silvacane in France. In England, it is the Cistercian abbeys which provided the noble ruins so beloved of the Romantic poets: Tintern Abbey is the classic example. The Yorkshire abbeys, drawing their great wealth from the sheep farms run by the lay brothers, are on a particularly grand scale; again, the sites are spectacular, even to-day. The biographer of Ailred of Rievaulx (who became abbot there in 1146) described how the monks who founded it in 1131 chose it for this reason:

High hills surround the valley, encircling it like a crown. These are clothed by trees of various sorts and maintain in pleasant retreats the privacy of the vale, providing for the monks a kind of second paradise of wooded delight. From the loftiest rocks the waters wind and tumble down to the valley below, and as they make their hasty way through the lesser passages and narrower beds and spread themselves in wider rills, they give out a gentle murmur of soft sound and join together in the siren notes of a delicious melody. And when the branches of lovely trees rustle and sing together and the leaves flutter gently to the earth, the happy listener is filled increasingly with a glad jubilee of harmonious sound.

Pastoral simplicity and puritanism are two elements of early

Cistercian philosophy; and yet it is the grandeur of many of their churches that impresses us today. If 'towers of excessive height' were banned, it did not prevent the whole ensemble of buildings being planned on a generous scale. This, together with the insistence on purity of line, gives early Cistercian architecture the air of being a forerunner of Gothic, whereas it is actually a return to a simpler and more restrained form of Romanesque.

Although some Cistercian buildings are in the Gothic style, such as the east ends of Rievaulx and Fountains (the latter being exceptional in having a magnificent sixteenth-century tower), it is by and large true to say that the great age of monastic building was over before Gothic became fashionable. The Cistercian expansion was exceptionally rapid; but it did not continue beyond the end of the twelfth century with anything like the same vigour. The thirteenth century was – as far as such generalizations can have meaning – an age of consolidation for the monasteries, while the fourteenth century was one of disaster: the Black Death and Hundred Years' War spelled ruin; communities dwindled, and were unable to maintain the spacious buildings bequeathed to them by their wealthy forebears.

Even in the thirteenth century, the pious began to look elsewhere for leadership in religious matters. Once again decay had led to reform, to a return to the original ideals; but St Francis of Assisi proposed a more dramatic and fundamental reversion, to the principles, not of St Benedict, but of Christ himself. His new order, the friars or 'brothers', were not to be 'enclosed', as were the monks – one of the criticisms levelled against the latter was that they withdrew from the world to save their own souls. The friars were to be the new apostles, working in the secular world but not of that world, living communally and in poverty in the midst of wealthy cities. The monks may have been vowed to individual poverty, but collectively, as orders, they remained exceptionally wealthy. The life of Francis and the early literature of the Franciscans are imbued with a new brightness of spirit which is impossible to convey in a few words, but which lay at the heart of their success. The English chronicler Matthew Paris records how, in the decade following the formal institution of the order in 1209–10, the new order was an immediate success:

About these days those preachers who are called Minors, under favour of Pope Innocent, suddenly burst forth and filled the earth. Living by tens or sevens in cities and towns, possessing nothing whatever, living by the gospel, showing extreme poverty in food and raiment, going barefoot, they showed an extreme example of humility to all men. On Sundays and holy-days they went forth from their hovels and preached the gospel in parish churches, eating and drinking at the table of those to whom they did this office of preaching. These men were found by so much the more clear-sighted in contemplation of heavenly things, as they showed themselves strange to the malice of this world and to carnal delights ... Wherever men are most wretched, stricken down by the most loathsome diseases, starved by famine or trodden down by the great, there went the friars of St Francis.

The Franciscans were soon followed by the Dominicans. St Francis had been primarily concerned with people who were supposedly Christian, living in towns where Christian worship was crowded out by the press of everyday business: St Dominic set out to attack a different problem, the heretics in southern France known as the Cathars or Albigensians, who posed a serious threat to religious orthodoxy. In a sense, the Dominicans drew their inspiration from their opponents; for the Cathar missionaries were also skilled preachers, living an austere and holy wandering life. The Dominicans were intellectuals, skilled in theology and often with a university training, because they had to counter the subtle arguments of the Cathars, arguments which still have a strong appeal even today (see p. 168 below): the Franciscans were above all popular preachers, able to breathe fresh life into familiar themes.

If the friars had kept to their original ideals, they would have left no memorials in stone, save perhaps the little chapel at **Assisi** which had sheltered St Francis in his early days and which still officially belonged to a nearby monastery. The chapel survives within the church of Santa Maria degli Angeli, built around it in the sixteenth century. But the fate of the new order is strikingly summed up in the great basilica built over St Francis's grave in the second quarter of the thirteenth century (albeit in the face of protests by some members of the order) and elaborately decorated by the greatest Italian artists of the day – Giotto, Cimabue, Simone Martini. The result is almost oppressive in its richness. The church was begun within two years of the saint's death by the Vicar-General of the Franciscans; by then there were probably several thousand friars, and the need for organization had

become imperative. By 1245 a convenient fiction had been introduced whereby the pope became the owner of all property belonging to the friars, and from this period onwards the friars began
to build churches in towns and cities, designed to hold the large
crowds attracted by their preaching, with the friary buildings
attached. They became popular burial places: the Franciscan
church in London (Greyfriars) was as notable as Westminster
Abbey in its day. Matthew Paris watched the progress of the friars
and wrote mournfully from the safe haven of his monastery at St
Albans in 1243:

during the last three or four centuries or more the monastic order has
not fallen so rapidly downwards as their Order; for it is now scarcely
twenty-four years since these brethren built their first houses in England;
and now their buildings rise to regal height. These are they who, in
sumptuous edifices which grow from day to day, and within their lofty
walls, spend untold treasures, impudently transgressing the bounds of
poverty and the foundation of their profession.

There is, however, more than a tinge of jealousy in his comments:
the very success of the friars not only laid them open to temptation
but earned them many enemies. The monks could rarely afford
to build on a lavish scale, and were hard put to it to maintain their
often decaying buildings; no wonder they were envious of the newcomers who could build so lavishly.

The typical friars' church is spacious and plain, and has something of the austerity of Cistercian architecture, particularly in the
early days; there was a strong puritan streak in the movement,
though its critics claimed that this principle was more honoured
in the breach than in the observance. Yet against the picture of
the jolly friar, indulging in all kinds of carnal delight, we should
set the austerity of churches like San Francesco at Siena, with its
huge aisleless brick nave and open wooden roof, or Santa Croce
at Florence – like Greyfriars, the burial place of many famous men
– which is at once grand and very simple, with the characteristic
wide nave and an open wooden roof. Dominican architecture is
often more conventional, though extremely plain: a good example
is the Dominican church at Regensburg, where choir and nave are
scarcely distinguished and the nave walls are almost devoid of ornament. As in the Franciscan churches, there is a sense of unity between the celebrant and the congregation which is often denied

in the architecture of other medieval churches. The Franciscans could use Gothic to good effect, as in one of their earliest churches, San Francesco at Bologna, or at Santa Maria Novella in Florence, but there is always the sense of welcome spaciousness as opposed to the spectacular soaring heights beloved of cathedral architects. The friars' churches are above all practical, designed to draw in listening crowds rather than to emphasize the mysteriousness of some ritual performed out of sight and earshot in the sanctuary.

So far we have dealt only with the masculine side of monastic life. The orders of nuns were numerous, but never so influential as those of the monks and friars, on whom they often depended for their rule and discipline.* Apart from a few exceptions where royal patronage was involved and where the nunnery became a royal mausoleum, nunneries were usually poorer and smaller than the houses of monks, and they suffered from one severe handicap: the nuns were always dependent on outside help in order to celebrate services, since no woman could enter holy orders. While the monks could live as a self-contained unit, nuns always had to have chaplains and priests to officiate; and on a practical level, they needed male servants to help them run their estates, and could not recruit lay brothers. This made their houses more difficult to administer, and wealthy patrons usually preferred to found monasteries for men, which were also less open to scandal: monks could rigidly exclude the opposite sex from within their walls, whereas it was impossible for nuns to do so.

The early nunneries were to be found mostly in England and Germany and seem to be related to the higher standing of women in Germanic society. In the early years of Anglo-Saxon Christianity, when the conventions of the continental church were not yet familiar and there was some degree of experiment in the air, we find such unusual institutions as the double abbey of men and women at Whitby, under the rule of abbess Hilda. Nunneries flourished in Mercia in the eighth century, under the guidance of St Werburga, who was remembered in the later Middle Ages as the patron saint of the great abbey at Chester. There was a major nunnery at Barking, for whose nuns the scholar-bishop

* The word monastery itself indicates that nunneries were relatively rare: it is often used today as though it applied only to a community of men, whereas its correct meaning is a community living under monastic vows, whether of men or women.

Aldhelm wrote his treatise *On Virginity* and which remained the largest house of nuns in England until the Reformation, with a church on a scale which rivalled the grandest churches of the monks. At Romsey, in the tenth century, a convent of Benedictine nuns was founded which became a refuge for members of the old Saxon royal house in the next century, when it was one of only nine surviving nunneries in England. Matilda, the wife of Henry I, was brought up there by her aunt Christina, and it was probably due to her that the church was rebuilt in 1120; it survives as one of the best Norman churches in England. Another creation of the Norman royal house is the Abbaye-aux-Dames at Caen, founded by William I's wife Matilda because her marriage was technically within the prohibited degrees. Although it was outstandingly well-endowed for a nunnery, it is none the less on a smaller scale than the Abbaye-aux-Hommes (see p. 202).

The tendency for nunneries to be on a smaller scale appears again and again, even in the Rhine valley and the west part of Germany, where there was an active movement in favour of the foundation of nunneries from the ninth century. The monastic capitularies of Louis the Pious, issued from 817 onwards, included regulations for enclosed houses of women, but they were far more common in the German lands of the empire than in France. Even here, an outstanding abbess, such as the mystic Hildegard of Bingen, might bring temporary fame to a nunnery; but only foundations with ducal or imperial patronage enjoyed a secure existence.

The predominance of nuns among religious orders today is a phenomenon which dates from the sixteenth century, as a result of the change of attitude towards the function of religious orders initiated by St Francis and St Dominic. The purely enclosed life of monks, with its emphasis on worship and independence of the world outside, had to be adapted, as we have seen, to make it possible for nuns. Even the institution of the Poor Clares, led by St Francis's disciple St Clare, did not make it feasible for them to fulfil the secular roles of nursing and teaching which are the main features of the modern orders, for the Clares, unlike the friars, were very strictly confined within their convent walls. The nearest approach to an order of nuns on the lines of the friars was the semi-official movement known as the Béguines, founded in about 1180 in Liège, where women lived in small houses within an enclosure. Their only vows were to perform good works and to remain chaste while living in the community. As with the monasteries, the movement underwent many vicissitudes; at various times the Béguines became mere beggars, indulged in extravagant scourging or simply fell into scandalous living. But a few communities survived, and the béguinage at Bruges (p. 312) retains much of its medieval appearance.

The monasteries suffered far more than any other religious buildings at the time of the Reformation in Protestant countries. The churches occasionally survived for parish use, and the conventual buildings were – even more rarely – preserved for private use, as at Much Wenlock and Lacock Abbey. But even in predominantly Catholic countries, monasteries came under attack in the eighteenth and nineteenth century. In Austria almost all the monasteries were suppressed in 1780. The French Revolution dealt a blow as severe as the English dissolution of the monasteries, not only to those in France, but also to those in the lands through which the revolutionary armies swept. In Spain and Portugal, the religious orders were dissolved in 1834–5, while the new state of Italy proclaimed its break with the religious domination of the past in 1866. In France, the Laws of Association of 1903 led to a renewed expulsion of the orders. However, none of these laws remain in force, and although very few communities can claim a continuous existence since their foundation, many medieval monasteries still fulfil the intention of their founders after five centuries or more.

5
Pilgrimage

The Christian tradition of veneration of saints' relics and shrines reaches back to the very early days of the church. References to the relics of martyrs can be found as early as 156 AD, and by the time Christianity became the official religion of the Roman empire the idea that the places where saints were buried had some special holiness was well established. It is a concept which has its roots in pagan practices. The great shrines of antiquity had their pilgrims, too: the temple of Apollo at Delphi with its oracle, the resplendent shrine of Diana at Ephesus, the Parthenon, dedicated to Athene, the Roman temples, all attracted worshippers from great distances, in search of physical or spiritual cures. Local shrines, such as that of Nodens at Lydney in Gloucestershire, or that of Sequana, goddess of the Seine, at Saint-Germain-Sources-Seine near Dijon, also had their devotees. The same pattern repeated itself in the Christian world, but instead of centring on spectacular natural sites or great cities, the basis of Christian shrines and pilgrimages was the relics of the saints and their burial places, with Jerusalem, the Holy City, as the greatest and best of such journeys.

The pilgrimage to Jerusalem, which was already being undertaken in the fourth century, lies outside our scope, though its effects on western Europe were profound. The crusades, which influenced much of western politics for three centuries and had widespread cultural and economic repercussions, were a direct outcome of the veneration for Jerusalem and the desire of pilgrims to see the place where Christ had taught and died. Early pilgrims undertook the hazardous journey out of spiritual ardour, but even in the fourth century St Jerome had to insist that it was not the destination but the manner in which the journey was undertaken that mattered. His comments foreshadow two of three kinds of medieval pilgrim: the devout and the curious. To these were added, in the ninth century, the penitents, for whom pilgrimage was a penance for crime and who were compelled to undertake the hazards of travel by a religious or even a secular court.

As the journey to Jerusalem became more and more difficult with the collapse of Byzantine rule in Palestine and the rise of Arab sea-power, so men turned to other goals. Rome, as we have seen, had always attracted pilgrims because of the numerous tombs of martyrs, but its reputation as a place of religion was always mixed. An Irishman wrote in the margin of his hymn book in the ninth century: 'going to Rome involves great effort and little reward, for the King whom you seek there you will not find unless you bring him with you'. Only with the institution of the jubilee years in the later Middle Ages did Rome appeal to the truly fervent pilgrim. By then other shrines had become its established rivals, for in the eleventh and twelfth centuries travel once more became easier and prosperity made pilgrimage possible for ever-increasing numbers. The overland route to Palestine was back in Christian control as far as northern Syria by 985. From 1099 until 1187 and again from 1229 until 1244, Jerusalem was in Christian hands, and pilgrims had open access to the holy places; even after it fell to the Egyptian armies, it was still relatively easy to make the journey. The eleventh century was the golden age of pilgrimage, both by individuals and by huge companies of pilgrims, sometimes well-organized, sometimes impetuous and leaderless, like the crowd which set out for Palestine from Autun in 1024–5. During these years, local shrines sprang up all over Europe, some of which achieved permanent fame, while others sank into obscurity after the initial excitement of the discovery of some relic.

Of these new shrines, by far the most successful was that at Santiago de Compostela in north-west Spain. This became in many ways the archetypal pilgrimage. Its popularity had far less to do with the sanctity of the place than the arduousness of the journey and the great distance. The shrine itself, where the body of St James the Apostle was said to lie, was discovered in the early years of the ninth century by an obscure Spanish bishop. It was then a neglected tomb in the hills a few miles outside the bishop's city. The discovery was probably inspired by the new cult of St James as patron saint of the renascent Spanish Christian kingdoms, which Beatus of Liebana had promulgated and which the kings of Asturias (see p. 214) had taken up. In fact, St James's association with Spain may stem from nothing more than a misreading of *Hispaniam* (Spain) for *Hieroselymam* (Jerusalem) in an account of the missionary activity of the apostles; and his body was already said to be either in Asia Minor or, more obviously, at Toulouse. The finding of the tomb was announced to the pope by the king of Asturias, Alfonso II, and was warmly received: it caught not only the imagination of educated men, but from the first seems to have inspired popular feeling. The Moors were after all a very real threat, and here was a relic which seemed to offer protection and encouragement against them. There is a parallel with the story of St Edmund in East Anglia, where, on a humbler level, his body became a talisman against the Vikings, and the abbey of Bury St Edmunds grew rich on pilgrims' offerings. But St James, despite the fact that his shrine was taken by the enemy and despoiled in 997, attracted attention throughout Europe. Before the sack of Compostela, pilgrims were already arriving from France, such as the bishop of Puy in Burgundy, who went in 950 to beg the apostle's help and God's mercy. By the early eleventh century, English or Scandinavian pilgrims may have been making their way to Compostela, while in 1072 the archbishop of Mainz was there, and foreign pilgrims were frequent at this time.

Compostela's real rise to fame, however, was largely the work of one man, Diego Gelmirez, bishop from 1100 to 1140. His predecessors had already begun to style themselves 'bishops of the Apostolic see' (much to Rome's annoyance), but Diego was supported in his ambitions by the then pope, Calixtus II, who was related to the kings of Castile. He became an archbishop and papal legate, and tried to become primate of Spain. Gelmirez was the king's chief councillor, one of the ecclesiastical barons whom the twelfth-century reformers so hated; but he used all his wealth and power to glorify St James and the shrine at Compostela. It was he who rebuilt the cathedral in the latest and most significant style. While the king, Alfonso VI, rebuilt all the bridges from the eastern frontier of Castile to Santiago, Gelmirez rebuilt towns and hospices along the road from France in order to make the pilgrim's way easier. The guardroom and dining room of his spacious palace can be seen, incorporated into a later building, to the north of the cathedral at Santiago itself.

The traffic of pilgrims to Santiago became so immense that by the fourteenth century a complete network of recognized roads existed which took the pilgrim not merely through Spain, but also across France (see Map 3, p. 14). Written guidebooks survive from as early as the twelfth century and continued until we find printed versions in the early sixteenth century. It is still possible to follow much of the great roads and find traces of the pilgrims along them. The twelfth-century guide, preserved in a manuscript at Santiago itself, begins:

There are four pilgrim roads leading to Santiago which meet at Puente la Reina on the borders of Spain. One road goes by way of Saint-Gilles-du-Gard, Montpellier, Toulouse and the Somport Pass; the second road passes Notre-Dame-du-Puy, Sainte-Foy-de-Conques, and Saint-Pierre of Moissac; another leads past St Mary Magdalene of Vézelay, Saint-Léonard-de-Noblat in the Limousin region, and the town of Périgueux; the last road goes by way of Saint-Martin of Tours, Saint-Hilaire of Poitiers, and Saint-Jean-d'Angély, Saint-Eutrope of Saintes and the town of Bordeaux.

On each road, the pilgrims would visit the local shrines, many of which became wealthy from these passing visitors, for a pilgrimage was by no means a journey to a predetermined place and back again. Whether as penance for sin or from pleasure in travel, pilgrims often made a tour of various important shrines; a man who murdered an Italian bishop in 1319 was sent to Rome, Santiago and Jerusalem, while Chaucer's wife of Bath, an inveterate and, one suspects, none too pious traveller, had been to Rome, Boulogne, Santiago and Cologne, which could represent a single journey of the kind undertaken by many pilgrims. The road through southern France was undoubtedly used by many pilgrims travelling between Santiago and Rome, and from the thirteenth century the abbey of Saint-Gilles stood on the crossroads with the route to Jerusalem, for many pilgrims to the Holy Land would embark at the nearby port of Aigues-Mortes (p. 316). Pilgrims were entitled by custom to hospitality on the way, and this was chiefly provided by monasteries such as Saint-Gilles, which, although they had to build spacious hospices and guest quarters to accommodate the crowds, could expect a substantial revenue in offerings in return. They also had to provide for huge crowds of worshippers, and at six places along the various roads, including Santiago itself, we find a particular church plan, with a spacious east end and ambulatory with radiating chapels, a nave with broad aisles, and wide transepts, designed to meet this need. The finest example, apart from Santiago itself, is at Saint-Sernin in Toulouse, which also contains superb twelfth-century sculptures in a conservative classical style. Its imposing octagonal bell-tower must have been a memorable landmark for the pilgrims. The road from Toulouse went on to the Somport Pass, where the hospice of Sainte-Christine, just below the summit on the Spanish side, stood ready to welcome them. Named as one of the greatest hospices in the world by the twelfth-century guide, nothing now remains except the foundations.

The second road began at Le Puy-en-Velay, the spectacular volcanic peak in the Massif Central, which had early connections with the pilgrimage to Santiago and was one of the places where pilgrims would meet to travel together in bands for safety. Here both the cathedral and the little church of Saint-Michel-d'Aiguilhe show Moorish influence, a reminder that in the twelfth century pilgrims travelling to Spain were going to a country where Moorish influence was very strong. The road led to the remote monastery of Sainte-Foy at Conques at the head of the Lot valley, where there is another 'pilgrimage' church on a plan similar to that of Saint-Sernin. It is the tenth-century golden statue of Sainte-Foy, however, which is the pride of the monastery; a large part of the medieval treasury has also survived. Most of these elaborate golden jewel-studded images have fallen prey to the greed of later generations; the statue of Sainte-Foy, which was paraded round the local villages on suitable occasions, is a reminder that the wealth of the great monasteries was not expended only on building and that many of them would have had treasures of this kind with which to impress worshippers. From Conques the pilgrim could go a few miles out of his way to the north, to Rocamadour, built on a dramatic hillside above the river Alzou. Deserted by the nineteenth century, it has once again become a place of pilgrimage, though the original shrine was destroyed; a small part of the church and much of the town is medieval. The route then led to Moissac (p. 133 above) and joined the other roads from western France at the pass of Roncesvalles.

The third road began at Vézelay, where the abbey church acted as a gathering point; indeed it was here that, in 1190, Richard I and Philip Augustus of France met when they set out on the Third Crusade. Vézelay had an important pilgrimage of its own, to the relics of St Mary Magdalene, and the church is suitably magnificent, set high above the rich countryside of Burgundy. It has an impressive entrance, with a spacious narthex or entrance porch leading to one of the masterpieces of Romanesque sculpture, the interior portal showing Christ in Majesty. The nave is on a generous scale (though the width of the stone vaults led to structural problems), leading the eye to the late-twelfth-century sanctuary, a typical Romanesque design which emphasizes the mystery of the rites performed there. The next major shrine on the road was that of Saint-Léonard-de-Noblat outside Limoges, where the church was given a spacious new apse in the twelfth century on the 'pilgrim-church' pattern; but the old nave was never rebuilt and contrasts sharply in scale with the east end. St Leonard was the patron saint of prisoners and his shrine attracted many famous pilgrims: Richard I made an offering here in 1197 in thanks for his deliverance from captivity. The road then led south-west to Périgueux (p. 70) and to Roncesvalles.

The westernmost road was used principally by pilgrims from northern France and England, though the latter often made the sea voyage to Bordeaux or even direct to Spain. The shrine of Saint-Martin at Tours has vanished, but the church of Saint-Hilaire at Poitiers has its original eleventh-century east end. The cult of Saint-Hilaire was largely a local one, but the church figures in one crucial moment of European history. According to legend, when Clovis, founder of the Frankish kingdom, met Alaric, ruler of the Visigothic domains in southern France and Spain, in battle outside Poitiers in 507, he saw a fiery light above the church of Saint-Hilaire, and, inspired by this, swept on to victory, killing Alaric with his own hand.

In the eleventh century, rebuilding was made possible by gifts from Queen Emma, wife of Canute, king of Denmark and England; she may have visited the church when he went on pilgrimage to Rome in 1026–7. From Poitiers, the pilgrims could follow the direct route to Bordeaux by way of Angoulême. On the edge of Angoulême Saint-Michel-d'Entraygues was built in 1137 to shelter pilgrims as well as to provide a place of worship for them. It is octagonal, with a vaulted cupola and a magnificent tympanum of St Michael and the dragon. The alternative route was via the now vanished shrine at Saint-Jean-d'Angély and Saint-Eutrope at Saintes, where only the east end is left. South of Saintes, at Pons, the vaulted entrance of the 'New Hospice' survives, founded by the lord of Pons in the mid twelfth century. The road still runs through the massive gateway, with its stone benches where pilgrims sat to await entrance to the hospice. As they waited, they scratched graffiti on the walls, including horseshoes, which perhaps reflect anxiety about finding transport, for many pilgrims would travel not on foot, but, like Chaucer's pilgrims, on horseback. Once they reached Bordeaux, they would be joined by their fellows who had chosen to sail down the French coast to Soulac near the mouth of the Gironde, when they would have given thanks for reaching land safely at the priory of Notre-Dame-de-Fin-des-Terres; here a vast church was built as early as 1079. From Bordeaux, the way led through the swampy desert of the Landes, and some pilgrims went by Bayonne; but the route along the mountainous north Spanish coast was hazardous and never as popular as the main 'French road' from Roncesvalles through Pamplona, Burgos and León. The twelfth-century guidebook does not mention the coast road at all.

Pilgrims coming over the Somport Pass and by way of Roncesvalles would meet at Puente la Reina in Navarre, where the five-arched stone bridge built for the convenience of pilgrims by an eleventh-century queen still stands. Many of the important places along the road grew up purely to cater for the pilgrims, and the maintenance of the road was regarded as an act of piety: the bridge at Najera, a little further on, was said to have been rebuilt by St Juan de Ortega, himself a disciple of the hermit St Dominic who built the bridge at the town which bears his name, Santo Domingo de la Calzada, 'St Dominic of the Causeway'. As his nickname implies, Dominic was also said to have been responsible for building large tracts of the pilgrim road itself. At Santo Domingo, the spacious pilgrim hospice next to the church has become a *parador*, one of the excellent Spanish hotels in historic buildings, and welcomes in its thirteenth-century hall a different kind of modern pilgrim. The church contains an interesting reminder of the miracle-tales which did so much to rouse pilgrims' enthusiasm. A young pilgrim at Santo Domingo was falsely accused of theft and hanged, but his parents, who had appealed to St Dominic and St James, found him still alive on the gallows on their return from Santiago. They reported this to the judge, who said that the roast chicken on his plate was as likely to come back to life as their son; but at this the chicken miraculously flew off, and the boy's innocence was established. To this day a cock and hen are kept in the church in memory of the event.

From Santo Domingo the way went on to Burgos (p. 93 above), capital of Castile, across the Castilian plain; here the pilgrim could find shelter at the Hospital del Rey, rebuilt in the sixteenth century by Charles V. At the same time, the hostel at León, the next important town on the route and capital of the old kingdom of the same name, was also rebuilt in spectacular style, though the old cloister was incorporated behind the Renaissance façade. This too is now a hotel, as is the hostel at Santiago, built by Ferdinand and Isabella, the 'Catholic Kings', in 1489. The last part of the journey, between León and Santiago, was almost as arduous as the crossing of the Pyrenees; the modern main roads no longer follow the pilgrim way, but even today it is not difficult to imagine the pilgrims' relief when they crossed the frontier passes into Galicia and made their way down to Santiago itself.

Santiago today guards its medieval secrets well. There is the usual rash of modern suburbs before you reach the charming six-teenth-century heart of the town, built of warm granite, a network of paved and arcaded streets redolent of a leisured and civilized age. And at first sight, nothing could be less medieval than the cathedral of St James, approached from the spacious square at the west end. A towering Baroque mass, down which there cascades a waterfall of the greenery that flourishes in the moist Galician climate, presents itself to view; it is at its best in the evening light, but even the most ardent admirer of Churrigueresque fantasies must admit that Richard Ford's description of it as a 'fricassee of gilt gingerbread' has some truth in it. It is striking in the way that a magnificent stage-set can impress us; and to that extent it prepares us for the more subtle glories within. But before we enter the cathedral, it is worth pausing to go into the western crypt, which houses relics of the earlier churches and the remains of parts of the present Romanesque church which have since vanished, including the stone choir-stalls of the canons and pieces from the original western façade. Mounting the Renaissance staircase, we come face to face with the far-famed Portico de la Gloria, im-mediately inside the eighteenth-century doors. Created in 1168–88 by Master Matthew, it owes its exceptional state of preservation partly to the local granite from which it is carved and partly to the way in which it has never been fully exposed to the weather:

before the new façade was built, there was an open vestibule with three great archways, so that the sculptures formed a kind of inner façade, as at Vézelay, to which they owe a good deal stylistically. The subject chosen is the vision of Christ in Majesty from the Book of Revelation; but Master Matthew emphasizes the triumphant and joyous aspects of the vision, and we have to search hard among the figures of the vault of the right-hand arch to find any reminders that there is punishment as well as reward. The subject of the vanished sculpture on the outer arcade may have been the Last Judgement. The Portico de la Gloria, in contrast, reassures the pilgrim that his long journey has been worthwhile and that his reward is at hand. St James, naturally, figures prominently here: he appears once among the apostles again, complete with jewelled copper nimbus, on the central pillar below Christ's feet, as if to welcome the pilgrim to his shrine.

Through the arches of the Portico de la Gloria the sweep of the Romanesque nave opens out, dominated but not overpowered by the golden Baroque altar built around the thirteenth-century wooden statue of St James. The kneeling figure behind the central arch, looking towards the altar with his hands folded in prayer, is that of Master Matthew himself, looking like an awestruck medieval pilgrim turned to stone at his first sight of the shrine. The rhythmical pattern of the brown granite arcades, lit by the spacious gallery above, is Romanesque architecture at its best, massive yet welcoming. The windows of the octagon above the crossing make the altar brilliant with light, in contrast to the usual Romanesque emphasis on mystery. It is a church which never fails to impress, whether seen almost empty or filled with worshippers at a festival. The pilgrims are fewer today, but the medieval attitudes to religion still thrive in this remote corner of Spain: there is a feeling of unshakeable tradition, of ancient familiarity, which is hard to find elsewhere in Europe. The crowd at a Palm Sunday service talking and moving around the nave, which was full of children with long palm fronds, was as relaxed and yet respectful as its pilgrim forebears. The festival of St James, with its dance of the giants, fireworks and the swinging of the great censer, or Botafumeiro, is a modern equivalent of the old celebrations of saints' days as popular festivals, though even here outside interest begins to make it artificial rather than spontaneous. The one moment when the old pilgrimage does revive is when the feast day of St James falls on a

Sunday; in these jubilee years, as many as two million pilgrims come to Santiago.

But to return to the cathedral as a building. It was completed some thirty years before Master Matthew created the Portico de la Gloria, and the sculpture within is therefore more primitive. There are fine capitals on the arches of the chapels off the apse and high in the transepts, and a doorway in the south transept which shows St James as 'Moor-slayer', appearing to lead the Spaniards to victory at the battle of Clavijo. Outside, only one of the three principal doorways described by the twelfth-century guidebook still remains in its original state. This is the Puerto de las Platérias, overlooking the little square where the goldsmiths used to have their shops. Baroque additions have masked the outer parts of the façade, so that the doorway now appears hemmed in between projecting buildings and shorn of its original upper storey; indeed, the first remodelling was carried out as early as the thirteenth century. Over the doorways, the whole surface is alive with statues, producing a rich play of light and shadow; the twelfth-century guide enables us to identify the marble figures of Christ and the apostles as original, while several of the other sculptures have been inserted here at different times from other parts of the cathedral, just as figures from the Romanesque choir-stalls were incorporated on the east end in the seventeenth century. The stylized foliage which separates the apostles is particularly eye-catching, and the background is filled with inscriptions, a commonplace of Romanesque art which rarely survives. The tympanum over the left-hand doorway is best described by the twelfth-century guide:

On the first level above the entrance is carved the Temptation of our Lord: there are in fact before Christ horrible angels like monsters who carry him up to the roof of the temple; others present him with stones, inviting him to change them into bread; others show him the kingdoms of the world, pretending to wish to give them to him, if, falling on his knees before them, he will worship them – which would not please God! But other angels, good angels, behind him and above him, sprinkle him with incense and serve him ... We must not forget to mention the woman who appears to one side of the Temptation of Christ: she holds between her hands the horrible skull of her seducer, who was beheaded by her own husband; she has to embrace it twice a day at his orders. O terrible and wonderful punishment of an adulterous woman, which should be told to everyone.

The author of the guide was a man of learning, but he or his fellow-clerics would have explained the sculptures to the wondering pilgrims in much the same words, who in turn would have told of these marvels when they reached home, encouraging others to set out on the long journey to Santiago.

For the less adventurous there were of course shorter and easier journeys to local or national shrines. Three examples will have to suffice, out of the thousands of places which attracted pilgrims. The cult of St Thomas Becket at **Canterbury** was the most spectacular example of how a cult could grow with astonishing rapidity. On the face of it, Becket was an unlikely candidate for popularity as a saint: proud and austere, his quarrel with Henry I I belongs to the history of the reforms within the church in the twelfth century. He fought for an ideal of church independence which few men in England would have supported, and although his exile in France gained him some popular sympathy on his return in 1170, he does not seem to have been a charismatic figure in his lifetime. It was his murder at the altar of Canterbury cathedral itself in December 1170, in which Henry I I was implicated, that made him a popular hero: the rights or wrongs of the quarrel were forgotten in the horror of the news of the archbishop's martyrdom. The monks of Canterbury, divided as to his merits in his lifetime, at once set about promoting his cause as a martyr and saint. The first miracles were reported within a fortnight of his death, and he was canonized only three years later; the exceptional rapidity was at least in part due to the pope's desire to make political capital out of the episode, but it also corresponded to a wave of popular enthusiasm for his shrine. But despite the fame of the Canterbury pilgrimage – in modern times largely due to Chaucer – it was by no means as consistently popular as Santiago. Fashions in such matters changed; some church acquired a new relic or some new and spectacular miracle occurred at a neglected shrine, and the crowds flocked elsewhere. Canterbury also suffered from political problems: royal patronage was not always readily forthcoming, because Becket had died in opposition to the king, and his name was on occasion invoked by forces hostile to the crown. Edward I I I preferred the pilgrimage to Walsingham, and the Black Prince's association with Canterbury was through the cult of the Trinity which Becket established there in 1162, rather than through the cult of Becket himself.

The immense and instant success of the cult of St Thomas is recorded in the books of miracles written by the monks and is visible in Canterbury cathedral itself. A year after his canonization, a devastating fire destroyed the east end of the existing cathedral, though the nave survived. The architect employed to rebuild it, William of Sens, had to retain the flanking tower-chapels of St Anselm and St Andrew, but he extended the plan well beyond the original area to include a reliquary chapel, possibly to house the fragment of Becket's skull broken away when he was killed, the 'Corona'; this is the most successful part of the rebuilding. The east end appears low because of the massive crypt below, where the saint's body was kept until 1220 and which is the reason for the impressive ascending flight of steps before the altar. Technically, the east end is interesting as an early example of Gothic in England, and for the use of Purbeck marble – a material beloved of English Gothic architects, with its lustrous green sheen when polished – for the first time. The work was completed in 1185, by which time there were signs that the pilgrimage was beginning to lose its popularity; but there is a striking memorial to its early heyday in the glass of the Trinity Chapel. Six of these windows, possibly the finest of the period in England, survive. Rich reds and blues predominate, with highlights of yellow and green, set in graceful tracery patterns. The medallions each show one of the early miracles of the saint. Many of the little scenes, which are provided with long inscriptions, show pilgrims travelling to the shrine, making offerings there, and – the commonest theme – the healing of the sick, often told in a sequence of pictures. In many of them, we can see the early shrine of the saint, a stone tomb with holes in the side, like the shrine at Salisbury said to be that of St Osmond. Later, a more elaborate structure was provided, an ark-shaped chest plated with gold and studded with jewels, like the shrines of the Magi at Cologne or Charlemagne at Aachen; it stood on a base about six feet high, and the shrine itself had a wooden cover which was suspended from the vault and could be pulled up at the times when the shrine was on display. For a pilgrim arriving at Canterbury did not simply make his own way to the shrine. In the fifteenth century, on arrival at the cathedral, he would wait to join a group of fellow-pilgrims and was then taken on an elaborate guided tour, with particular emphasis on relics of Becket, which culminated in the showing of the shrine: the keeper of the shrine would point out the different jewels on it with a white wand, and would name the donor of each.

Following the jubilee of 1390, when the pilgrimage enjoyed a massive revival, Archbishop Sudbury set about rebuilding the nave, replacing the Romanesque work of the late eleventh century by an ambitious new nave on the same ground plan. The first part of the reconstruction was only completed early in the fifteenth century, and further works went on until the end of the fifteenth century to complete the central tower. Its upper stages were designed by John Wastell and belong to the last and most beautiful flowering of English Gothic. But this building activity had little to do with the pilgrimage; rather, it reflected Canterbury's older and, in the end, more important function as seat of the primate of England. The jubilee years might have been good for Canterbury's prestige; but the records show that the pilgrims, who tended even in the early Middle Ages to be middle-class or poor folk rather than great nobles, cost the monks of Canterbury more in hospitality than they gave in offerings. The jubilee of 1320 cost £754, but brought in offerings of only £671; two hundred years later, in the debased Tudor currency, the annual offerings were recorded by Henry VIII's commissioners as £36 per year, an eighth of what the shrine at Walsingham drew in. The worship at Canterbury had been persistently attacked by the Lollards, and this may have had some effect. In 1536, Henry VIII's agents dismantled the shrine; the operation took several days and provided the king with several wagon loads of gold and jewels.

Our next example, **Marburg**, owes its fame to one person, St Elizabeth of Hungary. Before her arrival in the town, it was a small castle with a little community around it, which had only just obtained a town charter. Elizabeth, princess of Hungary, who had been religiously inclined from her earliest years, was married in 1221, at the age of fourteen, to Louis of Thuringia. Following the example of her aunt, St Hedwig, who was duchess of Silesia, she soon gained such a reputation for good works that her husband was converted and supported her endeavours. On his death in 1227, she and her children were ousted by Louis's brother; and although a counter-coup by some of the Thuringian barons led to her son becoming count, she herself refused all powers of regency and used her wealth only for charity, living for the most part in harsh conditions in a humble hospital at the foot of the castle at

Marburg. Her tendency to extreme penances was encouraged by her confessor, Conrad of Marburg, a not particularly attractive character; but her devotion in nursing the sick, as well as her acts of charity, won her widespread affection. When she died at the age of twenty-four in 1231, miracles were soon reported at her tomb, and in 1235 her brother-in-law Conrad, a leading member of the Teutonic Order of knights, obtained her canonization. A new church was already being built on the site of her hospital, and on 1 May 1236 the emperor Frederick II led the procession that bore the saint's body to its new resting-place. The emperor himself, barefoot and wearing a penitent's shift, opened the coffin and placed a golden crown on her head.

The church, built with all the resources of the Teutonic Order at its height – Conrad became Master in 1239 – was designed from the outset as a pilgrimage church. It has a triple choir, formed by rounding off the two transepts, and is admirably designed for ceremonial purposes. The nave is the first German Gothic example of a hall-church, where the aisles rise to the same height as the nave – an ideal solution for a church likely to be crowded by throngs of pilgrims. The arrangement of the choir windows in a double tier is a novelty for the time as well: the whole church bespeaks the latest architectural techniques, such as a wealthy patron like the Teutonic Order, with its international contacts, might draw upon. The result is almost unique, for only one other church offers a similar ground plan.

Both the exterior and interior of the church are severe, with little decoration, but the church houses a collection of rare treasures. The rood-screen, though shorn of the Crucifixion group, is a triumph of virtuosity in carving, intricate foliage that appears to defy gravity. Notice the 'green man' faces in the capitals, a mysterious motif found in sculpture from the fourth to the fifteenth century.

The north transept, or 'Elizabeth choir', contains the saint's mausoleum, a curiously Moorish construction of about 1250. The sarcophagus, of about 1350, shows Elizabeth on her bier; among the bystanders is the figure of Conrad, clad in the mantle of High Master of the Teutonic Order. Frescoes on the saint's altar nearby show Elizabeth putting a leper into her marriage bed, who appears to her husband as Christ; and the translation of her body in 1236 in the presence of Frederick II. In the south choir the counts of

Hesse are buried, from Conrad (d. 1240), shown with the knotted rope of a penitent, to William II (d. 1509), with a skeleton as 'memento mori'. The same motifs, particularly praying monks and friars at the feet of the effigies, recur throughout, even though the earliest effigy is almost Romanesque and the last Renaissance.

The choir proper is lit by a fine series of thirteenth- and fourteenth-century windows; the earlier of these are Romanesque in style, despite the general Gothic appearance of the building. That to the extreme left of the bottom row, showing Elizabeth in pauper's clothes beside St John the Evangelist, is exceptional in both colour and workmanship. Below, a hieratic Madonna and Child are adored by St Francis – Franciscan friars had helped Elizabeth during her time at Marburg. The third window from the left shows scenes from Elizabeth's life in a series of medallions set against a richly patterned background, but the finest work is perhaps that in the lower panels of the second window, showing, in brilliant colours and simple forms, the creation of the world and Adam and Eve.

The last of the church's treasures is the great shrine of St Elizabeth, in the sacristy. It is contemporary with the shrine of the Virgin at Aachen, and is extremely refined: minute filigree work, patterning of the utmost elaboration, and lifelike figures are added to the profusion of jewels and sheer splendour of the Romanesque shrines. If the final effect is not as powerful as that of the earlier shrines, it is perhaps because the sheer joy in mastery of technique has led to an overcrowding mass of detail.

The church of St Elizabeth stands out as a rare survival of an architecturally outstanding pilgrimage church built specifically for that purpose with many of its original treasures intact.

Our last example, **Mont-Saint-Michel**, on the borders of Normandy and Brittany, had a long but unexceptional history as an abbey, but its magnificent buildings are due to an almost unbroken tradition as a centre of pilgrimage. Few spectacles can equal that of Mont-Saint-Michel rising out of the misty shoreline as you come out of Avranches and look down on the bay in which it lies. The abbey and its complex stand on a rocky outcrop in the bay, rising 500 feet out of the surrounding seabed. Its nickname, 'St Michael in peril of the sea', comes from the extreme range of the tides, which rise and fall as much as forty-five feet, and used to make access to the Mont dangerous, because they flowed in so rapidly across the flat sands. It was the site that attracted the founders of the church and which has ensured its continuing appeal. Unlike the other great pilgrimage centres, its cult never centred on a personality and hence on specific relics, but only on the shadowy figure of the Archangel Michael. Of all the great shrines, it seems in retrospect the most pagan, dedicated to the *genius loci*, the spirit of the place, and distinctly lacking in an orthodox religious focal figure. It was a vision of the Archangel Michael which in the eighth century led Aubert, bishop of Avranches, to found a church on the mount, which was refounded by Richard I about 965 as an abbey; under a series of distinguished abbots from Jumièges and Bec, Mont-Saint-Michel established itself as one of the leading monastic communities of Normandy, reaching its zenith under Robert of Torigny, a monk from Bec, who wrote an important chronicle of Henry II's reign in addition to his work as abbot from 1154 to 1189.

The growth of the pilgrimage as a cult is difficult to distinguish from the growth of the abbey itself; it was certainly well established by the beginning of Robert of Torigny's rule, for Henry II and Louis VII of France both visited the abbey in the 1150s and 1160s. Robert was responsible for the first major expansion of the abbey; the second great period of building was in the early thirteenth century. The thirteenth and fourteenth centuries were the heyday of Mont-Saint-Michel; in the fifteenth century, the abbacy became a titular post, its rich revenues used to reward cardinals and other high-ranking secular clergy. In the wars of religion it became a fortress and it remained a garrison until 1667. The state continued to use the Mont as a prison until 1863.

Visiting Mont-Saint-Michel today, the first reaction may be one of horror at the immense throngs who crowd onto this tiny island each day, particularly in summer. Yet this is how it has always been, a magnet for travellers. When we enter the narrow street leading up to the entrance to the monastery, with its hotels, restaurants and tawdry gift shops, we are looking at a scene which has changed only in detail since the days of the medieval pilgrimages. If you substitute inns for the restaurants and change the gaudy souvenirs of today for the lead badges and provisions sold from a medieval stall, little has altered. (Even the tourist's quest for culture and a sense of identity with the past is perhaps not totally out of keeping with the medieval pilgrim's objectives.) Today, however, relatively few visitors stay on Mont-Saint-Michel, and the abbey buildings, once filled with guests from all ranks of life, now stand empty except in the daytime.

The church is the centre of the monastery and one of its oldest parts: the nave was begun on the orders of duke Richard II in 1023 and remains unchanged except for the demolition of three bays and one of the western towers in 1780. The choir is late Gothic. Each enlargement of the church and of the abbey buildings meant an immense operation. The rocky base on which they are built is roughly conical, with a small level platform at the peak, on which the central part of the church stands. Everything else is built on a huge sub-structure, either of stone and rubble or of a series of lower floors. The twelfth-century buildings, to the south-west, are now mostly in ruins; other twelfth-century parts are not open to visitors. So the overwhelming impression is one of a Gothic abbey, the creation of Raoul des Îles and his successors as abbot from 1212 onwards, when the lordship of the abbey passed into the hands of the French king. These buildings, on the north side of the Mont, are known as 'La Merveille', the marvel, and they fully deserve their title. They include a cloister with fine foliate carving and spectacular views, enclosing a small garden within a brilliantly conceived double arcade; a remarkable refectory whose windows, placed between fifty-eight pillars, are invisible from the entrance doorway; and spacious buildings for the reception of guests of varying rank. The architectural detail of La Merveille is unusual and is in a way an echo of the unusual role of Mont-Saint-Michel itself, originally a remote monastery on an isolated site which was drawn into the full tumult of secular life by its development as a place of pilgrimage.

6

The Military Orders

From 1099, with the capture of Jerusalem by the men of the First Crusade, until the fall of Rhodes in 1522, western Christendom was involved in military adventures at the far end of the Mediterranean. At their height, the four crusader states in the Near East constituted one of the most powerful forces in the region, and their ties with the west were close, because the settlers looked for support and reinforcement to their kin in the west. Not surprisingly, the impact of the crusades is still much more visible in Palestine than in Europe; but the crusader castles and churches lie beyond the scope of this book. The influence of these states on Europe was much more subtle. Even at its most obvious, in military architecture, the exact debt owed to new technology brought from the east is not always clear, as we shall see. The settlers in 'Outremer', the land beyond the sea, came into close contact with the Arab world, but no closer than the contact between Moor and Christian in Spain or Sicily.

But there was one institution which had a powerful influence on western Europe and which did arise out of the crusades. The origin of the military orders is an obscure and complex one; suffice to say that in the early twelfth century, encouraged by St Bernard and the new Cistercian ideals, a number of knights came together to form two new orders at once religious and military, designed to protect the pilgrims on the roads to Jerusalem, which were infested by brigands. They soon assumed a much larger role, the defence of Palestine as a whole against Arab onslaughts, and the Masters of the two orders, the Knights Templar and the Knights Hospitaller, became the major military figures in the kingdom of Jerusalem. The rise of the orders was rapid: they were given much land both in Palestine and in Europe; the revenues from the latter were used to support the knights fighting in Palestine, and soon the orders became involved in financial operations on an unprecedented scale. Because of their network of houses across Europe, they could accept money at one house and issue a letter to another house for its repayment. This kind of operation was the speciality of the Templars, who became the bankers of Europe in the twelfth century. Their prosperity, however, did depend to some extent on military success in the Holy Land; defeat meant not only loss of estates there, but heavy expenses for replacement troops and a loss of prestige which might diminish their income from gifts. Furthermore, the secular Christian lords of the east found that their huge castles were too expensive to maintain and garrison, and these – with the attendant costs – were gradually transferred to the orders. Yet the orders had such resources that when the Christians were finally ousted from the Palestine mainland in 1291 they remained among the wealthiest organizations in Europe.

This wealth, which had for so long been their strength, was now the downfall of one order, the Templars. Philip the Fair of France arrested all the Templars in his kingdom in September 1307, on dubious charges that the order was corrupt and heretic. Although no other king followed his example, Philip was able to coerce the pope into dissolving the order; most of its wealth in France went into the royal coffers, while in other kingdoms it was transferred to the Hospitallers, who had found a new base at Rhodes from which to wage war on the infidels. Here they became a sea-based power, at times dominating the eastern Mediterranean, but never achieving their dream of a renewed attempt on the Holy Land itself. The Hospitaller citadel at **Rhodes** is the best memorial to the military orders: the defensive works survive much as they were at the time of the siege, because Rhodes was of little strategic importance to the Ottoman sultans once they had driven out the Hospitallers. They are superb examples of Renaissance military engineering, and were of course designed to resist artillery. Earlier buildings do survive in the knights' quarter or *collachium*, principally in the so-called Street of the Knights, with the headquarters or inns of the various nationalities. This division of the order into national branches was both a weakness and a strength: in the heat of battle, rivalry between them could produce feats of bravery, but in peacetime it all too often led to intrigue and dissension. The street runs in a straight line up from the inner harbour to the palace of the Grand Masters, a narrow, cobbled thoroughfare flanked by buildings in honey-coloured stone. The inns of Italy, France, Spain and Provence face onto it, that of France, a much restored mansion of the late fifteenth century, being the grandest. At the foot of the hill are the inns of England and Auvergne, and the hospital (now an archaeological museum); this reminds us that the knights also had a duty, from the very beginning, to tend pilgrims when they were sick as well as to defend them on their journey. The Palace of the Grand Masters itself is really a fortress, commanding the ramparts and the whole town and harbour; damaged by an explosion in 1856, it was restored during the occupation of Rhodes by the Italians; the result can only be described as a Fascist film-set, vaguely based on the original plan and totally lacking any medieval atmosphere.

By the time that Rhodes had been rebuilt in its present form, the possessions of the order in the west were in poor shape. In Ireland at the end of the fifteenth century, the prior of the order was a rebel who once seized Dublin castle and refused to accept deposition by the Grand Master. Elsewhere, the practice of farming out priories to laymen had weakened the order's control and diminished its revenues. Like the monastic orders, they were swept away in northern Europe at the Reformation; but the traces of their commanderies, even in Catholic countries, are few and far between. Their buildings were often easily adapted to secular ends, and since their main interest in the commanderies was as sources of revenue, they did not build on the same lavish scale as the monasteries. Because the Templars were disbanded in the early fourteenth century, it is not surprising that their commanderies have not survived: most of them, outside France, passed to the Hospitallers. There is, however, a surviving group of eleventh- and twelfth-century Templar buildings at Loarre in the southern foothills of the Pyrenees near Huesca, with a walled enceinte, keep and church. But the most notable relic of the Templars are their churches (many of which also passed to the Hospitallers on the Templars' dissolution). Their circular plan makes them distinctive, because they are modelled on the church of the Holy Sepulchre at Jerusalem and on the Moslem Dome of the Rock, which was a church in the crusader period. The outstanding example is that at the Convento de Cristo at Tomar in Portugal, where the Templar property was taken over by the new Portuguese Order of Christ. Here the centre of the rotunda is taken up by an extraordinary octagonal sanctuary with Gothic murals and a faintly Moorish architecture. Otherwise, Templar churches are remarkable more for their uniformity: in England, there is a much-restored small example at Cambridge, and the Gothic Temple church in London also survives, notable for the tomb of William Marshal, whose remarkable career as a knight-errant took him from a humble position as a knight's younger son to that of regent of England under Henry III.

The Hospitaller commandery at Luz-Saint-Sauveur, high in the Pyrenees, is the unique example of its kind. Dating from c.1200, with a surrounding wall of the fourteenth century and later fortifications, it is a clear and practical group of buildings: there is a sculpture only on the church doorway, and the whole construction is very conservative. The church was consecrated in 1240, yet the exterior has nothing Gothic about it, and could be two centuries earlier.

The third of the great military orders, the Teutonic Knights, devoted themselves after the fall of the Holy Land to the conversion – forcible or otherwise – of the heathen peoples who lived to the east of Germany, in Prussia, Poland and the Baltic States. Their headquarters, at **Marienburg**, still survives, though it was much restored in the nineteenth century and damaged in the Second World War. It now lies in Polish territory and is known as Malbork. This vast palace-cum-castle covers over five acres. Here the Grand Masters entertained the lords from the west, who, like Chaucer's Knights, came to seek adventure in Prussia and Lithuania by joining the order's annual forays against the heathen. Marienburg, with the remnants of its luxurious interiors, where sculpture and ornament delighted the eye and comforts such as warm air ducted under the floors cosseted the body, would be the one place where one could gauge something of the wealth and aspirations of the military orders, but it, like the other castles of the order, including the equally grandiose complex at Marienwerder, which all lie in Polish or Russian territory, are both beyond our immediate scope and relatively difficult of access. In the latter Middle Ages, a would-be crusader was more likely to go to north Germany than to the Holy Land, and the combination of military might and splendid living offered by the Teutonic Knights was perhaps more influential than we can envisage today.

7

Heresy

Medieval heretics have recently attracted a great deal of attention, particularly the Albigensian or Cathar heretics of southern France. From scholarly works like *Montaillou* to popular novels, particularly in France itself, they have become something of a cult, perhaps because the ancient belief in two gods, one good and one evil, which lies at the heart of their teaching, is not unsympathetic to us today. But it is important to remember that heretics were very much a minority, even if a vocal one, in the Middle Ages, and their influence was limited, particularly after the church in the thirteenth century adopted the potentially heretical beliefs of St Francis and his followers and launched the Dominicans, who imitated the best features of Cathar life while preaching orthodox doctrines, against the Cathars themselves.

The history of medieval heresy is a long and complex one. The Arians, who believed in the unity of God rather than in the diversity of the Trinity, and the Pelagians, who denied the existence of original sin – to simplify some very complex theological arguments – both flourished in the latter years of the Roman empire and the early years of the barbarian kingdoms, when church doctrine was still being formulated. Indeed, Arianism at one time predominated in western Europe and North Africa; both the Lombards in northern Italy and the Visigoths in Spain in the early sixth century supported Arian rather than orthodox views, and persecuted orthodox Catholics vigorously and violently. But these were relatively minor arguments over the finer points of doctrine and there would have been nothing physically distinctive about a Pelagian or Arian church – if we can properly apply such labels to a building. Indeed, of the two baptisteries at Ravenna, almost identical in style and decor, one was Arian and one was orthodox. Again, at the end of the Middle Ages, the Lollards, Hussites and

Waldensians represent an age when doctrines were once again in question; the arguments are on points of theology, not on fundamental facts.

The Cathars, however, were different in that they belonged to a sect which challenged the basis of orthodox Christianity rather than arguing about details within a broadly accepted common framework. However, in terms of an inheritance visible today, there is almost nothing to see, because they deplored the very idea of a church with material possessions, tainted by the god who had created the world and whom they held to be evil. The church's answer to this challenge, when attempts at persuasion failed, was to suppress them by force, in the bloody Albigensian Crusade of 1208–29. The only traces the Cathars have left are at the remote defensive sites to which they retreated in the face of persecution, the most famous being Montségur, high in the Ariège, where the last of the rebellious Cathars were annihilated in 1244; Montaillou, brilliantly brought to life in the book by Leroy Ladurie, was the last village to harbour peaceful Cathar heretics in the 1320s.

At **Albi** itself, the cathedral is a memorial to those embattled times. Built in the last quarter of the thirteenth century, when heresy was not quite dead, it is an extraordinary edifice, a brick-red mass whose austere and defensive lines have been made more warlike by the addition of machicolations in the 1840s. But the military aspect is real enough, as the lower part of the western tower shows: here the lines are those of a keep, with battered foundations, circular buttress-towers, and nowhere the least indication that this is a place of peace and worship. The walls are uniformly massive, up to five feet thick, and there is only a single entrance, to the south. The interior is equally stark, a huge version of the friars' preaching churches. But against this austere and defiant background, the worldliness of the medieval church has ironically set magnificent sculpture in flamboyant Gothic; the south porch is fantastical and gracious, as sharp a contrast with the sheer walls rising behind it as one could imagine. The interior is richly painted with Renaissance frescoes, and the huge space is divided by one of the finest choir-screens of the early sixteenth century. Prosper Mérimée, the nineteenth-century novelist, who, in his official capacity, rescued many of France's great monuments from ruin, said of it that it made him 'feel ashamed of reason before this magnificent folly'. The mastery of the sculptor over his intractable material reaches its zenith in these five arches spanning the church, turning stone into patterns that float in the air like a spider's web. Folly, power, grandeur – all the things that the Cathars most hated about the established church: it is as if the builders of the cathedral at Albi had set out deliberately to illustrate them as magnificently as they could, almost providing the justification for the heresy they had fought so hard to suppress.

PART TWO

EMPIRE AND NATIONS

8

The Holy Roman Empire

The barbarians who swarmed across the ancient frontiers of the Roman empire on the Rhine and the Danube in the fifth and sixth centuries were not setting out to impose a new ideology on the west. Their kinsmen were just as likely to be found serving as *foederati*, troops recruited by the Romans from among the barbarians and used to defend the threatened frontiers, as among the invaders' ranks. If they were not already acquainted with life within the empire, they soon learnt something of it; and by and large their principal objective was to take over that empire and make it their own. Once they had gained lands and possessions, they were often careful to observe the outward forms of the Roman law of property; and after the initial period of raids and plunder, when the new peoples had settled in Gaul, Spain and Italy, the missionary activities of the Christian church brought another part of the inheritance of imperial Rome to them. So, although they retained their own, often very different, social structure, when they looked for a model for the government of a settled state it was to Rome that they turned. The Christian church, too, still acknowledged the imperial authority in the east, however distantly: the concept of empire remained, if no more than a long shadow thrown by Byzantium across Europe.

By the end of the fifth century, the broad areas of influence of the different tribes of invaders had more or less stabilized. What is now northern France was occupied by the Franks; southern France and much of Spain were held by the Visigoths; and Italy was fought over between the Ostrogoths and the Byzantine empire. The Franks were recently united under Clovis, who brought together the various warring tribes to form a powerful kingdom. We have already mentioned Clovis's victory at Vouillé in 507 in religious terms; politically speaking, it drove the Visigoths into

Spain and brought the Franks into contact with the Ostrogoths in northern Italy. The rare remnants of these cultures reflect their half-Roman, half-barbarian origins. At Ravenna, the mausoleum of Theodoric, the most famous of the Ostrogoth kings, stands on the edge of the present city, a massive domed building whose Roman origins would be clearer if it still possessed the colonnade which ran round the upper storey. The dome is made from a single stone, a technique found in eastern architecture, and there are other oriental features which remind us that the Ostrogoths were the 'Goths from the east'. But Theodoric had also spent nine years of his youth at Byzantium, and the masonry techniques are those of the Roman engineers. On the other hand, the treasure buried with king Childeric – in itself a barbarian custom – shows almost no Roman influence, but consists mostly of garnets set in a metal framework, somewhat like stained glass. Only the signet ring, crude though it is, has a hint of Roman authority about it.

But the pattern of barbarian settlement continued to shift until the end of the sixth century. The Ostrogoths were overwhelmed by new invaders, the Lombards, who came to form a north Italian kingdom and assorted dukedoms in southern Italy, owing varying degrees of allegiance to the eastern emperors at Byzantium. The Franks expanded their territory southwards to the Mediterranean, while the Visigoths were pushed back into northern Spain by the Byzantine reconquest of the south, and then, after 711, were almost annihilated by Moorish invaders from North Africa, who overran almost the whole of the Iberian peninsula in the space of eleven years – only the mountainous territory of the Asturias held out against them – and pressed on into France. Indeed, in the early years of the eighth century, it looked for a time as though the western half of Europe might become Moslem territory, leaving Italy as part of an encircled Byzantine empire. But once again a crucial battle near Poitiers decided the outcome. On 17 October 733, about ten miles north of the town, the troops of Charles Martel, the Frankish ruler, met the invading Moslems. They 'stood rigid as a wall and, like a belt of ice frozen solidly together, slew the Arabs with the sword', in the words of a contemporary chronicler. This defeat marked the northernmost point of the Arab incursion; their empire had become over-extended. They were defeated again near Lyon in 748 and were driven back beyond the Pyrenees in the following decade. Finally, in Britain, the Saxon kingdoms were beginning to coalesce into a single entity, and the Welsh and Scottish borders were by now well defined. Here Roman traditions were weak, because there had been a period after the Roman withdrawal when the pre-Roman civilization of the Celts had returned to supremacy. The Saxons took over from the Romans at second hand, and Britain was in any case less thoroughly Romanized than Gaul or Spain.

Of the three national groupings in the mid eighth century, Spain and England, on the edge of the Christian and imperial world, pursued their own political course, emerging, as we shall see, as nation-states with few links with the imperial past. The Frankish kingdom, however, thanks to the descendants of Charles Martel, was to revive that imperial tradition. Charles Martel was not king of the Franks; the kingship had become a mere title, with faint sacred overtones, while the real power was in the hands of the so-called 'mayors of the palace', of whom Charles Martel was the most effective. However, the kingship did still retain some value, for in the winter of 753–4 Charles's son Pepin persuaded the pope to crown him as king, in return for his intervention in northern Italy. The Frankish kings thus became the protectors of the papacy, and the customary prayers for the wellbeing of the emperor were replaced by prayers for Pepin and his successors.

Pepin's son Charles, known to his contemporaries as Carolus Magnus, Charles the Great, and to us as Charlemagne, succeeded his father in 768 and pursued an even more aggressive policy than his father. Pepin had consolidated the Frankish territories and had tentatively moved on to the offensive in Italy. Charlemagne's reign was one of almost continual wars; a major campaign was undertaken almost every year, and we know of over fifty in the forty-seven years of his reign, more than half of which were led by Charlemagne himself. After crushing the rebellious Lombard kingdom in northern Italy in the first years of his reign, his two main objectives were the pagans to the east and south-west, the Saxon tribes living beyond the Rhine and the Moslems beyond the Pyrenees. There was therefore a religious element in most of his warfare, just as the Moslem expansion into Europe had been fuelled by religious enthusiasm for Islam. Charlemagne's first attacks on the Saxons were highly successful: in 772 he destroyed their holiest sanctuary, containing an image of the Irminsul, or tree of the world, which in pagan belief linked the worlds of the gods and of men, and three years later he occupied Saxon territory, which stretched across what is now north-east Germany. In 777, he felt that Saxony was secure enough for him to intervene in Spain; this campaign was only moderately rewarding, because his supposed Moslem allies failed to welcome him as expected, and turned to near-disaster when his rearguard were ambushed by the Basques at Roncesvalles, an event recorded in the greatest of early French poems, *The Song of Roland*. In the later years of his reign, he mounted campaigns against the Avars, a nomadic people who had accumulated great wealth by raids on Byzantine territory and who lived on the eastern reaches of the Danube in what is now Hungary. To make the transport of provisions easier, Charlemagne attempted to build a canal linking the Rhine and the Danube, a feat reminiscent of Roman military engineering; but his resources were not equal to the task, and after about half a mile had been dug the project was abandoned, though the excavations can still be seen near Eichstatt in Bavaria and the linking of the two rivers will probably be achieved at long last in the 1980s.

This brief account of Charlemagne's wars cannot do justice to his exploits; but it does help us to understand the atmosphere of Carolingian civilization. The court of Charlemagne, unlike those of his predecessors, was in contact with the whole of the known world: his teachers were Saxon and Irish monks, his vassals ranged from newly converted heathens to the men of Rome itself, his embassies went to Byzantium and on one occasion to the fabled court of Haroun-al-Raschid at Baghdad, returning with presents the like of which had never been seen in the west – gold plate, ivory chessmen and an elephant named Abul Abbas which became Charlemagne's favourite pet. The elephant died in Saxony ten years later, but oriental fabrics decorated with elephants which may have been part of Haroun-al-Raschid's gifts survive in the treasury at Aachen. At Saint-Maurice-d'Agaune in Switzerland the abbey treasury contains a ewer said to have been one of the gifts made on the same occasion; interestingly, modern scholars suggest that it was in fact among the treasure seized from the Avars.

The culmination of Charlemagne's career came on Christmas Day, 800, when before the mass in St Peter's at Rome at which Charlemagne's eldest son was to be anointed as king, the pope approached Charlemagne as he knelt before the shrine of St Peter and crowned him with a diadem, while the nobles around him hailed him as emperor in the traditional manner and the pope saluted him in the manner reserved for the Byzantine emperors. The meaning and purpose of the ceremony remain obscure; but it marks the revival of the Roman empire in the west as an ideological force, the 'Holy Roman Empire' which was to survive in varying forms until 1792 and was to be imitated by both Napoleon and Wilhelm I of Prussia. But the particular character of this new empire, absent from both its predecessors and successors, is precisely its religious connotation: it is the Christian empire foretold in St Augustine's *City of God*, in which Charlemagne was to be the protector not merely of the papacy but of the whole of Christianity. The Byzantine throne was conveniently empty in 800, when Charlemagne made his claim, and so the nominal claim of Byzantium to fill this very role could be easily ignored. There was in any case the precedent of the division of the empire into eastern and western halves.

This new and ambitious political structure is reflected in the art and architecture of the Carolingian court. Little more than traces of the imperial buildings of Charlemagne's day have survived, with one important exception: the chapel of the palace which Charlemagne built at **Aachen**. Charlemagne may have been born at his father's palace here, built on the site of a Roman town. If it was indeed his birthplace, this would have been one reason why he chose to build a new and magnificent palace here between 777 and 786; another, more compelling, reason for creating a 'second Rome' here was that it lay at the heart of his imperial lands, while serving as a base for the wars against Saxony. In 794, having previously led a more or less nomadic existence as his endless military campaigns took him from Denmark to Spain, from Bavaria to Brittany, his court was settled here on a more or less permanent basis.

All that survives of Charlemagne's great palace are parts of the present town hall, and the cathedral, which is the chapel of his palace with a Gothic choir added to it. The design of the chapel was said by Charlemagne's biographer Notker to be his own: in fact it is closely based on the church of San Vitale at Ravenna, the imperial church of the last emperors of the west, whose heir Charlemagne claimed to be. Mosaics from Ravenna were sent to Aachen for use in the palace, so the link between the two cities was close and deliberate. In 812, ambassadors from the Byzantine emperor, who also claimed to rule in the west, recognized Charlemagne as emperor in a ceremony in the chapel.

Like San Vitale, the chapel at Aachen is basically octagonal; in the west this plan is almost unknown, but it is not uncommon in Byzantine architecture. In many details, the design recalls the rituals of the Byzantine court, notably in the emperor's isolation from the courtiers by seating him in the upper gallery behind the congregation, making him invisible yet at the same time a presence powerfully felt.

The outside of the church has a Gothic and later cladding which conceals most of the Carolingian work, except on the south side. The two great bronze doors of the west porch are Carolingian, the earliest such bronze doors to survive from the Middle Ages. Two lions' heads and restrained chasing round the panels are the only decoration, a sober contrast to the riches within. For this is one of those rare places where all the high history attached to a site is fully matched by what we see there. The immediate impression is of great richness and great age, of stepping into an unfamiliar world, where both forms and decoration are strange. The inner octagon, with its great square marble-clad pillars, half-conceals the altar, whose golden splendour is gradually revealed as we walk round the perimeter of the octagon, reading the inscription recording the building of the chapel which runs round the inside and is said to have been written by the great English scholar Alcuin. There are other treasures within: a huge circular bronze chandelier presented by Frederick Barbarossa, with an elaborate Latin inscription which proclaims it to be an image of the heavenly Jerusalem, its octagonal towers echoing the form of the chapel. The towers have engraved plaques as bases, each showing a scene from the life and teachings of Christ. As a tribute from the greatest German emperor to his even greater forebear, it is a fitting image: the rulers of the earthly kingdom looking forward to the celestial realms. Below, the massive golden altar front, which once shimmered in the flickering light of the forty-eight candles, is nowadays harshly but effectively lit. This 'cape of gold', or 'pala d'oro', completed early in the eleventh century, perhaps at the abbey of Fulda, is another masterpiece in metalwork. Christ sits in imperial majesty in the central mandorla, surrounded by the symbols of the evangelists, while the outer panels show scenes from the last days of his life, in a bold and unexpectedly lively style. Before this altar, thirty emperors, from Louis the Pious in 813 to Ferdinand I in 1531, were crowned.

The most impressive of the imperial relics, and one which was venerated by centuries of pilgrims, is Charlemagne's throne, in the gallery, looking directly down on to the altar. Its simplicity is in sharp contrast to the opulence below: white marble slabs without a trace of decoration, set above a plain flight of six steps. At this level the openings between the main pillars are filled by marble columns and a bronze railing, contemporary with the main doors and equally restrained and elegant in design. (The mosaics, as elsewhere in the chapel, are early twentieth-century.) In a chapel off the upper storey is the sarcophagus used for Charlemagne's remains until his relics were enshrined in 1165, made in Rome in the second century AD and showing the rape of Proserpina.

At the eastern side of the original chapel there opens out the Gothic choir, which turned the palace chapel into a miniature medieval cathedral. It is a daring piece of engineering, its walls more glass than stone. The glass has been replaced following war damage, but the colours and tones are suitably medieval. The soaring lines of its vaults are so completely different at first sight from the eighth-century building that it would seem difficult to find a common factor; but both have the same strong vertical emphasis, the striving heavenwards, that is typical of medieval architecture in the west. The east end houses two more great treasures. To the right is the 'golden ambo' or pulpit given by Henry II before 1014. For sheer profusion of wealth, it is unsurpassed. A formal framework divides it into panels, but within each panel order gives way to a riot of jewellery, ivory and even an antique glass tazza, the cup and cover being mounted separately as though they were huge precious stones like those in the central panels. It originally stood in the centre of the octagon, but was moved when the new choir was built.

Beyond, at the east end itself, is the shrine of Charlemagne, commissioned by Frederick Barbarossa but only completed in 1215, when Frederick II transferred the relics from an earlier shrine to this present one, a masterpiece by the Rhineland goldsmiths. Charlemagne himself appears on the end, while his successors are enthroned in serried ranks along the sides. The refinement of much of the work makes the golden ambo seem barbaric in its crude splendour. Here enamel work, pierced ornamentation and figures in high relief testify to enormous advances in technique.

Fittingly, this is one of the most magnificent of the great shrines, matched only by that of the Three Kings of Cologne.

The treasury, in a room off the cloisters, has yet more riches: the cross of Lothar, c.1000; an ivory probably carved at the imperial workshop in Aachen in Charlemagne's time; the reliquary head of Charlemagne, crowned with the emperor Charles IV's crown; another major shrine, containing a relic of the Virgin; the arms chest of Richard of Cornwall, resplendent in scarlet and gold heraldry; and the crown of Margaret of York. If in the end this profusion of treasure is overwhelming, we must remember that it was by such visual richness that the emperor was set apart from ordinary men in medieval eyes, and Aachen retains a fitting share of the pomp and awe of the Holy Roman Empire.

It is in fact in the arts of the jeweller, metalworker and ivory-carver that the best examples of Carolingian art have come down to us. Besides Aachen, there are only a handful of buildings, most of them restored, such as the oratory of the bishop's palace at **Germigny-des-Prés** on the upper Loire, a sophisticated miniature, square in plan with six radiating apses and four central arches, making it a very complex building for its small size.

The gateway at the monastery of **Lorsch**, east of Mainz, is similarly sophisticated, harking back to Roman architecture. It is a small freestanding ceremonial building, designed for processions and great occasions, and may even have been built for a visit by Charlemagne himself to the monastery in 774. Its bold patterned stonework seems unclassical to us, but in fact copies a Roman technique, *opus reticulatum*, exaggerated by the barbarian love of contrasts; the pilasters and triangular gables are typical of Carolingian imitations of the antique.

Imitation of the antique was a central feature in Carolingian culture: if the Roman empire was to be revived, then the appropriate style was also that of Rome. Roman influence can be seen everywhere – in manuscripts, in coins, in metalwork. Late-classical manuscripts were copied at Charlemagne's court, and the ornament and decoration of new manuscripts often includes elements from classical architecture, particularly in the formal opening pages. Charlemagne himself is portrayed in the style of a Roman emperor on his coins. At **Müstair** in eastern Switzerland, there is a statue of an idealized emperor, almost certainly intended to be Charlemagne, wearing the ceremonial dress of the Roman rulers.

Charlemagne's biographer Einhard presented a reliquary (now destroyed) to his monastery at Maastricht which was in the form of a Roman triumphal arch, the saints depicted on it appearing in classical dress. Other relics of this imperial style are the little statue, probably of Charlemagne, in the Louvre; this equestrian bronze seems a clear imitation of the great equestrian monuments of the later empire, one of which was brought to Aachen and stood outside the palace there: the doors on the chapel at Aachen echo classical bronzework. A piece of more mysterious origins, now thought to be Carolingian, is the so-called 'throne of Dagobert', an imitation of the folding stools used in Ancient Rome, now in the Cabinet des Médailles of the Bibliothèque Nationale in Paris.

Yet it would be wrong to think of the Carolingian period as one of slavish imitation. There is a new vitality in the art which comes from the mingling of barbarian and Roman traditions. Among Charlemagne's treasures were also the looted Avar riches, of which his sword, in the imperial treasury at Vienna, may well be an example. In manuscripts, a new script was introduced, the so-called Carolingian minuscule, which was easier to write and clearer to read than the old Merovingian script, and this remained the model throughout Europe for two centuries. For although Charlemagne's empire survived as a single unit only until his grandson's time, the cultural inheritance of Charlemagne's court can be traced not merely in France but in Germany and Italy as well. The shifting fortunes of the various claimants to the imperial lands, complicated by the Viking and Saracen raids of the ninth and tenth centuries, did not entirely destroy the old imperial ideal, and individual emperors could contrive to imitate the magnificence of Charlemagne. The elaborate altar canopy given by the emperor Arnulf to the monastery of St Emmeram at Regensburg in the 890s uses classical architecture and brilliant goldsmiths' work in the same combination as Einhard's lost shrine. Most astonishing of all is the massive golden altar front at Sant'Ambrogio in Milan, commissioned by the bishop of Milan not later than the middle of the ninth century, opulent and exquisite at the same time, with exceptionally fine figures in bas-relief and technically superb filigree work and chasing.

Within a century of Charlemagne's death, the empire as constituted by him was no more than a vague ideal, and the modern divisions of Europe were beginning to take shape, partly through new linguistic groupings. The universal Latin of official documents was challenged by the everyday speech of the different peoples: in a treaty between Charlemagne's grandsons in 842, the text is given in French, which is a kind of dialect Latin, and in German, which is Saxon and therefore close to Anglo-Saxon. In the end, it was the Germans under Otto I in the tenth century who were to inherit the ideal of the empire, which they called at first the 'imperium Romanum', then, in the twelfth century, the Holy Roman Empire; in the fifteenth, they added 'of the German nation'. Otto himself was elected king of the Germans in 936, under the system by which his two predecessors had been chosen, whereby the representatives of the five duchies which formed German territory elected one of their number as leader. His coronation took place at Aachen, and he was enthroned on Charlemagne's throne. But this ritual did not make him emperor: for that, he had to be crowned by the pope, and it was not until twenty-six years later that he achieved this. In the interval, he had united his domains in Germany and had acquired Lombardy; and he had resoundingly defeated the Slavs and the Magyars in 955, the latter at the famous battle of the Lechfeld outside Augsburg. Once again, the empire depended on a strong personality at the centre, a statesman and warrior of the first order. Otto was crowned in Rome in 962 with the imperial crown which can still be seen in the imperial treasury at Vienna. Originally a simple diadem, it has a hooped arch of pearls and gold added by Conrad II in the eleventh century. It is made up of eight hinged plates studded with gems *en cabochon* interspersed with pearls, mounted in filigree work. Alternate plates have enamels showing Christ enthroned and three Old Testament kings. It owes nothing to Roman models, something to the world of Byzantium, but is principally the product of a new and independent German culture.

With Otto's coronation, the Carolingian ideal of a western empire was revived, but in a changed form. Instead of the vast sweep of Charlemagne's domains, from the Atlantic deep into central Europe, the new empire was to be centred on Germany and northern Italy, claiming lordship of southern Italy as well. Otto's grandson, Otto III, extended its influence to Poland and Hungary, but he and his successor, Henry II, both died childless, and in 1024 the German princes elected Conrad, first of the Salian dynasty, to be king. Conrad came from the lower Rhineland: he was born in Worms and had lands in and around Speyer. After his coronation at Milan in 1026 (in the presence of king Canute of Denmark), he vowed to rebuild the cathedral at **Speyer** so that it would be the greatest church in the empire, and it remains the major monument of the Ottonian and Salian period.

Work began in 1029: the Carolingian cathedral was torn down, and the foundations for a huge basilica were laid out, in the shape of a great Latin cross, little different from the plan of the church we see today. It was remarkable both in its size and its use of a very long nave, a feature familiar enough in Gothic churches, but a novelty at this period. Neither Conrad nor his successor Henry III saw the cathedral far enough advanced to be dedicated, though both were anxious to press on with the work. After his death in 1039 Conrad was buried in the great crypt which runs under the east end like a second church, but his coffin was secured by iron bands lest the workers still busy in the cathedral should try to lift the heavy stone lid in search of treasure.

The ambitious plans of the original builders seem to have proved to be too much for their technical knowledge. Under the emperor Henry IV, the cathedral was virtually rebuilt, to a new plan prepared by bishop Benno of Osnabrück. While retaining the main outline of the original design, the foundations and walls were doubled and an elaborate architectural decoration was planned. A further refinement was introduced after Henry's return from Italy in 1096, bringing Lombard stonemasons with him. The problem of vaulting the huge nave had never been finally solved, and a new vaulting pattern was evolved (or re-discovered) to deal with it. Alternate pillars were strengthened, and six vaults used to cover the nave, while twelve vaults were used in the aisles. The cathedral, one of the most impressive and technically advanced buildings in the western world, as Conrad had intended, was virtually complete at Henry's death in 1106. Although the nave and west end were destroyed when Speyer was burnt by the French in 1689, the restorations carried out since then have preserved the basic early Romanesque form of the church, and in 1957 many of the later, incongruous details were swept away to give the pure lines and spaces that we see today.

The detail of the church largely speaks for itself. The use of rounded arches and classical pillars is carried to the greatest refinement, as in the north transept or the little baptismal chapel of 1055:

proportions are calculated to a nicety, to achieve perfect balance and harmony. The east end and the crypt are the outstanding parts of the church. From the outside, the east end conveys exactly the mixture of Roman and native majesty which was typical of Conrad's imperial ambitions. The rounded apse, with blind arcading, the use of galleries as a decorative feature (and as a practical method of access for repairs) and the quest for height in the elegant towers might at first seem too disparate to form a unified whole, but the plan succeeds, in a very individual and self-confident way.

The crypt, remodelled in 1906, contains the tombs of all the Salian emperors and a number of their successors. It was always planned as an imperial burial place, hence its elaborate vaulting and layout. Recent restoration has given it a powerful simplicity – the only sculptures are the imposing contemporary effigy of Rudolf of Habsburg, founder of the Habsburg dynasty, and two modern reliefs to the kings and emperors. The four Salian emperors lie under plain tombstones, inscribed only with a cross and their names; with them are buried four rulers of the empire who were never crowned emperor and thus remained simply kings of Germany: Philip of Swabia, Rudolf, Adolf of Nassau and Albrecht of Austria. No other cathedral holds so many of the rulers of the medieval empire; no other cathedral brings us so close to the emperors in their boldest and most confident mood, ready to set the pope on one side and proclaim themselves 'vicars of Christ'.

Under Henry III, the empire reached its zenith: no other emperor after him was able to preside over a synod which successfully deposed two popes and replaced them by a third, and for much of his reign the papacy was occupied by Germans. From his time dates the palace at **Goslar**, extensively rebuilt both in the Middle Ages and in the nineteenth century. It stands on the edge of the delightful sixteenth-century town, whose half-timbered buildings and narrow streets conceal tree-lined riverside walks and all kinds of fantastic gables and roofs. The palace is dull in contrast to the rest of the town, despite its claims to be based on twelfth-century architecture. The original building was damaged by fire in 1065 and again in 1132, when part of it collapsed during a ceremonial court. Almost the only remaining medieval part is the palace chapel, dating from the early years of the twelfth century. It is in the form of a Greek cross with an octagonal upper storey. Henry III's heart is buried here under a thirteenth-century effigy.

The most remarkable feature of the palace was some kind of great hall on the upper floor, though it was almost certainly less grandiose than the nineteenth-century reconstruction. But the present great hall still retains some pillars from the eleventh century and some late twelfth-century work. It was never glazed in the Middle Ages, and court ceremonials were held in winter in the room below, which was heated by a hypocaust under the floor. The hall now contains a monumental, if mediocre, cycle of fifty-four paintings setting out that vision of the medieval empire which inspired the foundation of the new empire in 1871, in a series of historical set-pieces, a reminder that the past can cast a longer shadow over the present than the crumbling ruins of palaces might lead us to believe.

Under Henry IV, the positions of pope and emperor were reversed by the church reformers: Gregory VII declared the emperor deposed when he tried to continue the policy of his predecessors, and excommunicated him, setting up a rival emperor; Henry IV deposed Gregory and installed an anti-pope. The duel lasted for nearly two centuries, from 1076 until 1250; but the end of the first stage was marked by the agreement sealed at Worms in 1122 by Henry V, by which the emperor retained many of his rights in the election of bishops. Two decades after Henry's death, Conrad III, first of the Hohenstaufen dynasty, did not go to Rome for coronation, remaining king of the Germans; the imperial coronation was never essential to establish the authority of a German ruler – yet another of the contradictions surrounding the existence of the empire. Conrad's successor, Frederick of Hohenstaufen, on the other hand, was crowned in Rome shortly after his election, and the imperial title was central to his thoughts and ambitions. Frederick 'Barbarossa' is the great national figure of Germany; it is he who will come again to reawaken the nation, according to a legend which reads very like that of king Arthur. Under his rule, the empire may not have reached the predominance it had enjoyed under Otto I, but Frederick's personal qualities made him a more charismatic figure. It was to his reign that later emperors looked back as a golden age; and yet there is relatively little in the way of physical relics that we can see today. Frederick's life was spent in long campaigns in Italy and in endless journeys across the empire. Of his palaces only **Gelnhausen**, a small building on an island in the little river Kinzig north-east of Frankfurt, survives as a more or less unified ruin; but little remains. It was founded by Frederick to strengthen his hold over the area and was the scene of a number of imperial assemblies. Oval in form, equipped with a huge watch-tower and probably moated, it was also partially a defensive site. All that is left is the entrance gateway, with a chapel above (and an odd capital on the inner face, showing a hare between two eagles). On the outer wall is a plain arcade with the remains of decorative plaques, possibly the site of the imperial throne. Other fragments of stonework are preserved in the gateway, and the nearby church of St Mary has a very fine arcaded chancel which must be related to the palace. Again, it is only the sculptured detail that gives an idea of the original richness of the palace.

Otherwise, we have to return to Aachen for evidence of Frederick as emperor. It was he who gave to the Palatine Chapel the huge candelabra, modelled on that made for Gross-Comburg in Franconia thirty years earlier, which also survives in its original place. Frederick was responsible for Charlemagne's canonization in 1166, and he also commissioned the shrine at Aachen, which was not completed until 1215. Just as Charlemagne looked back to the Roman emperors of antiquity, so Frederick now looked back to Charlemagne as his exemplar. The most striking image of Frederick himself, however, is a bust made in 1150–60, and later converted into a reliquary, which is in the church at **Cappenberg**, between Münster and Cologne. It derives from late classical busts of emperors, but its almost violent appearance, with its huge enamelled eyes (restored in the nineteenth century) and distinctive treatment of the hair, belong to a new and less restrained style. Originally a silver wreath surrounded the head. It belonged to Frederick's godfather, who gave it to the church after it had been converted to a reliquary, and it tallies with other contemporary portraits in seals and manuscripts, so it may well be a speaking likeness of the emperor; it is certainly unlike any other surviving work from the same period. Looking at it, we can imagine a personality forceful enough to rival Charlemagne's imperial accomplishments.

Frederick's ambitions had led him to arrange a match between his son Henry VI and Constance of Sicily, who claimed the Norman territories in southern Italy (see p. 205) as her inheritance. With the addition of this new dimension, the revival of the Roman empire seemed close at hand; Henry VI hoped to rule from Saxony to

Sicily. But he never established his wife's title and died leaving his three-year-old son Frederick as heir. It was almost twenty years before Frederick I I was able to make good his claim: he was elected king in 1212 and crowned in 1215, and proved an even more powerful character than his grandfather. In medieval times, it was he who was said to have slept under the Kyffhäuser mountain, waiting to lead Germany to a new golden age; only in the sixteenth century was the sleeping emperor changed to Frederick Barbarossa. His contemporaries called him 'the wonder of the world and a marvellous transformer'. Frederick's turbulent childhood and youth, the long periods he spent in Sicily, and a fierce intellectual curiosity made him into an unorthodox character whose attachments, if any, were to the Mediterranean world where Christian, Jewish and Moslem ideas intermingled. He was mistrustful, sceptical and inclined to value reason above belief, an attitude which on the one hand led him to make remarks about Moses, Christ and Mohammed as the three great impostors, and on the other hand to create the most impressive set of laws since Charlemagne's day, promulgated in 1231 for his Sicilian kingdom. He founded the university of Naples in 1224 to provide lawyers and administrators for his realms, a rival to the university at Bologna, where many members of the papal court were trained. He was the patron of philosophers and was in contact with the men who were bringing to the west the ideas of Moslem writers who had studied Greek philosophy, as well as with scholars working on mathematics. Leonard of Pisa, who introduced Arabic numerals and algebra to the west, was at Frederick's court. On the other hand, Frederick encouraged poets: through the influence of his wife, Constance of Provence, the poets of Tuscany and Sicily learnt the themes of the great Provençal poets, and Frederick's chancellor, Pier della Vigna, is sometimes credited with writing the first sonnet. Frederick himself is credited with several poems in Italian which follow Provençal models. He spoke six languages, was interested in medicine – he encouraged the famous school at Salerno – and wrote a classic treatise on falconry.

At the height of his power, Frederick ruled Germany, northern Italy and the Sicilian kingdom in the south of Italy, as well as Sicily itself and, briefly, the kingdom of Jerusalem. Typically, he had gone on crusade in 1228 and had regained Jerusalem by diplomacy, crowning himself king in March 1229. Yet his impressive intellectual and political achievements have left little mark in concrete terms. Like his predecessors, most of his life was spent in travel, quelling princely revolts in Germany, civic disturbances in northern Italy or papal intrigues in the south. The best examples of the style of his reign are in southern Italy. Scattered across Apulia are the ruins of his hunting lodges, at Gravina di Puglia, Lagopesole and Palazzo San Gervasio. **Lagopesole**, in the northern foothills of the Apennines near Potenza, was begun by Frederick in 1242, and he spent the summer of 1250 there, just before his death. Although much rebuilt, its massive, almost windowless walls, designed to keep out the summer heat and protect the cool inner courtyards, for it was both hunting lodge and summer residence, are typical of these lodges. The building was unfinished at the emperor's death. The spacious rooms are austere, with only traces of what would have been rich ornament. The curious keep, unrelated to the rest of the building, may have been here before Frederick began his building, while the chapel is the work of Charles of Anjou at the end of the thirteenth century. The finest civil monuments to Frederick's reign in this part of the world were the palace at Lucera, demolished in 1790, and the fortified bridge at Capua, a kind of symbolic gateway to the kingdom of Sicily, with a strongly classical central façade, with figures of the emperor, of justice and of judges. These survive in the museum at Capua, and are so classical in form that they were long believed to be genuine sculpture from antiquity which Frederick had re-used. This monumental entrance prefigures the triumphal arches of the Renaissance, with its programme of secular inscriptions: under the figure of Justice, 'At the command of Caesar, I stand as protector of the kingdom: how wretched I make those whom I know to be false'; under the busts of the judges, 'Those who seek to lead a pure life may enter safely'; 'I shut out the heretic [or faithless]: let him fear to be put in prison'. Frederick himself directed the composition of this remarkable monument; Richard of San Germano records that he 'signed the plan with his own hand'. The fragments, although artistically unexciting, are a vivid reminder of his dream of power and order.

For all Frederick's peaceable achievements, his reign was one of almost continuous struggle, chiefly against the popes, who desperately feared that the political basis of their power would be annihilated by this free-thinking emperor who had united north and south Italy and encircled their lands. The bridge at Capua hints at Frederick's concept of the empire as a rival to the papacy, arbiter in religious as well as civil life. The struggle was a bitter one, fought with propaganda of the most vitriolic sort; Frederick was excommunicated, not once but frequently, and in return the emperor denounced the church's wealth as a source of corruption and proclaimed the ideal of apostolic poverty, perhaps influenced by St Francis, whom he had met at Bari in 1220. The castle at **Bari** also represents the other side of the contest with the popes, the warfare which raged intermittently through Italy in Frederick's reign. Lying on the edge of the old quarter, the northern façade of the fortress has been restored to its appearance after it was rebuilt by Frederick in 1233–40. There is a fine doorway to the west and an elegant entrance hall, and the courtyard retains the thirteenth-century arcade.

The best-preserved of Frederick's castles, however, is that at **Castel del Monte**, fifteen miles west of Bari. Standing on an isolated hilltop in the once thickly wooded coastal plain, Castel del Monte is unlike any of Frederick's other castles, which were four-square and architecturally simple in plan, like Castel Ursino near Catania in Sicily or Foggia, where a fine doorway in the antique style remains. Castel del Monte is not merely octagonal; it has eight octagonal turrets at the angles, a plan as remarkable as the design for the bridge at Capua. Again, we seem to be face to face with Frederick's own concepts of architecture. The site is too remote for this building to have a public, propaganda-type, programme, though analogies with other octagonal buildings such as the chapel at Aachen have been suggested; the difficulties presented by the construction of an octagon meant that it was a form reserved for special structures, besides any special symbolic meaning it may have had, though the upper part of the palace at Lucera was octagonal. If Castel del Monte has a 'programme', it must surely be that it demonstrated Frederick's power and wealth; if he could afford to build in such style and luxury in the depths of the forests, what could he not accomplish elsewhere? As to the form, the octagon on octagon pattern of the towers looks like a *jeu d'esprit*, a building conceived as a pattern and created from an ideal ground-plan: this could have been Frederick's own contribution. The luxury of Frederick's world can be glimpsed here, whereas at other palaces and lodges similarly equipped the traces of floor mosaics and systems of running water laid throughout the building have long since disappeared. Even the lavatories had a simple flushing system. The walls were covered with marble and antique carvings. Again, only traces of ornament remain, notably the highly classical surround of the main doorway, another 'triumphal entrance' on a smaller scale, with its double-ramp staircase. The inner courtyard, also octagonal, is now bare, with only marks on the stonework to indicate the presence of a wooden gallery at first-floor level; the central fountain and pool have vanished. We need to envisage a wealth of ornament, perhaps plants and even carpets spread on the ground in the Arab fashion, to reconstitute the original effect. Again, in the interiors, which are now reduced to the bare Gothic skeleton of the building itself, we must imagine the richest possible furnishings, particularly in the so-called throne-room in the upper storey. The only surviving details of the decoration are the pillars of bluish and pink marble, and a few carvings; the interior was stripped in the early nineteenth century, before the building became state property in 1876.

Ironically, it was in this jewel-like building, more pleasure-palace than fortress, that the last Hohenstaufen princes lived out most of their lives as prisoners, after Frederick's son Manfred had been defeated and killed at Benevento in 1266 and the dream of a united German and Italian empire had been destroyed. The future of the Holy Roman Empire lay in Germany, which Frederick I I had never loved as much as his Italian lands. It was his son Henry who had looked after his interests there: he had built the palace at **Bad Wimpfen**, probably between 1224 and 1235, the best surviving group of Hohenstaufen palace buildings, crowning a ridge overlooking the river Neckar, in the heart of the Hohenstaufens' own estates. Here a delightful arcade with a wide view over the valley survives, a fragment of a great hall on the first floor. The royal chapel, though stripped of decorations, can also be seen, as can two fortified towers and a gateway. The palace was the largest of its kind, and its buildings were absorbed into the surrounding town very soon after Frederick I I's death, because it was sold off piecemeal to local lords and townsmen. It does not seem to have been a spectacular building, merely an ordinary noble dwelling enlarged to a royal scale. It is a reminder that the Holy Roman emperors, whatever airs and graces they might give themselves in distant Italy or Palestine, were in the end German princes, *primus inter pares*, unable to convert the empire into a hereditary possession. At the other end of the scale, their officers or *ministeriales* were successfully doing just that: the castellans appointed by the Hohenstaufens turned their appointments into a hereditary title, and the Hohenstaufen estates began to become ungovernable. This process was hastened by the anarchy of 1250–73, when no claimant to the empire became more than merely 'king of the Romans', and even that title was often disputed by rival claimants.

During the anarchy, a new power emerged on the eastern frontier of the empire, the kingdom of Bohemia, ruled by Ottokar II, and the anarchy ended with the choice of a Habsburg emperor, Rudolf, in 1273. But neither Bohemia's day nor that of the Habsburgs had yet come: it was not until 1346, under Charles IV, that Bohemia became for a time the centre of the empire, and the continous line of Habsburg emperors begins in 1438. In the meantime, the house of Luxemburg provided a great emperor, Henry VII, whose brief reign was spent mostly in Italy, though his most important action was the acquisition of Bohemia for his son John. But the vision of the empire was still as alluring as ever, and Henry achieved imperial coronation at Rome. The imperial supporters, or Ghibelline party, in Italy hoped for great things from him, and he appears in Dante's *Divine Comedy* as the paragon of emperors, reflecting Dante's view that the empire is a sacred institution, outside papal jurisdiction, and that it is the duty of pope and emperor to work together. Dante's ardent support for the empire as an ideal world government is balanced by a conception of the papacy as a purely spiritual office: his *bête noire* is papal avarice and greed for temporal power, the tendency towards theocracy which Jacques Maritain called 'the evil spirit of medieval christendom'. For Dante, the pope's role was that of the apostles and should be accompanied by apostolic poverty: the empire was the true ordainer of earthly life. In the *Paradiso*, Dante has a vision of the imperial eagle formed by the souls of the just rulers. There is no comparable vision of the papacy, but only the tremendous denunciation of contemporary popes spoken by St Peter.

For the struggle between pope and emperor for power over the clergy was now extended into the purely secular field. Pronouncements in the heat of the earlier contest were taken to their logical extremes, until Boniface VIII wore the imperial eagle on his vestments. Henry VII's successor, Louis of Bavaria, was crowned in Rome in 1328 while he was excommunicated; the ceremony was performed by a layman, a member of the Roman nobility. Later that year Louis declared the pope to have been deposed. With the pope now firmly under the control of the French king, it was obviously impossible to allow him any role in the empire which might have political repercussions. In 1338, the electors announced that the candidate chosen by them needed no papal confirmation. But even if freedom from papal interference was gained, there was an intangible loss: the empire began to abandon the claims put forward by Dante and to change its nature.

In 1346, Charles IV, grandson of Henry VII and son of the chivalrous John of Bohemia, who died in the same year at Crécy, was chosen emperor, and under his rule the focal point of the empire moved east to Prague. His involvement with the pope and in Italy was slight, but he did journey to Rome for an imperial coronation, and he remained on friendly if distant terms with the pope. He was above all a realist, and this is reflected in his attitude towards Germany. He saw that the empire could not become a unified kingdom on the model of France or England, because the crown did not have a sufficiently strong power-base of its own. Instead, he saw the empire as a confederation of states, with the emperor as *primus inter pares*. He was content to be effective king in Bohemia only and overlord of the rest of Germany, and this is reflected in the formal settlement of the empire's constitution, the Golden Bull of 1356, so called because the seal attached to the document announcing the new constitution was cast in gold. It attempted to give the empire a form of government which reflected 'the variety of customs, ways of life and language found in the various nations which compose it', and in this it succeeded, even if a distinguished nineteenth-century historian said that Charles 'legalized anarchy and called it a constitution'. It is the Magna Carta of Germany, though it is concerned not with individual rights, but with the rights and duties of the princes who elected the emperor and ruled the empire under him.

Charles was educated in France and spent much of his youth in Italy, and when he came to establish his court in Prague he employed the most fashionable artists in Europe to create a new imperial centre. His father had won Bohemia by force of arms from the last of the native rulers, but had not spent any length of time there: Charles often acted as his regent. Charles himself said of

1, 2. Contrasts in churches: the Gallarus oratory at Kilmalkedar, Co. Kerry, and Mont-Saint-Michel, the famous place of pilgrimage on the borders of Normandy and Brittany

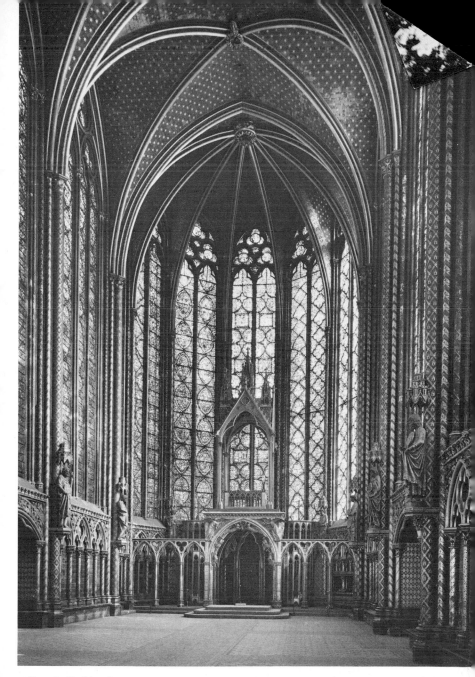

4. French Gothic: the east end of the Sainte-Chapelle, built by St Louis, with the reliquary altar designed to house the Crown of Thorns.

3. (*left*) Sicilian Romanesque: the strongly Byzantine chapel of the royal palace at Palermo built by the Norman kings.

5. Santa María de Naranco at Oviedo, part of the ninth-century palace of the kings of Asturias.

6. (*right*) Romanesque ornament at its richest: the exterior of the little church at Rioux, near Saintes, in Western France.

8. The towers of San Gimignano, a reminder of civic feuds: each noble family had its own fortified refuge.

7. (*left*) Civic pride: the fourteenth-century 'palace of the commune', or town hall, at Siena.

9. Towns, trade and communications: the cathedral, salt warehouse and twelfth-century bridge over the Danube at Regensburg.

10, 11. Contrasts in castles: a simple German fortress at Münzenberg and the immensely elaborate brick keep at Coca in Spain.

12. (*right*) Norman power: the keep at Rochester.

14. The church militant: Albi cathedral, in the centre of the lands
reconquered from the Cathar heretics.

13. (*left*) Burgos cathedral's Gothic west front with the early Renaissance
central tower in the background.

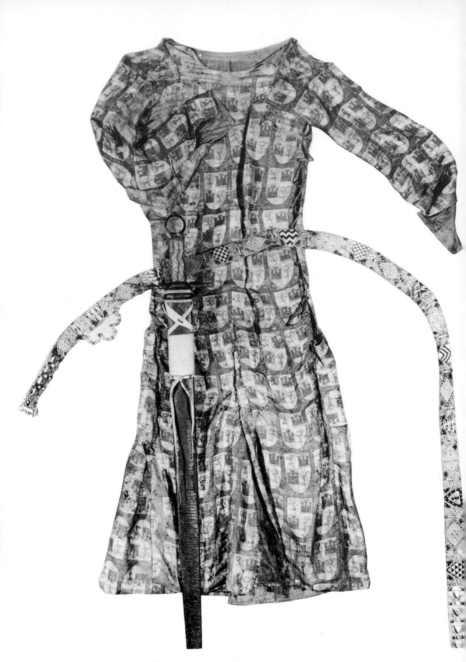

15. Princely splendour: the early thirteenth-century surcoat, sword and belt of Infante D. Fernando de la Cerda from the monastery of Las Huelgas at Burgos.

16. (*right*) The royal gold cup, made for Charles V of France; Parisian enamelwork on gold, set with pearls. The inscription on the neck is later.

17, 18. Medieval faces: (*left*) a relief depicting Christ and two disciples
on the road to Emmaus from the monastery at Santo Domingo de Silos
and (*above*) the tomb of Bertrand du Guesclin at Saint-Denis, Paris.

19. Medieval technology: the octagon at Ely, an extraordinary feat of masonry, carpentry and engineering.

it that he had 'found this kingdom so neglected that on our travels we met with no castle which had not been mortgaged, and all its crown lands with it, so that there was no choice but to lodge in a house in the town, like any other citizen. Worst of all, the castle at Prague, deserted since the time of King Ottokar, had fallen into such rubble and ruin that it was beyond repair. We therefore caused to be built at great expense a fine new palace, the palace men see there today.'

Charles I V's main residence was not in Prague itself, but eighteen miles to the south-west, at **Karlstein**. Here he created a new centre for his government in Bohemia, and it was here that the crown jewels and his collection of relics were kept. The castle, which held out against the Hussite rebels at the end of the fourteenth century when all other imperial fortresses had fallen, was both fortress and palace, not unlike Windsor in both its military and political functions, combining natural strength with imposing proportions. The castle as we see it today is largely the product of nineteenth-century restoration on the outside, and the detail is not necessarily accurate. The central keep, however, has retained its original interiors: these were the state rooms, the Hall of the Empire, and the chapel for the relics of the Holy Cross. The painting in the Hall of the Empire has vanished, but the rest of the decoration is more or less preserved. It is mostly based on Italian tradition, and there are early examples of *trompe l'œil* architectural effects alongside pure Gothic scenes and portraits set against a gilded background. But the main impression is of an individual and local style, not quite like anything else in Europe. Both in the chapel of the Holy Cross and in the Wenceslas Chapel in Prague cathedral, the walls are encrusted by semi-precious stones, an idea without parallel at this period (1357–67) but which may owe something to the pulpit at Aachen (Charles I V was responsible for the Gothic addition to the chapel at Aachen) or to descriptions of the Temple of the Holy Grail in contemporary poetry. The paintings in the chapel represent the highly individual side of Bohemian painting, combining Italian mannerisms with an almost Breughel-like depiction of character. The vaulting above is studded with embossed and gilded decoration, making the whole room a kind of jewelled casket for the precious relic which it once contained.

The Karlstein, despite its grandeur, is a reflection of Charles's private life. His work in **Prague** is public, the aggrandizement of his dynasty. We have already touched on the cathedral; the building of a new castle, the Charles Bridge and various monasteries all date from this period. He also founded the university and considerably extended the city itself by the creation of a 'new town' adjoining the old one and brought within a single set of walls. Relatively little work of Charles's time survives; even the Charles Bridge was only started by him, and was not completed until 1503. Parts of other buildings such as the city hall and the university are also fourteenth-century, but only the cathedral retains much of its original appearance. A number of fine Gothic churches elsewhere in Bohemia and luxurious illuminated manuscripts from this period also testify to the flourishing culture created by Charles.

Charles's two successors were unable to achieve imperial coronation at Rome, hampered by renewed civil war in Germany. His younger son, Sigismund, who was elected in 1411, did get himself crowned; but just as Bohemia had been Charles's strength, it was to be Sigismund's weakness. Under the influence of reformers and non-conformers, some brought to Bohemia by Charles himself, others disciples of Wyclif and the English dissenters, the Czechs evolved the first of the modern 'national' churches, in which reforming zeal, particularly over the forms and language of church services, went hand in hand with nationalist enthusiasm. The movement was more than mere anti-German feeling, however, and its supporters were to be found throughout the southern part of Germany. It would be truer to define it as anti-establishment, defying both pope and emperor. The open rift between the Hussites and the government began on 30 July 1419, when a mob in Prague hurled the councillors of the New Town from the windows of the New Town city hall. Within a year, the Hussites had armed and, under their general Jan Zizka, had inflicted a serious defeat on the emperor Sigismund outside Prague. In the years that followed, some of the Hussites changed from a moderate, reforming movement into a radical and revolutionary group, rejecting all outward forms of church service, except hymn-singing, communion and reading of scripture; they became violent iconoclasts and rejected all but the simplest forms of church hierarchy. They were able to uphold these extreme views because of their military successes, which included the defeat of a crusade sent against them in 1431. But the hardships of war led to a division in the Hussite ranks while negotiations for a reconciliation with the church were in progress. In 1434, the extremists were defeated by an army of moderate Hussites and orthodox Catholics, and two years later an agreement was reached with Sigismund and with the church. The struggle was far from over, and Bohemia remained politically and religiously isolated for the rest of the century; the Hussites became in effect a radical but still broadly Catholic church within the empire, a forerunner of the much larger upheavals of the sixteenth century.

The empire itself passed finally to the house of Habsburg on Sigismund's death in 1437. Frederick III was the last of the emperors to be crowned at Rome, but he did little more than rule his hereditary lands after 1444, leaving western Germany in the grip of increasing anarchy. His long reign of fifty-six years marks the end of the medieval Holy Roman Empire and its rediscovery by the men of the Renaissance. His son Maximilian, by his marriage to Mary of Burgundy, re-created the empire politically at a moment when new intellectual attitudes were favourable to the concept of empire; and so the vision of empire was reborn in a new guise. The dream of Charlemagne, Otto I and Frederick II was to survive until Napoleon replaced it by another, ephemeral, empire in the early years of the nineteenth century.

9
The Normans

The decline of Charlemagne's empire was hastened by the last of the great migrations of peoples to which the Roman empire itself had succumbed, the onslaughts of the Norsemen on western Europe which began in 793 at Lindisfarne in Northumbria and continued for two centuries. The reasons for the sudden movement – west, south and east – of the 'Vikings' are obscure; their activities began as raids in search of booty, made possible by their swift and seaworthy longships which could also sail far inland along rivers, and only after the middle of the ninth century did they begin to settle. Economic pressure, political unrest at home in Scandinavia, a growing and turbulent population – these were among the reasons for the raids, but we must also add daring, enterprise and a love of adventure. There is evidence, too, that the Norsemen came first as merchants and turned to raiding only when trade proved unprofitable.

The raids fell first and heaviest on lands which had little protection: the Norsemen were not haphazard in their choice, and did not attempt to challenge Charlemagne. They attacked the isolated monasteries around the coasts of Ireland, England and France first of all; then in the 830s and 840s their attacks grew more widespread and changed in character. Instead of attacking and withdrawing, the Norsemen established bases where they would stay, not for a season, but year in, year out, as at Noirmoutier on the mouth of the Loire; or they would begin to embroil themselves, as mercenaries or on their own account, in local warfare, as with the Norwegian war-leader Turgeis in Ireland from 840 to 845. In 845, Ragnar plundered Paris on Easter Sunday and was paid 7,000 pounds of silver by Charles the Bald to go home again, the first of the succession of hopeful payments called *danegeld* which only demonstrated the wealth of their victims and brought the Vikings back for more.

The success of this raid encouraged imitators, and by the 860s we hear of war fleets and of forces of 500–1,000 men attacking targets as far afield as Seville, Rouen and York. The towers built to prevent Norse raids up the rivers of north-west Spain can still be seen near Padron, on the Galician coast west of Santiago de Compostela. By 870 much of Ireland and two of the Saxon king-doms in England were permanently in Danish hands, as raiding turned to settlement; and by the end of the decade half England was theirs. Attacks on northern France were renewed in the 880s, and although the Norsemen were driven out at the end of the decade, they returned soon afterwards and in 910–11 attacked Chartres under Hrolf or Rollo; later that year Charles the Simple of France granted him and his followers the provinces facing the Channel, which we know today as Normandy, the Northmen's region. It is easy, given the history of Norse involvement with the west up to this point, to imagine them as mere pirate bands; but the organized nature of Norse society is immediately evident when we look at the work of Rollo and his successors as dukes of Normandy. He not only shared out the new domains among his followers in an orderly fashion, but enacted laws to ensure peaceful possession. He arranged the new social hierarchy in a way which testifies less to the democratic society of the north than to a shrewd realization on Rollo's part of the possibilities of French law; in effect, he created a pyramidal structure in which his companions owed loyalty to him and in turn gave estates to, and received loyalty from, their own group of subordinates. The settlers quickly adopted Christianity and the French language, and became, as peacefully as the times would allow, part of the kingdom of France, though they remained a distinctive cultural and political unit.

France was now almost immune from Viking raids; much of England was in Norse hands; the raids turned into warfare between the Norsemen of Ireland and York, with sundry adventurers joining in with an eye to the main chance. Recent excavations at York have shown us something of the city in Norse hands, reminding us that for all the coming and going of the petty kings who ruled there, there was also a solidly based community of tradesmen and craftsmen. The Norse kingdom came to an end in 954; but within twenty-five years the raids on England had been renewed, harking back for a time to the old pattern of pillage, destruction and *danegeld*, using Normandy as a base and plundering the rich

southern counties. Evidence of their success is to be found as far
afield as Gotland in the Baltic (see p. 301), where several treasure
troves of this period on display in the museum Gotlands Fornsal
are made up almost entirely of English coin. At the beginning of
the eleventh century, the desire for plunder became a renewed
ambition for conquest, a conquest achieved by Svein Forkbeard
in the winter of 1013–14 and consolidated by his son Knut (or
Canute) in 1015–16 after Svein's death. Knut created a Scandinavian empire, ruling England, Denmark, Norway and parts of
Sweden before his death in 1035; but it was a personal domain,
defying the logic of geography, and it quickly fell apart after his
death. Knut was the first of the Norse kings who became a truly
international figure, going on pilgrimage to Rome and winning the
favour of the pope; his daughter Gunnhild married the son of the
emperor Conrad. His successors held his lands for less than a
decade: in 1042, England returned to the old West Saxon dynasty.

Because the Norsemen of the ninth and tenth centuries were
essentially freebooters, owing allegiance to a chieftain, rather than
part of some wider political unit, their monuments are few and
far between: the ship found in a burial mound at Gokstad, with
carts and other goods, the carved stones commemorating individuals with their scenes from heathen mythology in Gotlands Fornsal
at Visby, the great earthworks at **Trelleborg** in Denmark which
represent either a garrison town and centre for the royal administration or a barracks for a professional army. All that remains is the
central ring earthwork and its outworks, which form a triangle
between the junction of two rivers; the layout of the houses is now
marked in concrete. It is an enlarged version of the kind of camp
that raiders on a 'Viking' journey must have set up, using natural
defences wherever possible and lying near rivers or the sea, which
is two miles away at Trelleborg.

The last incursion of the Norsemen into England was in 1066,
in that often-forgotten episode when Harald Hardradi of Norway,
who had a distant claim to the English throne by his descent from
Knut, sailed up the Humber and landed in the heart of Yorkshire,
aiming to seize the old Norse capital at York as his base, 'drawn
there', in Gwyn Jones's words, 'by the never-failing Viking com-
pulsions of land, wealth and fame overseas. His first battle had
been at Stiklarstader back in 1030; next came the great arc of sacks
and sieges, sea-fights and land-battles, from Poland through Russia

by way of Asia Minor and Bulgaria on to Sicily; then his bid for
a kingdom in Norway, wars through Uppland and along the
Swedish border, and seventeen years of hostilities against the
Danes.' But this last of the Norse adventurers was surprised by
Harold and the English levies at Stamford Bridge, and his army
was annihilated in a hard-fought battle.

The Norsemen won England in the end, all the same: Harald
Hardradi's invasion opened the way for the other claimant to the
English throne, William of Normandy. For once, a crucial event
in medieval history is recorded for us by a spectacular work of
art. It was made for the bishop of Bayeux, Odo, half-brother of
William the Conqueror, who had himself taken an active part in
the fighting. As bishop, the climax of his career was the dedication
of the new cathedral in 1077, of which only part of the west front
and the crypt survives. The dedication ceremony was a splendid
one, and the newly built church was decorated for the occasion.
The centrepiece of the decorations may well have been a huge wall-
hanging, nearly 250 feet long, one of the largest such works ever
made. Its subject was the recent past, from 1063 to 1066, one of the
most dramatic moments in the history of medieval Europe, when
the Norman duke and his followers had seized the English kingdom.

Today the **Bayeux Tapestry** is a household name. It was displayed in the elegant eighteenth-century Bishop's Palace, in a
specially constructed room, which became inadequate for the
huge numbers of visitors who flock to see it, and is now being
replaced. To see the tapestry itself is still a remarkable experience.
It is an extraordinary document, vivid, individual and impossible
to reproduce adequately even with modern photographic and print-
ing techniques. The word 'tapestry' is a misnomer: it is not woven,
but embroidered on a linen base in eight different colours of wool,
giving an effect of low relief as in sculpture. Indeed, it must have
resembled Romanesque sculpture very closely, for much contemporary stonework would have been coloured; and it is the slightly
three-dimensional quality of the tapestry that makes it so vivid
today.

Although scholars continue to argue over the standing of the
tapestry among early accounts of the Norman conquest of England,
there is no doubt that it is a historical record of the first importance.
It may indeed have influenced some of the early chronicles of the
conquest and is very probably the earliest source of the story that

King Harold was struck in the eye by a Norman arrow before he was killed, a story once discredited but now seemingly restored to historical favour. The problem is that, although the tapestry appears to be miraculously well-preserved, it has in fact been restored many times; the use of chemically dyed wool in the repairs carried out in 1842 is particularly noticeable, especially at the end. In the course of these restorations, details have inevitably been lost, misread or accidentally altered, and the arrow in Harold's eye might be such a point. But the general aspect of the tapestry has hardly changed in the nine hundred years since it was made, and in many cases it provides us with information unknown elsewhere.

Because nothing else like it survives, it is easy for us to regard the Bayeux Tapestry as an exceptional work of art made to celebrate an exceptional event. But it would be wrong to do so, because wall-hangings like these were not uncommon in eleventh-century churches and palaces, and fragments of others survive. What is exceptional is the scale of the tapestry, which does seem to have been an ambitious project: some scholars have suggested that as many as six separate teams worked on it. Furthermore, the artist responsible for the overall design was a draughtsman of great skill, working perhaps in a tradition of narrative picture-painting that had been developed at St Augustine's, Canterbury, in the years before 1066, to illustrate the Bible. The way in which a sense of continuous movement is given, of a kind of inexorable sequence of events leading to the Norman victory, shows that a master is at work. Notice, too, how the borders, at first decorated with scenes from fables or from rural life, change to become an echo of the slaughter at Hastings, filled with dismembered bodies and the debris of battle. The tapestry is also a marvellous record of how men lived in mid-eleventh-century England and Normandy. The most striking and clearly represented feature is the dress and armour of the nobles, followed by the ships and details of the military preparations. Even stylized features, such as the buildings, tell us something: Edward's palace is contrasted with the hovels of the humble folk in the scenes where the Normans forage for supplies.

If the tapestry was indeed produced in Canterbury for Bishop Odo, it serves as a reminder that, however dramatic the events of 1066 were, they were not a total revolution. After all England had been under foreign rule only fifty years earlier. It is true that there was a wholesale transfer of property from Saxon to Norman lords in 1066, and that Norman French quickly became the official language of the kingdom. But the Normans were no strangers to England: Normans had accompanied Emma, wife of king Canute, and there had been a strong Norman faction at the court since 1043, when Edward, recently returned from exile in Normandy, became king; and Harold had been the leader of the opposition to this Norman intrusion, and to the Norman claim that Edward had named William as his successor. So the battle of Hastings was in one sense the resolution of a struggle within the English court itself.

The vital importance of the events of 1066 was that England became a political and cultural part of continental Europe; otherwise it might have continued in troubled isolation or succumbed once more to a Norse invasion, for Svein of Denmark was to renew the Norse attacks in 1069–70. If Harold had been the victor at Hastings, England might have maintained an independent culture as well as political independence; but as it was, she became part of the lands ruled by the most successful entrepreneurs of the eleventh century.

For the Normans had learnt much in the century and a half since they settled in France. Unlike their Norse compatriots in York and Ireland, they had become part of a state with long traditions of administration, and had turned them to good use when they were little valued elsewhere in France. They were fortunate in possessing great leaders, for it was a Norman who wrote of his own people: 'when under the rule of a strong master the Normans are a most valiant people, excelling all others in the skill with which they meet difficulties and strive to conquer enemy. But in all other circumstances they rend each other and bring ruin upon themselves.' William himself had had to fight his way to the dukedom in the 1040s; civil war was to return to the Anglo-Norman kingdom at frequent intervals; and it was to plague the Norman kingdom in Sicily as well. But the ill-effects of these occasional convulsions were limited by the presence, from the early eleventh century onwards, of a feudal aristocracy linked by family ties to a vigorous clergy, whose interests lay in the long run in peace and stability. The settled aspect of Norman society and the piety of the dukes is best seen at **Caen**, which owes its importance to William. He realized the potential value of its site for the creation of a town which would command the border between the two halves of his duchy, upper and lower Normandy. From a collection of small villages in the early eleventh century, Caen grew during his reign to become one of the great towns of Normandy. It was not a cathedral city, and has never become one; and it is unusual in that its great monuments are those of its secular founder and of the merchants who later made the town prosperous.

The centre of old Caen has almost entirely vanished as a result of the bitter struggle for the town in 1944. Only the ruins of the castle and the civic church of Saint-Pierre remain. The rock plateau on which the castle stood has very little left of its medieval structures, except for the outer walls and the so-called 'Exchequer' building, a rare survival of a Romanesque secular building. Unfortunately it is not open, but is hired out for civic and private receptions, a sad fate for a monument of much interest which in a way represents the very origins of Caen: for this was the great hall of the palace which Henry I built here.

Almost equidistant from the castle to the east and west are the two great abbeys founded by William and his wife Matilda in expiation of their marrying without the pope's permission, because they were cousins and therefore needed his dispensation. The Abbaye-aux-Dames is the senior of the two by eleven years. It was dedicated in June 1066, while the preparations for the Norman invasion of England were at their height. The church survives in its original form. The monastic buildings, all much later in date, were until recently the local hospital. The church, dedicated to the Trinity, is the smaller of the two and has been considerably restored. The façade has been rebuilt, and the unfinished Romanesque towers have a most odd top storey from the seventeenth century. Inside, the severity of the plan is broken by surface ornament: blind arcades, a simple frieze around the arches of the nave, and, in the choir, capitals which portray creatures from the bestiary (including an elephant which the sculptor has given a nose instead of a trunk, putting a ring through it so that it can be led like a bull!). Below the choir is the simple but impressive crypt, the oldest part of the building; and at the entrance of the choir is a plain slab of black marble marking the resting-place of queen Matilda.

The Abbaye-aux-Hommes, despite the replacement of its choir in the thirteenth century and the collapse of the central tower in the sixteenth, is closer to its original state than the Abbaye-aux-

Dames. It is a remarkably austere piece of architecture. The twin towers of the façade, surmounted by thirteenth-century spires, rise from a plain wall almost bare of decoration, and grow only slightly more elaborate with each succeeding stage. Even the topmost of the Romanesque tiers is very restrained in style. It is a kind of ecclesiastical equivalent to a Norman castle, severe and powerful. The nave, too, has immense power and a minimum of decoration. A double arcade of equal height underlines the long perspective to the choir, a sensitive Gothic reworking of the same theme with pointed arches. The upper arcade is in fact the opening for a huge tribune gallery running the length of the nave. It is an austere and grand monument to an ambitious and hard man. William was once buried before the high altar, where the site of his tomb is marked by a simple slab. Even at his funeral there were extraordinary scenes, which it is easy to imagine in this sombre building. A local citizen, Ascelin, interrupted the service to claim that the king was about to be buried in ground which he had seized unjustly from him, and the assembled nobles had to promise compensation before the service could proceed. Then the attendants found that the corpse was too large for the stone coffin and, in trying to force it in, broke it open: the church was filled with such an overpowering stench that the service had to be brought to a hurried close.

Although the abbey was renowned for its rich revenues, its religious vitality seems to have been slight, which is perhaps why the church has survived so well; the only major restoration, following the collapse of the central tower, was faithful to the original, and all that is missing is the huge central tower, over 360 feet high. Another reason for the lack of alteration to what might otherwise have become a 'dynastic' church like Westminster Abbey or Saint-Denis (see p. 223 below) is that the dukes of Normandy after William were members of either the English or French royal houses and chose to be buried elsewhere. The Abbaye-aux-Hommes therefore remains as it began, the creation of a single powerful personality.

But as the structure of Norman society changed from that of newly settled raiders to prosperous and established lords, so opportunities for enterprise diminished. The habit of 'viking' was deeply ingrained, and it is not unreasonable to see the Norman expansion from 1050 onwards in terms of a renewal of the old impulses. England was their richest prize; but other groups made their mark as far afield as Spain, Jerusalem and Sicily. The Spanish adventurers were soon swallowed up in the general maelstrom of the conquest of Spain from the Moors, and left no great mark; the activities of the First Crusade, brutal and heroic by turns, are beyond our scope; but in southern Italy and Sicily, the Normans created an empire as striking as that based on their homeland. Once more a handful of adventurers like Rollo and his followers won wide estates in a totally alien land, and, using this as a base, went on to conquer a rich Moslem island, whose history might otherwise have belonged outside western Christendom. The Norman involvement in the south seems to have begun with a group of pilgrims or exiles who intervened in a local revolt against the Byzantine rulers in Apulia in about 1009–18, with the pope's encouragement. Although the revolt failed, some of the Normans remained in Apulia, and in return for their assistance in a local war the ruler of Naples granted their leader Rannulf a fief based on the hill fortress of Aversa, between Capua and Naples, where the east end of the cathedral built by the second Norman count, Richard, still survives. Richard eventually became prince of Capua, and his successes attracted many adventurers from Normandy to seek their fortune. One family in particular stands out, that of the Hautevilles, twelve of whom came south in this period; by 1047 one of them, Dreux, was count of Apulia, while his half-brother Robert Guiscard became the leader of the Norman advance in Calabria. In 1059, the popes, who had regarded the Norman incursion with deep suspicion, changed their attitude and enlisted the newcomers in their struggle against the empire, and Richard and Robert Guiscard became vassals of the Holy See. By 1071, Robert Guiscard had driven the Byzantines out of southern Italy, having arrived fourteen years earlier as a penniless adventurer.

Meanwhile Robert's younger brother Roger had found a new prize, the island of Sicily, which the Byzantine emperors had failed to recapture from the Moslems. In 1061 he captured Messina, on the north-east tip of the island, across the straits from Italy; and over the next ten years he established himself in the surrounding area. In 1071 he seized Catania with his brother's help, and went on to attack the capital of the island, Palermo, a city second only in the Christian world to Byzantium itself. After a five-month siege, the city fell to a Norman assault. It took Roger another twenty years to make himself complete master of Sicily. During this time Robert Guiscard's energies had been directed against the Byzantine empire, where his attempts to seize Illyria ended in failure, and against the German emperor, culminating in the sack of Rome by his troops in 1081. Robert died in 1085, and in due course Roger was able to make good his claim to his brother's lands. When he died in 1101, the adventurer who had arrived in Italy forty-five years earlier with little more than a sword to his name was the 'Great Count', the lord of Sicily and much of Calabria, and founder of a new dynasty, who were to reign as kings. The Norman world at the end of the eleventh century spanned the whole of Europe from Scotland to Sicily, and was to reach its furthest goal with the creation of the Norman state of Antioch in 1099. This world was united by a common loyalty to Normandy as the homeland of the far-flung adventurers, by narrow ties of kith and kin, and by ties of common culture: Geoffrey Malaterra, writing of the Norman conquest of Sicily, begins with the coming of Rollo to Normandy; families like the Echauffours could claim to be a race 'beheld with terror by the "barbarous" in England, Apulia, Thrace and Syria', while monks were brought from Normandy to found new houses in the hitherto Greek Orthodox and Moslem south.

Yet the influence of the local culture was to prove very strong, and the Norman ways of the north soon gave way to a very different society. The Normans were already renowned for their love of fine dress, luxury and rich surroundings, and what they found in Palermo encouraged them in their tastes, producing the most cosmopolitan culture of the medieval west, drawing on Latin, Greek and Arabic traditions. The 'Great Count' had quickly grasped that any ruler of Sicily had to show toleration to the very different religions which co-existed in the islanders; moreover, he was ready to make use of their skills as administrators. So his court contained both Moslems and Greeks. There were other points in the west, notably in Spain, where Islam and Christendom met; but nowhere was the mingling of varied cultures so evident as in Sicily.

The great period of Sicily was after Roger's youngest son, Roger II, who succeeded him in 1105 as count, had obtained for himself and his heirs the title of king, completing the extraordinary ascent of his family, in two generations, from adventurers to monarchs. To this period belong the cathedral at Cefalù and the palace chapel at Palermo, the memorials of one of the most extra-ordinary courts of medieval Europe. Roger himself, like his con-temporary Henry I, was a highly educated man; but he was also fired by a genuine intellectual curiosity, which made him the familiar friend of scholars. Like his Norman counterparts in England, he was a great law-giver, but he went beyond the mere business of everyday government. He set up a commission headed by the scholar Edrisi to gather all the available facts about the geography of the known world, interrogating travellers and recording the information which was eventually used to produce a great map engraved in silver and Edrisi's book on geography. Visitors to the Sicilian court included such men as Adelard of Bath, astronomer and tutor to the young Henry II. But, despite the presence of Arab poets and men of learning, it was to Byzantium that the Sicilians looked for their artistic inspiration.

Of the vast palace at **Palermo**, based on a Moslem fortress, which the Norman counts and kings rebuilt and embellished, only a little remains: the succeeding centuries have overwhelmed the Norman work with their own refashionings. But what there is, buried in the vast pile behind its austere façade, is of dazzling quality. From Roger II's time there is the Palatine Chapel, dedicated on Palm Sunday 1140. It is small, as befits a private royal place of worship, but overwhelming in effect. Maupassant called it 'the most surprising religious jewel ever imagined by human thought'. It draws on Rome, Byzantium and even Islam for its forms: Rome for the basilica plan, with antique columns and cosmatesque marble flooring, Byzantium for the style of the mosaics, in particular the Christ in Majesty in the cupola, Islam for the extraordinary pendant-studded wooden ceiling painted with miniature scenes from everyday life. Throughout, the mosaic inscriptions are in both Greek and Latin. The sheer opulence of the whole is strikingly different from the severity of the Norman buildings of the north; and yet the same sense of grandeur underlies both. Here the king of a rich realm proclaims his royal status with all the means at his disposal; at Saint-Denis a decade later abbot Suger was to attempt a similar gathering of earthly riches to the glory of God. The Palatine Chapel marks one of the moments of supreme self-confidence in the Middle Ages: the world can be conquered physically and intellectually.

On the second floor is the so-called Sala di Ruggero, King Roger's hall, which in fact dates from the reign of William I twenty years later. Here the dazzling art of the mosaic workers is turned to secular ends, to hunting scenes, affronted lions, peacocks and flamingoes, moving between palm-trees. This, together with two small pleasure-palaces on the Palermo outskirts, the Ziza and the Cuba (of which only the structure remains), is all – apart from the cloister at Monreale – that we have to remind us of the secular luxuries of the Norman kings, the cool recesses giving on to sun-drenched courtyards and gardens. The Ziza still has its marble and mosaics and the fountain of running water typical of Arab palaces; and even here there are touches of western tradition, in the impeccably classical pillars.

The cathedral at **Cefalù** dates from the middle years of Roger II's reign. It seems to have been his favourite project, and it was here that he wished to be buried, though in the end his tomb was placed in Palermo cathedral, where he lies among the emperors who succeeded him. Cefalù, between Palermo and Messina, must have been chosen for some private reason, as it was never an important centre, though it had been a minor bishopric in the days of Byzantine rule. The town lies under the shelter of the huge rocky headland which gives it its Greek name (*cephalos*, a head), and in the midst of its narrow streets rises the Norman cathedral. The exterior, restrained and simple, is very late Romanesque of about 1240, with a hint of eastern influence in its central arcade. The church itself lies across a small courtyard; it is a typical basilica in form, and its rows of columns have been cleared of the baroque plaster which until recently encased them. Only the bare stonework of the walls now detracts from the appearance of the church as a whole, but even this is a blessing in disguise, for it focuses our attention on the mosaic at the east end, completed in 1148. This overwhelming Christ in Majesty seems the archetype of all such portraits. The Byzantine stiffness so often found in these regal portraits of the Saviour here gives way to the fullness of humanity: there is warmth and tenderness as well as kingship in this haunting face. Below, more formal mosaics in traditional style portray the Virgin between angels, whose clothing is a direct imitation of that of Byzantine emperors. The choir itself has marble thrones for the bishop and the king, with a rich mosaic pavement. The rest of the church must have been set out in equal splendour, but to see the Sicilian artists working on a grand scale, we have to turn to Monreale.

Monreale, five miles outside Palermo, in the foothills of the mountains which encircle the city to landward, was built by William II between 1172 and 1176, though the mosaics and fittings were not completed until ten years later. Its dramatic site, overlooking the Conca d'Oro, is similar to that of many Greek churches, which are often placed in spectacular settings. The exterior is disappointing, partly because of rebuilding, partly because the east end, with its interlacing pattern of pointed arches studded with rosettes, is an incongruous mixture of Romanesque and Islamic styles. Two massive bronze doors of 1179 and 1186 guard the north and east doors: that to the north was cast by one of the great Pisan metalworkers, Bonanno. The interior, again in basilica form, is vast and spacious; it is bolder and simpler than the Cappella Palatina, less subtle in the interplay of light and shade, but more majestic. It is above all a public building, a place for ceremonial and processions, and the decoration is on a suitably magnificent scale. On the nave walls, above the antique granite columns, a boldly drawn cycle of mosaics depicts the story of the Creation and the main events of the Old Testament; those in the aisles portray the teachings of Jesus, while the choir walls have the story of the Passion. In sharp contrast to San Marco at Venice, which has the only other surviving mosaic cycle on this scale, the artists have not attempted to produce a detailed version in many small scenes, but have chosen to take crucial events and to make of each a striking composition. The apse is like that at Cefalù, but not as fine, partly because the sanctuary here is narrow, receding into mystery through a series of slightly pointed arches, and does not allow sufficient space for a figure conceived on a grand scale. Indeed, the real focal point is the Madonna, enthroned below Christ. Above the two thrones, for king and bishop, we are reminded that this is a royal church: to the left, William II is crowned by Christ, and to the right he is shown presenting the church to the Virgin. His robes and crown are strikingly unfamiliar: they belong to the ceremonials of the Greek emperors rather than to his western contemporaries, whereas the other figures have much in common with western Romanesque art. Among the saints around the apse is the figure of St Thomas Becket, one of the earliest known representations of him as a saint, carried out within ten years of his martyrdom. The huge cycle of mosaics was completed within ten years, in contrast to the centuries needed to embellish San Marco; the Sicilian kings were rich indeed to be able to summon the necessary craftsmen.

It is in the cloisters at Monreale that we can come closest to appreciating the palaces of the Sicilian kings. Built at the end of the twelfth century and surrounded by Moorish arches on white marble columns, they are a place of pure delight. The pattern-work which appeared so boldly and awkwardly on the exterior of the church is here refined and given a thousand variations: the pillars are alternately plain and decorated, some with spiral inlays of coloured marble, others with the complex filigree tracery beloved of Moslem artists, yet others with bold chevrons in pure Norman style subtly refined by delicate details. In the corner is a fountain, once the monks' washing place, formed of a single column with a terminal like some exotic fruit, playing into a circular basin; this is set within its own miniature cloister. From the foliate heads of the Corinthian columns spring charming figured capitals, which use motives from classical mythology as well as scenes from the Bible. The artistic force of Moissac or Santo Domingo de Silos may be lacking, but there is a grace and sense of style worthy of the finest Moslem architecture.

The Cappella Palatina, Cefalù and Monreale are the major monuments of the Sicilian kingdom, but they are far from being the only survivors. A host of lesser churches, notably several in Palermo itself, bear witness to the individual style of the Norman culture here; and across southern Italy we can trace the work of Roman- esque artists from the north. We have noted St Thomas Becket at Monreale; even stranger is a crude mosaic in the cathedral at Otranto showing king Arthur riding on a monster. For all the overlay of Arab and Greek civilization, there was still a strong element of the north, reinforced by the many French and English visitors to the island, and by marriage alliances such as that between William II and Joanna, daughter of Henry II of England, lord of another empire.

It is to that empire, the empire built up by the house of Anjou, that we now turn. The Anglo-Norman domains, reunited in the early twelfth century by Henry I, fell apart once more on his death: Normandy was gradually captured by partisans of his daughter Matilda, led by her husband Geoffrey count of Anjou, while England remained in the hands of his nephew Stephen. But two factors prevented a permanent division: the interests of the great lords, who held rich lands on both sides of the channel, and the energy and determination of his grandson Henry. Henry came to an agreement with Stephen which meant that he succeeded to the English throne on Stephen's death – he had already pulled off an astonishing coup by marrying the newly divorced queen of France, Eleanor of Aquitaine, in 1152, thereby gaining control of lands which stretched across south-west France. When Henry II was crowned king of England in 1154 at the age of twenty-one, his domains extended from Scotland to the Pyrenees. It was an astonishing personal achievement, and his thirty-five-year reign was spent first consolidating, then defending, his territories. The huge extent of his domains, to which he added in the 1170s part of Ireland and, by overlordship, Scotland, meant that he was incessantly travelling and that his energies were absorbed by law-giving and administration. However, in recent years, increasing evidence has been found that much of the exciting innovation in contemporary literature took place at the Angevin court, not only through Eleanor but also through Henry himself, and that it may have been a centre of artistic as well as intellectual activity. But almost nothing remains of the Angevin buildings. Chinon, Henry's administrative centre on the Loire, where he died in 1189, was rebuilt and is now an imposing ruin; Woodstock, the pleasure-palace, possibly modelled on those of Sicily, which he is said to have built for his mistress Rosamund, has vanished utterly; Clarendon, near Salisbury, scene of a famous confrontation with Thomas Becket, is no more than isolated pieces of masonry. Even his burial place, the abbey of **Fontevrault**, does not reflect his patronage. It was founded in 1100 by the eccentric but much-revered Robert d'Arbrissel, and was the centre of an important local order of nuns by 1119, when pope Calixtus II dedicated the church. The domed nave, in the style found further south in Aquitaine, was built in the 1120s. In this noble and spacious church, bare of all decoration save a few capitals, lie the effigies of Henry II, Eleanor, Richard Cœur-de-Lion and John's wife Isabella of Angoulême, probably carved in the early thirteenth century, at a time when the empire they had built and defended crumbled before the determined onslaught of Philip Augustus of France. John, Henry II's youngest and favourite son, lies across the Channel at Worcester; having lost his French domains in 1204 he died at the height of a civil war in England in 1216.

Ten years earlier the Norman kingdom of Sicily had ceased to exist, and had become part of the Holy Roman Empire. The

Norman domination of Europe had come to a sudden end, leaving only the accursed inheritance of the English claim to wide lands in France and the imperial claim to Sicily, which were to dominate the political scene in centuries to come. But their exploits had brought both England and Sicily within the orbit of mainland Europe, and had permanently changed the dimensions of Europe.

10

Monarchies and Nations

The Reconquista *in Spain*

The Roman rule in Spain ended in 409, when the barbarian hordes, invited into the empire by one claimant to the imperial office in order to fight off his rival, swept into the peninsula and established independent kingdoms for themselves. They were followed by the Visigoths, who, acting nominally for Rome, drove some of them out into north Africa and conquered the rest. Spain became an extension of their southern French domains based on Toulouse; by 475 they controlled the whole of the country except Galicia in the north-west. A century later, forced into retreat from Gaul by the Franks, Toledo had become the centre of their lands, and in 587, with the conversion of king Reccared from Arianism to orthodox Catholicism, Spain was established as a unified state, ruled by elected monarchs and owing religious obedience to Rome. Under Reccared's successors Spain prospered despite Byzantine attempts at reconquest, the political turbulence caused by the problem of electing new kings, and a lack of loyalty to the crown as such: Visigothic kings were all too often treated by their nobles as one of their number, a rival rather than an overlord or leader.

The Visigoths produced a highly individual culture, little-known outside Spain, of which there are still considerable traces. They were the first of the 'barbarian' races to strike coins of their own design, under Leovigild (568–86), instead of imitating those of Rome. They also made good use of their classical inheritance: Isidore of Seville, who died in 636, wrote the most influential encyclopaedia of the Middle Ages, the *Etymologies*, which was the basis for many later works of the same kind. Like Bede in England a century later, Isidore was a polymath who also wrote the history of his own people. The architecture of the period can be studied in half a dozen well-preserved churches in old Castile, León, Galicia and Portugal. They are for the most part humble buildings, of massive masonry roughly squared to size, with classical columns and the elegant Visigothic horseshoe arches (which have a long pre-history in Spain, going back to the second century AD) and simple geometric patterns as decoration. Santa Comba de Banda, once a small monastery, was never more than a rural outpost; but San Juan de Baños near Palencia preserves an inscription in the crude capitals of the period declaring it to be a royal foundation, the work of king Recceswinth, dating from 661. It has lost its original and unusual plan, with three square apses arranged like crenellations, but the nave is intact; once again, the elegance of the Visigothic arches is most striking, and there is an exterior door-way with pleasing decorations in low relief. These patterns occur at Quintanilla de las Viñas, near Burgos, where only the east end of a once substantial late-seventh-century church survives, with a marvellous triumphal arch at the entry to the apse and simple but haunting carvings of saints and angels in a totally distinctive, almost childlike style. The most complete of this group of churches is that of San Pedro de la Nave on the Portuguese border, moved fifty years ago from its original site. It is closer in style to Santa Comba; the classical columns of San Juan de Baños are replaced by rough four-square masonry pillars; but we can at least see the overall form of a late Visigothic church. It also contains some of the first 'historiated' capitals, quaint vignettes of Abraham and Isaac and Daniel in the lions' den, as well as fine patterned work based on Roman originals.

A fortunate find near Toledo in 1859 means that we know a good deal about Visigothic metalwork. The hoard of Guarrazar, now in the Museo Arqueológico Nacional in Madrid, contains sacred jewellery, possibly from Toledo cathedral itself. Among the crosses and liturgical pieces were two votive crowns, offered by the Visigothic kings at a shrine. One of these survives; it was probably given to the shrine of St Felix by king Recceswinth, founder of San Juan de Baños. It is a golden circlet, made in two halves, with an inner and outer plate; the outer plate is pierced and set with sapphires and pearls, while below, as in a chandelier, are suspended the letters of the king's name, each with a pendant of a square stone, a pearl and a rock crystal.

The hoard at Guarrazar was almost certainly buried in anticipation of disaster, the disaster which overwhelmed the Visigothic kingdom in 710–18, when in the course of a civil war the Moslem armies which had swept across north Africa in the preceding decades were invited to cross the straits. As with the Saxons in England, they were expected to take their booty and depart; but, having defeated king Roderick at Guadaletz in the far south, they invited their fellow-religionists to join them and rapidly swept through Spain. Only in the Cantabrian mountains on the north coast did a few Christians, under the leadership of a certain Pelayo, hold out; their fastness was secure enough to enable them to beat off Moslem attacks. The majority of Christians in the peninsula settled down under Moslem rule, paying a special tax but otherwise free to practise their religion and becoming 'almost Arabs', Mozarabs. But the handful of Visigoths in the north held out, creating the kingdom of Asturias. Under Alfonso I, Pelayo's successor, the counter-offensive was begun, taking advantage of quarrels among the Arab invaders, and by the end of the long reign of his successor Alfonso I I the Asturian kingdom extended all along the north coast, from Santander to the mountains of Galicia, and well into the plateau of central Spain. Alfonso I I's reign marked the high point of the kingdom based on Oviedo; it was in his time that the tomb of St James at Compostela was discovered; and his ambassadors forged a close alliance with Charlemagne despite opposition from his nobles. But what had taken seven years to lose was to take seven centuries to regain.

Because the capital of Christian Spain was moved southwards as the reconquest proceeded, the royal buildings at Oviedo erected by Alfonso I I after he moved the capital there in the 790s were never swept away in the interests of later fashion by his successors. Asturian art is a development of the Visigothic style of the seventh century, but because there were no great examples of the latter in the new kingdom, it is also based on early Hispano-Roman architecture, together with some influences from Charlemagne's realms: once again, Spain offers a distinctive and eclectic style. In the centre of **Oviedo**, despite the devastation of the civil war, the church of San Tirso and the Cámara Santa (the cathedral treasury) survive, much-restored; on the outskirts, the enchanting palace-church of Santa María de Naranco and the apse of San Miguel de Lillo bear witness to the taste of Alfonso's successor, Ramiro I. The Cámara Santa was originally part of the palace built for Alfonso II by the architect Tiuda, but its exact function remains unclear: it may have been a martyrium, or martyr's chapel, in honour of St Leocadia, to whom the crypt is dedicated, or it may simply have been the palace chapel. It now contains a brilliant collection of medieval jewellery, the accumulated treasures of the cathedral. The most spectacular pieces are the earliest ones, which re-create the splendours of this small kingdom in a way that the traces of elaborate but faded frescoes of San Julián de los Prados (to the north of the town) cannot do. But it is worth remembering, here as elsewhere, that the survival of jewellery and architecture of high quality should be set against the lost riches of paintings and embroideries. A delightful legend tells how Alfonso II entrusted the precious materials for the 'cross of the Angels' to two passing pilgrims who offered their services as jewellers, and how they were angels in disguise, who vanished, leaving behind the finished cross. It seems that the true origin of the cross is north Italy; its exquisite filigree work, finely balanced settings and elegant proportions are close to Lombard work, but have no real parallels in Visigothic art. The much larger 'cross of Victory' bears an inscription telling us that it was made at the castle of Ganzon and presented to the cathedral by Alfonso III in 908. It relies for its effect on a totally different technique, that of cloisonné enamel. Studded with a variety of precious stones, it is grander and more elaborate, but less refined, than the cross of the Angels. Two years later, the cathedral was given a reliquary coffer, perhaps by two nobles; this seems to have been made locally, but incorporates on the top an enamel plaque which may well be from Charlemagne's imperial workshop.

On the edge of Oviedo, on a site which recalls – or rather foreshadows – that of Monreale in relation to Palermo, Ramiro I built a palace and two churches on the slopes of mount Naranco. Two buildings survive: and there has long been doubt as to what one of them is. San Miguel de Lillo is clearly a church; but what is the other, now known as Santa María de Naranco? The most recent opinion seems to prefer a palace, though it has been argued that it is a kind of ceremonial royal church. It may even have been both, a ceremonial hall with a chapel in the crypt. It had certainly become a church by the twelfth century. We know that there were villas here in Roman times, and the exquisite building at Naranco seems to me to be their latter-day successor. It faces exactly south, with a cool and lofty central hall on the first floor approached by a double staircase; at either end are colonnades which make perfect belvederes, commanding the whole valley in which Oviedo lies and the high mountains beyond. Nothing quite like it survives anywhere else in Europe; its appeal lies in the combination of a small scale with a grand design. It is unmistakably a building fit for a prince, beautifully decorated and the work of a highly skilled architect; and yet it remains intimate, a place surely for relaxation rather than ceremonial. The central hall, with its stone vault, was a prodigy in its time: two chroniclers note that no wood was used in its construction. Again, it would be a perfect retreat in summer, away from the heat of the valley. There are no religious motifs among the carvings; instead the rosettes contain strange beasts in interlacing patterns which are a more sophisticated version of the patternwork we have seen on earlier Visigothic buildings, and other reliefs show secular figures and armed horsemen. The only religious element is the altar, bearing an inscription describing the restoration of the building in which it was placed; but bearing in mind that one of the early chroniclers speaks of a palace and *two* churches here, it could easily have come from the lost church.

San Miguel de Lillo, a few hundred yards away, is nowhere near complete: about one third of this very complex church remains, a building on the grand scale appropriate to a palace complex. The central portion and the whole of the sanctuary have gone, leaving only the west end. The west door is flanked by two stone plaques whose designs are based on a Roman ivory of the early sixth century; other carvings preserved in the local archaeological museum are clearly religious, which reinforces the argument that Santa María de Naranco was originally secular. Inside, two flanking stairways lead up to a tribune gallery, a typically Carolingian arrangement found in other Spanish churches of this period. On the outside, only the superb tracery of the windows remains to remind us of former splendours, work which shows a command of geometry which even the greatest Gothic architects might have envied. These miniature rose-windows with their delicate colonnades were obviously exceptional pieces – there is no sign of them at the elegant and sophisticated little chapel at Santa Cristina de Lena, twenty-five miles south of Oviedo, which survives intact, with a tribune and a raised sanctuary to the east, marked off by an arcaded screen.

In the early tenth century, the sons of Alfonso III divided the little kingdom between them, creating separate states in León, Asturias and Galicia; but the king of Galicia soon reunited it with León, and made his capital at the city of that name in 914. Meanwhile, the counts of Castile, whose power was based on Burgos, rebelled against the kings of León; but when Castile did emerge as a kingdom in 1035, its ruler was the son of the king of neighbouring Navarre. In 1037 Ferdinand I conquered León and Galicia, and from then onwards the initiative lay with Castile; León retained a purely nominal separate existence until 1230. As at Oviedo, the century or so of León's apogee has left remarkable monuments, preserved because the capital moved to Toledo in 1085. At **San Miguel de la Escalada,** east of León, is one of the finest Mozarab churches of Spain, rebuilt in 913 by the local abbot, who had come from Córdoba. It uses the traditional basilica plan, but the horseshoe arches give it a totally different atmosphere, and the three horseshoe-shaped apses cut out of a rectangular east end have nothing to do with the classical pattern. If this seems a highly individual building compared with early Romanesque elsewhere, it is only because other examples are scattered throughout Spain, many in remote places; it is in fact, apart from the east end, a typical if very refined example of its kind.

At **León** itself, Ferdinand I, persuaded by queen Sancha, chose the church of St John the Baptist as his burial place. It was rededicated to St Isidore when, in 1063, the body of the famous writer was brought here from Seville. The present church of St Isidore is a much restored twelfth-century building; but the burial place of the kings of León and Castile, the so-called Pantheon, is in the earliest part, which forms a kind of narthex or western porch. It dates from the time of Ferdinand I, but its most striking feature is the remarkable series of frescoes on the ceiling executed in the reign of Ferdinand II (1157–80); sheltered from the light in this cool dark space, they retain much of their original freshness, and are the finest and most extended cycle of the period to have survived. Working on a prepared white background, the artist employs simple colours, and gold is reserved for Christ's halo. The other colours are mostly derived from natural sources, though some azure may have been used, now appearing as grey-blue. The major biblical scenes owe something to Byzantine art; they are all taken from the gospels and the Apocalypse, and include a bold Annunciation and Last Supper. At the foot of the Crucifixion, one of the few parts which have deteriorated, appear the figures of the king and queen. The central vault has a powerful Christ in Majesty in a mandorla surrounded by the evangelists, shown in Visigothic fashion as men with the heads of their symbolic animals. In contrast to the usual regularity of Romanesque art, the surrounding border is daringly freehand, almost abstract. The most engaging scenes, however, are the Annunciation to the Shepherds, which the artist uses as an excuse to take us into the countryside of León: shepherds and goatherds play pan-pipes and blow horns, or feed their dogs from wooden dishes, while the sheep follow a belled ram, the goats browse on young saplings, and the pigs appear to catch falling acorns in mid-air!

All this is rendered in a free and confident style, whose simplicity hides considerable talent and sophistication. On the inside of one of the arches is an early example of the 'labours of the months', in which the tasks appropriate to each month form a series of vignettes; here the formal framework produces a more conventional result, though the pictures of February, huddled in his cloak before the fire, and December, cheerfully feasting on the fruits of his toil, stand out. We know nothing of the artist, who, although he was clearly in touch with the mainstream of twelfth-century painting, seems to have been a native of León. By this time, the pilgrimage to Santiago was well established, and it may be that this is another example of the influence of the movement of pilgrims on the art of Spain and France.

During the century between the building of the Pantheon and the completion of the paintings, the fortunes of the *reconquista* had ebbed and flowed dramatically. By 1082, Alfonso VI had raided as far as the south coast, but a new Moslem army from Africa drove the Christians back to Toledo and threatened to push them even further north. In the 1090s Ruy Díaz de Bivar, better known as 'the Cid' (from his Arabic title 'el Sidi') carved out a lordship for himself by conquering the Arab kingdom of Valencia. His principality vanished on his death, but his deeds were commemorated in the great *Poema del Mio Cid*, and as recently as 1942 his body was reburied under the crossing in Burgos cathedral as a mark of honour. To the west, Alfonso's grandson created the kingdom of Portugal, while the old French territories in the northeast became by 1162 the kingdom of Aragon, centred on Barcelona and Saragossa. A renewed offensive by the kings of Castile at the end of the twelfth century led by Alfonso VIII resulted first in a disastrous defeat at Alarcos in 1195, and then triumphant victory at Las Navas de Tolosa in 1212. Córdoba and Seville were captured by Ferdinand III in 1236 and 1248 respectively, and only his death in 1252 saved the last Moslem kingdom, based on Granada, from extinction. This time, the Moslems did not mount a counter-attack, but the fourteenth and fifteenth centuries were largely taken up by the endless dynastic quarrels of the Christian kingdoms and it was to take another two and a half centuries to drive the Moslems from the peninsula.

Throughout the reconquest, Castile had taken the lead; and the kings of Castile continued to look to Burgos as their home, even though Toledo was the capital of the combined kingdom of León and Castile. Alfonso VIII founded a convent just outside Burgos, at **Las Huelgas**, and it is here that the Castilian kings are buried. Built in the style of the great Cistercian houses, many of the abbesses were of royal blood. It was here that the kings of Castile, from Ferdinand III in 1219 to Juan I in 1379, were knighted; in the fourteenth century an articulated statue of St James was used to perform the dubbing ceremony, and this can still be seen in a chapel with an ornate Moorish wooden roof in the convent garden. The tombs of the royal family are in the convent church, those of Alfonso VIII and his wife Eleanor of England, Henry II's daughter, being in the central nave. The real riches of Las Huelgas are kept in the rooms off the cloister. The chapter hall contains a spectacular Moslem standard captured by Alfonso VIII at the battle of Las Navas de Tolosa in 1212, woven in gold, blue and green thread on a scarlet base, with the intricate patterns and inscriptions from the Koran typical of Moslem textiles. It has the confident splendour of a faith whose lands stretched from Iraq across north Africa, whose armies had just driven the Christians out of Jerusalem. Its state of preservation is remarkable; but there is something about the air of Las Huelgas which favours textiles, for, a few rooms further along, there is displayed the most astonishing collection of thirteenth- and fourteenth-century royal robes, found in the royal tombs. We can see the extraordinary rich shroud brocades and cloths of Eleanor of England; the heraldic tunic of Fernando de la Cerda (the oldest son of Alfonso X, who died in 1275), patterned with the arms of León and Castile, and his beret, studded with pearls forming heraldic patterns; and a brilliant blue, gold and red cloth which was the shroud of one of the first patrons of the monastery, who died in 1196. Once again, we are reminded how much is missing from our conception of medieval life, and how the colour and spectacle are the hardest elements to recapture when it is the grey bones of architecture which are our commonest experience of medieval art and life.

The skill in textiles displayed at Las Huelgas was due in great part to Arab weavers of silks and fine cloths; and it is time to look briefly at the Moslem civilization of southern Spain and its interplay with Christian Spain. For all the warfare between the two religions, the crusades and military orders, there were also long periods of peace and trade: scholars went to and fro, though the artistic and intellectual debt was almost always from the Christian side to the Moslem artists and philosophers, and to the flourishing Jewish intellectual life throughout Spain, to which the synagogue built by Samuel Halevi at **Toledo** in the mid fourteenth century bears witness. The interior is a masterpiece of Moorish woodwork, transforming a plain, square building into a glowing casket with shimmering surfaces; the windows have nets of finest tracery and rest on Moorish polylobe arches and alabaster columns. The synagogue survived because it became a church on the tragic expulsion of the Jews in the wake of Christianity's triumph over the Moslems at the end of the fifteenth century. At **Córdoba** we find the same process applied to a Moslem holy place. The Great Mosque, begun by Abdu'r-Rahman in 786 and enlarged by his successors up to 987, was one of the wonders of the Moslem world, with its vistas of endless arches, one tier above the other to give additional height, and the dazzling white marble and the maksourah or caliph's enclosure with its mosaic-encrusted domes. In the midst of this forest of Arab arches rises the Christian cathedral, built in the sixteenth century; although the mosque became a church in the thirteenth century, it was only after 1492 that substantial changes were felt to be necessary. Even then, the emperor Charles V is said to have protested that the canons of the cathedral had destroyed a masterpiece in order to create something ordinary. For the mosque at Córdoba is technically and artistically unique; it contains solutions to the problems of vaulting which lie at the basis of Gothic architecture, and its decorative stonework is unsurpassed, for instance in the smaller outer doorways with their patterns of contrasting red, green and white, interlaced arcades and surface ornaments that look like designs for a rich brocade. When the mosque was built, Córdoba was one of the greatest cities in the world, with half a million inhabitants, capital of the caliphate of the west and ranking only after Baghdad and Constantinople. It boasted seven hundred mosques and three hundred public baths, and a huge royal palace above the town at al-Zahrā, whose ruins have recently been excavated and restored.

Córdoba's years of greatness came to an end long before it fell into Christian hands, and in the twelfth century **Seville** predominated. As a great port and former capital of Spain, it had always been a rival of its western, landlocked neighbour; and while Córdoba remained a provincial city, Seville was a dynamic centre of trade until the Guadalquivir silted up in the eighteenth century. As a result, little of Arab origin remains; but on the site of the old pleasure palace of the Moorish kings, Peter the Cruel built a new Alcázar, using Moorish craftsmen, whose lofty rooms are decorated with ornamental woodwork and carved stucco. It is at **Granada**, the much smaller city on the foothills of the Sierra Nevada, the last stronghold of the Moorish kings, that we come face to face with Moorish art at its best. The sultans of Granada were never powerful or even secure on their throne – many were deposed only to regain the throne, and one of them even reigned for three separate periods – and in one sense their architecture reflects their precarious hold on power. They built in flimsy materials, rubble and poorly laid brick; all that mattered was the brilliant surface, the impact of the moment. Decoration is everything in the art of Granada, because of the observance of the Moslem ban on portrayal of the human figure. Much of it is carried out in stucco, which yields spectacular results with far less labour than stone or wood. In the courts of the Alhambra, which occupies a fortress-like position but is otherwise as unlike the lowering castles of northern Europe as possible, the atmosphere is that of an immensely wealthy but languid civilization, escaping the sweltering heat of the Andalusian summer in shaded pavilions overlooking pools and fountains. Patterns shift and repeat themselves like a kaleidoscope, patterns of light and shade, of sparkling water, of walls like carpets, of ceilings like frozen cascades. There is no feeling of purpose, hardly even a feeling of grandeur or opulence: beauty is everything, whether in a geometric interlace or in a jet from a fountain. Beside the Alhambra, the gardens of the Generalife preserve something of their Moorish aspect, with terraced water-gardens and little pavilions. Only the quarrels of the Christian kings kept Moslem Granada in being. When at last Ferdinand, the husband of Isabella, queen of Castile in her own right, inherited Aragon in 1479, Christian Spain was united and the Spanish nation was born. Granada's days were numbered; but none the less, it took ten years to reduce the Moslem state, and Granada itself held out against a long siege, in which the military orders fought with their old vigour after a long period of decay, and the Spanish war-cry of 'Santiago!' was heard for the last time against the infidel on Spanish soil.

With the 'Catholic kings', we leave the medieval world. The end of the *reconquista* coincides with Columbus's landfall in the West Indies, and a new vision of the world and of Spain's part in it. The Moorish and Jewish inheritance of medieval Spain was rejected; both Jews and Moslems were expelled or forcibly converted, and Spain, once the gateway to the eastern world and its intellectual life, became the champion of a reactionary, introverted church, closed to all ideas and influences which were not impeccably orthodox.

England and France

Spain and Germany became 'nations' in the modern sense of the word only at the very end of the Middle Ages; and in Germany and Italy political unity was not achieved until the nineteenth century. In England and France, however, political unity and the idea of nationhood as a political term were much more closely linked. After 1204, when they lost their lands in northern France, the English kings were much less involved in affairs in France, though their claims to be the greatest single vassal of the French king were only dormant, and they still held extensive territories in south-west France, ruled from Bordeaux. Henry II and Louis VII had seen themselves as personal rulers: a kingdom was different from a dukedom only in that a king owed homage to no one and was answerable to no higher court, despite the pope's claims to judge all earthly rulers. But during the thirteenth century, partly as a result of Henry II's administrative work, kingship acquired a new status as an institution: it became monarchy, where the king was at the head both of a pyramid of feudal ties and also of a political and administrative structure quite independent of the feudal system. At the same time, the concept of the king's role as a sacred office was strongly emphasized: instead of the elected monarchy of the Holy Roman Empire, where consecration as emperor lay in the pope's hands, the monarchy in England and France was hereditary, and consecration became automatic, enshrined in the increasingly elaborate rituals of coronation which reached their most complex development by the end of the thirteenth century; that drawn up for Edward I I in 1307 was to be the model for all future English coronations. An indication of the strength of the new administrative organization with a hereditary ruler at its head is the fact that both the English and the French thrones were occupied by minors in the early thirteenth century. Henry I I I came to the throne aged nine in 1216, and Louis I X became king of France at the same age in 1223. At the same time, the titles of the English and French kings changed: Henry I I I was the first English king to have the title 'king of England' on his great seal instead of 'king of the English', and Louis I X's title in contemporary records changes likewise from 'king of the French' to 'king of France'.

Both Henry I I I and Louis actively promoted the idea of hereditary monarchy as an institution which was more than the leadership of a group of great barons. Henry I I I, in so doing, was unfortunate in that he was faced by a determined opposition who saw his proper role as precisely the latter, and tried to limit his power; but when Louis I X was asked to arbitrate between Henry and his opponents at Amiens in 1264, he roundly declared in his settlement that the king of England was to 'have full power and unrestricted rule within his kingdom', clearly agreeing with Henry's view of the matter. Both kings erected royal pantheons, in Westminster Abbey and the abbey of Saint-Denis, and it is here that we can see the image of thirteenth-century monarchy most clearly. Both were in a sense national shrines, the place where the sacred and the secular government came together to celebrate the monarchy.

The abbey of **Saint-Denis** now lies in an unattractive northern quarter of Paris. Once it stood outside the city walls, just as Westminster Abbey was outside the City of London. St Denis, the apostle and first bishop of Paris, was said to have been buried after his martyrdom in c.250 in a Gallo-Roman cemetery on the site;

the monastery later erected in his memory was patronized by the last great king of the Merovingian dynasty, Dagobert, during his brief reign of ten years from 629. The new Carolingian dynasty in the eighth century continued this patronage, and, like Dagobert, chose Saint-Denis as their burial place, but with the massive expansion of the empire under Charlemagne and his preference for Aachen, Saint-Denis was temporarily eclipsed. It was not until the accession of the Capetians that Saint-Denis became the accepted royal burial place: after 996, only three kings were ever buried elsewhere.

The monks of Saint-Denis were in close touch with the royal court, and during the fourteenth century acted as the official chroniclers to the monarchy, compiling the *Grandes chroniques de France* under the auspices of Charles V. They were the guardians of the royal regalia and of the sacred banner of France, the *oriflamme*, the great scarlet flag which in peacetime hung over the tomb of St Denis. It was first used by Louis VI in 1124, and its last appearance was at Agincourt in 1415. Medieval writers claimed that when it was unfurled it was a sign that no quarter was to be shown. The war-cry of France was also derived from the abbey: in the fourteenth century it was *'Montejoie, Saint Denis!'*

For their part, the kings of France encouraged and rewarded this devotion to their dynasty with wide grants of lands and revenues. Indeed, ambitious monks in the thirteenth century forged a charter to prove that Charlemagne had given the kingdom of France itself to Saint-Denis as a fief, and the king himself was the abbey's vassal. But even St Louis's generosity did not go this far: his most enduring contribution to the abbey was the commemoration of his ancestors. The royal tombs had been placed at random throughout the abbey, with a group before the altar of the Trinity. St Louis commissioned a series of effigies and new tombs to be placed below the rebuilt crossing of the church; the kings and queens are all portrayed in thirteenth-century clothing, including St Louis himself. Even though his arrangement of the tombs was soon disrupted, and at the Revolution two of the effigies were destroyed, fourteen still survive, replaced under the crossing. They are a remarkable witness to the medieval idea of a royal dynasty and to the awakening of a royalist nationalism in France which was to survive the disasters of the fourteenth century.

Of the other medieval effigies, the most striking are André

Beauneveu's masterly portrait of Charles V, the figure of Bertrand du Guesclin, and Pierre de Thoiry's effigies of Charles VI and Isabella of Bavaria. Beauneveu's likeness of Charles V brings out the practical and austere nature of the man who rebuilt the kingdom after the debacle at Poitiers in 1356 and the wild years of the peasant rebellion known as the *jacquerie*, while his great commander, du Guesclin, youngest son of a poor Breton knight, is portrayed with the utmost realism. The same realistic vein recurs in the effigy of Charles VI, whose madness plunged France once again into chaos: the sculptor is clearly trying to present a favourable image, but the result none the less hints strongly at a disturbed mind.

The church itself has been rebuilt many times since St Genevieve's first edifice on the site in the fifth century. Yet the bulk of the surviving architecture represents the work of two men: abbot Suger and Pierre de Montreuil. As one enters the church, the immediate impression is that the entire building is a unity, in High Gothic style of the thirteenth century. In fact, substantial portions of the twelfth-century fabric of abbot Suger's day survive. The façade and west porch date from this period, but have suffered so severely over the centuries as to be almost unrecognizable as Romanesque. At the east end, the lower storey of the apse, one of the earliest examples of the new Gothic style, is from Suger's period.

In Christopher Brooke's words, 'Suger was a monk, an administrator, a royal minister, a notable author and a great patron of artists and architects. The combination is at once unique and characteristic of the age.' Indeed, 'royal minister' is an understatement, for Suger was effectively regent of France in 1145–7 while Louis VII was on the Second Crusade; it was he who laid the foundations of the French royal administration and consistently acted as chief adviser until he died in 1151. Suger's own account of the rebuilding of the abbey is a vivid glimpse of the problems involved in an ambitious project of this kind. Faced with a crumbling church whose fabric had to stand up to hordes of pilgrims to the shrine of St Denis, he had to find his own sources of stone and timber; but merely to reconstruct was not enough, and what Suger created was the first Gothic church. He claimed to have desired above all to harmonize old and new work, but after the construction of the west end he seems to have turned to a new architect for the choir, an architect whose designs included the earliest known Gothic vaulting, supported by slender pillars which give the effect of space and light for which Suger strove. His new church was to be full of light, but not the austere white light of the Cistercians: Suger sought light coloured by stained glass, reflected from precious stones or sparkling from golden vessels. Some of the church furnishings survive, adapted from antique treasures: a porphyry vase mounted on an eagle, a water-jug and another vase in the Louvre, a chalice of sardonyx in the National Gallery at Washington and a copy of the base of Suger's great cross in the museum at Saint-Omer. He himself appears as donor in a stained-glass window in the central chapel of the choir, a window made to his order between 1140 and 1144 and thus among the earliest stained glass to survive, ranking with that of Chartres. Sadly only fifteen panels of the original series, which included a depiction of the First Crusade, have survived.

Pierre de Montreuil's rebuilding of the upper part of the choir, the crossing and the nave is entirely in the spirit of Suger's original concept of light and space, albeit in the fully developed Gothic idiom. The large dimensions of the transept were specifically designed to contain the royal tombs, but the nave, too, is generous in scale, lit at all three levels instead of allowing all the light to come from the clerestory, as in Romanesque designs. This gives the nave a unity which, with the quality of the details and refinements such as the gradual increase in the size of the pillars towards the choir, make the late-Gothic work at Saint-Denis a masterpiece in its own right. But it is the presence of the royal tombs and the inheritance of abbot Suger that makes Saint-Denis what it is – a monument to one of the outstanding figures of the Middle Ages and a focal point for the cult of the French monarchy.

Saint-Denis, which so narrowly escaped destruction in the French revolution and was extensively restored and tidied up in the mid nineteenth century, is in sharp contrast to **Westminster Abbey**. At Saint-Denis the royal effigies are in neatly ordered rows and there are a mere handful of other memorials: the architecture predominates. Westminster Abbey, despite the Reformation, has in many ways a more continuous history than almost any other major European church, in that it has been the national shrine for nine hundred years and the memorials of succeeding generations have accumulated without interruption. The eighteenth century, which is rarely in evidence in other medieval churches except as a time of decay and neglect, crowded Westminster Abbey with a host of commemorative effigies, which, fine as they may be individually, are as unpleasing to the eye *en masse* as the excesses of a French provincial cemetery; nor is the atmosphere improved by the arrangements made – necessarily – for the throngs of tourists who visit the abbey each year. Yet the patient and persistent visitor can get glimpses of what its original builders intended, and how it developed up to the Reformation.

The original church at Westminster was founded at an uncertain date in the Saxon period, and we know almost nothing about it except that there was a monastery of some substance at Westminster when Edward the Confessor set about rebuilding the church in the decade after 1040. Edward's motives for doing so are also obscure; according to one account, when his magnates refused to let him go on pilgrimage to Rome, he expiated the vow he had already made by refounding a monastery dedicated to St Peter, while another version ascribes it to his intention to be buried there and implies that a close link already existed between the crown and Westminster. Edward's church was an avant-garde example of Romanesque design based on that found in England and Normandy at the period but unlike anything else in England at the time. It had twin west towers as an integral part of the building, a long nave leading to a central tower over the crossing, with short transepts and a small apse and ambulatory. Of this church, traces have been found during excavation; parts of the monastic buildings of the same date still survive, notably of the refectory and dormitory. A stylized representation of the abbey as it was in 1066 can be seen on the Bayeux Tapestry.

Henry III rivalled, indeed excelled, his contemporary St Louis in piety; he was said to hear mass up to five times a day, and he seems to have had a special devotion to Edward the Confessor, who had been canonized in 1163. The miracles wrought at St Edward's shrine had made it one of the major pilgrimage places in England, and Henry's new church centred on a single royal figure rather than a dynasty. Where St Louis had commissioned a series of effigies of his predecessors, Henry III rebuilt the shrine of St Edward and placed it to the east of the high altar, where throngs of pilgrims could more easily be accommodated on feast days. A number of other features – the provision of a large sacristy where robes and treasures could be kept, the adaptation of the undercroft of the chapter house as a royal treasure vault – were determined by the abbey's special status. Henry III's architect, Henry of Reynes, was an Englishman with considerable knowledge of French Gothic; the style is an international one, with the exceptionally high, narrow nave of the period, and original handling of some of the details. No expense was spared on the work: the piers of the nave are of Purbeck marble, while before the high altar is a mosaic pavement of *opus alexandrinum*, executed by a master craftsman from Rome named Oderic in 1268. But Henry was unable to complete the work despite the huge sums lavished on it, and when he died in 1272 the rebuilding was abandoned; the west end of the Norman nave survived until about 1388. In the last years of Richard II's reign, the lower part of the west end was built, and despite a brief spell of activity under Henry V the nave was only completed and paved just before the Reformation. The towers were built between 1725 and 1745.

Meanwhile, the existing fabric of Henry III's abbey underwent complete changes, mostly to do with the building's now accepted role as royal mausoleum. Of the kings of England from 1272 until the Reformation, only Edward II, Henry IV, Henry VI and Edward IV are buried elsewhere: Richard III's grave at Leicester was destroyed at the Reformation. In fact, the tombs in Westminster Abbey commemorate above all the later Plantagenets and the Tudors. The Plantagenet tombs are tightly grouped around the shrine of Edward the Confessor, which, together with the Coronation chair of Edward I, was the great symbol of the English monarchy. The seven bays behind the altar between St Edward's chapel and the ambulatory are each occupied by a king or queen. Henry III lies under a bronze effigy portraying him as a young man, in a tomb of porphyry brought by Edward I from the east as he returned home on learning of his father's death. Edward's own tomb is of plain black stone; it bears the inscription '*Pactum serva*', 'Keep the agreement', which is said to be a reminder that the king's body was, according to his last wishes, to be carried in front of the English army until Scotland was conquered. Less romantic historians have ascribed it to Edward II's meanness; but Edward probably intended it as a reminder to his son and the English nobles that they had sworn in 1306, a year before his death, to reconquer Scotland. By contrast, the tomb of his grandson, Edward III, carries one of the greatest of all medieval effigies, a striking if conventional portrait, perhaps by Jean de Liège, which captures the aura of grandeur associated with the king. The effigy of Richard II, made by two London craftsmen, is more realistic, and perhaps artistically the finer achievement; originally his effigy and that of his beloved Anne of Bohemia were shown with right hands clasped. The tomb was ordered before Richard's death, in 1394–6, a practice which was not uncommon at the time; it cost no less than £933 6s 8d. Richard's body was brought from Pontefract to Westminster only in 1413, fourteen years after his death: Henry V, who was responsible for this reburial, was so anxious to be buried in St Edward's chapel that he remodelled the whole of the east end of it, taking down the great reliquary cupboard that closed the eastern bay and building a chantry chapel above the vacant space. His tomb, with a plain wooden effigy, lies beneath the chantry chapel: the effigy was once silver plated, but was long ago stripped of its covering. An ornate grille closes the entrance to the chapel made by Henry V.

When Henry VII came to choose his burial place, there was no longer a suitable position in the chapel behind the altar. With typically Renaissance grandeur, his solution was to build a Lady Chapel yet further to the east, beyond the already complex arrangements of the existing east end. Its astonishing fan vault, richly carved stalls and elaborate fittings contrast sharply with the severe nave of the original building; yet what we see today is as nothing compared with the chapel in its heyday, filled with images, metalwork and rich fabrics, as well as the richest stained glass obtainable, 'painted, garnished and adorned in as goodly and rich a manner as such a work requireth and as to a king's work apperteineth'. The careful planning of the tombs and altars, however, which included a tomb for Henry VI at the far end of the chapel behind the altar, was disrupted by Henry VIII, who failed to complete Henry VI's tomb and chantry, altered the site of the great bronze grille surrounding his father's tomb and inserted a classical altar instead of a Gothic one. The bronze grate and the effigies by Torrigiano of Henry VII, his wife and (in the north chapel) his mother Lady Margaret Beaufort all mark the end of medieval art and the beginning of the Renaissance, as does the emphasis on princely magnificence. Even the vault, Gothic in origin, is drawn into this display; its marvels – 'the most wonderful work of masonry ever put together by the hand of man' – seem dedicated less to the glory of God than to a demonstration of human skill.

The very diversity and richness of the monuments and chapels of Westminster Abbey, and the contrast with the unsatisfying effect of the building as a whole, show how easily great architecture and the requirements of everyday religious use can be at cross-purposes, and remind us how often we see medieval churches through the eyes of nineteenth-century restorers and rearrangers. Many great churches at the end of the Middle Ages would have resembled Westminster Abbey with its clutter of chapels and tombs, haphazard layout and general accretions of time, accretions which have only survived because of Westminster's continuing function as a royal mausoleum until the eighteenth century.

Pantheons such as Saint-Denis and Westminster Abbey reminded men of the glorious past of the English and French royal houses. Their present power was reflected in their palaces, that of Louis IX on the Île de la Cité in Paris and Henry III's palace at Westminster. The palace of St Louis has largely vanished; we can see its towers and spires in one of the most famous illuminated manuscripts of the fifteenth century, the *Très Riches Heures* which belonged to the duc de Berry.

In the calendar, June is represented by reapers in the fields on the banks of the Seine, with the Île de la Cité in the background. At one end is a water-gate, and it is surrounded by ramparts; but the buildings within are decorated with pinnacles rather than fortifications. Little of this delightful group remains; the **Sainte-Chapelle** is now overshadowed by the surrounding law-courts, grim modern replacements for the medieval royal courts within the palace, and the buildings to the north still have a largely medieval façade overlooking the Seine, including three restored towers, one of which has a clock dating from 1370. Inside the palace, now known as the Conciergerie, one huge guards' hall built in the early fourteenth century survives as the base for more recent rooms above.

Much of the palace already existed in Louis's day, and the Sainte-Chapelle was his great addition, memorial to that piety which eventually led to his canonization in 1297. The Sainte-Chapelle was built in 1241/3–48, to house the Crown of Thorns with which our Lord was crowned before his crucifixion. This relic is first mentioned in 409 by Paulinus of Nola, the Roman consul from Bordeaux who became a Christian and later a parish priest in Spain; it was venerated for centuries in Jerusalem, but was taken to

Constantinople in the eleventh century. Baldwin, the Latin emperor of Constantinople, visited France in 1237, and Louis began negotiations to buy the crown from him; even though Baldwin was anxious to gain Louis's support, the negotiations, through Venetian intermediaries, took two years, and it was two years before his envoys brought it back in triumph, having paid the enormous sum of 13,500 livres for it. The Sainte-Chapelle is conceived as a vast reliquary for this precious object. Externally, it has very much the shape of a chest for relics such as can be seen at Aachen or Cologne, though the proportions are heightened to meet the requirements of Gothic architecture.

The interior is a single, unified space, whose focal point is the canopied altar. The brilliant glass, depicting scenes from the Old Testament, is the equivalent of the enamels on a relic-chest; as at other shrines, the glass includes the expected Old and New Testament picture-cycles, but that of the first bay of the nave on the right has episodes showing the history of the precious object, culminating in its display before the king and queen. The nineteenth-century restoration of the sculpture and painting, although accurate in many ways, has a slightly dead feeling about it. But it is the architecture and glass which is the Sainte-Chapelle's chief glory: everything is subordinated to the creation of a perfect, richly decorated vaulted space. The glass in particular has survived almost intact, a complete 'programme' almost without parallel. It reflects the mixture of wealth and piety, public activity and private devotion which comes across so clearly in the earliest biography of St Louis, by his friend and confidant Jean Joinville. Louis well knew that kings could not afford to behave like St Francis, and must maintain a regal presence. Almost puritan in his attitude towards the common diversions of courtiers, disliking minstrels and banning dice from the court, he none the less wore rich robes and a cape of peacock's feathers. The 'rich robe' of the Sainte-Chapelle is another aspect of this royal magnificence, one which impressed Henry III so much that he is said to have wished he could load it on a cart and wheel it away.

Of Henry III's rival palace at **Westminster**, almost nothing remains save the crypt of St Stephen's, a few fragments of the fourteenth-century decoration now in the British Museum, and the great hall built by William Rufus and rebuilt in Richard II's reign between 1394 and 1399. The original hall was clearly an unimpressive place; William Rufus, on seeing it completed, is said to have commented that it was only fit to be the kitchen of the hall he had wanted to build. The hall was redesigned by Henry Yevele, and new walls and façade were built on the original foundations; the massive hammerbeam oak roof, spanning nearly seventy feet, was constructed by the king's carpenter, Hugh Herland. Ironically, this very hall was to be the scene of Richard II's formal deposition in 1399, just as it had been the scene of Edward II's abdication in 1327. Its chief use was as a law-court: no less than three courts sat here, the Courts of Common Pleas, of Chancery and of the King's Bench.

The theme of princely magnificence, already noted in the Lady Chapel at Westminster Abbey, is best seen in England in other religious works from the very end of the Middle Ages, such as King's College Chapel at Cambridge, in the same form as the Sainte-Chapelle, but exuberant in its decoration where the latter is restrained, its fan-vaulting appearing to defy gravity. St George's Chapel, Windsor, rebuilt by Edward IV as part of his renewal of the Order of the Garter, is another masterpiece resulting from royal patronage, a fitting monument to the greatest of all royal orders of chivalry.

Royal power, for all its splendour, did not go unchallenged in the fourteenth and fifteenth century. A king could be faced with rival claimants to the throne, or with vassals who had grown over-mighty. Both played their part in the shaping of the English and French nations, above all in the long-drawn-out struggle we call the Hundred Years' War. In 1328 Edward III found himself in the position of being both an over-mighty vassal of, and claimant to, the throne of France. His claim, as a nephew of Charles V through his mother, was in many ways better than that of Philip VI, the late king's first cousin. But practical considerations enabled Philip to gain the throne, and little was said of Edward's claim until a renewed dispute arose over Gascony. The resulting wars underlined the differences between the two kingdoms, which until then had formed a cultural unity, speaking the same languages and sharing many similarities of outlook: in the thirteenth century the best English scholars had gone to the university at Paris, and many French abbeys had estates in England. But by the end of the fourteenth century the English universities had largely replaced those of Paris. English was increasingly the language of the court, if not of the highest nobility, and the old religious links had been broken by the seizure of alien estates. The court culture of Edward III and the Black Prince was essentially French and chivalric, with its enthusiasm for Arthurian romance (also mainly a French genre), the Order of the Garter, closely paralleled by the ill-fated French Order of the Star, and its patronage of men like Froissart, who moved easily between the courts of Flanders, England and France.

Of all this splendour, there are few material remains: the royal accounts are full of lists of jewels given and received, but little goldsmiths' work of the period escaped melting down in later financial crises. One of the best examples of the kind of object which graced a fourteenth-century royal household is the so-called *Goldenes-Rössl* at Altötting in Bavaria. Originally a New Year's gift from Isabella of Bavaria to her husband Charles VI in 1404, it was given in the fifteenth century to the church at Altötting and therefore survived. It is an elaborate fantasy in which the Virgin and Child, attended by the king's children in the guise of St Catherine, St John the Baptist and St John the Evangelist, sit in a tower of gold foliage studded with pearls and precious stones. At their feet kneel the king and queen, and the royal marshal, bearing the king's tournament helm, while below a page holds the king's impatient horse. It is an outstanding piece, not only for its sumptuousness, but for the lively and tender expressions of the figures and endearing details, such as the lamb which leaps up at St John the Baptist. Related pieces of almost equal splendour are the reliquary of the Order of the Holy Ghost in the Louvre, and the reliquary of the crown of thorns in the British Museum.

Another piece which demonstrates the goldsmiths' skill at this period is the Royal Gold Cup now in the British Museum, commissioned by Jean duc de Berry in the last decades of the fourteenth century. Standing about nine inches high, its shape alone is masterly. The actual metalwork is simple, ornamented only by a chaplet of pearls around the foot and (originally) around the top of the cover, and a row of pearl-centred rosettes on the stem. The foot, cup and cover are enamelled with finely drawn scenes from the life of St Agnes as described in the *Golden Legend*, the great anthology of saints' lives compiled by Jacopo de Voragine. The whole is remarkably well preserved; its bright realistic enamels echo the finest achievements of contemporary French miniaturists.

In terms of pure jewellery, a number of badges, insignia and collars of chivalric orders survive, among them the famous Dunstable Swan jewel of the mid fifteenth century and collars of the orders of the Golden Fleece, and obscurer orders such as the Tress. More elusive and more spectacular is the family jewel of the princes of Hohenlohe, kept at the museum of Schloss Neuenstein, which is a collar of this type, but made to the very highest standards in a style which is related to very late Gothic architecture: eight sapphires, each in a setting of leaves, are linked by naturalistic intertwined branches, and as a pendant there is the mysterious emblem of a fool's head in a rose, the significance of which has never been satisfactorily explained. The piece undoubtedly relates to the Burgundian art of the period (p. 236 below).

For a brief moment in 1420 it seemed as though England and France might be brought together by Henry V into a single realm of great wealth and power. But the differences now ran too deep; the Gascon lords had hated the alien officials of the Black Prince in the 1360s, and so now the Parisians disliked these foreigners, even more distinctive because of the increasing use of English among them. With Joan of Arc's campaigns in the 1420s, we have reached the stage of open nationalism: the French throne belongs to a French king, and 'France' is the focus of loyalty, rather than the puppet-figure of Charles VII. Yet the paradox of this emergence of nationalism is that the fifteenth century is the age of the great lords rather than of the kings. Cardinal Beaufort and Warwick 'the kingmaker' in England, the dukes of the royal family in France – these are the leading figures in fifteenth-century politics and culture. And it is at this time that the greatest of the vassal states appears, the duchy of Burgundy, originally created for the youngest son of John II of France, Philip the Bold. Philip and his three successors made Burgundy into an independent power, rivalling France itself, by a series of dynastic marriages which brought them control of the rich towns of the Netherlands. They created their own elaborate culture, whose principal feature was feasts and festivals of unmatched splendour, which we can only dimly imagine from accounts in the chronicles.

Burgundy as a European state lasted for just over a century and disappeared with the death of Charles the Rash in 1477, so its monuments are relatively few and far between; as with the royal house of France, the chief memorial of the dukes of Burgundy are the remains of a pantheon, the Charterhouse at Champmol at Dijon, where the dukes are buried, just as in England the Beauchamp chapel at Warwick commemorates the Kingmaker's power, albeit on a smaller scale. The Charterhouse (a Carthusian monastery) was decorated by craftsmen from the Netherlands, and two huge gilded wooden altarpieces can be seen in the Musée des Beaux Arts at Dijon; conceived in elaborate architectural terms, they have the realistic, immediate but rather sentimental figures typical of northern late-Gothic sculpture. More remarkable is the work of Claus Sluter, equally realistic but fired by a stronger artistic vision. Of his statues, those around the base of the Calvary survive, though the actual Crucifixion group was demolished during the French revolution. Even more dramatic are the white marble figures of mourners by Sluter around the base of the tomb of Philip the Bold, portraits of simplicity and strength which can stand comparison with the greatest work of the Italian Renaissance. The tomb is also in the Musée des Beaux Arts, as are those of his successors.

The other survivals from the Burgundian court are a number of paintings, again by Flemish artists, now scattered in museums throughout the world, though the majority are in the Netherlands. Panel-painting appears here as the chief art-form for the first time – until now, most of the great painters had worked on manuscripts, as miniaturists, or on frescoes. There was already a strong artistic tradition in the Netherlands in the late fourteenth century, but most of the major artists, especially the miniaturists, had been forced to seek patronage at royal or ducal courts outside the Netherlands, because, wealthy though their native towns were, even the wealthiest merchants could not rival the resources of princes. However, Philip the Good, after his installation as duke of Brabant in 1430, gradually came to regard Brussels as the capital of his domains, and from 1440 onwards he was frequently there. From 1459 until his death in 1467 it became his usual place of residence. He spent long periods at Bruges as well; Burgundy itself naturally occupied much of his time; but unlike his predecessors, he spent very little time in Paris. The court of Burgundy was moving away from the orbit of France and creating its own culture in the process, a culture based primarily on the Netherlands.

Philip inherited from an earlier duke of Brabant his court painter, Jan van Eyck, who entered his service in 1425 and remained with him until his death in 1441. Van Eyck enjoyed the duke's special favour; Philip stood godfather to one of his sons, and when in 1435 there was an argument between the duke and his parsimonious officials about granting him a pension, Philip insisted that it should be done, 'for we should never find his equal in artistic skill'. Van Eyck was working in a tradition of panel-painting of which the greatest exponent had been the 'Master of Flémaille' (probably Robert Campion of Tournai), who had been among the first to adopt a realistic approach to religious art: in the Mérode altarpiece (now in the Cloisters Museum in New York) he depicts the Annunciation with the Virgin settled comfortably on the floor in front of a spacious fireplace, leaning against a cushion on the fireside settle. This combination of genre painting, hitherto found only as an incidental element in the illumination of manuscripts, with the development of the technique of painting in oil on panel, is what gives Flemish art of the mid fifteenth century its striking novelty and power. Even in its most majestic moments, such as the great altarpiece in the cathedral of St Bavo, carried out by Jan van Eyck and possibly Hubert van Eyck in 1425–32, there is a feeling of immediacy which earlier artists had never been able to capture. The Annunciation, on the shutters, is once again set in a familiar, if luxurious, interior, while the altarpiece itself ranges from portrait to landscape and still life, all meticulously set down. Only in the background are there hints of the fairy-tale world of fourteenth-century Gothic miniatures, though the detailed symbolism and careful theology are entirely medieval in spirit, and the central panel, *The Adoration of the Mystic Lamb*, departs from worldly realism to give us a glimpse of paradise itself. Yet even here the grass is meticulously painted with identifiable wild flowers.

The increasing emphasis on the portrait is reflected in the vivid series of royal and ducal images from this period, beginning with the anonymous portrait of John II of France in the Louvre, that of Rudolf of Habsburg in the cathedral museum at Vienna, and those of John the Fearless at Antwerp and Philip the Good at Dijon. In England, the court painters of Richard II produced the picture of the king enthroned in Westminster Abbey, but this is a formal image still, a sharp contrast with Burgundian art. The finest of the Burgundian series – for it is a conscious series, recording the likenesses of each succeeding ruler – is that of Charles the Rash by van Eyck's successor, Rogier van der Weyden, now in Berlin. Van der Weyden's most famous portrait is that of an anonymous lady in the

National Gallery at Washington, and he is the first painter whose reputation rests mainly on his achievements in this field.

The Burgundian dukes never established a single capital in their domains; as we have noted, Philip the Good distinctly preferred Brussels in the latter part of his reign, but Dijon remained important and was the centre of much of his administration. Partly because of their peripatetic existence, little in the way of architecture has survived. The château at Hesdin in Artois was one of the few places on which any of the dukes spent great sums, and this has completely vanished. We know that it was richly ornamented by Philip the Bold, and that in Philip the Good's time there was a gallery full of medieval mechanical devices for playing practical jokes, the account for which survives:

[The painter] also made a bridge in this room, constructed in such a way that it was possible to cause anyone walking over it to fall into the water below. There are several devices in this room which, when set off, spray large quantities of water onto the people in it, as well as six figures, more than there had been before, which soak people in different ways. In the entrance, there are eight conduits for wetting women from below and three conduits which, when people stop in front of them, cover them all over with flour. When someone tries to open a certain window, a figure appears, sprays the person with water, and shuts the window. A book of ballads lies on a desk but, when you try to read it, you are squirted with soot; if you look inside it, you can be sprayed with water. Then there is a mirror which people are invited to look at, to see themselves all white with flour; but, when they do so, they are covered with more flour. A wooden figure, which appears above a bench in the middle of the gallery, announces, at the sound of trumpets, on behalf of the duke, that everyone must leave the gallery. Those who do so are beaten by large figures holding sticks ... and those who don't want to leave get so wet that they don't know what to do to avoid the water.*

The most characteristic feature of Burgundian culture was undoubtedly in this ephemeral vein of display, sometimes aided by stage-machinery of the kind described above but put to a more serious purpose. Of the great ceremonies with which the dukes of Burgundy laid claim to a place among the monarchs of Europe, all that survives are the chroniclers' descriptions of jousts and feasts, solemn entries and civic receptions, surrounded by elaborate

* Translated by Richard Vaughan, *Philip the Good* (London, 1970), p. 138.

allegories and tableaux. A few tapestries – the most portable of art forms – survive, notably a floral tapestry in the Historical Museum at Bern; and we can hear modern reconstructions of performances of music by the great court composers – Binchois, Ockeghem and Josquin des Pres. As a parting image of this complex, luxurious, ill-fated court, let us take the book of hours of Charles the Rash, devout and impulsive, last of the Valois dukes. This manuscript, in the Austrian National Library at Vienna, is written throughout on pages stained black, the lettering being in white and gold, with the usual richly illuminated borders and full-page miniatures, all carried out, in an almost perverse tour-de-force, in colour on the same black background and yet attaining a very high artistic standard. This extraordinary piece of luxurious book-production stretches to the limit medieval skills and techniques. There was no way forward from this achievement, just as in the end there was no way forward for Burgundy itself, which, after Charles the Rash's death, passed into the Holy Roman Empire with the marriage of Charles's daughter to Maximilian of Austria.

PART THREE

LORDS · PRINCES
AND VASSALS

11
Castles

Just as the medieval church evolved a formal hierarchy to overcome
the problems of organizing and regulating its members in an age
when communications were difficult – a hierarchy which has survived in the Catholic and Anglican churches to the present day
– so the medieval rulers of Europe developed a hierarchical system
to ensure control of their territories. It was not always a conscious
development, and the kings were in some senses as much products
of a gradual evolution of this system as the lords and vassals beneath
them. The church had one great advantage in this process of
organization: loyalty to a common belief. In secular politics there
was none of the fervent belief in nationalism which has been used
as a rallying-point in modern times; instead, a complex interlinking
structure was built up on the simplest loyalty of all: that of one
man to another.

The origins and development of feudalism are a long and complex
subject, and can only be outlined here. Its beginnings can be traced
back to the fifth and sixth century, when the power structure of
Europe was in chaos. On the one hand, the invading barbarian
war-bands depended for their coherence on the loyalty of warriors
to their chief, celebrated in Anglo-Saxon poems such as *Beowulf*,
which opens with a description of a ruler and his men:

> Hrothgar won honour in war,
> glory in battle, and so ensured
> his followers' support – young men
> whose number multiplied into a mighty troop.
> And he resolved to build a hall,
> a large and noble feasting-hall
> of whose splendours men would always speak,
> and there to distribute as gifts to old and young
> all the things that God had given him . . .

The ruler offered gifts, the prospect of victory and rich feasts to his men in return for their service as warriors. The equation between feasting and bloody service in war was made even more directly in the early Welsh poem *The Gododdin*:

> Never was made a hall so acclaimed
> so mighty, so immense the slaughter.
> You deserved your mead, Morien, fire-brand.

The other element in feudalism was that of protection for the non-warrior: a man would bind himself to a lord and offer to serve him with whatever skill he possessed, in return for protection, both physical and economic. This was a development from late Roman society, when the spacious villas in the countryside became increasingly the focus of local economic activity and also of rudimentary defence for the local population. Such an *ad hoc* institution was bound to develop in varying ways throughout Europe, and what is surprising is not the differences between French, German, English and Spanish feudalism, but the common factors to be found among them. By the eleventh and twelfth centuries we can find everywhere, to a greater or lesser degree, a pyramidal structure of feudal society. In broad terms, serfs and freemen alike owe service to a local lord, who in turn owes service to a baron; the baron owes service to a yet greater lord, who – perhaps with further intermediate stages – owes homage to the king himself. This simple structure reflects the pattern of landholding, for the economic element in both the payment of the war-band and provision for the artisan, steward or farmer has been commuted by this time to a grant of land enabling the vassal to support himself. But life is never as simple and schematic as this, and from an early period we find men owing homage to more than one lord as they acquire scattered lands, and instead of the simple pyramid we have a series of overlapping pyramids in three dimensions. Even at the highest level there were complications: as we have seen in the relationship between the kings of England and France, one king could be the vassal of another in respect of parts of his territory. In England, the feudal structure can be seen in a very simple form in the redistribution of lands after the Norman conquest; but even here loyalties were complicated by the requirement of an oath of loyalty to the king, to be sworn by every freeman, from peasant to lord.

The monuments of feudalism are its castles: here we find the three elements of reward, protection and interplay with royal government at their clearest. Kings both used feudalism and tried to restrain its excesses by invoking greater principles, which were eventually to lead to the concept of national monarchy which replaced it. They granted lands – and hence sites for castles – as a reward, tried to protect their subjects by building castles and tried to control the building and misuse of castles in the interest of the people at large. All these actions played a part in the history of castles.

The origins of the castle lie in the simple fact that, in an age when war-bands were armed with spears, bows and swords and techniques for using heavier missiles were largely unknown, any kind of built-up defence was a formidable deterrent. There is evidence for rudimentary fortification of Roman villas in France in the fifth century; old Roman camps and Iron Age hill forts were re-used in Britain and France. Such defences as were added consisted usually of a wooden fence of stakes driven into the ground and a ditch. Sites with natural defences, hilltops or islands, were at a premium. These defensive positions and their crude structures were direct descendants of Roman and barbarian military encampments: the very word castle is related to the Roman *castrum*, a camp. They are distinct from the fortified towns – again Roman in origin – in both scale and function. Not only were they smaller, but they were primarily refuges, not places of permanent occupation. On the other hand, if a war was prolonged, such fortresses had an important military role to play, particularly in a defensive war. Charlemagne and his predecessors in the eighth and ninth centuries had difficulty in conquering Aquitaine, the Auvergne, Brittany and Saxony because of fortresses in the countryside, and took severe reprisals against those who had defended them. They themselves did not build royal castles because their opponents after 770 were largely on their frontiers, not within the kingdom, and it is only with the gradual collapse of Carolingian power that the castles reappear, as defences against Viking, Arab and Magyar raiders. These raiders in turn built fortified encampments, the Vikings on the island of Noirmoutier, the Arabs at Garde-Freine near Fréjus. In England, defensive *burhs* were built against the Viking invaders, and in Saxony a similar network of fortresses was created as a defence against Slav raiders.

It is in tenth-century France, however, that the castle, as opposed to the mere temporary defensive enclosure, really emerges. From the time of Charles the Bald, Charlemagne's grandson, fortresses were given to trusted retainers, and in the tenth century this became a common reward for faithful service. They were manned by soldiers, who lived more or less permanently in the castle, as a garrison; and lands were granted with the fortress so that it became a local power-base as well. By the eleventh century, techniques were evolved for creating a strong fortified position in an area where no natural defences existed. These are the elements that distinguish a castle from a Roman or modern fortress; it is the place of residence of the local lord, to all intents and purposes his private property, permanently manned and constructed with advanced engineering techniques. The earliest surviving castles which conform to these criteria are to be found on the Loire, at Doué-la-Fontaine and at Langeais. The latter was built by Fulk the Black, count of Anjou, great-grandfather of Henry II of England, and an enthusiastic castle-builder: he also founded the castles at Amboise and Montbazon on similar lines, using a natural promontory, cutting a moat across the neck and building a wooden keep. At Langeais, the wooden keep was soon replaced by the stone structure which survives today. At Doué, there was already a ninth-century stone hall, which had been burnt; the shell was incorporated into a new defensive system in about 950, the lower entrances were blocked up and it was heightened, to form a tower. The simplest form of early castle, which could be erected almost anywhere, was that of a motte and bailey, a circular or oval enclosure surrounded by an artificial ditch, the soil from which formed a defensive mound. The keep and palisade were all of wood. This type of castle was used by the Normans on many sites in England after the Conquest, when large numbers of castles were built in a short time in order to control the country: most were later rebuilt in stone and extended, but the original plan can easily be seen at Launceston in Cornwall. The Normans in southern Italy also used this technique as they conquered new territory, and examples of motte and bailey castles are to be seen on the Bayeux tapestry.

Fortifications such as these were easily built at relatively little expense, and in periods when royal control was weak local barons were able to construct their own strongholds as bases from which to impose their own rule. As early as 864, Charles the Bald ordered the destruction of private fortified sites, and this struggle to impose a royal monopoly, by which castles could be built only under royal licence, continued into the twelfth century and revived when royal authority was weak. At the end of the civil wars between Robert of Normandy and Henry I and again between Stephen and the supporters of the Angevin cause, the destruction of 'adulterine' castles built without permission was a major operation: the wars had shown that many such fortresses were able to withstand a prolonged siege, and under Stephen the period of anarchy had been long enough for stone castles to be built. Twenty years later, in the civil war between Henry and his sons, the barons who had taken part in the rebellion had their castles razed to the ground after Henry's victory.

A network of castles in loyal hands was thus essential to the security of a country. At the beginning of the twelfth century, when duke Frederick of Swabia invaded the west bank of the Rhine, in the words of the chronicler Otto of Freising, 'he halted each time he found a site suitable for a castle which would dominate the surrounding countryside. Then he went further on and built another one. He did this so thoroughly that it was said everywhere that duke Frederick always pulled a castle along with him at his horse's tail.' By the mid twelfth century, however, it was commoner to find the newly installed victor taking over existing castles. One of Henry II's first acts after his accession was to recover from his barons the royal castles they had seized, even at the risk of alienating his own supporters. The confiscation of rebel castles was the other side of the coin as far as royal control went, because any legitimate castle licensed by the king could be built only on certain terms, one of which was that it should not be used against him. In France, however, the crucial power to license and control castle building was in the hands of lesser lords, and the long struggle for power between Henry II and his sons on the one hand and Louis VII and Philip Augustus on the other was marked by endless strategic castle building, notably along the Norman border, and by attempts on both sides to control castles built by independent or openly rebellious petty lords.

However, during this period of interminable minor campaigns, truces and renewed campaigns, it became apparent that stagecraft was beginning to catch up with the castle-builders' engineering. Henry II acquired a reputation for being able to reduce the most impregnable castle with extraordinary ease: he took Chinon rapidly in 1155; Thouars, north of Poitiers, reputedly impossible to take, was reduced in three days in 1158; at Castillon-sur-Agen in 1161, 'a castle fortified by both nature and artifice', the siege lasted less than a week. The two elements in his success seem to have been surprise and the use of mercenaries and a professional siege-train. By the end of the twelfth century, castles were being designed with complex arrangements against surprise and against the siege techniques of the day, and were thus becoming much more elaborate and expensive.

We can get an impression of what an early twelfth-century castle looked like from a number of ruins: Arques, Domfront and Loches in France, the last with the bulk of its massive keep still largely intact, towering above the thirteenth-century outer defences added by Philip Augustus after he had captured it in 1206. There is little from this period in Spain and Germany that has not been rebuilt in later centuries, and the finest examples are to be found in England, though some of the Irish castles of the following century preserve features from the twelfth century. **Richmond** was the centre of the vast earldom held by lords of Breton descent from the Norman conquest until the fourteenth century. Built on a triangular plateau overlooking the river Swale, it contains a rare example of an eleventh-century residence, 'Scotland's Hall', in the southern corner of the enclosure, a two-storey building which is relatively lightly fortified, relying on its site for safety, as the longest side overlooks the river. The tower-keep, converted from a gatehouse in the twelfth century, is virtually intact, as are the curtain walls. Richmond, although relatively remote, is typical of the surviving castles of the period, in that it is associated with a town of some substance. The similar keep at nearby Scarborough was built to protect the port; the castle at Newcastle upon Tyne defended an important town used as a base in Henry's wars against Scotland; Dover was again a port defence; and bishops' castles like Rochester were based in towns because these were the seat of the bishop's power. Castles could be built to overawe towns and cities as well as to defend them: this was the case with William I's Tower of London and 's Gravensteen at Ghent (see p. 314), where the counts and the townspeople were at odds throughout the Middle Ages.

In several cases, these 'town' castles relied on existing fortifications. The **Tower of London** was built in the south-east angle of the Roman city walls, originally as 'certain fortifications completed in the city against the fickleness of the vast and fierce populace' shortly after William's coronation on Christmas Day 1066. By the end of the following decade, a stone keep, now called the White Tower, was being built under the supervision of the bishop of Rochester, Gundulf, an expert on stone buildings and creator of Rochester castle. The size of the White Tower was due to its use as a royal residence. It had a basement and two upper floors, the entrance being on the first floor by a wooden staircase, a defensive arrangement common in castles of this period. The top floor, containing the chapel of St John, was the king's residence. This has been altered by the insertion of an extra floor, and the exterior, too, has changed, with eighteenth-century windows and cappings to the turrets; only the chapel of St John gives some impression of the Romanesque grandeur of the original interior, its massive arcading, the principal architectural feature, echoing the Abbaye-aux-Hommes at Caen. By the end of the eleventh century, a stone curtain wall had been built, but this was replaced by Richard I and Henry III, who extended the outer defences beyond the line of the Roman wall which had originally sheltered the keep. It is from Henry III's reign that we first have a reference to the keep being whitewashed, and a new inner precinct was built south of the White Tower, to enlarge the royal quarters. The Wakefield Tower survives from this period, but the great hall has vanished. Edward I completed his father's work by closing the collapsed west inner curtain wall, and building the complete outer wall and moat, with the formidable entrance defences to the west of the barbican, as well as the Middle Tower and Byward Tower. The total cost of the works commissioned by Edward was over £21,000, more than the sum spent on building a new castle in Wales from the foundations up. The new moat was on a huge scale because of the natural disadvantages of the site, and a further defensive entrance, St Thomas's Tower, acted as a water-gate to the river. The Tower, as we see it today, is largely Edward I's creation, and it belongs in many aspects to the style of his great Welsh castles (see p. 253 below).

But we have moved on, well beyond the twelfth century. The White Tower type of keep is to be found at **Dover**, built in 1168–88 by Henry II on the site of a fort used by Iron Age people, Romans and Saxons in turn. Later work, particularly for military reasons in the last two centuries, has altered the general aspect of the castle substantially, but the keep and ground plan are basically those of Henry II's reign, with one important change. In 1216, the French took advantage of the troubles of king John's reign to mount an invasion, and were able to undermine the east tower of one of the gates. The castle held out, but this and the capture of Rochester by the mining of the south-east corner a year before had shown up a vital weakness, and in 1227 a new main entrance, the Constable's gate, was built, using the latest principles of design, and in 1243 a barbican was added. Thereafter little work other than maintenance was done on this first bastion of England's defence, the most powerful castle of the realm when it was given its final shape in the mid thirteenth century. Other square keeps – part baronial, part royal – in England and Normandy which share a common pattern are those at Falaise, Castle Rising and Norwich. Norwich has fine Romanesque arcading on the outside, giving it a highly decorated appearance.

The attacks on Dover and Rochester had shown up a basic weakness in the rectangular keep design which had been discovered in the mid twelfth century. If the attackers concentrated their efforts on the angle of the tower, it was very difficult to get a proper aim at them from the battlements or from within the castle, and if a corner was undermined, the damage to the structure was even greater than a breach in a curtain wall. So experiments were made with multi-sided keeps, leading eventually to the adoption of round towers. One of the earliest examples of this type is the octagonal keep at **Gisors**. There is uncertainty about the date of this massive tower, which stands within a twelfth-century ring-wall. What seems certain is that the castle was started by William Rufus in the 1090s and the keep was built either by Henry I or Henry II, and that the rest of the fortifications belong to the period after it had fallen into French hands in 1193. The architectural style would certainly point to Henry II's reign, because Gisors strongly resembles the castle at **Orford**, which can be dated to 1166–72, and which is the best surviving example of a small group of polygonal tower-keeps of this period in England. However, the advantages of the polygon plan are offset at Orford by three projecting towers, square in section, which reintroduce the very blind spots which the design seems intended to obviate. The keep, standing above the once-busy port on the Suffolk coast, has survived intact and unaltered, because it has only once seen military action, in the rebellion of 1173–4. As at Dover, the projecting staircase tower also contains the first-floor chapel. The living quarters are spartan – a warren of minute cubicles in the thickness of the walls and two huge rooms in the centre of the first and second floors. In France, there had been experiments with poly-lobed keeps: at Houdan, thirty miles west of Paris, the lords of Montfort built a circular keep with four projecting circular turrets as early as 1130. Nearby, at Étampes, the royal castle is on a four-leafed clover pattern, with a vaulted first-storey hall. But these seem to have been products of a local fashion, without direct successors.

At Framlingham, not far from Orford, the castle was rebuilt in the 1190s with a curtain wall linking a series of square towers, leaving an oval enclosure in the centre, and from the early thirteenth century onwards the curtain wall plays an increasingly important role in major castles, even where there is a central keep. **Château Gaillard**, Richard I's supposedly impregnable castle dominating the Seine at Les Andelys on the Norman–French border, incorporated all the most recent ideas on military architecture when it was built at vast expense and great speed in 1196–8. It was built on a site seized from the archbishop of Rouen under Richard's personal supervision, in defiance of the church's anathemas: the king's enthusiasm for the work was such that one chronicler wrote: 'if an angel had descended from heaven and told him to abandon it, that angel would have been met with a volley of curses and the work would have gone on regardless'. Richard was a very experienced commander, and had spent most of his adult life in active campaigning: he had seen siege warfare in France, Sicily and the Holy Land, and the design of Château Gaillard was based on this experience. The approaches are defended by a massive redoubt, all but one of whose five towers have vanished: this stands outside the forty-five-foot deep moat cut across the neck of the projecting spur on which the main part of the castle stands. The irregular curtain wall of this inner bailey is designed so that there are no blind spots, and the massive keep, with walls sixteen feet thick, is specially strengthened on the landward side against missiles fired from siege-engines. The footings of the keep are cut into solid rock, to hinder any attempt at mining. Yet despite Richard's boast that he could hold Château Gaillard even if it were built of butter, this masterpiece of engineering – on which he spent one and half times the total expenditure on English castles in the whole of his reign – was taken in March 1204, less than five years after his death. A determined assault by Philip Augustus of France and a garrison dispirited by the inactivity of king John undoubtedly weighted the odds in the attackers' favour, but, even so, the means used were relatively simple, though laborious: the filling-in of the outer moats, a surprise attack through the latrine tower, and finally the use of a trebuchet or stone-throwing engine against the walls of the inner bailey where they had been weakened by mining and counter-mining through the rock below. Given time and energy – it had taken Philip Augustus six months with a large army – no castle was impregnable, but despite the lesson of Château Gaillard, designers of castles continued to search for the ideal of a fortress which would resist all assaults.*

By and large, it is true to say that from the thirteenth century onwards, major castles are only common in areas where there was strong central government. The castles of Germany and south-west France, areas of relative anarchy, tend to be far more numerous but on a smaller scale, often with a single tower and rudimentary outworks. In the absence of strong central authority, the castle became the focus of local government, a trend reflected in the names of great families: both the Hohenstaufen and Habsburg dynasties took their names not from their territories, but from the castle which was at the centre of their power. Excavations at Staufen show that the castle there in the early twelfth century was a simple square tower and a stone hall within a ring wall, against which wooden buildings were erected. It is as if the Bigod earls of Norfolk had renamed themselves Framlingham after their castle there. And the emperors unconsciously emphasized the often symbolic nature of their power when they built palaces, which were unfortified, rather than great strongholds.

Imperial castles, such as that at Nuremberg (p. 297), were often administrative centres, or relatively small in scale, such as that at **Trifels**, perched high above the little town of Annwater in the Wasgau forest of the Rhineland on a conical peak which rises a thousand feet above the floor of the valley. It is a fortress designed as a refuge or place of safety rather than a strategic garrison

* But in 1418, Château Gaillard, which had scarcely been altered, held out for sixteen months against the English, and surrendered only because of lack of water.

point; true, it commands the valley below, which is one of the lines of communication between the Rhine and Alsace, but the sheer length of time needed to get men down from the castle would have made it impracticable as a defensive base. It was originally built as an inaccessible refuge by some unknown independent-minded baron in the tenth century, and a stone building first appeared here between 1040 and 1060. At the end of the eleventh century it was in the hands of the opponents of the emperor, Henry IV, but in 1113 it was handed over by the archbishop of Mainz, whom Henry had captured. The archbishop was promptly imprisoned at Trifels, and the almost impregnable security which the castle offered was at once realized and put to good use. Twelve years later, as Henry was dying, he gave instructions that the imperial insignia were to be taken to Trifels, and they remained there for nearly a hundred years out of the next century and a half. Many of the items listed in an inventory of 1246 (by which time the jewels of the Norman kingdom of Sicily had been added to the imperial collection) still survive in Vienna, notably the crown, orb and imperial cross, as well as many of the ceremonial clothes of the emperor. (Replicas of the most important items are on display in the castle.) Because the insignia were at Trifels, in the years when the empire itself was in dispute, the saying ran, 'Whoever possesses Trifels, possesses the empire.'

Trifels, like the Tower of London after the medieval period, combined the functions of treasure-house and state prison. Its most famous prisoner was Richard I, captured on his way from Palestine by Leopold of Austria in revenge for a pretended insult at the siege of Acre two years earlier. Leopold sold his prisoner to Henry VI, and Richard was brought to Trifels while his fate was decided: a huge ransom was demanded from England, and counter-offers to prolong his captivity were discreetly sought from Philip Augustus of France and John. From Trifels, Richard was taken to appear before the emperor at Speyer, where he impressed every-one with his proud bearing and eloquent answer to the trumped-up accusations made against him. Some writers have tried to associate the legend of Blondel, the minstrel who set out in search of Richard, with Trifels; but the obvious impossibility of approaching Trifels unseen and the fact that the king's whereabouts were known by the time he reached the castle means that the story, if it belongs anywhere, should be attached to Richard's time in captivity at Dürrenstein in Austria. Richard was at Trifels from March 1193 to March 1194.

For a place with such remarkable associations, the actual architecture of Trifels is unspectacular. The castle had fallen into almost total ruin by the end of the nineteenth century, and the bulk of what we see today is a reconstruction. Most of it is unexceptionable and reasonably conservative: the lower floors of the main keep are original, and it is quite hard to distinguish between these and the upper floors. Only the great hall is a failure, reminiscent of (and contemporary with) Mussolini's rebuilding of the Castle of the Knights at Rhodes, with an unconvincing marble floor and staircase. There is good evidence that the hall did have a marble floor, but it would not have had the mechanical smoothness of this restoration. The overall impression of the castle is, however, a faithful one, with its massive central tower – a typical *Bergfried*, to give it its German name – distinct in appearance from Norman work by the rusticated stonework and the lack of battlements.

Throughout Germany, control of the countryside rested with the hundreds of lesser castles in the lands of imperial officials or *ministeriales*, who all too easily became independent barons. Other factors which tended to make German castles different in scale and style were the terrain and the local system of inheritance. As in south-west France, both of these led to smaller, shared castles: hilltop sites with good natural defences, but relatively small in area, were common, while inheritances were divided equally among heirs, instead of being passed down through the eldest son. Both in Provence and Germany, we find a number of families living in one castle as co-owners; as many as fifty or sixty families might have a share in the property.

In Italy, where the towns were more powerful than the local lords in the fourteenth century, the majority of surviving castles date from the fifteenth century, with the exception of the Hohenstaufen castles in southern Italy already discussed (p. 189). Only a state like England under Edward I was able to bear the expense and carry out the necessary organization for castles such as those built in north Wales in the late thirteenth century. These form the most remarkable surviving group of medieval castles, and their origins and construction are worth looking at in some detail.

The age-old enmity between Saxon and Welshman was inherited

by the Normans after their conquest of England, and border warfare was frequent in the eleventh and twelfth centuries. The
marcher lords, whose lands lay along the borders ('marches') of
Wales, enjoyed a degree of freedom from royal interference, in
return for their activities in holding the Welsh at bay or extending
Norman rule into Welsh territory. The first major attempt to
conquer Wales was made by Henry II in 1157, but met with little
success, and Henry abandoned conquest in favour of a policy of
supporting and befriending the Welsh rulers. However, the
emergence of a powerful Welsh state under Llywelyn the Great
between 1195 and 1240 changed the situation. Llywelyn united
five of the lesser lordships into a substantial principality in north
Wales, and although he still acknowledged Henry III as his lord,
he was too powerful a vassal for the king, and too threatening a
neighbour for the marcher lords, who at the time were weak and
divided. As a result the king's justiciar, Hubert de Burgh, took
a hand in marcher affairs: although he was defeated, Wales became
an area where the royal power was directly involved. Royal castles
began to be established, at Cardigan, Builth, Carmarthen and
Montgomery, replacing the fortresses held by marcher lords.

Llywelyn the Great's principality disappeared at his death, only
to reappear during the English civil war between de Montfort and
Henry III in 1257–67. The new ruler, also called Llywelyn,
assumed the title of Prince of Wales, and reconquered almost the
whole of Wales, including much marcher territory. His title was
recognized by Henry III in 1267. However, Henry's son Edward
had emerged as victor in the civil war, with the help of Roger
Mortimer and other marcher lords. When Edward came to the
throne, Llywelyn failed to do homage in the prescribed form, and
it became clear that Llywelyn's ambitions were a threat to the
English hold on Wales. War broke out in 1277, and Llywelyn's
gains in the 1260s were retaken: parts of south Wales which had
never previously been occupied now fell to the English barons,
and Edward at once ordered fortresses to be repaired or built to
act as royal strongholds. Llywelyn's power was now restricted to
north Wales, and the danger of north and south acting in concert,
which had defeated the English on so many previous occasions,
was eliminated. Edward himself laid the groundwork for the
conquest of north Wales by building a castle at Flint, the first of
the group with which we are concerned: a second was planned

at Rhuddlan. However, Llywelyn now sued for peace, and a treaty was made, leaving Llywelyn with his title and lands which consisted of Anglesey, Snowdonia and little else.

Edward now set out to impose some kind of order on his newly acquired lands; but the replacement of the loose tribal laws of Wales by the formal justice of England led to disturbances, which Llywelyn's brother David used as a rallying-call for a revolt, which broke out in March 1282, and much of Wales was overrun. Edward, who had been on good terms with both Llywelyn and David, was taken by surprise. He was heavily engaged elsewhere, in Gascony and Scotland, and reacted swiftly and sternly to the news from Wales. A summons to the army went out at once, and his forces were ready in August. By October he had reversed the situation, and only the mountains around Snowdon remained outside his control. Efforts were made by the archbishop of Canterbury to get agreement between Llywelyn and Edward, but these came to nothing. A month after the breakdown of talks, Llywelyn was killed in a skirmish in mid-Wales. The following spring, Edward's forces encircled Snowdonia and in June David was captured. He was tried and hanged in October.

The conquest of Wales was complete, but the land had to be made secure against future revolts. Edward spent most of 1284 in Wales, making his arrangements. The mountains of Snowdonia could not be effectively occupied and garrisoned, but instead Edward created a ring of castles along the coast, stretching from those already begun at Flint and Rhuddlan to the castle at Aberystwyth in mid-Wales which he already held. Conwy, Caernarvon and Harlech were the new sites, with an additional castle at Beaumaris on Anglesey, which was the last to be started, in 1295. Work on all these castles was supervised by one man, the king's 'master of the works in Wales', James of St George, who came from Savoy on the borders of France and Italy. James of St George had originally been in the service of the counts of Savoy, and had worked on the count of Savoy's castle and town at Yverdon on Lake Neuchâtel. Five of the new castles in north Wales were similarly planned as integral parts of towns, because the English presence in the area needed more personnel than could be contained in the castles.

The first of the castles, **Flint**, was started in 1277. Its plan is unusual, consisting of a square enclosure with four corner towers, the largest of which is designed as a separate keep, divided from the rest by a moat. The lower part was for storage, while the upper floor contained accommodation grouped round a central well, an arrangement paralleled only in Castel del Monte in southern Italy (p. 189). The separation of the tower is perhaps explained by its nearness to the sea: it could be used as a last refuge if the rest of the castle were taken, like any other keep, but with this arrangement it would also be possible to supply it or evacuate the occupants by sea even after the loss of the outer works.

Rhuddlan, on the river Clwyd, was the farthest inland of the new castles, and a new canal had to be dug to the sea to make it accessible to sea-going vessels. This was the first work to be done, from 1277 to 1280. It was largely completed in 1282, when it was attacked by the Welsh during their last great revolt and severely damaged. It was rebuilt without alteration after this, and work ended in 1285. Its plan is concentric and fairly conventional for a thirteenth-century castle: the four-square inner ward, however, has two gatehouses, to east and west, each elaborately equipped with defences. Interestingly, all six towers have identical internal arrangements: symmetry is the hallmark of the design despite an irregular site. There were plans for Rhuddlan to become a cathedral town and centre of the shire, but these never materialized, and intended town walls never developed beyond a wooden palisade.

Conwy was captured by the English in 1283, and its possibilities were at once realized: commanding the Conwy estuary, the abbey of St Mary stood on a spur of rock which formed a natural stronghold. The additional expense involved in moving the abbey was offset by the fact that it was the burial place of Llywelyn the Great and had enjoyed the patronage of his house: its removal would underline the change of dynasty. A new site was found seven miles away, and the abbey's new buildings were ready in October 1284. Meanwhile work had already started at Conwy itself. The plan of both town and castle was determined by the lie of the land: the castle is almost oblong, following the line of the rock, its long walls strengthened by intermediate towers and the gateway set so that a right-angled turn has to be made before entering. Because the site is so narrow, it has a single massive outer wall, and is divided by a cross-wall into two wards. A water-gate provided direct access to the inner ward, which contained the royal apartments. This royal ward was marked off by four turreted towers, from which royal standards would be flown when the king was in residence. Another impressive feature was the Great Hall, built of stone and 125 feet long. Conwy was designed as one of the centres of royal power in Wales, and the associated town is known to have housed royal offices and officials. Its walls, with their twenty-one towers, slope up the hillside to the north and west of the castle, with three gates, one of which is on the quayside. They and the castle were designed as a single unit and were built at the same time. The design is such that each section of wall can be isolated, so that, even if attackers gained a foothold on top of the wall, they could be contained before they overran the whole defences. The whole fortified enclosure is almost a mile in circumference, the most ambitious single project of its kind undertaken in Britain in the Middle Ages, and also one of the best-preserved examples of its kind.

Harlech and Caernarvon were both captured in the summer of 1283, and in both cases work on the castles began very quickly. **Harlech**, on a beautiful site overlooking the Irish Sea, is perhaps the most 'orthodox' of all the north Welsh castles. Its plan – four-square, with corner towers and a twin-towered central gatehouse on the side – is not dissimilar to that of Villandraut in Gascony, built for Clement V by James of St George, who had been at Conwy in 1295. Just as James drew on recent continental work, so even from this outlying corner of Europe his achievements were noticed and had their influence elsewhere. But the gatehouse at Harlech is on a more massive scale than either its predecessors or successors, a miniature four-turreted keep. (Two turrets are in fact apses rather than complete towers.) This is largely due to its position: the sheer cliffs on all sides except the east make the line of attack predictable, and James of St George and his associates provided the necessary defence. The moat in front had to be cut through solid rock, which was an expensive operation. The accommodation inside the castle was fairly extensive, but this was not designed as a royal castle, and the apartments are correspondingly less spacious than at Conwy or Caernarvon.

At **Caernarvon** there was already an earlier castle, founded by Hugh of Chester in 1090 and used by the Welsh princes; but only the site of this was used by Edward. It stands on the mouth of the river Seiont, whose name is a reminder that this is the Roman fort of Segontium. Edward's new castle was also to have Roman and Byzantine echoes: perhaps inspired by the discovery of what was believed to be the body of Magnus Maximus, the father of the emperor Constantine, in the town in 1283, he and his architects chose as a model for the new castle the sixth-century town walls of Constantinople, with their patterned masonry of bands of different-coloured stone and their polygonal towers. They were also perhaps influenced by a description of a great Welsh city in the Welsh romance 'The Dream of Macsen Wledig' (i.e. Magnus Maximus).

He saw how he came to an island, the fairest in the whole world, and after he had traversed the island from sea to answering sea, even to the uttermost bound of the island, he could see valleys and steeps and towering rocks, and a harsh rugged terrain whose like he had never seen. And from there he saw in the sea, facing that rugged land, an island. And between him and that island he saw a country whose plain was the length of its sea, its mountain the length of its woodland. And from that mountain he saw a river flow through the land, making towards the sea. And at the river mouth he could see a great castle, the fairest that mortal had ever seen, and the gate of the castle he saw open, and he came to the castle. Inside the castle he saw a fair hall. The roof of the hall he thought to be all of gold; the side of the hall he thought to be of glittering stones, each as costly as its neighbour; the hall doors he thought to be all gold. Golden couches he saw in the hall, and tables of silver.

The castle is later named as Aber Seint, and a great fortress is built there for Macsen, with earth brought especially from Rome. So the design of Caernarvon could be a conscious attempt to re-create Magnus Maximus's fortress, appealing to the Welsh traditions in the same way as the fact that Edward's first son was to be born in Wales and become the first of the princes of Wales. Once again, Edward's architects created something new and remarkable; because the circumstances which dictated the design were exceptional, Caernarvon has no close medieval parallels, though one of the count of Savoy's castles does have polygonal towers set in a curtain wall.

The plan of Caernarvon is not unlike that of Conwy: the castle has an oblong shape, with two separate wards inside, and forms the angle of the town walls nearest to the water. The accommodation, except for the great hall, was largely in the seven towers and two gatehouses; but the buildings in the inner ward were never completed. The towers are linked by massive walls equipped with elaborate wall-walks and galleries. The huge scale of operations meant that the work was only partly completed when the Welsh rebelled again in 1294, and much damage was done; however, building began again in 1295 and continued into the early part of the fourteenth century. Yet, despite its intended role as a kind of Welsh equivalent of Windsor, it was never visited again by a king of England until the twentieth century, and only in the investiture ceremonies of 1911 and 1974 has it been used in the way that Edward I seems to have intended seven centuries ago.

The last of the castles, **Beaumaris**, dates from after the revolt of 1294. James of St George was commissioned to begin work early in 1295 on a castle which would secure Anglesey against future revolts. Once again a shore site was chosen, on level ground to the north-east of the island. It is the only castle where the site imposed no restrictions, and the symmetry evident at Rhuddlan appears again. The site has no natural defences and St George's answer to this is a forest of towers: the outer wall has eight bastions, four towers and two twin-towered gatehouses, the inner ward six towers and two apses and towered gatehouses nearly on the scale of that at Harlech, giving a huge inner defensive unit containing what are virtually two keeps. The dock, essential to the castle's survival, has its own carefully worked-out defensive system. The accommodation was on a fairly lavish scale, and the lovely vaulted chapel still survives, as a reminder that castle interiors could be elegant as well as practical. But as building progressed, so the threat of Welsh rebellion receded, and by 1330 work had ceased. The original plans were remarkably ambitious: the actual cost of over £14,000 for the castle, which was only half-finished when work stopped, was equal to that of the whole of the walls and castle at Conwy.

The Edwardian castles in north Wales were the results of a remarkable effort; royal accounts indicate the vast reserves of men and money that Edward poured into their building. Even though they were never completely finished, they are a fitting memorial to an architect of genius and an energetic king.

Apart from Flint, none of the Edwardian castles has a keep as such: the idea of a powerful central building as an unassailable refuge had largely given way to a series of defences which left the garrison with a much wider range of tactical options. The gatehouse becomes the centrepiece of the castle, defended by elaborate barbicans. A magnificent example of such a gatehouse can be seen at **Villeneuve-lès-Avignon**, the royal stronghold across the Rhône from the Papal city, where the Fort Saint-André has an entrance which is almost a small keep in itself, built in the 1360s. It has five machicolations, a system of projecting defences at the top of the tower (replacing the earlier battlements and hoardings) which contained slits opening downwards so that attackers at the foot of the wall could be bombarded from above. These stone projections evolved from wooden hoardings, which were liable to be set alight by flaming projectiles fired by the enemy. There are other minor improvements in design, but there is no architectural revolution in castle-building in the fourteenth and fifteenth century, merely increasingly intricate variations on the basic schemes of the previous centuries. The function of the castle begins to diverge, however; there is a sharp distinction between the royal and princely residences, which retain the outward defences and appearance of a castle, but become more and more palatial inside, and the purely practical military works, the *châteaux-forts* or fortresses which were eventually to become the forts of Renaissance Europe, designed to resist artillery fire.

Of the two greatest royal residences in England and France, **Windsor** has been so greatly altered that its medieval core is almost impossible to distinguish. Edward I I I's work at Windsor cost over £50,000 between 1350 and 1377; of this the bulk, however, was spent on royal apartments. Work on the projected great round tower of the early 1340s, designed to house his new order of chivalry, was suspended in 1346. When the new order was finally formed a year or two later, it consisted of only twenty-six knights, and the great tower was abandoned. Otherwise, Edward's new buildings were contained within the existing fortifications dating back to William I.

Across the Channel, however, it was a different story: the Hundred Years' War was fought almost entirely on French soil, and was aggravated by the activities of independent mercenaries and by the violent peasant uprisings of 1358–9, known as the *jacquerie*, as well as by revolts in Paris itself. Security was therefore much more important to the French kings, and Charles V not only ordered a general inspection and strengthening of all royal fortresses in 1367, but created a fortress-palace for himself at **Vincennes**. A miniature for December in the calendar of the *Très*

Riches Heures of the duc de Berry shows us the castle as it was in the fifteenth century, laid out in a huge rectangle with towers at each corner, the curtain wall having three intermediate towers on the south side and one to east and west. To the north, the dramatic keep, nearly two hundred feet high, had its own defences, a low curtain wall at the foot with small corner turrets. Because intermediate towers on this side could have been used to attack the keep, they were omitted, and the curtain wall is broken by the moat which surrounds the keep. The interior of the keep was appointed in palatial style, panelled and vaulted in wood and made as comfortable as such a fortress could be. All except one of the outer towers have been reduced to stumps, the keep has been denuded of its crenellations, and this former hunting lodge has now been swallowed up by the suburbs of Paris; but it was once at a safe distance from the troubled capital, while near enough to be in touch. The layout of the castle, with the central stronghold given its own defences, reflects an increasing preoccupation with treachery from within as well as rebellions outside the walls, a foreboding all too often realized in the turbulent politics of the fifteenth century.

Charles V's son, Louis d'Orléans, created not one but a string of great fortresses to the north-east of Paris, in the county of Valois. Between 1392, when he was given the county, and his death in 1406, he rebuilt six castles, at Crépy-en-Valois, Béthisy, Vez, La Ferté-Milon and Pierrefonds. Of these, Vez, with its massive archaic square keep with corner towers, survives relatively intact, while La Ferté-Milon was never completed and was partly demolished in the sixteenth century after a four-year siege. Here the curtain walls are as high as the towers, to provide a level and easily accessible defensive walk behind the battlements. This feature is repeated at **Pierrefonds**, but with a further set of battlements on the towers at a higher level. Pierrefonds as it is today is chiefly a monument to Viollet-le-Duc, the architect who explored and analysed French medieval buildings until he knew almost as much about them as their creators. Viollet-le-Duc was commissioned in 1867 by Louis-Napoleon (later Napoleon III) to reconstruct Pierrefonds, which was then a massive ruin, with one tower intact and the remainder in various degrees of decay. The exterior is largely successful. Experts may disagree with points of detail, but the overall appearance is close to that of the original château in the fifteenth century. The interior, however, is often more nineteenth-century than medieval (as is true of his work at Roquetaillade, south-east of Bordeaux, where the exterior is highly correct, but the interiors are a delightful fantasy on medieval themes). But the reaction of the nineteenth century to the Middle Ages needs a guidebook of its own. The important point about Pierrefonds is that the exterior was a very careful reconstruction based on excellent data, and the result is considerably better than, say, Rhodes or Trifels.

The last of the group of princely castles in this tradition which we shall look at is **Tarascon**, on the banks of the Rhône south of Avignon. Tarascon was begun about 1400 by the duke of Anjou, who also held the title of king of Naples; his son, king René, completed the fortress. Here the curtain walls are raised level with the towers, but there is no battlement walk: instead, there is a huge open platform, enabling the garrison to move instantly from one side of the castle to the other. On the river side, where attack by bombardment was unlikely, the state apartments have large windows, and the interior has galleries and tracery which foreshadow the Renaissance châteaux on the Loire. Centuries of use as a prison, however, have given the interior an unduly grim appearance: it is difficult to imagine the gay and lively court of René d'Anjou, renowned for its culture and chivalry, in these bare echoing halls. Restoration since 1926 has however given us back the medieval exterior of the castle; the moat has been filled with water, and later additions have been cleared away to reveal the massive bulk of the castle with its four-square silhouette.

Turning to the lesser castles of the fourteenth and fifteenth century, these follow the general pattern of the royal castles in their architectural conservatism and tendency to become predominantly residences rather than fortresses. The one major innovation is use of brick, which, although found in the castles of the Teutonic kingdom as early as 1300, was very rare until the late fourteenth century elsewhere in Europe, partly because the technique of building in brick was not understood. But by the end of the century Sicart de Lordat had built the huge brick keep at Montaner near Pau for the count of Foix, and smaller brick castles were to be found in the Rhineland and in the Loire countries, where stone was scarce. Muiderslot, east of Amsterdam, is a beautifully preserved example, rebuilt in 1386 to an old-fashioned square plan with round corner towers. Doornenberg, a square moated keep

totally rebuilt after its destruction in 1945, is even more conservative. In England, brick castles are rare. **Tattershall**, the most
impressive of the survivors, may have been built by a north German
architect in direct imitation of the tower-castles of the Teutonic
knights. This form allowed for spacious interiors, lit by relatively
large windows. In defensive terms, particularly against artillery, the
brick castle was not of much value, and the tower at Tattershall
is the ancestor of purely domestic Tudor architecture rather than
the forerunner of a new trend in military building. It is in the
same vein as the great defensive houses of the 1470s and 1480s
like Middleham and Kirkby Muxloe. Caister castle, built by Sir
John Fastolf, the veteran commander of the French wars, is a
mixture of the rectangular, low-built castle and the tower type,
with a single corner tower containing Sir John's private chambers.
Held for his heirs, the Paston family, by an inadequate garrison,
it was taken with little difficulty by the duke of Norfolk in 1469
using a small artillery train.

Even in the far more disturbed conditions in France, where in
some areas warfare was endemic from 1337 until the 1430s, the
same trend towards more luxurious living quarters can be found.
Effective artillery appeared earlier in France than in England,
however, so there is also a contrary trend towards building even
more massively, and towards adapting buildings for use by defensive artillery. The artillery train devised for Charles VII by
the Bureau brothers in the 1430s and 1440s had amply demonstrated what the new bronze cannon, firing metal balls, could do.
One fiercely independent lord's answer to this new warfare was
to build a castle which was almost purely military in purpose, and
which attempted to forestall all possible assaults. **Bonaguil**,
between Bergerac and Cahors in south-west France, was created
in the late fifteenth century by Berenger de Roquefeuil, as a fortress
conceived in terms of a feudal world that had almost vanished.
He is said to have been threatened with the confiscation of all his
lands by Louis XI and to have built the castle to resist an assault
by the royal army itself. The castle is built on solid, hard rock,
out of range of any artillery which could be sited on the neighbouring hills, on a spur defended by a massive barbican, capable
of withstanding a separate siege, and with its own garrison and
supplies. There was even an escape passage to the inner keep in
case of disaster. The main body of the castle has been partly

demolished, the chief loss being the living quarters. The diamond-shaped keep, designed to offer a minimal profile to enemy artillery mounted on the barbican or the spur beyond, is intact, as is the great tower, a hundred feet high. Everywhere blind alleys and concealed openings are placed to defend doorways, so that only a suicidal attack could succeed and a mere handful of men could hold the castle against hundreds of attackers, even if the outer defences were taken. Such devices had been developed throughout the Middle Ages – and some modern guides tend to see them where they do not exist* – but at Bonaguil these elaborate traps reach their ultimate refinement. It was, of course, never attacked; Berenger de Roquefeuil was no trouble to the king, however defiant he might be, as long as he sat inside his impregnable fortress. The castle had become a self-imposed prison.

The existence of earlier and still very powerful castles in England and France meant that fewer new castles were built there in the later Middle Ages. The same was true in Germany, where castles still remained relatively small: even the largest of the seventy or so Rhine castles, **Marksburg**, is not on the same scale as its Anglo-French counterparts, and is the result of haphazard growth over three centuries, from a simple square tower to a semi-palatial building relying on its unassailable hilltop site for protection. The defences are therefore unsophisticated, and consist of a series of gateways on the twisting approach which climbs up to the castle proper.

It is in Spain that we find the greatest castle-building activity in the fifteenth century. Spanish castle building, drawing on Moorish traditions, was somewhat isolated from the mainstream of European military architecture, and Spanish castles often seem a combination of very archaic ideas with unexpected innovations. In the far south, Moorish castles survive: the Alhambra at Granada is one of these, and if we regard it as a fortified residence based on an earlier castle, a Moorish equivalent of Windsor, it fits well into the military and social context of the later Middle Ages. But this dual purpose is typical of the castles of the region: at Málaga, the great double fortress of the Alcazaba and the Gibralfaro contain gardens and a palace built of the same perishable materials as the

---

* A guide at Carcassonne once assured me that the treads on the stairs on the battlement walk were calculated to make access difficult to anyone wearing foot armour – which would have hindered the defenders rather more than the attackers.

Alhambra. The strength of the Alcazaba derives from its site
on a natural spur overlooking the harbour, and its defences – as
in similar German castles – consist of a series of gateways on the
steep winding approaches. Huge curtain walls link the two
fortresses; these are later work, for the main fortress is tenth- and
eleventh-century, and the linking walls are fourteenth-century.
Other examples of Moorish castles with later Christian additions
are at Baños de la Encina and Alcalá de Guadaira. **Baños de la
Encina**, on the Guadalquivir east of Córdoba, is built out of a
pebble and mortar mixture dried in the sun, which sets extremely
hard – a technique only possible in the hot climate of southern
Spain. The design of the castle, using a curtain wall studded with
towers and without a keep, antedates anything of this kind in
Christian Europe by two hundred years, because Baños was built
in the golden age of the caliphate of Córdoba, under Abd'ur-
Rahman III (912–61). The great gateway, with its double-
horseshoe arch, immediately identifies it as a Moorish fortress; after
the Christians took it, during the campaign which led to the great
victory at Las Navas de Tolosa in 1212, they added the keep and
a redoubt, but the basic shape of the fortress survives unaltered.
Alcalá de Guadaira is also built of pebble and mortar, with square
towers: the unusual feature here is a detached eastern tower, linked
only to the main castle by a bridge to the upper levels and commanding the whole of the entrance defences. Again, this ingenious
eleventh- or early twelfth-century design has no contemporary
parallel in Christian Europe.

The classic castles in Spain belong to the period of anarchy in
the late fourteenth and early fifteenth centuries, when the Spanish
kingdoms were not only at war against each other, but were also
torn by civil strife, beside which the English Wars of the Roses
seem a simple and straightforward affair. The style of castle is
quite distinctive: a central keep with a massive curtain wall with
towers at the angles and at intervals along it. The keeps were square
in form and usually very high. There had been experiments in
the fourteenth century, such as the circular castle at Bellver, near
Palma in Majorca, which is entirely concentric in plan except for
a great round tower between the outer moat and main circular
keep.

Symmetrical designs such as Bellver or the square plans of Coca
and Manzanares el Real are typical of castles built in a plain, where

there are no restrictions imposed by the site. Yet there seems to be a special insistence on symmetry in the Spanish castles, particularly in the finest group of all, in the south of León and in old Castile, between Valladolid and Madrid. Montealegre, an almost square shell with four square corner towers and intermediate round towers, is the earliest, and exceptional in its lack of a keep; it also had very little in the way of outer defences, relying on sheer strength and its position on a low hill to resist the attackers' assaults, which it did successfully when Pedro the Cruel attacked it soon after it was built in the late fourteenth century.

Coca, La Mota at Medina del Campo and Manzanares el Real are the exemplars of the absolutely four-square plan. They are all palaces as well as fortresses, and the basic planning is not unlike that of Vincennes. Coca and La Mota are built of brick, and have affinities with the brick towers of northern Europe or Montaner while remaining quite distinctively Spanish. **Coca**, built by Moorish workmen (*mudéjars*) living as Moslems in Christian Spain, is a square within a square, the square keep being set on the corner of the inner rectangle, which has the broad wall-walk typical of the period. This rigid and economical plan, created in defiance of an irregular hillside site, is turned into a fantasy by the decorative brickwork and by the elaborate and far from practical battlements, all executed in brick with endless concave and convex fluting and ornamentation. Each battlement becomes a pinnacle, and the corner towers are studded with bartizans, turrets which project from the face of the brickwork making each angle into a miniature keep of its own. The walls are pierced at intervals by gun loops, a reminder that we are in the age of artillery, and positions for heavy cannon are also provided. Coca was never besieged, which accounts for its good state of preservation: the walls are solid enough to have withstood contemporary artillery, but the embellishments would certainly have suffered.

La Mota is a much simpler and more austere version of Coca. There is no fantasy here, but merely an austere and awe-inspiring keep, added when an earlier castle was almost entirely rebuilt in the fifteenth century. The square towers of the original fortress were retained, but an outer curtain wall, with provision for artillery, was built. This was designed so that access from the inside to any point on the walls was as easy as possible: there are two complete walks built inside the walls, with vaulted ceilings, and with connecting stairs in the towers. The only ornamental features are the bartizans and machicolations at the top of the keep, which none the less have an entirely practical purpose.

At **Manzanares el Real**, however, the vein of fantasy reaches its peak. Here the machicolations are added purely for architectural effect, to make the building look like a castle: there are no slits through which the defenders can hurl missiles. The deliberately rough stonework is studded with apparently embedded cannon balls, in what looks like a deliberate visual pun. A beautiful gallery in flamboyant Gothic style crowns the walls on one side, and the overall impression is of hesitation between military power and aesthetic enjoyment. The castle is undoubtedly powerful, and is defended by well-placed gunports; but the upper parts have almost no function other than embellishment. When the duke of the Infantado was building this stronghold, the period of anarchy was drawing to a close, and the Catholic kings, Ferdinand and Isabella, had begun to curb the power of the nobles. The duke seems to have been hedging his bets by commissioning a palace which could be used as a castle, but which did not look practical enough to pose a threat to royal power. Ironically, the great monument to the royal power of Renaissance Spain, the Escorial, was to be built only fifteen miles away across the hills.

Peñafiel, fifty miles to the north, was rebuilt ten years before Manzanares, but is purely military in purpose. Pedro Girón, who was responsible for the rebuilding, was the master of the military order of Calatrava, leader both of numerous raids against the Moors and of several rebellions against the king of Castile, Enrique IV, and his favourites. He died just before – dispensed from his vows – he was to have married Isabella, the future Isabella the Catholic. His career reflected both the old anarchic ways of the early fifteenth century and the new resolve which was to make the order of Calatrava, under his illegitimate son Rodrigo Telles Girón, a powerful force in the final stages of the *reconquista* (p. 212). The castle is built on a hilltop above the Duero valley, and its layout is determined by its site: it occupies a narrow plateau, and its elongated plan is that of a great ship, a design found in other Spanish castles. The curtain wall is studded with twenty-six towers of varying sizes, and there is a lower outer defence. The architecture is very conservative: the curtain walls and general layout are less technically advanced than in the average thirteenth-century English castle, and there are machicolations only on the towers, which also break the level of the wall-walk. Inside, the keep is entirely traditional; like Vincennes it has its own moat and is completely separated from the rest of the castle. There is no provision for gunports and no reinforcement of the walls against artillery, though the site would have made it difficult for an attacker to mount cannon within range. **Fuensaldaña,** just outside Valladolid, is an unfinished square 'plains' castle of the same type as Peñafiel, though here there are small gunports. Its keep is particularly impressive and is almost intact, with angle towers running the full height of each corner. The tower seems designed to make the maximum impression; unfortunately, its owner aroused the jealousy of the king's favourite and was murdered in 1453 before he could complete the castle. Within fifty years, the power of the nobles was broken, and both intrigues and castle-building were suppressed. The Spanish grandees became royal officials or sought adventure in the New World or in Habsburg Spain's newly created European empire.

So far we have looked at the castle mainly in military and technical terms. But it was also part of the community, a symbol of the lord's superiority but also of his responsibilities. When John, third baron Cobham, built his castle at Cooling in the 1380s he placed an inscription on the archway of the gatehouse which reads in modern English

> Know, all who are and shall be,
> That I am made to help the country.
> In knowing of which thing
> This is charter and witnessing.

Even if, in the wake of the Peasants' Revolt, he may have been anxious to emphasize that this was not a new tyrant's fortress, Cobham's inscription underlines one aspect of the castle that we have not yet touched on: its role in the safety of the community as a whole. Cooling is on the coast near Rochester, and raids on the Kentish coast by the French occurred several times in this period. Cobham himself was ordered on 30 June 1377 to provide for the defence of Kent, with other lords. In the event of an invasion, the local inhabitants would be expected to take refuge in the castle, both to help to man it, as they were required to do, and if possible to bring in all available food and livestock, so as to deprive the enemy of supplies. This explains the often disproportionate size of the area within the outer walls, which otherwise has no logical purpose and serves only to extend and hence weaken the defences. It also explains the long-established obligation of the local population to work on the construction, maintenance and manning of a castle. Examples of the duty of paying for or physically helping with the building of a new castle can be traced back to the eleventh century, and this duty continued as a means of maintaining the castle once it was finished. Castle-guard was a duty which applied not to the peasants but to the local knights, who in the twelfth and thirteenth centuries might have to spend up to four months a year on duty, though a more common figure was forty days.

Castles could also become the focal point of a new community: a site originally chosen for strategic reasons might, a century later, be the centre of a new village, with its own church and market, and could eventually grow to be a town. Watermills were also sometimes built as part of the castle complex, using the water which fed the moat, as at Ardres in Belgium. It is all too easy to see the castle in military terms: if there were indeed long periods – in France during the Hundred Years' War in particular – when castles were almost continuously on a war footing, as fortresses or refuges, there were far longer times of peace, when the castle was the focal point of a lordship, a centre where men went peacefully about their business.

12

Manor-Houses and Villages

Just as the great lords held their lands from the king, so at a lower level the lord's knights were rewarded for their service by landholdings, as were lesser men. In the ninth and tenth centuries, all kinds of service were paid for by grants of land: we find the lord's steward, his officials and even his cooks and his painters paid in this way, but in the succeeding centuries, with the increasing use of money, the granting of land came to be restricted to the class immediately below that of the lords, and a fourteenth-century German lawyer could define the system very simply: 'The fief is the pay of the knight.'

The knights formed the core of the lord's household; many of them lived permanently within the castle walls and were fed and housed by him. These household knights did not need a grant of land on which to live, though they often received it all the same. The knights who lived outside the household on their own lands reproduced the lord's household in miniature; their house was the focal point of a smaller estate run in a similar way to that of their lord. This pattern of feudal holdings was overlaid on the existing pattern of settlement, the villages, which had been established following the barbarian invasions. Throughout Europe, the general pattern of settlements in the country today is not radically different from that in 1000 AD, and few of the village sites are older than 500–600 AD. Broad patterns are always dangerously simple, but there is good reason to see the settlement of Europe in three rising stages: villages from 500 to 1000 AD, castles from 1000 to 1200, and towns from 1200 to 1400. The patterns overlap and there are many exceptions, but if we want to assess the likely age of a settlement, this is a reasonable guide.

The pattern of villages is surprisingly dense: in France, during the period of the great English raids between 1346 and 1361, it is estimated that most peasants were within twelve miles of a castle or walled town in which they could take refuge, which means that castles could be as much as twenty-four miles apart, and were certainly – except in special circumstances – ten miles away from each other. Villages in lowland England are often under a mile apart, even where naturally favourable sites are hard to find, and the vast bulk of these sites are Saxon. So they are the basic unit of medieval society, and the oldest of our contemporary social institutions.

But there is little that is obviously medieval in a village today, whether in Scandinavia or in Spain, apart from the parish church. Medieval peasants' houses varied from daub and wattle hovels to rough stone-built cabins; they were first and foremost '*machines à vivre*' and as a result were continuously adapted and rebuilt, particularly in the increased prosperity of sixteenth- and seventeenth-century Europe. Local historians and archaeologists can point out occasional survivals from much earlier periods embedded in the fabric of later houses, but clearly visible evidence, such as the cruck end-framing of a cottage at Didbrook in Gloucestershire, is rare.

As with the parish church, the medieval buildings that do stand out in a village today are the relics, not of the villagers themselves, but of men and institutions with wider horizons. The manor-houses of northern Europe represent the feudal system; the great tithe barns and granges represent the monastic orders with their huge farming enterprises. The pattern is of course far from uniform: the grouping of manor-house, church and cottages typical of northern Europe is unknown in southern France, Italy and Spain, where different factors prevailed. In France generally, where towns developed earlier and more quickly, many twelfth- and thirteenth-century knightly families would have lived in a town house rather than on their estates; in Italy, the newly wealthy middle classes in the towns actively bought land in the surrounding countryside. We shall meet Francesco di Marco Datini, the merchant of Prato, in his real context of trade and cities, but when he returned to his native town as a wealthy man in the late fourteenth century, he bought about 300 acres in small plots over the course of a dozen years. Even in France, some land had remained outside the feudal system, land technically held 'in allod', free of any feudal obligations; but the term would have been meaningless in Scandinavia, Saxony or Spain, where feudalism had scarcely penetrated and the typical settlement was a group of buildings at the centre of a farm, as in the farmhouse and fortified barns at Voss in Norway or in the farmhouses of Saxony. Inheritance systems also played their part: in southern France, the equal division of estates among heirs meant that holdings were continuously fragmented, whereas the primogeniture system of the north meant that estates passed intact. Furthermore, the presence of a sizable lord's house in the village was determined by the richness of the land: only in the most fertile parts of Europe – England and northern France – could the lords farm efficiently enough to produce a saleable surplus over and above their own needs.

English manor-houses survive in very large numbers: there are often three or four of medieval origin within a single village, and their history can be traced in architectural terms from the early thirteenth century. At Boothby Pagnell in Lincolnshire, a fine stone house consisting of a raised upper hall above a vaulted cellar survives almost unaltered. It is interesting to compare it with the not dissimilar farmhouse at Störa Hästnäs on Gotland, where similar space and accommodation is provided. Although Boothby Pagnell is built on two floors and Störa Hästnäs is a tower-house, both have a division of the living quarters, a raised entrance, and large storage areas, and a similar preoccupation with defence against casual raids without actually being fortified. Boothby Pagnell derives from castle and monastic architecture, and is on a grander scale than most manor-houses of the period. The majority of the latter would have been built in timber, the traditional northern building method: indeed, the Anglo-Saxon for 'to build' is *timbran*. A number of castle halls were built in wood, to a design which gave an aisle along each side under the lower parts of the roof slope, and this was copied in later, smaller houses throughout southern and eastern England. The wooden hall is itself a very early building type, celebrated in Anglo-Saxon poetry as the house of the chieftain where he dispenses mead and gifts to his followers. Reconstructions of such early halls can be seen at West Stow in Suffolk and at Löjsta on Gotland, where the original dated from c.1000 AD and was a very primitive form of aisled hall. The typical English medieval aisled hall is often sophisticated, with elaborate tracery in the spandrels and trusses where these are visible. In the late fourteenth century, the central part of the hall was roofed by a new type of truss, which did away with the need for aisle supports and gave a central area which was the full width of the building, in parallel with the development of more sophisticated forms of church roofing at this period. Smaller examples of these buildings are almost always private homes; for a grand example of an aisled hall, we must go to Oakham castle in Rutland.

In the fourteenth and fifteenth centuries, the size of the manor-house tends to increase, and the distinction between castle and manor becomes one of technical detail, as at Stokesay in Shropshire, where the basic design is that of a great house and the defences are incidental rather than integral to the building. The great hall is typical of that found in many fourteenth-century manor-houses; it is smaller than that at Dartington Hall in Devon but nearly twice the size of that at Bradley Manor near Newton Abbot. Great halls continued to be built in the larger manor-houses until the mid sixteenth century, but the general trend was already towards greater subdivision and privacy. The first room to be divided off was the lord's bedchamber or great chamber, sometimes called a solar, which strictly means no more than a room above ground-floor level. This separate room is already present at Boothby Pagnell as a mere division of the rectangular hall block. At Stokesay it has become a separate feature, a tower at the end of the hall block; the solar is half the size of the hall itself, and has its own fireplace. At Bradley Manor, we can see the next development, that of private sitting rooms: the oriel, originally a projecting bay added on an upper storey, became an integral part of the house, while at the same time the lord and lady withdrew from the great hall to dine in a separate parlour. Such arrangements would be found only in the largest manors and were closely related to developments in contemporary town houses. Where we find large-scale houses in the country, they often belonged to men with considerable but scattered estates, who might also have town houses. The Pastons in fifteenth-century Norfolk, with houses in half a dozen villages and in Norwich, would have expected a similar standard of comfort wherever they went. Like the kings in the early Middle Ages, they travelled from manor to manor partly to manage their estates and partly because it was easier to move house than to move produce from one manor to another.

In France, the equivalent small houses were almost always fortified at this period. Timber survivals such as the manor-house at Canapville near Lisieux, built for the bishops of Lisieux, are limited to Normandy, and even there are mostly to be found in the Auge region. Late-fifteenth-century stone manors such as Courboyer near Bellême in the Perche region are close in appearance to the Scottish fortified houses of the following century, with massive towers and elegant turrets. Further south, the *manoir* disappears, and in its place we have the small *château*, a building whose English equivalent would be 'hall' rather than 'castle', but which is more substantial than all save a few English manors. The small manor-house is missing here, as elsewhere in Europe.

Of the other buildings of the village, barns survive in surprising numbers: like houses, they are often disguised by later additions or rebuildings. The most spectacular examples are usually tithe barns, where the tenth of each crop due to the church was gathered in and stored, or the barns of monastic estates or granges. The Templar barns at Cressing in Essex date back to the twelfth century, while at Great Coxwell in Berkshire there is a thirteenth-century barn which belonged to Beaulieu abbey, built on the aisled hall principle. The barn at Bradford on Avon, dating from a century later and once the property of Shaftesbury abbey, has a more sophisticated single-span roof.

13

Towns and Trade

The town is perhaps the greatest innovation of the later Middle Ages. The Romans gave us the great cities of Europe, the barbarian invaders in the fifth and sixth centuries the bulk of our villages; the town as a self-governing, dynamic entity belongs to the thirteenth and fourteenth centuries. The government of the Roman empire had been based on a systematic network of cities connected by military highways, and the very word 'civilization' implies that life in a city (*civis*) is superior to that of the village or countryside. The barbarian tribes who overwhelmed the empire were literally 'uncivilized', in that they did not live in cities and were prepared to work as farmers or soldiers, tasks which the Roman citizens had come to abhor. The Roman city in its ideal form depended on a highly developed economy and a powerful imperial defence system for its existence: it was spacious, with superb public buildings, and its inhabitants lived in stone-built houses, ranging from vast tenement blocks to elegant houses on the edge of the town served by paved roads and municipal sewerage systems. Food and supplies of all kinds were often brought from considerable distances: Rome itself depended on north African corn to supply its population. The inhabitants led a leisured life, in which public entertainments played an important part: every Roman city had its arena or amphitheatre as one of its public buildings. Many towns had no walls, because attack was unthinkable far from the great frontier garrisons on the Rhine and Danube.

This picture of calm – admittedly a somewhat idealized one – was rudely shattered by the first barbarian invasions of the latter part of the third century AD. The towns were now fortified; in Gaul, where sixty cities were destroyed in 276, cities as far west as Saintes, almost on the Atlantic coast, hastily erected walls at around this time. The cost of building extensive walls meant that parts of the city were often excluded; wealthy men who had once lived on the edge of the city left their unprotected houses for country villas, a trend encouraged by agricultural and social changes which favoured the creation of great estates. Roman cities had never had a wealthy merchant class; their great men were essentially government officials and administrators, and their prosperity depended on that of the imperial state itself rather than on trade. As public order decayed, owing to corruption within and barbarian attack from without, so the towns and cities fell into decline. Public buildings and works ceased to be maintained, and the focus of economic life moved to the countryside.

The new barbarian rulers, having sacked the towns in the process of conquest, saw them in a different light. It was the towns, fortified and often strategically placed, which had offered most resistance; they were strongholds, with a definite military value. There are few, if any, examples of a major medieval town without defensive walls, but the military aspect of towns is often ignored: they could resist attack just as successfully as any other kind of fortification, and this remained true throughout the Middle Ages. Otherwise, the Merovingian, Lombard and Visigothic kings valued towns as symbols of their power, and as convenient centres from which to govern. They took over the palace buildings of the Roman governors, or established a comrade-in-arms, the *comes* or count, as their deputy in a provincial city. As soon as the kings became Christian, the cities had an added importance as the seat of a bishop, and many places owed their very survival to their new role as a religious centre; those which did not become bishoprics often disappeared completely. In England, where the re-establishment of orderly government took far longer, correspondingly fewer towns survived; we have seen that many of the English bishoprics were based outside towns, with minsters at their centre. In Spain, the decaying towns of the south were revived by the Arab invaders, whose civilization was favourable to great towns based on trade: Baghdad, Cairo and Damascus far outshone their western counterparts in the ninth and tenth centuries.

The fate of a great city in the uncertain centuries between Constantine and Charlemagne can best be seen at Trier (p. 291 below), not far behind the imperial frontier on the Rhine. Salvian, writing in the fifth century, speaks of it as having been sacked four times and wiped out. Rapid decline under attack in the fourth and fifth centuries was followed by a period when the town was almost deserted, as the presence of a hermit living in one of the Roman gates suggests. In Trier's case, the medieval revival was modest: the Liebfrauenkirche is much smaller than the cathedral, basically a fifth-century building, and no attempt was made to replace the latter, as would have been done elsewhere, while the medieval walls were only half the length of the Roman ones and followed a very different course.

The re-emergence of towns in the later Middle Ages can be dated in broad terms to the tenth century and beyond. Charlemagne's revival of imperial ideas did not include a vision of the empire based on a network of administrative centres. His government was that of the late empire and copied only the highest echelons of the imperial civil service, the 'leaders', *duces* or dukes, who were his deputies, on the model of Roman provincial governors. The administrative unit for the Carolingian empire was the imperial estate or *villa*; although the modern French *ville* derives from this word, the relationship between these huge farms (for which precise if rather unrealistic instructions on management were issued by Charlemagne) and the later medieval town is negligible. The *villae* were established on sites suitable as farming centres, not necessarily convenient for communication or defence; nor did they bear any relation to the pattern of church administration.

The crucial element in the reappearance of the town is that of trade. Roman towns had in a sense been administrative collecting points for the huge supplies required by the state to maintain its armies, drawing on a relatively unsophisticated agricultural economy. Changes both in technology and attitudes meant that medieval towns were essentially centres for exchange, supplying specialist goods to the countryside in return for produce. Furthermore, the role of the towns as religious centres encouraged this: both the celebration of church festivals and local pilgrimages to shrines and relics were occasions which drew people to the towns; and in the ninth century, with the spread of monastic life, a number of major monasteries appeared just outside the town walls. Under Roman law, burial within the town or city itself was forbidden, and Christians had their own distinct cemeteries, as in the catacombs on the Appian Way at Rome. We have seen how, in Rome itself, churches were built over the burial sites of saints; and this process was repeated throughout the former imperial lands. By the tenth century, these often humble churches had become the nuclei for new monasteries; most great medieval towns have one or more monasteries within their walls, drawn into the town itself as the ring of defences was expanded to accommodate a growing population.

The Romans had relied primarily on land communications; they had never been greatly interested in seafaring as a means of transport. With the decay of the roads, river and sea routes became increasingly important, and ports and river-towns flourished even in the eighth century, when their landlocked counterparts were in the deepest decline. It is from this period that the prosperity of the Low Countries and the Rhine cities dates; at the heart of Charlemagne's empire, they were ideally placed for long-distance trade anywhere from central Europe to Britain and the North Sea coast. Men from what is now north Holland were famous as sailors from the sixth century onwards, and their trading settlements reached as far south as Mainz: Ghent, Maastricht, Namur and other Low Countries towns date back as trading centres to this period. The successors to the Friesians, the Vikings, whom we tend to remember as destroyers of organized life and hence of commerce, were traders as much as raiders. Their great settlements at Birka, Hedeby and Duurstede in Holland have been excavated, revealing spacious warehouses, shipyards and farmsteads, and a wealth of exotic imported goods from as far afield as Russia and Persia. They established trading-posts across northern Europe and deep into Russia; their word *vik* or *wik*, originally meaning a bay which provided anchorage, came to mean merchant settlement, and dozens of place-names still contain this element. A tenth-century glossary defines *wik* simply as 'a village where merchants dwell'. It was used of non-Viking settlements such as Quentowic on the French coast near Boulogne. When the Norsemen destroyed this town, it was refounded as Étaples, 'the place of storehouses', and traders continued to come there. The five ships found at Skuldelev in 1962 and preserved at Roskilde include two cargo ships, a reminder of how important coastal trade was to the Vikings themselves.

Merchant quarters could also be found in the ninth century much further inland in German territory. At the Roman Rhine fortress of Castra Regina, now Regensburg, a merchants' quarter is recorded in the late ninth century. It was substantial enough to be fortified in 917 and joined to the old Roman fortifications. On the other hand, they are rare in France; but much depends on the survival of records. The merchants of this period, although they enjoyed royal protection and were subject to special royal officials, were not members of formal associations and did not build communal halls. Only detailed archaeology can distinguish the merchants' quarter of an early medieval town, as in the recent excavations at York, if we have no documentary evidence of it.

The privileges granted to merchants under Louis the Pious in 825 and 828 foreshadow the independence of traders throughout the later Middle Ages. Merchants are to be free from service in the army, their ships are not to be seized and they are to be tried in special courts, forerunners of the English courts of 'piepowder' or *pieds poudrés*, referring to the travelling merchant's dusty feet. These were not general privileges, however; they had to be obtained by individuals, and it was only in the eleventh and twelfth century that a specific body of law relating to merchants came into being.

By the end of the eleventh century, town life had once more become an important feature of European society. The increased economic activity following the end of the raids by Norsemen and the settlement of the raiders in England and Normandy was largely channelled through the towns, while in Germany a deliberate policy of encouragement of trade under the Ottonian dynasty had led to the creation of twenty-nine new royal markets in central and eastern Germany between 936 and 1002, mostly in smaller towns which became important as a result of their market charters. In Spain, after the recapture of Toledo in 1085, towns were founded by Alfonso VI and his successors in northern and central Spain, usually for military reasons but also to re-populate the deserted frontier regions which the Moslems had neglected in favour of the rich lands of Andalucía. Segovia, Salamanca, Ciudad Rodrigo and Ávila, which retains its original walls, all date from this period. Other new towns across northern Spain, such as Puente la Reina, grew up along the pilgrimage road to Compostela. Gradually, skilled artisans began to group themselves in towns to be nearer to the markets: until the early eleventh century, most handicraft work had been done on the rural estates, and the trade was in raw materials rather than finished goods. Industrial specialization developed only gradually, but it was to be a very important factor in town life.

But the towns as yet lacked any formal organization. The

merchants had set up associations as long ago as the eighth century; the first of the guilds, mentioned in an edict of Charlemagne in 779, were societies which aimed to help their members in need and were purely religious and charitable. By the early eleventh century, we hear of such a guild acting in concert in trading affairs, merchants from Tiel in Guelders who traded with England; and within fifty years such societies of traders were common in Flanders and the Rhineland.

Clearly such merchant bodies, whose individuals were already recognized as enjoying a special legal status, could not fit into the system of feudal law and tenure; and the same was to a lesser extent true of towns as a whole, because feudal procedures relied largely on the tenure of productive land. Towns were often subject to ancient royal or episcopal sovereignty, and it was not easy for a lord to lay claim to them, even if they lay within his lands. The attempt was made, however, but it was relatively short-lived. By the end of the eleventh century, towns began to develop their own political organization, effectively outside the feudal system. The inhabitants united into communes and became the collective feudatory of their lord, whether he was king, bishop or noble. In Spain and Italy, where the feudal system was less powerful, we find towns gaining exemption from royal or imperial jurisdiction as early as the tenth century; the 'town peace' gave responsibility for the maintenance of order, and hence control over certain areas of government, to the townspeople themselves, as at Genoa in 958. The earliest French commune was that of Cambrai in 1076, and between then and 1270 many French and English towns gained their own charters. The end of the twelfth century was a particularly rewarding period, as an indirect result of the Third Crusade: Philip Augustus delegated royal authority in major towns to a provost and four citizens before his departure for the east in 1190, and in the unrest of Richard's and John's reigns in England, many English towns acquired some degree of formal independence: London, which had had a charter in the early twelfth century but had lost its freedoms in 1141, was able to buy a new charter of liberties in 1199 for 3,000 marks.

Besides giving legal independence and some degree of self-government, charters often granted freedom from tolls to merchants from a particular town. Tolls were a major source of income to owners of markets, fairs, bridges and roads, and were also exacted on the actual buying and selling of goods. Freedom from tolls, whether granted in respect of a few local places or – much more rarely – in general terms throughout the kingdom, was a great commercial advantage, and was usually purchased from kings or lords short of ready cash, who were in effect realizing their revenue in advance.

The personal freedom of townsmen was also an encouragement to the growth of towns. Once a man was accepted as a citizen – often after residence in the town for a year and a day – and had taken the oath usually required of all citizens, he was outside the feudal system, even if he had been a serf. '*Stadtluft macht frei*' ran the German saying: 'town air makes you a free man' – free in some respects, but also bound by the oath to your fellow-citizens. But it was a powerful attraction to ambitious or able men whose only other hope was a career in the church as a means of escape from their ties with the land. The town walls thus became not only a defence, but a boundary line between the feudal and non-feudal worlds. The gates were guarded to prevent unauthorized entry and to collect tolls, and they would be shut at night; a bell would be rung to warn citizens that this was about to happen. (Bells were the usual method of signalling civic events: hence the great belfries of the Flemish town halls, and the *grosse cloche* at Bordeaux, which is still used to signal the beginning of the vintage.) The citizen's life was regulated in a multitude of other ways: edicts prescribed the way he should build his house, how he should dress, what live-stock he could keep, while trade regulations covered the minutest detail of his commercial activities.

Because towns were potential sources of revenue and control of townships was both a political and military advantage, we find numerous examples of deliberate new town foundations throughout the twelfth to fourteenth centuries, where no town or even settle-ment of any kind existed before. Military and political town founda-tions go back to the Anglo-Saxon *burhs* or boroughs, fortified sites with a sufficient population to fulfil the strategic and administrative needs of Alfred and his successors; they are rare on the continent until the eleventh century because Charlemagne's policy had been based on the *villa*, and there was no tradition of such foundations. The market charters of the Ottonian emperors, already mentioned, did not imply the foundation of a town, and the deliberate founda-tion of trading towns comes later. One of the earliest examples is Freiburg im Breisgau, founded by the duke of Zähringen in 1120, in imitation of the great trading towns on the Rhine. The inhabitants were all to be traders or merchants, and the town was laid out with a broad market street running across it. Only the ground plan and the south-eastern gate of the original town survives; the market street is now the Kaiser-Josef Strasse. The magnificent town hall and merchants' houses are all sixteenth-century, but these and the cathedral bear witness to the success of the venture. Lübeck (p. 302 below) was virtually a new foundation in 1158. But the new towns of the thirteenth century were usually on a more modest scale, and the best examples as a group are to be found in the **bastides** of south-west France. Here political, economic and military factors all come together. They are grouped on the thirteenth-century frontier between English and French territory along the Dordogne, Garonne and Lot valleys, and represent a planned effort by both sides to establish their lordship over disputed territory while providing for its settlement and exploitation. Continuing warfare in the area meant that the bastides were also, but incidentally, used as military strongholds: this was not their prime function. A number can be identified by their 'gridiron' layout: a typical bastide of this kind is square in plan with a central roadway in each direction and is completely contained by a surrounding wall. The church and market place are in the centre of the town, and the market usually has covered arcades, while the houses are separated by narrow spaces designed to prevent the rapid spread of fire, which so often devastated medieval towns. In all, there are nearly two hundred bastides, built by French and English royal officials between about 1250 and 1300; of these, some eighty were founded by the king of England, acting either alone or in concert with a local lord, and about two out of five are built on some form of grid plan.

The classic example of a bastide is **Monpazier**, founded in 1284, south of the Dordogne between Bergerac and Cahors. Here much of the outer wall and three of the six gates remain, and the ground plan is virtually unchanged. The grid pattern is clear, and many of the houses still occupy their exact thirteenth-century sites, so that the system of fire prevention by narrow spaces, or *androndes*, between the buildings can be seen. A few of the original façades survive, notably at no. 39 rue Notre-Dame on the main north–south axis, and in the market place, where the arcades survive, though the wooden market building is much later. (This market hall contains the local set of weights and measures, a reminder of the general lack of standardization in medieval times.) The original church has been replaced by a late Gothic building, but is on the original site adjoining the market square. At other bastides, such as Monflanquin and Beaumont, the church is used as part of the town's fortifications, while at Domme the site of the bastide is determined by strategic considerations. Almost all the bastides are set in open country, a reminder that their inhabitants were primarily engaged in agriculture, though there was a mint at Domme, and Libourne, the largest of all the bastides, was a port near Bordeaux.

By the late thirteenth century, a number of towns succeeded in developing their political identity to the point where they were in all but name independent states. In Italy, the towns owed only the very loosest allegiance to the Holy Roman Empire (and were often at war with the emperor); in Germany, a number of towns threw off the only effective control over them, that of their local bishop, and became 'free imperial towns', again owing obedience only to the emperor. Whereas in Italy there were few, if any, towns which were not independent, the 'free imperial cities' were rarer and were the exception rather than the rule. They were to all intents and purposes free of feudal taxes and tolls; they were self-governing, had their own armies and could form alliances, and the emperor's hold over them was very slight. Such towns naturally had great trading advantages over their less free rivals. The most important were Worms, Speyer, Basel, Strasbourg, Augsburg and Magdeburg. Regensburg and Nuremberg (pp. 292, 296 below) owed much of their prosperity to this special status.

In Italy, the old civic institutions of Roman times had lingered on, if only as a focus for opposition to the bishops, who were usually the lords of the towns in the eighth and ninth centuries. But the real impetus towards independence came with the formation of communes in the tenth and eleventh centuries, and the revival of east–west trade, in which Italy was the vital geographical link. Pavia in the early eleventh century was dealing with French and English traders on the one hand and merchants from Venice and southern Italy on the other. We have noted the charter given to Genoa in 958; Venice, founded in the marshes of the Po delta in the fifth century by refugees from the mainland, was self-governing from the beginning, owing nominal but unenforced allegiance to the

Byzantine emperors and emerging as a fully fledged republic in the tenth century after the Byzantine withdrawal from northern Italy. The mainland cities, without the protection of Venice's lagoon, had more difficulty in shaking off ambitious lords, and there is a long interval between the first appearance of consuls, at Pisa in 1085, and their achievement of unchallenged control in the cities. But in the twelfth century both Otto of Freising, closely in touch with the imperial court, and an outside observer, the Jewish writer Benjamin of Tudela, were struck by the way in which the cities ran their own affairs, under the leadership of officials – usually consuls and a great council – elected by the populace. But this did not mean that there was no feudal hierarchy within the cities; throughout their history, there is a perpetual tension between the nobles and their fellow-citizens. It is simply that feudalism never became the predominant form and carried none of the automatic superiority that it did elsewhere. In Bologna in the thirteenth century a writer contrasted the barefoot nobles with the merchants who travelled in coaches or on horseback. In Genoa in 1173 and in 1211 the consuls actually dubbed knights and raised their own cavalry force in this way. But equally the nobles had resources which the common people lacked: perhaps their most powerful weapon was the desire of the newly wealthy merchants to join the ranks of the nobles, so that the natural leaders of their rivals the *popolo* or common people were perpetually defecting to the other side. Just as the tradespeople had their guilds, so the Italian nobles had sworn associations, either by kindred or by rank, and many of the feuds which bedevilled the Italian cities were between these noble factions. Bologna and San Gimignano (p. 326) retain the visual evidence of this, the multiplicity of towers once typical of Italian towns, in which the owners could defend themselves against attack. There were other reasons for this style of building, however, such as shortage of land within the city (as with the office blocks of today) and a love of display. At intervals attempts were made to limit or destroy such towers by the city officials, but they were never successful.

The self-evident wealth and power of these communities, coupled with the inherited traditions of Rome, made them the focal points of fierce patriotism. The wider *patria* (fatherland) of the Roman poets became narrow pride in the immediate community. There are a number of panegyrics on individual cities, but the quality of Italian civic patriotism, which was to influence the later national patriotism of the fourteenth and fifteenth centuries, can best be seen in Dante's love-hate relationship with his native Florence, from which he was exiled. In his *Divine Comedy* he looked back to a golden age of the city, when life was simpler and men less greedy and ambitious. Again, it is a concept taken from classical literature, but Dante regards the golden age as very recent, and presents it as his great-grandfather's description of life in the city in his own time: an age when the greatest magnates were content with simple clothing and homespun ways instead of seeking foreign luxuries and riches in trade. But Dante's vision was an illusion, as much as William Morris's similar vision of medieval London –

> ... small and white and clean
> The clear Thames bordered by its gardens green.

The more tangible aspect of this civic pride was in the public buildings of the Italian cities, which also owed their being to the new patriotism and to the old Roman traditions of public building, dormant for many centuries but still remembered. We have seen how in any medieval town, including those of Italy, the cathedral could be a focus for civic pride. In Italy, however, we find also the first great secular civic buildings: the Palazzo Comunale in Siena, with its famous *campo*, completed in 1346, in front of it, and the Palazzo Vecchio in Florence are the best surviving examples of a form which first appeared in Lombardy in the mid twelfth century. In Florence the Bargello, the palace of the city governor, also survives. Of the grandest of all the medieval civic palaces, the Doge's Palace at Venice, only the fourteenth-century façade is left; the wealth of Venice in the sixteenth and seventeenth centuries meant that the interior was remodelled as fashion dictated. At Siena, however, the great frescoes by Lorenzetti and others show that lavish interiors were by no means exclusive to later centuries. Attempts were also made at Siena to regulate building around the *campo*, so that houses would have a uniform window pattern; but standardization and an architectural concept of the city as a whole were a Renaissance ideal. True, the walls gave the city a clear identity and visual unity when they were newly built, but the same can be said of castles, and in the case of cities, suburbs quickly grew up to dispel any visual effect the imposing ring of towers and battlements might have had. The cities were too dynamic;

Florence's original Roman walls were trebled in extent in the twelfth century, and these walls were in turn almost trebled two hundred years later. Between each rebuilding, the suburbs grew to be larger than the city itself. Public works were also a point of civic pride, notably the fountains and aqueducts which were essential for the cities. The Fontana Maggiore outside the cathedral at Perugia, with bas-reliefs by Nicola Pisano, built in 1277–80, and the imposing aqueduct at Spoleto, on a scale worthy of Roman civil engineering, built in 1362–70, are two of the finest examples.

The features of the Italian city-states were not unique to them, even if the political freedom of the northern towns was more limited. In the Low Countries and north Germany, as well as in great trading centres such as London, we find impressive public buildings. But it is noticeable that trade is the crucial factor in determining the size and wealth of a medieval town. There are cities and towns where other elements are more important or as important, but they never rivalled the great trading centres: Avignon and Rome, as the church's administrative centres, Bologna or Oxford as university towns, Santiago or Canterbury as pilgrim centres, never attained the same prosperity as the trading towns. If Paris and London had been merely centres of government, they too would have remained relatively small. For the medieval world, towns and trade were synonymous; but within the world of commerce there was immense diversity of emphasis. Some towns were the centres of international fairs, a development of the local market on a grander scale. These originally developed to deal with the sale of seasonal goods, primarily wool at the end of the shearing season; but increasingly they became major points of contact for trade between northern and southern Europe. The most important group were the four towns in Champagne, which from about 1180 onwards held six fairs spaced throughout the year: one at Lagny, one at Bar-sur-Aube, two at Provins and two at Champagne. As each fair lasted for up to two months, from the arrival of goods to the final settling of debts, commercial activity in the area was almost continuous. The French and Flemish merchants brought textiles from the manufacturing areas spread across northern France and the Low Countries, while the Italian merchants paid for their purchases both in exotic Mediterranean goods needed by the cloth-makers, such as alum (used as a cleansing agent) and rare dye-stuffs, as well as in spices and other luxuries. As the fairs developed, so formal organizations appeared to deal with the problems of contracts and of the safety of merchants travelling to and from the fairs: officials were appointed to supervise contracts, which were recognized as valid everywhere on pain of being banned from all the fairs, instead of merely within the limited jurisdiction of the lord of the place where the contract was made, while the count of Champagne organized safe-conducts through France and Burgundy for merchants travelling to the fairs. Despite their immense prestige, the fairs were by nature institutions which have left little trace behind them: at Provins, there is the tithe barn, or Grange aux Dîmes, which was used as a covered market, and at Bar-sur-Aube a wooden portico around one of the churches in which the traders' stalls were set up. For all their crucial importance in the development of trade, the fairs themselves declined from the mid thirteenth century onwards: Provins was deprived of its privileges after a riot, and although the other fairs continued they ceased to be the main means of exchange of goods.

The merchant of the early Middle Ages was a traveller, moving around with his goods in great caravans, like his oriental counterpart. From the late thirteenth century, however, the growth of international institutions and the improvement in communications brought about by the rise of the fairs – many Alpine roads were rebuilt in the early thirteenth century to cater for this traffic – meant that the merchant could control operations from his home, relying on a network of contacts for his business and on professional carriers to convey his goods. Trade-routes were built up along the Rhône, and the routes down the Rhine were extended into central Germany and linked up across the Alpine passes with Italy, while Flanders and England developed a very close producing and manufacturing link: England produced the raw material, wool, and Flanders converted it into cloth. Meanwhile the merchants of the north German towns and of the Baltic were linking the trade with Russia with that of the Rhine and the Low Countries. The old pattern of self-sufficiency or of manufacturing at the point where raw materials were produced was being replaced by the basic pattern of modern industry and trade, where imports or exports of raw materials are balanced by exports or imports of finished goods. At the same time, specialist trade services such as insurance and banking developed.

In the later Middle Ages, we first find merchant towns which traded entirely in foreign commodities, having no substantial natural resources of their own. Some were ports, such as Venice, Lübeck, Visby and Aigues-Mortes; but others were inland towns, such as Florence and Siena. The latter depended for their wealth on the use of credit and banking facilities, which had first been developed at the end of the twelfth century. Eleventh-century trading was often by barter; but money was always an element in trade, and money-changers were important at the fairs. They began to issue letters of credit to avoid the need for physically transferring coin over long distances, and gradually a network for exchange and settlement of foreign debts grew up, in parallel with the system of banking for government and ecclesiastical purposes which was often in the hands of the monastic orders. By the second half of the thirteenth century, however, commercial credit was much more sophisticated than that offered by the Templars, and with the suppression of the latter in the early fourteenth century, banking became a secular trade. The loans made were often huge, and against poor security; the collapse of the great Florentine banks of the Bardi and Peruzzi in the 1340s was due to their lending nearly one and a half million gold florins to Edward III to finance his French wars. Most of it was spent on buying a 'grand alliance' which failed to win a speedy victory in 1338-9 and came to nothing, with the result that Edward stopped repayments and the banks collapsed. This disaster was followed by the years of plague and a general decline in economic activity, due partly to depopulation and partly to the devastation of wars in France and Italy, which led to radical changes in the patterns of production and consumption, while new elements, such as imports of rye and iron ore from eastern Europe, made their appearance.

For a vivid image of a merchant's life at the end of the fourteenth century, we have the business papers of Francesco di Marco Datini, over 150,000 of which were discovered in his house at the little Italian city of Prato in 1870, and from which Iris Origo brilliantly re-created his life in her book *The Merchant of Prato*. A small portion of the archive is displayed in the town hall, but only the expert can decipher the technical language of the endless letters of instruction which went to and fro between Datini and his agents in Pisa, Avignon, Spain and elsewhere. His house, which he left to charity, still stands, completely rebuilt inside but with traces of fifteenth-century frescoes on the outside; but it is difficult to recapture the grandiose impression it once made on his fellow-citizens. Datini was the leading merchant of his small city, but on an international scale he could not compete with the greatest trading companies or with individual merchants. Nor had he their political ambitions: we find Italian merchants on the French royal council and high in the favour of the English king, and merchants from the Hanse advising the Black Prince. The most impressive memorial to such an individual is the house of Jacques Cœur at **Bourges**. Jacques's fortune was founded on his work as royal moneyer at Bourges, and he later became master of the Paris mint; but between 1430 and 1450 he traded with the east, buying cloth and linen at Rouen, Troyes and Bruges and importing sugar, spices and silk. His network of contacts dwarfs that of Datini: he helped to found a French consulate in Alexandria, owned banks at Rouen and Bruges, sent ships not only across the Mediterranean but also down the Atlantic coast. Even if the capital with which Jacques Cœur traded may have been in part the royal revenues for which he was responsible, his range of activity was extraordinary. In the end, he became too obvious a target for intrigue: the king was deeply in his debt, having borrowed 200,000 gold crowns for his Normandy campaign in 1449. In 1451 Cœur was arrested and accused of various financial malpractices, and his goods were seized by the king.

Cœur's career is therefore exceptional, and the palatial house he created at Bourges must have been almost without parallel in its time; indeed, it is still referred to as the 'palace' of Jacques Cœur. It is in some ways closer to the Renaissance châteaux of the Loire than anything else, with decorative turrets and a spacious interior courtyard. But on closer examination it is seen to combine the luxurious and the practical in a way which, though strange to us, was typical of merchants' houses in this period. Even such a grand figure as Jacques Cœur lived 'over the shop'; the richly ornamented street façade, with its *trompe l'œil* figures of a man and a woman watching from balconies, has two entrances, one for carts and one for pedestrians. Three sides of the irregular courtyard are simple: a glazed gallery above a portico – like that at Bar-sur-Aube, but in stone – where merchants could display their wares. The other two sides, marked off by staircase towers, contain the living quarters. At one end were the kitchens, the heat from which was used to provide steam baths on the floor above; in the centre was

the banqueting hall; and at the other end a private suite of rooms
with its own staircases to a similar set of rooms above. On the
first floor, above the banqueting hall, was the great hall, and in
the tower at one corner of it, Jacques Cœur's office and treasure
chamber. In all there were over thirty rooms, including a private
chapel over the entrance which could be used by both the family
and by visiting merchants. In this chapel we can glimpse the richness of the interior decoration, because the glorious painted ceiling
has survived. It was probably the work of a French master who
knew the work of the great Flemish artists. Against the star-studded
deep blue of a night sky, angels carry texts from the Old and New
Testaments in praise of Christ. The vaulting is complex for such
a small roof, and the way in which the elegant figures have been
composed to fit the elongated spaces is very impressive. Elsewhere,
only occasional features have survived the use of the building first
as the town hall and then as law-courts. A magnificent turreted
chimneypiece and handsomely carved doorway in the banqueting
hall are the best examples of the wealth of sculpture that once
adorned the house. Corbels with secular scenes, such as that which
represents an episode from the romance of Tristan, reflect the taste
of the owner, while the contemporary fashion for mottoes and
devices is evident from the hearts on the façade and inscriptions
such as 'To a valiant heart nothing is impossible' and 'Speak, act
and keep silent'. Jacques Cœur's earlier career as a merchant in
the east is commemorated in the decoration of exotic trees on the
central courtyard tower. Ironically, his career was to end there:
banished from France in 1453, he found employment as commander of a fleet sent to assist the Hospitallers at Rhodes, and
died on the island of Chios in 1456.

On a small scale, but of equal splendour, is the **Ca d'Oro** in
Venice, built between 1420 and 1434 for Marino Contarini, a
member of the family from which several doges came. Contarini's
notebooks for the building accounts survive. He seems to have
designed the house, but he employed two companies of stone-
cutters, including Matteo Raverti and Giovanni Bon, famous for
their work on Milan cathedral and the Doge's Palace respectively.
The house follows the traditional Venetian pattern, where the façade
of porticoes and loggias is flanked by enclosed rooms to left and
right. The Ca d'Oro, probably because of lack of space, is asymmetrical: the enclosed rooms are to one side. The porticoes, as in

Jacques Cœur's house, were places to do business, where wares could be spread out and examined, while the rooms included both store-rooms and living quarters. The Ca d'Oro is spectacular in the opulence of its decoration: flamboyant Gothic tracery, door-ways with a hint of oriental designs, and rich marble facings from an earlier building combine to make up a façade like that of a rich casket. The façade was originally painted and gilded: the gilding was mostly on the tracery and on the pinnacles of the 'battlements', with vivid red and blue paintwork elsewhere. The whole effect must have been highly theatrical, even in an age renowned for magnificent display of wealth. The entrance is to one side: a plain doorway gives on to a courtyard where an impressive portal makes up for the lack of outer display; in the centre of a pinnacled tympanum an angel holds the Contarini arms. An open staircase leads to the upper floors, which formed the living quarters. The interiors have all been completely rebuilt, and the Ca d'Oro now serves as a museum of sixteenth- and seventeenth-century Venetian art; some of the furnishings, notably the chests or *cassoni*, are of the correct date, and there is a fifteenth-century staircase brought from elsewhere.

Another survival from this period with a less impressive exterior but with fine interiors is the **Palazzo Davanzati** in **Florence**. This was built by the Davizzi, who were prominent in civic life, in the 1330s; it housed not one, but several, families, a practice similar to that of dividing inheritances equally among heirs. The clan, rather than the modern nuclear family, was the social unit. But this division did not imply squalor; pooled resources, on the contrary, made a more impressive building possible. It is built round a central courtyard, with the spacious and well-lit formal rooms on the façade. The ground floor is the working area, with storage space and servants' quarters; the rooms on the upper floors are luxurious by the standards of the period, with their original stone fireplaces – a recent innovation when the palace was built – and delightful late-fourteenth-century decoration: one bedroom is painted with a tile pattern of lions, while in the frieze courtly life is depicted in an arcade. Other rooms have floral patterns, with different friezes – garden views, a chivalric story – while parakeets perch in the foliage below. The murals are clearly related in general style to those at Avignon, and, like those in the papal palace, imitate the themes of tapestries. There is a study or writing room, im-

portant to a family with much civic business to look after. The
kitchen also survives more or less in its original state, with shelves
built into a recess in the wall. The furniture is a diverse collection,
mostly of a later date.

But such buildings as these are the exception, not the rule, and
most of the apparently medieval townscapes that we see today are
in fact no earlier than the sixteenth century. Most towns have
suffered a major fire at some time in their history; war, changes
in fashion and sheer decay have done the rest. As Howard Salzman
says, 'rare indeed is the *Altstadt* that can boast a secular building
older than the fifteenth century, and many are the *vieux quartiers*
dating almost wholly from the seventeenth century or later'. Of
all the aspects of medieval life, the aspect and atmosphere of a
medieval town is perhaps the hardest to recapture.

Trier

Trier is one of the rare towns where the link between the classical
past and the medieval world is clearly in evidence. Beside the
famous Porta Nigra, Germany's finest monument from Roman
times, stands a delightful Romanesque cloister, founded for the
hermit Simeon, who had established himself in the Porta Nigra.
The Romanesque arcades echo the arcading of the gateway itself.
Even the most spectacular modern buildings in Trier have an
ancient background: witness the theatrical effect of the gilt, purple
and white stucco of the bishop's palace, like a flat stage-set against
the rebuilt civic basilica of Constantine, which was adapted as a
palace by the early Frankish rulers of the city in the 470s. The
Rhineland Museum is full of magnificent classical statuary, monuments and mosaics; by contrast there are a mere handful of the
barbarian weapons which conquered the empire, and, tucked away
in a corner, a relief of a Roman horseman and a mounted barbarian
locked in conflict, a suitable symbol for a city which was sacked
four times by the Franks between 411 and 427. If you take the
central point of the modern city, the market place and cathedral,
the Middle Ages come sharply into view, and in the museum by
the Porta Nigra, the tenth-century headstone of the market cross
deservedly has a room to itself. The cathedral summarizes Trier's
whole history. Its central portion, to a height of about twenty-five
feet, is still the original Roman building, an audience hall adapted

as a church by bishop Niketus in the sixth century. This was extended, and in the adjoining cloisters there is a good plan and reconstruction of the early form of the church as it was before it was partially destroyed in a Norse raid in 882; it was rebuilt in the tenth century, and from then on each age has made its additions until it has become an encyclopaedia of different styles: a Gothic choir and vaulting, an extensive Baroque remodelling, and finally a recent restoration which has removed much of the Baroque work, but in the process has produced a new style of its own, with the walls stripped to bare stone. It is a valid enough remodelling, but it gives no idea of what the medieval or Roman church, with its plasterwork and frescoes, would have been like. (Roman frescoes from the crypt survive in the Episcopal Museum.)

The glory of medieval Trier is the Liebfrauenkirche, just beside the cathedral. It is a rarity, a Gothic church in the shape of a Greek cross, with four equal radiating branches connected by chapels in the angles to create an almost circular building which is as high as it is wide. Writers have called the Liebfrauenkirche a '*rosa mystica*', linking the hymns to the Virgin with its remarkable ground plan: its dark and soaring interior, after the spacious lines of the cathedral, makes the image doubly apt. It owes its form to the builders of Reims cathedral and to churches across the border in north-east France. It was in fact the herald of the new Gothic style in Germany.

One other, civilian, monument deserves to be mentioned, the squat mass of the Frankenturm just off the market square, an eleventh-century Romanesque tower, built with Roman materials. It is named after a fourteenth-century owner, not after the sixth-century Franks, and is typical of noblemen's houses in medieval towns, as we shall see at Regensburg, Siena and San Gimignano. Even within the walls of a town, a nobleman did not feel secure without his fortifications, and here the original entrance was well above street level, approached by a ladder which could be drawn up in case of attack.

Regensburg

Regensburg owes both its name and much of its present town plan to the Romans, who established a garrison town on the bank of the Danube at the end of the first century AD, calling it Castra

Regina. As at Trier, many of the Roman buildings remain visible; but here they are fragments, incorporated into later medieval constructions, because, unlike Trier, medieval Regensburg outstripped its Roman predecessor in size. By the fifth century there was a bishopric at Regensburg, and in the early sixth century the town became the capital of the Agilolfing dukes of Bavaria, who seem to have been related to the Franks and who ruled from 555 to 788. In the eighth century Bavaria was brought under Frankish domination by Charles Martel, who was able to depose two rebellious dukes in succession and established an imperial palace here. There was Frankish influence in the religious sphere as well: the missionary bishop of Poitiers, St Emmeram, who established a number of Bavarian monasteries and died in about 685, is buried at Regensburg. There were links, too, with the Anglo-Saxon world through Christian missionaries: St Boniface re-established the bishopric at Regensburg, and the Schottenkirche still bears witness to the presence of the Scotti, or Irish.

At the end of the ninth century, Bavaria became part of the east Frankish kingdom ruled by Charlemagne's descendants; weak rulers left it open to Hungarian attacks until Otto I's victory over the latter at Lechfeld in 955. Regensburg remained the ducal capital until the thirteenth century; in the twelfth century, it was one of the richest towns in the region, with stone walls and impressive towers. There was an early tradition of civic self-government here, culminating in Regensburg's becoming an imperial free city in 1245. Freed of the restrictions imposed by the duke's presence, the natural advantages of its position at the crossroads between the great trade-routes running from north Germany to Venice and from eastern Europe to France came into their own, and the citizens of Regensburg became for a century key figures in European commerce: the merchants' quarter, which lay originally to the south of the cathedral, around St Cassian's church, and later moved to the shores of the Danube, finally came to take up most of the western part of the town. However, the glory of the town was relatively short-lived. The new town walls, taking in the monastery of St Emmeram, which, like so many abbeys elsewhere, had been in the suburbs, were built in the 1320s. But civil war in the duchy in the late fourteenth century, the Hussite wars in the early fifteenth century, and the rise of rival towns such as Nuremberg put an end to Regensburg's prosperity as the trade-routes were disrupted or taken over by rivals. Despite the presence of the 'perpetual diet' of the Holy Roman Empire in the town from 1663 onwards, the town became a minor provincial centre under a prince-bishop; an indication of its stagnation is that it did not expand beyond the medieval town walls until the 1850s. But it is this very stagnation – and the town's escape from damage in the Second World War – that has preserved so much of the medieval town. Today Regensburg is a flourishing, lively city, with a new university, so it is by no means a museum town, but a place where Roman, medieval and modern meet. A fitting symbol of this is the section of Roman wall uncovered during the building of a multi-storey car park, of which it now forms the end wall, with excellent signs explaining its place in the plan of the Roman garrison town.

The oldest monument of medieval Regensburg is St Emmeram's church, once a Benedictine monastery. The church itself is heavily disguised under a Baroque coating of 1731–3, which conceals a largely intact Romanesque building. Its crypts have been left largely untouched, with the exception of the Ramwold crypt of 980 to the east of the church. That of St Emmeram dates from about 740, while the St Wolfgang crypt dates from 1050, as does the most important piece of sculpture in the church, the carvings on the doorway into the St Rupert church. Above the door is a striking Christ enthroned, framed by a rectangular inscription which makes the composition look like a leaf from a manuscript, an impression reinforced by the survival of the original colouring. Beneath Christ's feet is a medallion portrait of abbot Reginwart (1049–69), which dates this statue and the companion pieces of St Emmeram and St Denis as among the earliest medieval works in Germany, showing the influence of the hieratic art of Byzantium. The church is the burial place of the late Carolingian rulers of Germany, Armulf of Carinthia and Louis the Child, but their tombs have disappeared. That of queen Emma, wife of Charlemagne's grandson Louis the German, who died in 876, is marked by a Gothic monument of c.1280, as are the tombs of St Emmeram and St Wolfgang.

The St Jakobskirche or Schottenkirche is another church which bears witness to Regensburg's international connections in the early Middle Ages. This was the church for a monastery founded about 1090 by a certain Marianus, an Irish Benedictine monk who arrived at Regensburg in about 1070. It became the mother-house of a

number of south German monasteries, of which its abbot was
visitor-general. It survived the general dissolution of German
monasteries in 1803, only to be disbanded in 1862. Nothing survives of the early cloister buildings, but the church is largely untouched. The towers are part of the original fabric. The nave had
to be rebuilt shortly after the church was consecrated because much
of it collapsed owing to faulty construction. There are fine capitals
and details throughout the church, but the north doorway or
Schottenportal, occupying nearly a third of the nave wall, is outstanding. The programme of the sculpture is obscure; it is possibly
the work of sculptors from Pavia in northern Italy. Some details
can be readily identified, such as Christ and the apostles in the
upper frieze, the Virgin to the left and an unidentified emperor
to the right. Other forms and figures seem to belong to the world
of myth, such as the dragon of the underworld swallowing the globe
below the emperor's feet. Just inside the door is a delightful and
endearing portrait of the doorkeeper, Rydan, in his monk's habit,
carrying a door-bar and a great key. Two of the wooden sculptures
also deserve mention: a magnificent rood at the entrance to the
choir, dating from 1200, and a late-twelfth-century crucifix in the
right aisle, reminders of the rich furnishings with which the citizens
of Regensburg endowed the church.

The same citizens were responsible for providing funds for the
building of the cathedral, begun in 1250. Like so many enterprises
on this scale in the Middle Ages, the building operations dragged
on until the Reformation. Even so, the towers were not completed
until the nineteenth century. The style is that of French Gothic,
and although it is the best example of Gothic in Bavaria, it ranks
only with the minor provincial cathedrals of France, showing how
pervasive French artistic influence was at this period and how a
city at the height of its prosperity would turn to France for such
a work.

Yet the citizens also had considerable cultural links with northern
Italy, and Regensburg is remarkable as being the only town north
of the Alps with the tower-houses typical of Bologna, San
Gimignano and other north Italian towns. In Italy such tower-
houses had defensive or even offensive intent. Here in Regensburg
they seem to have been adopted in imitation of Italian fashion,
without the need for protection from warlike rivals, and were
symbols of the wealthy patrician dynasties which emerged in the

twelfth century: some families were prominent in the town for as long as two hundred years. Originally there were some sixty such towers, but now only twenty survive, often truncated and disguised by later layers of rendering. Most of these are in the old merchant quarter west of the cathedral. Immediately opposite the west end of the cathedral, behind the Kaiserhof hotel, is a group of four such towers in the Watmarkt and Wahnstrasse, the finest being the Barenburger tower with elegant early Gothic windows. Other buildings which bear witness to Regensburg's ancient prosperity are the huge salt warehouse at the end of the stone bridge over the Danube, and the bridge itself, which, although the upper part has been rebuilt and heavy traffic now roars across it, is still substantially unaltered since 1146, when it was completed after eleven years' work. Only one of its three defensive towers remains, next to the salt warehouse. For its time, it was an astonishing feat of engineering, and in the sixteenth century the Nuremberg poet Hans Sachs could still say of it that it had no equal in all Germany.

Nuremberg

The great German imperial cities were one of the most unusual institutions stemming from the Holy Roman Empire. Elsewhere, the great cities were either independent states, as in Flanders or Italy, or owed their power to their position within a kingdom. The Hanse association demonstrated the power of the north German towns as a group: Augsburg and Nuremberg in the south could afford to stand alone as immensely rich trading and financial centres, owing loyalty to none but themselves and the emperor. Augsburg, home of the great banking family of the Fuggers, was transformed in the sixteenth century, but Nuremberg survived as a largely fifteenth-century city until the end of the Second World War, when the majority of the old half-timbered houses were destroyed in bombing raids. Yet enough remains to give something of the atmosphere of the medieval period.

Nuremberg is unusual among medieval towns in that it seems to owe its existence to the royal castle built there in the mid eleventh century, which still dominates the town. We hear of a market in the late eleventh century, and it was called a town by 1163. By the end of the twelfth century it was a favourite residence of the German emperors, and in 1219 Frederick II made it a free imperial city, ten years after its first walls had been built. Ruled by a self-perpetuating oligarchy, the town's rise to fame was a gradual one. In 1356, the famous Golden Bull of Charles IV was issued here, a reform and re-statement of the constitution of the Holy Roman Empire which was to remain in force as the basis of the empire's government until its dissolution in 1806. But this did not imply that Nuremberg was anything more than the imperial residence when the bull was issued, and the choice of the moment for an assembly of the empire's electors. Nuremberg's true fame was to be commercial, and this came about at the very end of the medieval period. Hans Sachs and the mastersingers, famous from Wagner's opera, were medieval survivals in an early Renaissance world, though their attitudes were indeed those of the great patrician families of the Middle Ages. By Sachs's day, in the mid sixteenth century, the proverb ran that 'Nuremberg's hand was in every land'. Its wealth was founded not on native industry, but on commerce, the same commerce from north to south and east to west which had made its neighbour Regensburg great in earlier centuries.

The massive fortifications which still surround the city date from 1452 and symbolize the new-found power of the city. Although adapted to withstand artillery attacks in the following century and partially destroyed to meet the needs of modern traffic, nearly three-quarters of the perimeter survive, probably the largest single remaining medieval fortification. The gates, however, are part of the sixteenth-century remodelling. Inside the walls, the quarter south of the river has little of interest; the chief vestiges of both imperial and civic Nuremberg in the Middle Ages are grouped in the north-east corner of the old town. The old centre of the town was the Hauptmarkt, where the famous 'Schöne Brunnen' (Fair Fountain) still stands. Made in the fourteenth century, the successive tiers of figures are the seven electors of the empire (round the base), the Nine Worthies, and the prophets. The Nine Worthies, three from the Old Testament (David, Joshua and Judas Maccabeus), three from pagan antiquity (Alexander, Julius Caesar and Hector) and three from the Christian era (Arthur, Charlemagne and Godfrey of Bouillon), were a popular theme in pageants and civic art, and this is one of the finest representations of them.

Just off the Hauptmarkt to the south is the hospital, or Heilig-Geist-Spital, with a well-preserved arcaded central courtyard. In the other direction, towards the castle, is the Sebalduskirche, a graceful Gothic building with an ornate east end, reminiscent in its display of civic wealth of Saint-Pierre at Caen. The main works of art are sixteenth-century, but there is a fine early bronze font – complete with built-in hearth for warming the water.

The castle, which forms part of the town defences, stands on a hill overlooking the city. It has been severely altered and damaged over the centuries; recent restoration has had to be reconstruction rather than repair work. The most interesting feature, among some rather indifferent imperial rooms of the sixteenth century, is a Romanesque court chapel on three levels. Below, the servants could stand and hear the service through a central opening in the roof; above, the courtiers assembled, at the same level as the altar, in an elegant square nave with four central pillars; and from a tribune behind the nave the emperor looked down on both courtiers and celebrating priest, through a perspective of pillars and arches which centres on the altar. Indeed, the strange proportions of the chapel make sense only when viewed from the imperial tribune. From the castle, there is a well-preserved section of covered walk along the outer wall; both here and from the top of the remaining tower there are fine views over the town, which still retains something of its medieval aspect in its irregular town plan and broken roof-scape.

Carcassonne

Carcassonne is the finest surviving example of a medieval fortified town. A place of considerable military and economic importance, first under the counts of Toulouse in the twelfth and thirteenth centuries and then as a French royal stronghold on the border with Aragon, it lost its *raison d'être* in the seventeenth century when, in 1659, the French acquired Roussillon and extended their frontier to the Pyrenees; the economy of the region, based on cloth manufacture in the Middle Ages, had long since declined. As a result, there was no incentive to remodel or even to demolish the medieval fortifications, on which very little work had been done since they were completed in the thirteenth century. Carcassonne had only once – during the Black Prince's great raid across southern France in 1355 – had to withstand a serious attack since the present defences were built: the inhabitants of the lower town, beyond the river Aude, fled into the citadel, leaving their homes at the mercy of the English army. The prince stayed for only two days and did not attempt to attack the fortress; had he known that there was almost no water there, a situation aggravated by the vast influx of refugees, he might well have acted differently.

The city today presents an aspect very similar to that which the Black Prince would have seen. It has been extensively restored, it is true, both by Viollet-le-Duc in the 1840s and 1850s, and more recently, when some of Viollet-le-Duc's more fanciful reconstructions were modified, in particular the replacement of slates by roof-tiles on the towers. The defences are based on Roman and Visigothic work, which is clearly visible in places: the different periods of construction can be distinguished, because the Roman work is large blocks of stone laid without cement, that of the Visigoths stone and brick intermingled, the latter in a herringbone pattern, while the early medieval stonework is irregular and cemented together. The last stage is that carried out under Louis IX and Philip III, even but rough-faced stonework with regular joints. It was this last stage, carried out after the last count of Toulouse had been driven back when he attempted to take the city in 1240, that made Carcassonne into a fortress on an exceptional scale. The site is a classic one, on a projecting spur above the river Aude, and double walls were necessary on the south, where the approach is almost on level ground. But these were continued as a complete circle of walls and towers, with a winding approach road and huge twin-towered barbican at the entrance, to produce the largest concentric defence system in Europe; the double wall is present even on the northern side, where the lie of the land is in itself a major obstacle to an attacker. The low outer wall is separated from the much more formidable inner defences by a broad dry moat; the inner line of walls follows for much of its length the line of the Roman walls, and on the north-west corner the base of the walls and even one of the towers is original Roman masonry. The castle of the counts, to the west, with its own access to the lower city, is mainly twelfth-century, with some additions of the time of St Louis, while the great sweep of wall to south and east, including the gateway, was built under Philip III. The engineering is fairly conventional: open-backed towers rise above the lengths of curtain wall, though the later sections are virtually level with the towers. The south-east corner, the weakest point of the site, is defended by a huge, almost detached tower on the outer defences, and the main gateway has massive double towers with projecting reinforcements (*becs*) on the outer side, while the gate itself has the usual apparatus of portcullises and drawbridge. Throughout the wall walk, particularly in the towers, there are blind alleys and points for ambushes (though perhaps not quite so many as the ingenious local guides manage to find for the benefit of tourists).

It is the scale and complexity of the defences that sets Carcassonne apart; once we are inside the gateway, we find ourselves in a townscape typical of medieval towns rebuilt gradually over succeeding centuries. However, the castle of the counts, remodelled under Louis IX, is unusual in that it forms an integral part of the town defences. At Conwy, the nearest surviving parallel, the castle is in effect an extension of the town walls: here the castle sits four-square in the centre of the western wall. It is a stronghold within a stronghold, of which the interior has largely been gutted. The eastern façade, within the city, is formidable, with a simpler version of the city's own gateway in the centre. The dry moat, designed to prevent the use of battering rams, was originally deeper, while the timber hoardings along the battlements are conjectural reconstructions by Viollet-le-Duc.

The church of Saint-Nazaire is in sharp contrast to all this massive military architecture – an airy thirteenth-century Gothic building, created by northern artists, as if this was the only safe religious style in a region infested by heretics. It is notable for its glass, including a late-thirteenth-century rose window and a fourteenth-century Tree of Jesse window, and for its sculpture, particularly the statues in the choir, which are masterpieces of the northern French style of the mid thirteenth century. However, the most remarkable carving in the church – one hesitates to call it sculpture – is a strange bas-relief in one of the chapels, said to represent the siege of Toulouse in 1218, at which Simon de Montfort, the leader of the crusaders against the Albigensians, was killed. His body was brought to Carcassonne for burial, and this could be a fragment of his monument. The last strongholds of the Albigensians, the mountain-top castles of Corbières, lie to the south of Toulouse. The ruins of Quéribus (which held out until 1258, eleven years longer than the more famous Montségur), Peyrepertuse, Puylaurens and Aguilar form a line some twenty miles long marking the old border with Spain; and after their recapture from the heretics, they reverted to their role as frontier defences.

Towards Perpignan, the massive fort at Salses, built by Ferdinand in 1497, marks the Spanish side of the border: it only came into French hands in 1642. It is this wild frontier territory to the south, not apparent as one approaches Carcassonne along the peaceful valley of the river Aude, that determined the character of the city.

Gotland and Visby

Gotland, lying in the middle of the Baltic, has from the earliest times had a distinctive culture of its own. While the rest of Scandinavia followed the Viking pattern of raiding, trade and primitive farming, in Gotland the warlike element seems to have been absent. Its inhabitants can be distinguished even in their graves in far-off Estonia by the absence of the Viking panoply of weapons; and on the island itself over half the Dark Age coin-hoards to be unearthed in Sweden have been found. In the museum at Visby the heaped-up coins lie, their labels – Arabic, English, Byzantine – echoing the far-flung network of trade that brought them here. Some, no doubt, were the profits of Viking raids used to buy goods here in Gotland; but the fact that the hoards were buried underlines the image of a civilian community hiding its wealth in the face of an armed enemy.

To anyone used to the Mediterranean and Near Eastern pattern of town traders and country farmers, it comes as a surprise to find that Gotland appears originally to have been a trading community without an urban centre, and that its wealth was established before Visby was built. The typical Gotland merchant, even in later years, lived as both farmer and trader, perhaps at home for the spring sowing and the harvest, but travelling at other times. The best examples of these farms and warehouses combined are to be found at Bringes, near Norrlanda, and at Störa Hästnäs, just outside Visby. The former is a ruin, but **Störa Hästnäs** is well preserved. It was probably built in the early fourteenth century, though it belongs to a traditional style going back to the ninth or tenth centuries, and is on four levels: a cellar, with its own separate entrance, a ground-floor warehouse, again with a separate entrance, and then two living floors, probably living quarters below and a sleeping chamber above, approached by a ladder up to a doorway high in the east wall. This arrangement is defensive, and inside there would have been a trapdoor and a hole in the ceiling through which intruders could be attacked. The surrounding farm buildings have disappeared, but the surviving tower-like building would have been part of a substantial stone-built complex.

The traders from Gotland had established very wide contacts by the twelfth century, fanning out in all directions. They traded with the great Swedish settlement at Birka, west of what is now Stockholm; to the east, they had an establishment at Novgorod, where they had founded a church dedicated to St Olaf at some time before 1080. They went westwards to England, and southwards into the German empire, where Lothair III had granted them his imperial protection and exemption from customs in 1134. Equally, foreign merchants were to be found on Gotland, particularly from Russia. The presence of these foreigners and the need for a proper port led to the establishment of the town of Visby in its present form; there had been a small, earlier settlement on the site, which offered the best natural harbour on the island, but it only developed fully in the late eleventh and early twelfth century. Furthermore, by the mid twelfth century, the old Viking ships, narrow and shallow in draught, were replaced by a new type of ship, the cog, built in Lübeck and the north German ports, which was wider and deeper, and easier to sail, but which needed a proper harbour, whereas the Viking ships could be beached or lifted out of the water.

Despite the increasing activity of the German towns in the twelfth century, Gotland retained its position as the chief trading centre in the north. In 1161 Henry the Lion of Saxony made peace between the Germans and the men of Gotland after a series of wars, extracting in return the right for German merchants to visit Gotland. These in turn settled in Visby, where their community remained a separate one for some years, the 'community of Germans resident in Gotland'. However, they soon merged with the existing settlement to form a single town dominated by the Germans whose wealth made it the greatest seaport in northern Europe. From the sea, its appearance must have been very striking, with houses of up to eight storeys built in stone, buildings of this size being practically unknown elsewhere.

Trade in Visby was further encouraged by fairs, so that it was both a permanent trading centre and one which attracted a large additional influx of visitors at certain times of the year. The town reached its present extent by the mid thirteenth century, when a defensive wall was put round it for the first time, further evidence of the peaceful nature of the Gotland community. The wall is some two miles long, interspersed by shell turrets. Earlier fortifications such as the so-called Powder Tower by the harbour were included in the walls, and in places houses were incorporated. All except two of the original turrets remain; they are supplemented by later towers astride the wall. In the early fourteenth century, the walls were heightened, but this did not prevent the first serious attack on the town, by Waldemar Atterdag of Denmark in 1361, from succeeding. After this, Gotland became a Danish possession, its trading position further undermined by the hostility between the Danish kings and the Hanse (see p. 304 below).

By this time Visby was in any case overshadowed by the German Hanse towns. Although it had become a member of the Hanse as the Gotland community disappeared, its central place in the Baltic was no longer so advantageous: the advances of the Teutonic Knights in Prussia meant that the coastal route from Russia was less hazardous, and ships could hug the land without fear of falling into pagan hands. Trade tended to go directly from Russia or the eastern Baltic ports to Lübeck, and at the end of the thirteenth century responsibility for the Kontor, or foreign merchants' trading post, at Novgorod was transferred from Visby to Lübeck.

Even now **Visby** only just fills its medieval walls, though twentieth-century development has taken place to the east and south. From the fourteenth century to the nineteenth the town slowly declined, retaining its medieval form but none of its medieval vitality, the last flickers of which were extinguished by a devastating siege by the Lübeckers in 1525. All save one of the eighteen churches were abandoned: only the Marienkirche, originally built by the German community, continued in use. This plain, largely Gothic church has unusual features which betray its origin: a tribune, probably for the use of the leaders of the community, in the west end, tower and spire details which recall the churches of the Rhineland and, above all, a huge attic store-room above the vaulting. The vast gargoyle at the east end of the church is in fact the wooden crane for hoisting goods into this storage space.

Partly because the other churches are ruined, Visby has no great architectural splendours to offer. But almost every house is medieval, however disguised, and occasionally a fine unspoilt building appears, such as the so-called 'old apothecary's house', a medieval warehouse which later served as a chemist's shop. This has a large vaulted lower room with rooms for clerks above, and the owner's fairly simple accommodation behind it. Another striking building, and a somewhat mysterious one, is the church of the Holy Ghost, built as a round church with a choir extending out to the east, the round part having two storeys. It was possibly a guild church, the upper part being for the masters, though their view of the altar would have been very restricted. Alternatively, it may have been built by a military order, such as the Knights of the Sword from Lithuania, who eventually became part of the Teutonic Knights; this idea is supported by the architectural details, which are closer to those of palace chapels than of civic churches elsewhere. Visby's curious status, as almost a colonial outpost of the German merchants, meant that no great civic buildings were put up; the only important one, the Rathaus, was demolished in the last century.

The wealth of Gotland is perhaps most in evidence in its country churches. These range from the rather pathetic church at Västergam, where the Gotlanders, jealous of German Visby's prosperity, seem to have tried to create their own trading-centre, to the great churches in minute villages, such as Gothem, with its frescoes of knights, Stånga, with its fragments of gigantic sculptures intended for a façade, or the much-restored Dalhem. Most of them are unusual in form, the high nave being almost square in plan and with central pillars. The sculpture, too, is idiosyncratic, probably the work of local masters who had learned their craft abroad. They are a reminder of how even a wealthy medieval community with many links with the outside world was none the less isolated and inward-looking if geography so dictated. The churches also underline the relative brevity of Gotland's prosperity in the twelfth and thirteenth centuries: there is little sign of the rebuilding or extending of churches found elsewhere. The farmer-traders of Gotland could not compete with the organized skills of the German Hanse merchants in their heyday.

Lübeck and the Hanse

Lübeck lies at the south-western corner of the Baltic; today it is almost on the border between East and West Germany, but it has always in some sense been a frontier town. It was a trading-post between the Christian west and the pagan east when it first appears in history, in the eleventh century. Destroyed by Slav raiders, it was rebuilt on a more secure site about 1143. Encouraged first by Henry the Lion of Saxony and then by the Hohenstaufen emperors, the town became a free imperial town in 1226, a status which it held until 1937. Forty years later, the Lübeck merchants were to be found everywhere, and in England Henry III granted them the privilege of forming a Hanse, or trading association, like that enjoyed by the Cologne merchants. By the end of the century, Lübeck had become the leader of a much wider 'hanse', a loose association of German trading towns which cooperated to defend and develop their trading interests. For the next two hundred years, the Hanse dominated northern European and Baltic trade, bringing furs, wax, timber and grain from Russia, Prussia and Poland and selling in return fish, salt and wine. From England they shipped wool to the Flemish weaving towns, selling Baltic timber in return. Other products that figured largely in their affairs included German beer and Swedish copper and iron. All this was carried out by individual entrepreneurs, who owed allegiance only to their towns, who in turn belonged to the Hanse on a very informal basis. There was no written constitution of the Hanse, and few formal letters of alliance: in 1469, the council of the league claimed that the Hanse had no legal entity, being neither *societas* (association) nor *collegium* (union) but merely 'a firm *confederatio* of many cities, towns and enterprises for the purpose of ensuring that business enterprises by land and sea should have a desired and favourable outcome, and that there should be effective protection against pirates and highwaymen'; they went on to point out that they had no common seal, but usually sealed their letters with the town seal of Lübeck.

This remarkable institution disappeared only in the late seventeenth century, having for most of its existence defended its interests by purely economic means, such as sanctions and blockades. However, Dutch competition and the closing of the Russian markets, coupled with the problems of the religious wars of the sixteenth and seventeenth centuries, led to ineffectiveness and apathy, and Lübeck, once powerful enough to wage war on Denmark, was left to become merely another northern European port, overshadowed as a commercial centre by its old sparring-partner, Hamburg. As a result, much of the medieval town survives. The merchant wealth of medieval Lübeck is best reflected in the

Marienkirche and in the Rathaus, or town hall; in so far as the Hanse ever had a headquarters, it was the Rathaus at Lübeck. The Marienkirche was built by the town council in the thirteenth century, using the new and fashionable French Gothic style, adapted to the requirements of brick construction. It is both larger overall, being the largest of the brick Gothic churches of the north, and more artistically impressive than the cathedral at the other end of the town, whose massive Romanesque interior is in sharp contrast to the grace of the Marienkirche. As befits a merchant community, the adaptation of French Gothic is overlaid by parallels with English Gothic, as if the builders had deliberately tried to attain an international style.

The Rathaus, a complex and much-restored building, has a curious double façade, its fifteenth-century brick front (with great oculi as windvents in the towering wall) overshadowing a Renaissance loggia added in the following century. The state rooms in the south wing have been several times restored, as an inscription records and the newness of their glazed brick betrays. The upper part has another façade with windvents, surmounted by turrets, the basically four-square massive plan made light and cheerful by the use of elaborate detail, a proliferation of blind windows and arcades, and by patterning in two colours of brick. The result is a very individual building, rich, conscious of the latest fashions, yet standing apart from the mainstream of European architecture.

There are more practical survivals from the age of Lübeck's greatness. Parts of the town's defences survive, notably the great Holstentor and the Burgtor. The Holstentor was built between 1469 and 1478, partly as a defensive work, partly as symbol of the town's wealth and power. The towers are massive enough, but the central arcading, façade and terracotta decoration are peaceful rather than warlike; the inner face is entirely arcaded. It houses a small museum devoted to the town's history. It was soon after the building of this grandiose gate that Lübeck embarked on its unsuccessful military campaigns. The Burgtor, at the north end of the town, is less dramatic. Here stood the custom-house, and this was the old main entrance to Lübeck. Walking from the Burgtor to the cathedral, down the main axis of the town, we find the most important buildings of medieval Lübeck: the Heiligen Geist hospital, with its magnificent low brick façade surmounted by minaret-like towers; the old Shipman's Hall, now a restaurant, which retains its sixteenth-century hall with the original benches and tables; the Marienkirche; and the Rathaus. The Holstentor backed on to, and defended, a more practical area of the town, the warehouses along the quays. Just behind the Holstentor a small group of these survive; the quays in front of them, once piled high with merchandise, are prettily overgrown with grass and willows.

Throughout the town, but particularly in the streets south-east of the Rathaus, the old brick façades survive, with their characteristic stepped gables, a style to be found throughout the lands where the Hanse traded, from Bruges and Ghent in the west to Cracow – also a Hanse town – in the east. There are also charming courtyards containing almshouses in the Wahmstrasse, their extent being more or less that of a merchant's *hof*, his house and yard, since these were private houses left for charitable purposes and adapted accordingly. In the Heiligen Geist hospital, a remarkable fourteenth-century mural portrays just such charitable merchants, founders of the hospital.

Artistically, Lübeck can offer little to rival the Flemish achievements, though there is a magnificent Memling *Crucifixion* in the St Annen Museum, bought by merchants and presented to the cathedral. Its own artists specialized in elaborate carved and painted triptychs in high relief which are technically skilful but which I personally find highly unattractive. The St Annen Museum has an extensive collection, and there is an imposing rood screen by the late-fifteenth-century sculptor Bernt Notke in the cathedral. Notke is the finest exponent of Lübeck woodcarving, and his masterpiece is the great St George and Dragon (1498) in the Störkyrka at Stockholm. Here the freedom of a detached group eliminates the awkward postures of the triptychs – yet even so, as Sacheverell Sitwell writes, 'In the more intriguing bypaths of Gothic ... is it possible to conceive of a work of art stranger or more backward-looking? ... It seems hardly possible that it is not a century earlier in date, so charged is it with the runes and *kraken* of the North in the very spikes and convolutions of the serpent's tail, and yet this sculpture is the product of Lübeck, a mercantile city in the forefront of its time.' Here though is the paradox, and the key to Lübeck as it has come down to us: for all its enduring commercial vitality, it was an intensely conservative city, even in its heyday; and the weight of the medieval past and its glories falls like a shadow across the pages of Thomas Mann's *Buddenbrooks* (written about his native town) in the twentieth century:

Tony looked at the grey gables, the oil lamps hung across the streets, Holy Ghost Hospital with the already almost bare lindens in front of it. Oh, how everything was exactly as it had been! It had been standing here in unmovable dignity, while she had thought of it as a dream worthy only to be forgotten. These grey gables were the old, the accustomed, the traditional, to which she was returning, in the midst of which she must live.

Bruges

Set in the flat polderlands of north Belgium, Bruges has completely changed in character since the Middle Ages, like the English Cinque Ports across the Channel. The endless fields, broken only by lines of poplars, were then estuaries and open sea; and a nature reserve to the north of the town marks the site of the mouth of the river Swijn, where Edward III inflicted a crushing naval defeat on the French at the battle of Sluys in 1340. Medieval Bruges was one of the great ports of Europe, and the peaceful lake known as the Minnewater was its inner dock, crowded with shipping and flanked by warehouses: up to 150 ships could pass through in a single day. It had begun as a simple fishing port in the ninth century, but soon became a commercial centre. In the thirteenth century, the rise of English wool exports to the weaving towns of Flanders rapidly made it one of the most important commercial centres in northern Europe, but although it was ideally placed for the English trade, this was only one aspect of its activities. On the formation of the Hanse, Bruges, with its neighbour Damme, was one of the towns where the Hanse merchants of Germany enjoyed special privileges under a charter from the countess of Flanders in 1252–3. In the latter part of the thirteenth century, wool from England and Spain, cattle from Holland and wine from western France were the chief cargoes. With this growing trade came the Italian bankers who had once traded at the inland fairs in north-eastern France, and who now made Bruges the financial centre of northern Europe. By the fourteenth century, luxury goods were arriving in quantity: spices brought directly from the east in Genoese or Venetian galleys, furs, wax and corn from eastern Europe and Russia.

But Bruges lay outside the Holy Roman Empire and was never

an actual member-town of the Hanse. It was dependent on the presence of German merchants, and did not in fact generate its own trade. The rise of Dutch commercial enterprises at Antwerp and the gradual silting-up of the Swijn estuary led to a decline in Bruges's fortunes; this was made worse by quarrels between the Hanse merchants and the authorities in Bruges, and by 1475 the town was less important than Antwerp. In 1520 the head-quarters of the Hanse in Flanders was moved to Antwerp.

By the marriage of Philip the Bold and Margaret of Flanders in 1369, Bruges had become part of the Burgundian empire and, as one of the great towns of Flanders, was both the scene of great ducal ceremonies and also uneasy under the new-found power of its lord. Two episodes from the reign of Philip the Good illustrate this fluctuating relationship. It was at Bruges in January 1430 that Philip held his marriage feast after his wedding to Isabel of Portugal. The ducal palace, which stood on the site of the present Palais de Justice, was transformed by wooden buildings erected in the courtyard, and huge heraldic beasts pouring fountains of wine, hippocras and water were set up. Isabel made her entry through streets hung with crimson, and a spectacular banquet followed, full of the allegorical 'devices' beloved of the Burgundian court. Three days of jousting followed, in the market place; and on 10 January the creation of a new Order of Chivalry, the Golden Fleece, was announced. This was modelled on the English Order of the Garter and consisted of twenty-four knights who were also the king's chief councillors. Although chapters of the order were usually held elsewhere, the Order of the Golden Fleece appears everywhere in Bruges, on monuments, buildings and pictures; until 1794, a salvo in its honour was fired from the walls on the order's original meeting day, 30 November.

In contrast to this peaceful and festive occasion, Bruges was often at loggerheads with its lord. In 1437, after a year of discontent over a long-standing quarrel about civic rights, Philip the Good attempted a show of force in the town, but he was driven off with heavy losses and he himself narrowly escaped. One of his chief councillors, the sieur de l'Isle-Adam, was killed. However, Philip was able to bring Bruges to heel by withdrawing her commercial privileges, and in February 1438 the citizens made their peace on Philip's terms.

Modern Bruges is still dominated by the huge belfry of the town hall. The lower part of the tower and the market behind are thirteenth-century, with fine Romanesque windows; the upper part is Gothic, replacing a wooden spire that was burnt down three times. Its octagonal shape sits slightly awkwardly on the four-square Romanesque part, which has been 'Gothicized' by the addition of four corner turrets. At every street corner in the town, the belfry reappears between the roofs, a reminder of the pride and wealth of medieval Bruges. Surprisingly, the town hall is on a much more modest scale, though extremely elegant. It was started in 1376, the first to be built in Flanders, and completed in 1402: its present aspect, like much of Bruges, owes a lot to nineteenth-century restoration. The façade is reminiscent of an elaborate jewel casket in the way that the soaring lines of Gothic windows and pinnacles have been adapted to a relatively small secular building. Inside, the old council chamber or 'Gothic Hall' has suffered from drastic nineteenth-century restoration, which added a programme of historical paintings, yet much of its original character survives. It has a magnificent wooden ceiling with pendant vaulting, built by Jean de Valenciennes in 1402, and a fine set of bosses representing the four elements and the twelve months. These vivid three-dimensional carvings, set at an angle so that they can be seen from below, include two delightful vignettes of a courting couple and of a knight and squire. The decoration of the room as a whole does to some extent reflect the brilliant colours and sumptuous effect that it would originally have had. Yet much of the original impact must have depended on the contrast between these high colours, gold and scarlet, and drab greys and browns of the city outside. The other great Flemish town halls are to be found at Brussels and Louvain; Ghent and Middelburg also have fine examples from the late fifteenth century.

Beside the town hall, a covered passage leads to the quays along the canals, lined by old houses, almost all of brick with the characteristic stepped gables which make each into a miniature formal façade. Their appearance has changed little since the fifteenth century, though it is not easy to date any particular house, since the traditional style of brick building continued into later centuries and much restoration has been carried out in the last hundred years. This is the world of Rodenbach's symbolist novel *Bruges la Morte*, which was illustrated by engravings of old Bruges, a dead city whose atmosphere permeates the lives of the pro-

tagonists, and of Korngold's opera *Die tote Stadt* based on the novel.
Seen in winter, they retain their almost ominous stillness, the stillness of the long centuries of decline. In summer, busy with boats,
they are nearer to their medieval function as the main arteries of
the town; only then the boats brought goods for merchants' warehouses, instead of sightseers. The most impressive of the surviving
houses is the town house of the Gruuthuse family, now a museum
of applied arts. Again, the building was substantially restored in
the nineteenth century; its palatial lines give an excellent idea of
Bruges's wealth. A portrait of Louis de Gruuthuse, its owner, can
be seen in the Musée Groeninge; governor of Bruges and knight
of the Order of the Golden Fleece, he was rewarded by
Edward IV of England for his support of the Yorkist cause with
the earldom of Winchester. Other important secular buildings,
north of the market place, are the burghers' palace and the old
customs house, now a library; the arms over the door include the
badge of the Order of the Golden Fleece. These form an attractive
group at the head of the Spiegelrei canal.

The life of Bruges was not merely commercial. For her spiritual
and artistic glories, we need to turn southwards again, to the church
of Notre Dame and the Béguinage. The magnificent brick of Notre
Dame overshadows the Musée Gruuthuse, rising to almost as great
a height as the belfry. A sombre exterior conceals a spacious interior.
The treasures of the church are the tombs of Charles the Rash
of Burgundy and his daughter Mary of Burgundy. Charles the Rash,
the last ruler of the Burgundian state, spent his life in a duel with
the great towns of his domains. Bruges, however, was not one
of the towns with which he had quarrelled; it had been the scene
of 'the most splendid and extravagant festivities in the annals of
Burgundy' in 1468, when he married Margaret of York. After his
overwhelming defeat and death at Nancy in 1477, his body was
found only after two days' search on the battlefield. The mausoleum
at Notre Dame was built after his daughter's death in 1482; both
tombs date from 1491–8. Their elaborate brass and black marble
bases echo the Burgundian fashion for using black (see p. 238 above).
These sumptuous tombs mark the death of an ambitious dynasty,
who had sought to create – and nearly succeeded in so doing –
a new state in Europe.

At the other extreme to this princely magnificence is the Béguinage, just north of the Minnewater and therefore in the heart of

the old commercial centre. The Béguines were women who, though they did not take vows, devoted themselves to a religious life. Founded in the 1180s by a priest in Liège, they were once widespread in northern Europe, and were to be found as far south as Italy. Now only the establishments in the Netherlands and Belgium survive, and that at Bruges, although architecturally the finest, is now occupied by Benedictine sisters. (That at Ghent is still an active community.) Although the Béguinage is still on the original site of its foundation in 1245, what we see today is largely sixteenth-century or later. The atmosphere of calm within the heart of a city remains, characteristic of the Béguines themselves, who would work among the citizens by day and return to their quarters at night, living in the world but not of the world.

Two other religious monuments deserve a brief mention. One is the chapel of the Holy Blood, where a relic brought back from the Second Crusade in 1150 by the then count of Flanders is kept. Each year on the Thursday before Whitsun, it is paraded through the streets accompanied by a huge and colourful procession. Another reminder of the Holy Land is the fifteenth-century 'Jerusalem church' commissioned as a replica of the Church of the Holy Sepulchre by a returning pilgrim.

The finest religious monuments in Bruges are also her artistic masterpieces, to be found in the Musée Groeninge and the Memling collection in the former hospital of St John. Jan van Eyck's great paintings are now widely dispersed, and only the Virgin and Child, commissioned by Canon van der Paele, and a portrait of his wife remain in Bruges. It is the Memling pictures which predominate: in the Groeninge Museum, the Morcel triptych stands out among a group of lesser Flemish masters, sharing the same aversion to the fantasy of High Gothic painting. The interiors are domestic and down to earth; even the extravaganzas of the legend of St Ursula by an unknown master end with a little picture of pilgrims at her shrine, complete with symbolic votive offerings hung up beside it. It is this attention to detail, coupled with the discovery of new techniques in oil painting (in particular the use of a white ground), which set apart the Flemish masters. They point the way forward into the Renaissance, with the individuality of their portraits and the realism of their details; and yet the world they portray is often still firmly traditional and medieval. Contrast the highly praised *Reliquary of St Ursula*, a painted version of the jewelled reliquaries of the Rhineland (which seems very much overrated), with the *Virgin Adored by Martin van Nieuwenhoren*. The one looks back to a tradition three centuries old of great reliquary chests, as richly adorned as possible; the other looks forward to the Madonnas of Bellini's later style and to the great Italian masters. The Virgin remains a hieratic image, but van Nieuwenhoren is portrayed in an entirely realistic way. In the huge *Mystic Marriage of St Catherine* the Virgin is enthroned in secular splendour; she has no nimbus, and is shown as an entirely human figure, attentive to her devotions. The two saints seated before her are said to be portraits of Margaret of York and Mary of Burgundy, while Charles the Rash is said to appear as one of the Three Kings in the *Adoration of the Magi*. Whatever the truth of this, we are looking at paintings which are concerned to convey character and individuality, not great schematic theological ideas. Yet turn to the right-hand wing of the *Mystic Marriage* and we are back in the Middle Ages: in brilliant colours, hard and jewel-like as any miniaturist could have desired, the visions of the Apocalypse are unfolded in a way that a twelfth-century artist would have recognized.

Ghent

Ghent remains today what it has been since the fourteenth century, an active centre of trade. From the monotonous northern approaches along the Scheldt, with all the dismal apparatus of a modern port, to the bustling commercial heart of the city, it has none of the feeling of remoteness in time of Bruges. Yet amidst the roaring traffic and the crowds, much survives of the city that dominated fourteenth-century Flanders.

Ghent's citizens succeeded in establishing a commune as early as 1126, and the counts of Flanders encouraged Ghent and the other trading towns in their domains by establishing a stable currency and uniform weights and measures. An Italian merchant, writing in the fourteenth century, noted that most great towns had a number of different systems, 'but in the cities of Bruges, Ghent, Ypres, Lille and Douai, there is only one set of weights and measures, except for corn'. But economic and political well-being brought in its wake pride and independence: already in 1180 Philip of Flanders rebuilt the old castle 'to humble the excessive pride of the people of Ghent, their pride in their wealth and their houses, which were like fortified towers'. In the fourteenth century, it was Ghent which led the revolt of the Flemish towns against their pro-French count, Louis de Nevers, whose policies had brought about a ban by Edward III on wool exports from England to Flanders in 1336. As the chief trade of the Flemish towns consisted of buying raw wool and turning it into cloth, this was a serious matter; and the merchants in the towns were in any case pro-English. By early 1338, Ghent, under the leadership of Jacob van Artevelde, and in league with Ypres and Bruges, had driven out the count and had made an alliance with England. The revolt led to internal quarrels and van Artevelde was murdered in July 1345, just after a meeting with Edward; but the English allegiance remained, until Louis de Nevers's successor eventually adopted a policy of neutrality towards both France and England, acknowledging France's over-lordship but maintaining the trade links with England. Ghent's prosperity continued under the Burgundian dukes, but was disturbed by the religious wars of the sixteenth century, and its medieval wealth disappeared with the decay both of the cloth trade and of its port in the seventeenth century.

All the different aspects and periods of Ghent's history are mirrored in its surviving monuments. The earliest is the castle of the counts of Flanders, extensively but carefully restored in the late nineteenth century. The plan of the castle is perhaps derived from the early crusader castles in Palestine, which count Philip had seen when he went to the east in 1177–9. Its most distinctive feature is the outer wall, with semi-circular turrets above the buttress piers; each turret has two 'storeys' for defensive purposes. This system is ideally suited to the castle's situation, where an attack was likely to be made by an ill-disciplined but numerous mob rather than a small assault force of trained soldiers. Inside, the keep is built on the remains of an eleventh-century castle, whose first and second floors form the cellar of the present keep. The upper floors of the keep were used primarily for state functions; the massive outer walls contain two very large rooms, both suitable for large gatherings, as well as living quarters of the garrison, a reminder that these early castles had a triple function as fortress, residence and meeting place. Few such Romanesque halls survive, but their architecture is unremarkable without the splendid tapestries and furnishings used at a medieval feast. The little chapel over the gateway is the most interesting architectural interior in the castle, with an east window in the shape of a cross. To the east of the keep, the so-called castellan's apartments have two fine rows of Romanesque arches on the outside.

One other secular building of the twelfth century survives in Ghent: it is only a façade, but in many ways it is even more striking than the castle, simply because of its rarity. This is the Staple House, among the justly famous sixteenth-century houses of the Quai aux Herbes, where corn levied under the staple taxes was stored. Its form is that of the flat rectangular façade surmounted by a stepped gable typical of medieval and early modern Flanders, but in place of windows and brickwork there are stone pillars and wooden doors. Not far away to the north is the Great Shambles, to use a suitably medieval name, the long stone building of the meat market built in 1404, again with stepped gables and with stone gable windows as well. A few hundred yards further on, the huge open plain of the Friday Market is a reminder of the sheer size of the great medieval trade markets.

As at Bruges and half a dozen other Flemish towns, the belfry is the symbol of Ghent's medieval civic pride. Isolated in a swirling sea of traffic, yet hemmed in by surrounding buildings, it does not dominate the city as does that at Bruges. It was begun in the thirteenth century, finished a hundred years later, and much altered and restored ever since. The gilt copper dragon at its summit, it has been suggested, is a distant relation of the treasure-guarding dragons of Norse myth, a symbol and protector of the city's wealth. At the base of the great tower, and forming part of the belfry, is the fifteenth-century cloth market.

Across a small square, the tower of St Bavo's cathedral challenges the belfry for supremacy of the skyline. It is a very late Gothic building, begun in 1353, but largely built in the first half of the sixteenth century, in a simple, very archaic style. Of earlier buildings on the site, all that remains is the Romanesque crypt, with its simple square pillars. The cathedral's greatest treasure, however, is *The Adoration of the Mystic Lamb* by the brothers van Eyck (see p. 236), a reminder that just as much of the wealth of the Burgundian court derived from the revenues of Flanders, so the Flemish citizens could rival their duke when it came to matters of artistic patronage.

Aigues-Mortes

The port of Aigues-Mortes lies on the delta of the Rhône, in the Camargue. Built as a new town by Louis IX from 1241 onwards, it has been preserved for us by the silting-up of its harbour little more than a century after its foundation. Aigues-Mortes was ideally placed to take advantage of the trade-route down the Rhône valley, and Louis's motives in founding it were largely commercial: there was no royal port on the Mediterranean, and he was therefore unable to profit from this lucrative source of revenue. He also had in mind the usefulness of such a port in his crusading projects. The Rhône marked the eastern frontier of France, and both for this reason and as a protection against casual piracy the new town was heavily fortified. Its site was doubly vulnerable because it lay deep in the marshes, connected to the mainland only by a single causeway; it was perhaps the most isolated of such new towns throughout Europe. It was also the precursor of a huge increase in the number of new towns founded in France, a phenomenon which reached its peak in the 1270s and died away only with the Black Death in the 1350s.

Despite the attempts by Louis IX and Philip III to enforce the monopoly of Aigues-Mortes as the one port of entry for France, 'the obligatory outlet for national trade' linked with the fairs of Champagne, the port never prospered dramatically; the nearest great town (and the compulsory depot for goods going through Aigues-Mortes) was Nîmes, and the only purely local industry was the salt-pans of the Camargue. It never outgrew its original walls, and there are no great merchants' palaces here. Yet despite the silting-up of the harbour it remained a viable centre of sea-trade until Sète was built nearby in the mid seventeenth century.

The causeway across the marsh (now the D46) was defended by an isolated outpost, the 'Tour Carbonnière', two miles from the town itself. From the top of this tower there is a good view of the port in the distance; the tower is designed as a miniature self-contained fortress. The causeway reaches the town through its modern suburbs, at the Porte de la Gardette, a typical twin-towered gateway, which is matched by three similar, smaller gates to the south and east which originally gave on to the dock area. These defences were completed only under Philip III in the last decade of the thirteenth century, but the construction was all to the original plan, and the fortifications are unusually regular and consistent in appearance. The original defence for the new town was the Tour de Constance, to the north-west, which forms an independent keep, with its own moat, not unlike the arrangement at Flint forty years later (see p. 253). It has elaborate defences, including a gallery round the ground-floor room designed so that any enemy troops who penetrated that far could be picked off from above. It has its own arrangements for provisions and water supply, and was used as the royal residence on the two occasions when Louis IX himself came to Aigues-Mortes, on his way to the east as a crusader, in 1248 and 1270. It is possible that Louis had this long-planned expedition in mind when he actually ordered the building of the port, and the departure of the two crusades were certainly the high points of its history. In 1248, the king spent a week or so in the town, and set sail with thirty-eight ships; this was only part of the flotilla, and other lords made their own way to the rendezvous at Cyprus. In May 1270, there was a longer delay, since the fleet that was to leave from Aigues-Mortes was larger. Louis, now a sick man, stayed at Saint-Gilles, while the common soldiers fought among themselves in the oppressive atmosphere of the crowded port: apart from its marshy site and inadequate supplies of fresh water, it was also prone to sandstorms. Louis had to move down to Aigues-Mortes to quell the riots, but he sailed shortly afterwards. The crusade ended disastrously with the king's death at Tunis less than two months later.

The Tour de Constance also acted as a lighthouse for the harbour; although the upper part of the tower has lost its defensive works, the great iron cage for the light remains, reminiscent of the masthead braziers by which the ships of the crusading fleets used to keep in touch with one another. The building of the rest of the town's defences was provided by financiers from Genoa, the Boccanegra family, who received a share of the revenues from customs in return; the layout is almost exactly rectangular, with circular towers on the corners and lesser towers on the north side. There are also five lesser gates, which correspond to the grid plan of streets within the walls, a plan which can be clearly seen from the top of the Tour de Constance or by walking round the ramparts, which are still largely intact. A feature of the plan, which underlines the military role of Aigues-Mortes and rarely survived later development elsewhere, is the wide space immediately inside the walls and the large street linking the north and south gates, all of which were designed to make rapid troop movements possible in response to an attack. The moat outside has disappeared, and where the waterfront used to be is now a dusty open space to the south. The best general view of the town is from the road south to Le Grau du Roi, 'the royal river-mouth', a name which recalls the canal between the port and the sea which was needed even in the earliest days. Here there are no railways or modern buildings to obstruct the medieval silhouette. Within the walls, the population is now a quarter of what it used to be in the early fourteenth century; it remains a local centre for the old salt-trade but little else. Only the shadow of the walls, almost unchanged since they were built and never drastically restored, are a reminder of Aigues-Mortes' brief heyday.

Florence

'There is the noble city, the queen of the Middle Ages. It is inside these walls that civilization began again.' So wrote Stendhal in January 1817 on first seeing the city, unconsciously indicating the problem which any description of medieval Florence must at once face. It was here that the Renaissance, the revival of interest in classical humanism and secular learning, began; and whereas elsewhere we can often draw a tolerably clear line between the medieval and Renaissance world, it is far from easy in Florence, the home of Dante, Giotto and Petrarch, where the new culture developed gradually and imperceptibly from the old. I have simply regarded medieval Florence as coming to an end in 1400 – nearly a century earlier than in northern Europe and Spain – and what follows is primarily concerned with Florence in its republican days, before the great merchant families (and eventually the Medici) replaced the commune.

The earliest of the public buildings of Florence is the baptistery, a free-standing building opposite the cathedral. This fact alone betrays its early origin: it belongs to the period when such buildings were separate chapels rather than part of a larger complex, like the fifth-century baptistery at Poitiers. It escaped total rebuilding in the fourteenth and fifteenth century because it was believed to be of Roman origin, but, although built on a Roman site, the earliest parts of its fabric are actually fifth or sixth century. The main structure is Romanesque, c.1059–1128, with decoration – arcades, pavements and mosaics – of the thirteenth century. It set the style for much later Florentine work, particularly their delight in patterned marble (which became a minor art in its own right – as witnessed by the Museo dell'Opificio de Pietre Dure). The sources of inspiration for this were buildings such as the Palatine Chapel at Aachen and, in the case of the corners, the banded marble used at Lucca and Pisa. The interior is similarly treated, and if it seems exceptional today, it is because so many medieval buildings survive structurally intact but stripped of their marble facings. The richness of the patterning works well in this otherwise very austere space. The bronze doors to the south are the original ones, designed by Andrea Pisano, of the famous family of sculptors. They contrast sharply, in their treatment of the scenes from the life of St John the Baptist as miniatures from a manuscript, with the early fifteenth-century doors by Ghiberti to east and north. Andrea Pisano was also in part responsible for the building of the campanile, designed or at least begun by his predecessor as master of the cathedral works, Giotto. It was built between 1334 and 1359, and is basically Romanesque in style, despite its date, with its graceful lines and well-proportioned arcades.

The earliest of the civic buildings of Florence is the Bargello, originally the palace of the *podestà*. This post may seem curious to us until we compare it to that of a chief executive: the *podestà* had to be a foreigner, from at least fifty miles away, and held office for only a year. The idea was to have a chief officer who was independent of all local factions, and could carry out his function – mainly the administration of justice – without fear or favour. The earliest examples of this institution in the Italian cities date back to the 1160s, when the emperor appointed a *podestà* in several Lombard towns, but in general the *podestà* was chosen by the city rulers themselves, and by the early thirteenth century the office was common. It eventually became a specialist career: one Milanese held office in different towns for seventeen terms. But it was by no means an easy task, and many such officers were thrown out, justly or unjustly, before their time had ended.

The façade of the Bargello dates from 1255 and incorporates an earlier tower. The palace became the *podestà*'s seat in 1261 and was gradually enlarged during the next century. The exterior rises fortress-like from the narrow surrounding streets and is crowned by battlements: the large and elegant window of the great hall is the only break in the solid wall, an alteration made in 1345. The entrance leads into a huge vaulted guardroom and thence into the courtyard, whose severe lines are broken by a loggia and balcony of elegant proportions, with an open staircase to the first floor. The stone coats of arms of the successive *podestàs* enliven the walls, and along the arcade are the emblems of the different wards of the city, a reminder that civic pride was tempered by narrower local loyalties. The Bargello is now a major museum of sculpture, and a ground-floor room contains a fine assembly of fourteenth-century pieces. Leading off the balcony on the first floor is the great hall, restored in 1887, the vaults of which were built by Neri di Fioravante in the 1340s, during the French duke of Athens' brief tyranny in Florence: the duke's arms decorate the keystones. The rest of the interior has suffered from the use of the building as a prison in the sixteenth and seventeenth centuries, and by the requirements of the museum, so that any impression of the private residence or public offices of the *podestà* is hard to obtain. The chapel contains nineteenth-century reworkings of frescoes said to be by Giotto.

The Palazzo Vecchio and the cathedral, even in this age of tower blocks, remain the dominant features of Florence's skyscape. Brunelleschi's brooding dome belongs to the early Renaissance, but the silhouette of the Palazzo Vecchio is entirely medieval, a fortress within the city very like the Bargello. Despite its name, it is fifty years younger than the Bargello. It was originally built for the seven priors from the different guilds who ruled the city, and was planned in the early 1280s. Work began in 1299, using men from the cathedral building yard, and in fact it seems that work on the cathedral stopped for a time while the priors' palace was completed. In 1314 all except the tower had been built. From the beginning, the Palazzo Vecchio was – and still is – the centre of the city's administration, and as such it has undergone radical alterations. During the brief rule of the duke of Athens in 1342–3 the main door was fortified and additional defences built. After the demolition of these, it remained substantially unchanged, though under varying names, until the sixteenth century. As the constitution of Florence altered, so it was known first as the Palazzo del Popolo, then as the Palazzo dei Signori, briefly the Palazzo

Ducale in the 1540s and finally 'the old palace' when the Medici dukes moved to the Pitti palace across the river. Behind the medieval façade, only the ground-floor guardroom remains intact; the upper rooms were entirely rebuilt and refurbished first by the *signori* and then by the Medici.

The square dominated by the Palazzo Vecchio, the Piazza della Signoria, was the setting for much of the public life of medieval Florence, and was an open space even before the latter was built, a reminder of the defeat of the emperor's partisans, or Ghibellines, in 1268: the palace of their leaders, the Uberti family, was torn down, and it was decreed that nothing should ever be built on the site. In front of the Palazzo Vecchio is the stone platform, the *aringhiera*, or haranguing-place, added to the palace in 1323, but much reduced in size in 1812, from which the city's official used to address the people. Open-air speeches and ceremonies all the year round need a better climate than that of Florence, and in 1376 the vaulted Loggia dei Lanzi was begun; it was finished six years later. It is still used for welcoming distinguished visitors to the city on state occasions. Its semicircular arches anticipate the Renaissance architecture of the following century, and its open aspect contrasts sharply with the closed and forbidding façade of the Palazzo Vecchio; but Florence in the 1370s was at the height of its power and self-confidence, and did not need to conduct its public life behind massive walls. On the other side of the Palazzo Vecchio the original façade of the Tribunale della Mercatanzia, or court of commerce, completed in 1309, has survived the rebuilding of the rest of the square.

Florence's suburbs spread beyond the Arno at a very early date, and in 1172 a new town wall was started which spanned the river and enclosed a small but significant area on the south bank. The city's bridges were therefore not gateways to the outside world, as at London or Paris, but internal and vital links. The Ponte Vecchio, built in 1345, brings medieval Florence vividly to life, though the restriction of the shops on it to goldsmiths and jewellers was due to a Medici decree in 1593; the corridor linking the Uffizi and Pitti palaces which runs along the upper part of the bridge was also of their devising. But the central thoroughfare, with its shops built into the stone superstructure of the bridge, is little changed, even if some shops have gained space by building out over the river, until the whole structure seen from the outside looks like a great overloaded ark. Inside, the spaces are so small that the miniature art of jewellery seems the only one which could possibly fit into rooms on this scale, and one wonders how the butchers who rented the shops in the fifteenth century could have managed. The bridge was maintained by a special agency, responsible also for the city's mills, walls and offices, and for confiscated rebel property. Of the old city walls, only the Porta San Frediano survives, isolated in Oltr'arno near the Ponte Vespucci.

There are many other medieval monuments in Florence, notably the churches of Santa Croce, Santa Maria Novella and San Miniato; but these are not civic monuments: they owe their existence to organizations which gave their loyalty to more universal ideals than the glory of Florence. Despite the later splendours of the Florentine Renaissance, we can still see why Dino Compagni, writing in about 1310, could underline his pride in his native city by praising its buildings, describing how even then 'many people came from distant countries to visit Florence, not through necessity but on account of its crafts and the city's beauty and adornments'.

Siena

The civic buildings of Siena form a more coherent whole than those of any other Italian city. They are late in date, and are the result of very conscious planning: just as the vast unfinished cathedral (p. 103) was designed as a monument to the city's splendour, so the councillors in their debate on the new city hall, or Palazzo Pubblico, observed that

it is a matter of honour for each city that its rulers and officials should occupy beautiful and honourable buildings, both for the sake of the commune itself and because strangers often go to visit them on business. This is a matter of great importance for the prestige of the city.

The deliberations were protracted: a site had to be chosen and plans agreed, all of which took some sixteen years. Its placing, on low ground, is due to the rivalry between the *terzi* which occupied the three hills within the town, which meant that neutral territory had to be chosen. The Campo in front of it is also a neutral meeting place, where the three hills converge, and acts as a kind of amphitheatre in which the Palazzo Pubblico is the stage set. Both natural and artificial means have combined to produce an extraordinary unity: the ideal shape of the site has been complemented by conscious planning decisions. As early as 1297, when the plans for the palazzo had only just been approved, a decree was issued that buildings facing on to the Campo should not have balconies and the windows should be framed by small columns. This imposed unity is reinforced by the apparently natural unity of the building material, the warm red brick which is the hallmark of Siena. But this too was a conscious decision, because stone buildings were not uncommon in early medieval Siena. Brick was cheaper and more readily available, however, and in 1309 it was decreed that all new houses should be built in brick.

At the foot of the Campo the ground fell away quite sharply, and the new palazzo had to be built on a vast artificial mound held in by foundation walls. By 1310 the main body of the building and the wings were completed, but work continued for another thirty years before the building had been raised to three floors and the tower was complete. The basic design is not dissimilar to that of the Palazzo Vecchio in Florence, but the forbidding aspect of the latter is considerably modified. The front follows a gentle curve, and the battlements are purely ornamental. The windows, with the double columns and ogive arches, are both decorative and spacious; whereas the Palazzo Vecchio, like a castle, is lit from the inside, here the façade has abandoned all defensive pretensions. These windows are echoed in the Palazzo Sansedoni, which was given a new façade in 1339. Seven years later, in 1346, a local chronicler wrote:

On 30 December they finished paving the Campo of Siena in stone, and it is considered the most beautiful square with the most beautiful and abundant fountain and the most handsome and noble houses and workshops around it of any square in Italy.

By this time, the graceful bell-tower on the Palazzo Pubblico was almost complete: its stone capping was finished in 1348, and in 1360 a clock was installed. It is the forerunner of the great *carillon* towers of the Flemish town halls, though here the exceptional height is due to a desire to bring the tower up to the level of the highest point of the cathedral.

The interior of the Palazzo Pubblico is of exceptional interest, because it retains the original programme of frescoes, which are not only masterpieces in their own right, but also tell us much about the civic ideals of medieval Siena. The great public rooms on the first floor were decorated very soon after the completion of the building by some of the greatest Sienese artists, and despite the ravages of damp we can still imagine their original splendour. The most beautiful of the series is in the Sala del Mappamondo, the *Maestà* by Simone Martini, finished in 1315; it is an early work, clearly modelled on Duccio's famous image in the cathedral, and a reminder of the special devotion of the Sienese to the Virgin. Duccio's composition is more restricted and stiff: Martini uses the freedom of the expanse of wall to depict the Virgin under a broad canopy of honour, and he sets this against a blue background instead of the flat gold of the earlier painting. The Virgin is seated in an elaborate Gothic chair, and two kneeling angels pay graceful homage. It is a reminder that the city was formally dedicated to the Virgin, traditionally in a moment of dire crisis in 1260. Sienese coins bore the inscription in Latin 'Siena city of the Virgin', and Mary was regarded as the head of the city's government. The same room once contained – as its name implies – a world map by Ambrogio Lorenzetti, symbolizing Siena's role as a centre of international trade. This has vanished, but on the opposite wall to the *Maestà* is another work by Simone Martini, *Guidoriccio da Fogliano at the Siege of Montemassi*, painted to commemorate the Sienese captain's victory over rebellious nobles in the neighbouring countryside. This splendid figure was originally part of a frieze commemorating all Siena's victories since 1314; as we see it today it appears too heroic and individualistic to be appropriate to a strongly republican commune. It is also perhaps a deliberate reminder not only of the commune's power and authority but of the problems and dangers which the employment of a successful captain could bring: Guidoriccio's figure is isolated, framed by the panoply of military might.

The Hall of the Nine, the seat of government of the nine elected leaders of Siena, is next to the Sala del Mappamondo. Here the hints on good government in the previous room become a full-scale lecture on the subject, in Ambrogio Lorenzetti's cycle of frescoes representing *The Allegory of Good and Bad Government*. These were painted between 1338 and 1340, and the symbolism is addressed directly to the members of the nine. The central fresco, representing good government, is interesting in two respects. Firstly, Good Government is shown as a single lordly figure, in contrast with the republican constitution. But the inscription below clarifies this: 'Wherever this holy virtue (justice) reigns, it unites many souls, who, once united, constitute the Common Good which rules them.' So the regal figure is indeed a ruler, but is symbolic of the whole body of citizens joined together in quest of the common good. More specifically he is robed in black and white, Siena's colour, and bears Siena's arms, while the Roman she-wolf, the city's ancient symbol, crouches at his feet between Romulus and Remus. Justice is shown to the left, in a scene which is given almost equal weight, and Common Good is accompanied by the six virtues, seated on a richly hung bench with the figure of Peace stretched out at ease against a cushion on the left. The three theological virtues, faith, hope and charity, hover above him, while twenty-four Sienese elders come to pay homage. Concord is seated below Justice, holding the cords of justice and thus binding society together. It is an elaborate, philosophical composition, with complex undertones: the theories of republican government and the vision of the City of God in the Book of Revelations all contribute to the imagery.

On the right, the effects of Good Government on the city and its surrounding countryside are portrayed. This is one of the first major landscape compositions in western art. To the left we see the city, with its narrow streets, squares, shops and houses, palaces and workrooms, and the citizens going about their business. In the background workmen are building a new house; girls dance with linked hands in the foreground, while merchants go about their business, and a wedding procession makes its way through the streets. Between the two worlds of town and country appears the naked figure of safety, whose scroll reads: 'Let all free men go their way free from fear, and let everyone toil and sow likewise, while this lady holds sway over such a community; she has taken all power away from the wicked.' The vision of peace and prosperity is continued by the depiction of the countryside, where each man goes about his allotted task. In the distance, as we move away from the city and hence from good government, ominous castles appear and the landscape grows emptier. Again, there is much complex symbolism: the activities shown in two scenes represent the seven mechanical arts of medieval philosophy – the making of clothes, the working of metals and materials, trade, agriculture, hunting, medicine, and dancing and music.

The frescoes which represent the antithesis, bad government and its evils, are very much decayed, and only the general scheme can be made out. Common Good is replaced by Tyranny, the virtues by the vices, and Justice is shown bound. Fear rules instead of safety, and lawlessness and desolation are rife. Soldiers plunder where the merchants traded and the peasants tilled the fields. Above the picture was placed the coat of arms of France, the leader of the Guelph cause in the fourteenth century – for the Sienese, good government could be found only under the Ghibelline, imperial, banner.

Elsewhere in the Palazzo Pubblico, these themes are taken up again, notably in a cycle of paintings by Taddeo di Bartolo outside the chapel, while artists of a much later period were to re-echo them. Historical paintings of the twelfth-century struggle against the emperor were added in the fifteenth century, and the tradition was revived in the nineteenth century with paintings on the theme of Italian unity.

But a mere fifteen years after Lorenzetti's frescoes were completed, the Nine were overthrown, because they were unable to ensure the proper administration of justice, and Charles IV entered the town in 1355. Popular rule never fully revived: at the end of the fourteenth century the city fell into the hands of the Visconti tyrants of Milan. The medieval ideal flickered on until 1555, when after a prolonged siege the city surrendered to Charles V. Two years later Philip of Spain sold Siena to its old rival, Florence, and it became part of Cosimo de' Medici's dukedom of Tuscany. His arms are set boastfully on the façade of the Palazzo Pubblico, but the true ideals of Siena are still proclaimed by Lorenzetti's frescoes within.

San Gimignano

The little town of San Gimignano lies between Florence and Siena, on a hilltop overlooking the Valle d'Elsa. The silhouette of the town from the road below at once suggests that here is something out of the ordinary: above the usual muddle of tiled roofs rise thirteen slender towers. More than any other Italian town, San Gimignano has retained its medieval aspect. Its history is brief and obscure: a commune grew up here, possibly around a castle, and survived as an independent political entity until Florence established lordship over it in 1353.

Most of the buildings date from the late thirteenth and early fourteenth century. The Porta San Giovanni, by which we enter the town, is the best-preserved of the gates, dated 1262: it leads into the main square or Piazza della Cisterna, by way of the fourteenth-century Palazzo Pratellesi and – in the square itself – the Palazzo Tortoli. On the adjacent Piazza del Duomo is one of the finest palaces, the original Palazzo del Podestà, whose tower, 167 feet high, was used as the maximum height to which other towers could be built. A few of the houses retain their attractive pillared windows with brick arches, but most of the buildings are in the local yellowish-grey stone, huddled close together, with none of the regular lines of the medieval new towns. The towers – there are said to have been seventy-six originally – are in some cases so slender as to have no practical use except as a very temporary refuge, and they seem to have been built for prestige here, rather than for practical and defensive reasons, as they had once been. Most of the towers have lost their battlements and other finials, leaving them gaunt and four-square when seen close to, with only a minute window here and there to break the monotony of the smooth stone surface. From the highest of the towers, that of the Palazzo Comunale on the south side of the Piazza del Duomo, there is a fine view of the other towers and of the town, perched on its small hilltop in the rolling Tuscan landscape, which has changed little since it was the *contado* or subject territory of San Gimignano and other towns. A walk of no more than five minutes brings us right through the town. Descending the hill and looking back to the west, there is a dramatic view of the towers silhouetted against the sky, an imposing sight familiar to the peasants who lived and worked under the lordship of the town.

Even a small town like this, less than a quarter of the size of Siena or Florence, could count for something in the artistic and political world. Dante is said to have spoken in the Palazzo Comunale, in the council chamber, seeking an alliance between San Gimignano and Florence, in 1299. The room contains a *Maestà* by Lippo Memmi obviously commissioned in imitation of that painted for the Palazzo Pubblico in Siena by his brother-in-law Simone Martini. It was completed two years after the Sienese painting, in 1317. Earlier frescoes, dating from 1292, show hunting scenes and battles, while in the *podestà*'s room in the tower are a set of love scenes, possibly by Niccolò di Segna, dating from the mid fourteenth century.

The churches in the town are relatively modest. The Collegiata, a collegiate church which is also the cathedral, is basically Romanesque, but with Renaissance extensions; it contains works by minor Florentine and Sienese painters, showing how the town was never exclusively within the sphere of one or the other, even though it acknowledged the lordship of Florence. The Gothic church of St Augustine, on the edge of the town, also has Renaissance frescoes. The most delightful of the churches is the modest San Iacopo, in the Pisan Romanesque style. Just to the south of this, through the gateway, are the medieval wells, or *fonti*, sheltered by an arcade.

But it is above all for its streets that San Gimignano is famous; here as nowhere else you can feel the atmosphere of a medieval town, close-knit, almost oppressive – particularly if you imagine another sixty-three towers on the skyline, overshadowing the narrow streets. Even on a bright day, the houses shut out the light; the shadow-filled town contrasts sharply with the open brilliance of the light in the countryside beyond. For medieval men town life and country life were very different ways of existence, divided by the thin line of the town walls.

PART FOUR

THE WORLD OF
LEARNING

14
Schools and Universities

Medieval education was exclusively under the control of the church: though the actual degree of supervision exercised by the ecclesiastical authorities varied widely, every school, from the parish priest's humble class to the highest university debate, was conducted by men who were in holy orders or under the church's jurisdiction. The roots of the church's involvement in education go back to the period, in the sixth and seventh centuries, when the bishop was often the only local personage with any authority. In some towns, the bishop took over responsibility for the public schools; elsewhere, in the absence of any schools, informal teaching was provided within his household, because a priest had to be able to read and write, and the bishop needed scribes and literate administrators to help him to run his diocese. Elsewhere, the monasteries preserved the traditions of higher learning, copying manuscripts and, even in the worst periods of barbarian raids, continuing to add new commentaries and works to the small store of religious and classical literature in circulation. Monks, too, had to be able to read and write, and the monastic schools became very important. Linked to the monastery, which had its own buildings and corporate life, they had a firmer foundation than the bishop's *ad hoc* schools.

Under Charlemagne, the bishop's teaching responsibilities were formalized, and in 789 it was decreed that 'in every bishop's see, and in every monastery, instruction shall be given in the psalms, musical notation, chant, the computation of years and seasons, and in grammar; and all books used shall be carefully corrected'. Twenty years later, this decree was repeated, ordering the bishops to 'set up schools where letters and the science of the Scriptures shall be taught'. At a lower level, the bishops issued instructions that the priests should open schools in the towns and villages where anyone could be taught letters free of charge. At the highest level, there was the palace school where Charlemagne himself laboriously learnt to read and write and where the greatest scholars of the age assembled. In 782 Charlemagne appointed the Anglo-Saxon scholar Alcuin, who had been master of the cathedral school at York, to take charge of it. Enough documents from the school have survived to give us an idea of the range of learning it offered. The basic instruction was by catechism, the system of question and answer which is still used in both the Roman Catholic and Anglican churches to teach church doctrine to laymen. The main subject taught in this way was grammar – in other words, Latin grammar, for the native speech of the nobles' sons who attended the school would have been Frankish, and Charlemagne himself loved to listen to the old Frankish songs. Arithmetic was briefly touched on, but more advanced teaching, in the form of lectures and debates, added only one new subject, theology (which included logic and philosophy). Otherwise it was further instruction in grammar and the art of speaking. Rhetoric included some study of classical literature, which ostensibly survived only as a literary model, because of its pagan elements, but which, to judge from Alcuin's own lyrics, was also appreciated in its own right. The slender flickering flame of secular Latin literature burned on throughout the Middle Ages, until it became the blaze of Renaissance humanism; but it was a secret appreciated only by a handful of scholars. To the ordinary pupil, the great classical authors were represented by tags and quotations in their grammar lessons.

Throughout the Middle Ages, teaching was done almost entirely by word of mouth. The teacher either interrogated pupils, who recited their lessons, or spoke on a given subject. Books were valuable, and even in a cathedral school there might be no more than a dozen or so, all in the teacher's possession. Writing was done on a wax tablet; parchment was scarce, and even paper, after its introduction in the fourteenth century, was often difficult to obtain: Margaret Paston, writing to her husband in the 1450s, excuses a cramped letter by a postscript – 'paper is hard to come by'. The master alone had a desk; his pupils sat on the floor or on the benches. So the medieval schoolroom was merely any convenient empty space. Even in the great monasteries or in cathedral buildings, it is impossible to identify with certainty rooms which may have been purpose-built as schoolrooms, and we have to go as far afield as the Hanse town of Wismar in Prussia to find an intact example of a medieval town grammar school, a long narrow brick building with the typical stepped façade of the civic architecture of the time. In form it is not unlike the schools at Higham Ferrers, built by archbishop Chichele in the 1420s, and at Wainfleet in Lincolnshire, founded by the bishop of Winchester in 1484; all are single-cell buildings, oblong in plan, and although the architectural styles vary from Gothic chapel to miniature town hall, the function is the same: to provide a large open hall and little else. But such buildings were rarities. At Bristol and Oxford we find teachers holding classes in rooms over the town gates or in their own houses. At Ewelme in Oxfordshire the grammar school and almshouses founded by William de la Pole, duke of Suffolk, in the 1440s forms an exceptional group of medieval buildings. On an altogether unusual scale, very close to that of the university colleges at Oxford and Cambridge of which they are the twin foundations, are the buildings of Eton and Winchester.

The humblest schools were those which taught elementary learning: the ABC, followed by the main prayers and then the psalms, were the standard course of reading, designed to give a good grounding in Latin. This was coupled with singing, which was the other element of church services; but writing was usually left until a later stage and was not normally part of the curriculum of the 'song school'. Some such programme would have been used in the collegiate churches with schools attached, like Ottery St Mary (p. 111), if only to train the choristers, while in the country the parish priest – if he was sufficiently skilled – would instruct children in these basic skills. The greater churches and monasteries also had song schools, but they could offer higher learning as well, taking in grammar and writing. The distinctions were never clearly made – to the medieval mind all educational establishments, from song school to university, were simply 'schools' – and the range offered at any given place depended very much on the teacher in charge.

The basic instruction in grammar and rhetoric could lead to a career as a parish priest, or would serve for a merchant, who could acquire more specialized skills such as accounting during his apprenticeship. Although the grammar school curriculum did become broader in the fifteenth century, any kind of higher education was reserved for the universities, which were a wholly medieval creation. The basis of medieval educational theory was the late Latin idea of education as concerned with the seven liberal arts, divided into two groups of three and four. The *trivium* of grammar, rhetoric and dialectic was the basic course, though dialectic, or logic, was neglected in the early Middle Ages. The *quadrivium*, consisting of arithmetic, geometry, astronomy and music, retained only a nominal place in practical teaching: it became an area for specialists only. Just as important as this theoretical basis was one overriding practical fact: because all instruction was in Latin, education was truly international. There were no linguistic barriers restricting study within western Europe until the end of the fourteenth century. Hence when a particular centre of study attained pre-eminence, it attracted men from all over Europe.

The emergence of 'advanced' schools dates from the mid eleventh century, the beginning of that period of peace and economic and intellectual revival which we have already noted as a crucial development. The first impetus came from the new energy of the monasteries: at Monte Cassino in central Italy, classical writers were copied afresh, and Arabic writers on medicine were translated into Latin, while at Bec in Normandy two of the early abbots were famous as theologians: Anselm's work was more literary, but became the basis of much later teaching, Lanfranc had an established reputation as a teacher, and opened a school which rapidly attracted an international following. Unlike Anselm, he taught laymen as well as monks. Like the monasteries, the cathedral schools relied for their reputation on individual teachers. They were always more accessible to outsiders and from 1100 to 1150 they were the main centre of intellectual advance, particularly the group of schools in the Île-de-France, centred on Paris, including Orleans, Chartres, Laon and Reims. These were paralleled on a lesser level by cathedral schools in England and Germany; in Italy we find urban schools, some of them beginning to specialize in law, as at Pavia, or medicine, as at Salerno.

One of the most important elements in the new intellectual activity of the late eleventh and early twelfth century was the readiness of both masters and students to travel in search of knowledge. The Celtic monks, who had traditionally pursued their aimless spiritual quest, the 'wandering scholars' of Helen Waddell's book, now became the exemplar for itinerant masters and students established far from home. The relationship between a great teacher and his followers outstripped any formal and institutional bounds at first, and then gave rise to a new and unprecedented organization. The best-known example of this is of course the career of Peter Abelard, made familiar through his autobiography, which, quite apart from the romantic drama of his love for Heloise, is of major importance as a picture of the world of learning in the early twelfth century. Abelard's early training was as a wandering student, after his father had disinherited him for refusing to give up learning and become a knight. He finally came to the cathedral school at Paris, attracted by the fame of William of Champeaux, who was one of the leading philosophers of the age. Abelard not only opposed his master's views, but succeeded in setting himself up as a teacher at Melun, seemingly without the approval of the authorities, which was always required in such cases. After a brief period at Paris, during which he established his reputation as the leading philosopher of the age, but was only able to teach outside the cathedral school, at Sainte-Geneviève, Abelard turned to theology. Once more he set up as a teacher in opposition to his master, Anselm of Laon, and was forced to stop lecturing. However, he was finally able to establish himself as a recognized master at the school of Notre-Dame in Paris. His later career, as lover and condemned heretic, does not concern us here. What is important is that Abelard was able to constrain the conservative teachers who opposed him to admit him to their ranks by the sheer popularity and force of his lectures. The organization of higher learning was still very informal, and even the church's control over the licensed teachers was difficult to enforce in the face of a genuine wave of enthusiasm for the new spirit of inquiry. When Abelard retreated to the wilderness of Brittany, his followers still sought him out.

By the mid twelfth century, Paris had not one, but three schools: at Notre-Dame, at Sainte-Geneviève and at Saint-Victor, the last founded by Abelard's old master, William of Champeaux. However, it was the old cathedral school at Notre-Dame which outlasted its rivals, and it was the chancellor of Notre-Dame who came to grant licences for fee-paying schools under independent masters in the late twelfth century. These became even more common after a papal decree in 1179 which forbad the taking of payments for such licences, which were to be given free to any properly qualified person. How was this qualification defined? We have seen that even in Abelard's day there was an informal system in operation: a would-be teacher had to study with an established master for a reasonable time, and obtain that master's permission to set up as a teacher. By the 1170s this system was becoming formalized, and the masters had formed themselves into some kind of guild. In the early thirteenth century this had become a corporate body, with rights and privileges and a legal existence. We can trace its activities more clearly when the masters came into conflict with the Chancellor of the cathedral school in 1219–22. The canons of the cathedral tried to break up this new association, which they regarded as a threat to their privileges and authority. From the lawsuit which resulted we learn that the guild was organized in 'nations', and in the following decade we hear of a 'rector' of the whole university. At the same period we first meet the term 'university': it originally meant simply 'the whole body' of masters or students, but rapidly came to be used as a name for the new institution.

Paris was created as a university by its masters; at Bologna the institution was the result of the students combining into an organized body. In Italy a tradition of lay education, in which masters and students were often, but not always, in holy orders, seems to have survived from the seventh to the eleventh century. The school at Bologna was famous as an arts school in the 1130s, and its school of law seems to have developed as an adjunct to this. Italy belonged to the area where written law, based on the old Roman laws, predominated; the rudiments of these, and the art of writing legal documents, needed to be learnt in schools rather than by practical experience. Soon afterwards, canon law, the written law of the church, came to be taught at Bologna as well, and the teachers began to involve themselves in questions of legal theory as well as mere practicalities. They were, however, free from all restrictions: anyone could set up as a teacher, as long as the would-be students would pay to listen. There was no apparent system of licensing, but the masters seem to have formed a guild by the end of the twelfth century. A master's success, however, depended entirely on attracting customers: he was not paid by the cathedral authorities, as in northern Europe, and was in effect hired as a private tutor to a group of men who might well be of mature age – Bologna was in many ways a postgraduate university, for those who already in effect held degrees in arts. Furthermore, the students had little protection as individual foreigners under the law of the city-republic of Bologna; but by forming themselves into corporations, they could gain legal standing. So societies and groups of societies sprang up, which in the early thirteenth century had resolved themselves into four bodies or 'universities', for Lombards, Tuscans, Romans and those from beyond the Alps. In the mid thirteenth century this was reduced to two, Italian and non-Italian. The earliest such society seems to have been formed by the German students for their mutual protection, and from this germ the others grew; but scholars from Bologna itself were always outside the 'universities', which underlines the fact that the 'universities' were associations of foreign students. Likewise, the professors, who were originally citizens of Bologna, were also excluded from the 'universities' because they were not foreigners; but this division was made sharper by a series of quarrels between the students and the professors, partly over teaching arrangements and partly over questions of jurisdiction, which were not resolved until the late thirteenth century. The final form of Bologna's constitution in the later Middle Ages differed in theory rather than in practice from that of the northern universities.

The grouping of students by nation which first appears at Bologna was common to most medieval universities. So also was the weapon which the students used at times of crisis, that of secession. The students at Bologna used it against the civic authorities and the professors, while in northern Europe it was used mostly against church authority. In 1204 a group of students left Bologna to establish themselves at Vicenza. The same happened in 1215 to Arezzo, in 1222 to Padua, and in 1321 to Siena. Of these, only the migration to Padua was of lasting effect. In the north, the rise of Oxford was given a major impetus by a migration of students from Paris, recalled by Henry II during his quarrel with Becket, who attached themselves to existing schools at Oxford, about whose origins we know little. In 1209, disturbances at Oxford led to a suspension of studies by the masters, and the dispersal of themselves and their pupils to Reading, Paris and Cambridge. The choice of the last-named is obscure, as it was no more than a market-town of some size, but without any ecclesiastical or administrative importance. Some scholars remained here after the revival of Oxford studies in 1214, but it took a further exodus from Paris to Cambridge in 1228 to establish a sufficient body of students.

By the mid thirteenth century, these loose associations of students and teachers had become sufficiently recognized as desirable and useful for attempts to be made to found new universities by charter. The first such 'charter' university was created by Frederick II at Naples in 1224, to act as a training-ground for administrators, free from the pro-papal leanings of the lawyers at Bologna. Like so many of the later attempts, this instant creation failed to take root; throughout the Middle Ages, no university founded by this method came to rival the earlier and more spontaneous foundations.

The early accounts of the universities give the impression of a relatively relaxed discipline, an atmosphere more of a gathering of enthusiasts for learning than of an organized and regulated body. In many ways, the fully formalized university, with officials, appointed teachers and enrolled students, emerges only in the mid fourteenth century. Supervision of student life began with regula-tion of attendance at lectures at a very early stage; outside the hours of teaching, the student, who was usually of mature age, was left to his own devices, to find his own lodgings and lead his own life. But serious disturbances between students and townsmen, at Paris, Oxford and Bologna, compelled some kind of discipline of student life as a whole – students were usually clerics in minor orders, and hence exempt from ordinary secular jurisdiction. Furthermore, there was an increasing trend to provide lodgings not only for poor scholars, but for monks who were studying at university. Gradually this system of halls developed into the collegiate system familiar in the older English and Scottish universities, a system once wide-spread on the continent but now almost entirely vanished there. College buildings survive at Bologna and Salamanca. In both cases, the buildings have been given Renaissance façades, though the in-terior of the Collegio di Spagna at Bologna, built in 1365 by Matteo Gattapone for the great Spanish prelate Cardinal Albornoz, is unaltered. Only parts of the Colegio Viejo at Salamanca still exist, but the original schools (Escuelas Minores) retain an interior court-yard of 1428 behind a late fifteenth-century front. A vivid monu-ment to university teaching in fourteenth-century Italy is the tomb of Cino de' Sinibaldi (c.1360) in Pistoia cathedral, near Florence, which portrays him both delivering a formal discourse to his fellow-doctors and reading a lecture to students, who follow the text which he is expounding in their own copies with varying degrees of attentiveness. A similar theme is to be found in the memorial to Giovanni da Legnano, a lecturer at Bologna who died in 1386; a bas-relief from his tomb, now in the Museo Civico at Bologna, shows three students seated at benches, books open before them, while others crowd in the background. In northern France, similar scenes can be found on incised grave slabs commemorating teachers, such as that of Guillaume de Saint-Remy, doctor of theology, who died in 1340, now in the Musée Bossuet at Meaux, where he was a canon of the cathedral.

At Oxford and Cambridge, by contrast, a considerable portion of the colleges are still housed in their original medieval buildings, and parts of the original schools survive. At **Oxford**, the earliest foundations were University College, Balliol and Merton; of these, Merton was actually the first to obtain a charter, and it was also the first to have a completed quadrangle. 'Mob Quad', as it is now known, is entirely fourteenth-century, but was built over a long period, from 1304 to 1378, and seems to have evolved into this shape rather than being planned: the north and east sides were the earliest, and the quad was closed by the addition of the two other sides in 1371–8. The treasury, in the older part, is a curious box-like structure embedded in the north corner, entirely of stone, including the ceiling of the first-floor room, and was designed to resist both the risk of fire common to all medieval towns and the local hazard of riots between 'town' and 'gown': it is a reminder of the turbulence and uncertainties of medieval university life. The library, in the south range, has many of its original windows and the original north doorway, but its furnishings are all seventeenth-century, as are the coffered ceiling and the dormer windows which provide most of the light. Medieval libraries must often have been cramped and dark like this one; indeed, the idea of a special room for reading would have been an innovation when Merton library was built, and many great monasteries stored their books in cupboards in the cloister and elsewhere. At Merton the books were kept in a library chest with three locks, still to be seen there, as are the chest's successors, desks to which some of the books are even now chained. North of Mob Quad is the hall, completed by 1277; of the original building only parts survive, chiefly the undercroft and west wall. It was heavily restored by Sir George Gilbert Scott in the 1870s but the hall door has its old scrolled ironwork, as stylish as the decoration in the margin of a Gothic manuscript. The chapel is notable for its great tower. Oxford abounds in these towers, the work of a group of architects and masons in the late fifteenth century, using the Cotswold stone which was readily available. We shall see that Cambridge, on the other hand, specialized in gatehouses. In both cases, competition between the founders of increasingly well-endowed colleges in the late Middle Ages lies behind these architectural displays.

The supreme example of a medieval college is New College, founded by William of Wykeham, clerk of the king's works, keeper of the privy seal, chancellor and bishop of Winchester under Edward I I I, a man who had made his career in government service and had had no university education himself. His twin foundation of Winchester College and New College in 1382 and 1379 respectively was to be the model for Henry V I's linked foundations at Eton and King's sixty years later. Until the mid fourteenth century, the halls had been exclusively undergraduate residences, under a warden or master responsible for discipline, who had no teaching role. At King's Hall, Cambridge, by 1370, there were students living in what was otherwise a 'college' of fellows; and Wykeham's statutes were the first to provide for this arrangement from the beginning. The fellows continued to teach in the university at large, but assumed special tutorial responsibilities towards the undergraduates of the college. Furthermore, Wykeham provided for all the necessary ancillary buildings which distinguished a college from a mere hall of residence. New College was planned around a great quadrangle containing a communal dining hall, a chapel and a library. New College is curiously isolated from the world outside; its site, in the angle of the old city walls (which the college is responsible for maintaining), is today even more cut off by the approach down College Lane, leading to the squat tower above the gate, which has its original outer door. The quadrangle within, Great Quad, is on an appropriately ambitious scale, and the buildings are relatively little changed, save for Georgian windows and a seventeenth-century battlemented upper storey on three sides. The medieval façades, lower and with narrow windows, would have offered a much stronger contrast with the airy perpendicular architecture of the chapel and hall to the north, and the towers would have stood out more boldly. The second tower, in the north-east corner, is the muniment tower, almost as defensive in aspect as the treasury at Merton. The scale of Great Quad is matched by that of the chapel, whose simple five-bay interior is one of the largest in Oxford, with a spacious ante-chapel. A door between the gate tower and the chapel leads through to the cloister, peaceful with its great ilex, which was designed as a burial-ground and was added by the founder two years after the college had opened; it was completed in 1400. Above it rises the bell-tower, a detached campanile whose simple lines harmonize with the restrained tracery of the cloister walk. All in all, this is a place remote and still, echoing the ancient monastic predecessors of the college. Wykeham's foundation, even allowing for the very generous scale of the buildings, provided for a much larger body of scholars than any previous Oxford or Cambridge college, though it could have been matched in size at Bologna or Paris. It looks forward to the great expansion of university buildings in the fifteenth and early sixteenth century, when pious creations for charitable purposes became more frequent as patronage moved away from the traditional institutions such as monasteries towards memorial foundations, from small chantry chapels to the great collegiate bodies. A college, as we have seen, was not only a university body, and to the medieval mind there was little difference between a college of priests and a college of students and fellows in minor orders. In 1470, Sir John Fastolf's intention to found a college of priests at Caister castle near Yarmouth was transmuted by another bishop of Winchester, Fastolf's executor, into part of the endowment of his new college of St Mary Magdalen.

All Souls, whose entrance is in the turmoil of the High Street, was founded seventy years after New College, but looks backward rather than forward. It is the only college of fellows, a lone survivor from early medieval practice, and it is on the small scale of medieval colleges, consisting of a warden and fifty-four fellows. Yet its plan owes much to New College, with gateway tower, hall and chapel on the north side of the quad, which is designed as an enclosed unit. The quad itself has never been added to (apart from the battlements of 1510), and although the façade on the High Street has twice been altered, the interior of the quad has its original proportions: neither the gate tower nor the chapel rise much above the roof-level of the living quarters.

Oxford possesses the best example of a university (as opposed to collegiate) building of the fifteenth century, in the Divinity Schools. It began as schools only, in the early 1420s, but the plans were extended to include space for the library given by duke Humfrey of Gloucester to the university. This was to be housed on the upper floor, which is now within the Bodleian library, of

which the room for the duke's library – but, alas, neither his books
nor the fittings – is part; it has a resplendent painted wooden roof.
The roof, too, is the glory of the Divinity Schools, otherwise a
spacious, echoing lecture-hall, an extraordinary example of what
is technically known as a lierne vault, intricate in structure and
ornamented with bosses. It is not as graceful as the finest fan-vaults,
with massive pendants that really seem to defy gravity, but it is
none the less striking, and in contrast to the sobriety of Oxford
Gothic in general.

Oxford's great Renaissance college, Christ Church, whose scale
dwarfs New College just as that foundation had dwarfed its predecessor, is a monument to the ambition of Cardinal Wolsey, the
last of the private patrons of the late Middle Ages and a splendid,
if low-born, example of princely magnificence. But it, and other
new building of this period, is in pure Gothic, of a local kind which
resists the flamboyance of King's College chapel at Cambridge –
except in the Divinity Schools roof – and relies instead on elegance
of proportions, as in Magdalen's justly famous tower. Gothic was
to survive at Oxford until the seventeenth century, in work at Jesus
College, Exeter College, and elsewhere; and Oriel was rebuilt in the
old style between 1619 and 1642. This was probably due to the
successes of the group of architects based in Oxford from 1475 to
1525. William Orchard, designer of the Divinity Schools and of the
chapel and cloister at Magdalen, seems to have been head of a firm
which acted as building contractors as well. John Lebon and
William Redman designed Christ Church hall, and William Vertue
Corpus Christi College – sober enough compared with his work at
Westminster. With such examples, the innately conservative
university world had no ambitions to embark on classical flights of
fancy or extravaganzas like those of the Elizabethan gentry.

The medieval survivals at **Cambridge** are more varied; there
is no evidence of a traditional school of architecture, as seems to
be the case at Oxford. The earliest complete court or quad at either
university is the Old Court at Corpus Christi College, a modest
range of buildings which were originally no more than a two-
storeyed range, whose architectural distinction lay in the fact that
they were the first fully planned closed quadrangle. 'The rooms
had in the first instance bare walls and the windows were probably
half-shuttered, half-glazed. On the ground storey they had clay
floors. On the first floor they were open to the roof . . .' The church

of St Benet, to the north of the court, served as college chapel. The court is solidly built of stone, with prominent buttresses, as befitted a college founded by two wealthy town guilds in the aftermath of the Black Death; it was for five centuries the whole of the college, a reminder of the small scale of medieval colleges, which had often begun as little more than private lodging-houses for a dozen students. The oldest of the Cambridge colleges, Peterhouse, has its original hall, refurbished in 1868–71 by Sir George Gilbert Scott, complete with William Morris & Co glass to Burne-Jones designs; if the decoration is recent, the building itself is remarkable in having served the same secular function for nearly seven hundred years. Other colleges have some medieval work. The medieval court at Trinity Hall is disguised by an eighteenth-century classical facing on the interior, though the outside is unaltered. Queens' has a gatehouse of 1451, and the first court is contemporary with it, while the second court has a cloister of 1460–90, more typical of Oxford quads. Gatehouses were a distinctive Cambridge speciality: within the next fifty years, Jesus, Christ's, St John's and Trinity all had gatehouses. Each became more grandiose and richly ornamented than its predecessors: the heraldry at Jesus is modest, while at Christ's and St John's the arms of Lady Margaret Beaufort and her various devices are prominently displayed in stone. Trinity caps all of them with a statue of the founder, Henry VIII, over the great gate; as befits the largest of the colleges, it also has an earlier and smaller gatehouse, now by the chapel, which had been the entrance of King's Hall; Henry VIII had created Trinity by merging this college with Michaelhouse and two smaller hostels, and the earlier gatehouse dates from 1426–30. Similar gatehouses are a feature of contemporary monasteries and of grand domestic architecture, a distant derivative of the castle entrance flanked by twin towers, but the scale of college architecture has made them into something more ostentatious and substantial. Because they are so close to each other, there is a distinct sense of competition, each proclaiming the lavishness of its benefactor.

The glory of Cambridge, and the culmination of late Gothic architecture, is of course King's College chapel. Henry VI, wishing to imitate the great foundations of William of Wykeham and to provide an education for clerics in the traditional mould, as a counter to the rising tide of Lollard ideas, laid his plans on a truly regal scale. He ignored the existing King's Hall, which was primarily a training ground for the royal household and for laymen, and endowed a new college in 1441, the building of which began with the chapel. It also virtually ended there: the chapel was finally glazed and furnished in 1535, and no more work was done for two centuries. The modest court built when the college was founded, which lay to the north of the chapel, contrasted strangely with the vast and splendid creation in whose shadow it lay. The plan of the college seems to have been that of the king himself, and the execution of it was in the hands of Reginald Ely from 1446 until Henry VI's defeat and capture by Edward IV in 1461, when work stopped. By this time, the original source of white limestone had given out, and the second stage of the work, carried out under Edward IV and Richard III, can be readily identified. By 1485, the five eastern bays were complete and had been roofed in, and a temporary wall had been built to make this part available for use. The seven western bays had risen no more than ten feet above ground level. Henry VII attended a service in the chapel in 1506, and in 1508 he provided funds for work to be resumed. When he died a year later, he instructed his executors to make payments as necessary, and, under the direction of the great architect John Wastell, the western part was completed by 1512. Between 1512 and 1515, the daring and astonishing fan vault was built, and the extravagant display of Tudor heraldry lining the nave walls was completed. The final effect is of a vast and spacious interior devoted as much to the glory of the royal house as to the glory of God: we are in the full flood of Renaissance thought, where the secular dominion of the state is commemorated in a way that in earlier centuries had been reserved to sacred matters. King's College chapel is the last master-piece of Gothic architecture, but it is also arguably the first master-piece of the English Renaissance in its overall conception. Even the celebrated west front has strong secular overtones, being closer in form to a great gatehouse, with its twin flanking towers and heraldic display over the doorway, than to any previous style of church building.

King's College chapel in its final form has little to do with university life and much more with Tudor royal display. Yet it had arisen out of a genuine interest in education; Eton College, its counterpart for scholars, gives some idea of what Henry VI might have achieved at King's if he had had the time and money, but it also reminds us that there was a change in attitudes towards education at this time. William of Wykeham's twin foundation of Winchester and New College, Oxford, sixty years earlier, belongs to the very first stages of the process. Just as university teaching had become highly specialized, so education outside the universities was increasingly a matter, not for clergy, to whom it was an additional duty, but for specially trained professional teachers. At Cambridge we find students younger than the university undergraduates acquiring the degree of master of grammar as a licence to teach; and from the fourteenth century onwards, but more generally in the late fifteenth and early sixteenth century, we find the private, secular grammar schools.

15
Law and Medicine

How far did higher learning impinge on everyday life? The main body of graduates were masters of arts, in other words, holders of a general degree; a smaller number went on to specialize in theology, which included philosophy and such natural science as was studied, or in law, which was largely theoretical. Medicine did not necessarily require an arts degree; at Montpellier an arts graduate merely took five years instead of six to attain his medical degree, and in the early Middle Ages Salerno was scarcely a formal university. In all three disciplines, the circle of experts was very small and the learning very specialized; the theologians might settle obscure disputes within the church, the lawyers might advise on international conflicts, and the doctors might propound general theories of health; but by and large theirs was an esoteric world, with little practical application. The parish priest at mass, the judge or magistrate in an ordinary court, the barber-surgeon treating the sick, held no degrees, and what they taught and practised was only rarely influenced by the deliberations of the university doctors. Canon law, which regulated a cleric's life down to minute details, did have a strong practical influence, but the spread of Roman law and of theoretical ideas about medicine as ideas which played a large part in day to day life (and which eventually became the basis for modern continental law and for medicine everywhere) were both the result of the Renaissance and of the wider education which followed in its wake.

The worlds of law and medicine outside the universities are difficult to recapture in visual terms. Both were part of wider institutions: law went with government, medicine with the care of the poor and aged. So surviving law-courts, such as Westminster Hall or the Palais de Justice at Poitiers, are parts of palaces, used incidentally for legal purposes. Law-courts retained the mobility of early medieval government longer than any other institution: the English judge of today on circuit is working in the same way as his medieval predecessors, travelling round the country and holding courts in different towns as necessary. Until the nineteenth century, county assizes were usually held in any convenient large building (usually the town hall), as were the deliberations of the higher courts in London – the concept of a special court building is an entirely modern one. Even Parliament, the highest court of the realm, met within the royal palace of Westminster. These are English examples, but the same was true abroad. At Poitiers, the ducal palace, built by the Plantagenets in the twelfth century, is unusual in several respects. It is not a fortified building, though there is a keep next to it, and it was for a long time the centre of an administrative area as great as that controlled from Paris or London, both in the twelfth century and again in the late fourteenth and early fifteenth century. The hall, an echoing space a hundred and fifty feet by fifty, was primarily used for state occasions, and in the late fourteenth century Jean duc de Berry had the end wall rebuilt with three monumental flamboyant Gothic chimneypieces, with a balcony above and new windows in the same style, as well as statues of himself, his wife and the king and queen, masterly examples of French Gothic portraiture. In the 1430s the *parlement* of Charles V I I sat here while the Paris *parlement* was under English control, and in 1453 the trial of Jacques Cœur (p. 288 above) took place here. By contrast, when Joan of Arc was examined at Poitiers in 1429 by a commission of the *parlement*, the hearings seem to have taken place in the chief advocate's lodgings, underlining again that it was the presence of certain people which constituted a court, rather than the place in which it assembled. At the other extreme of the judicial system there were courts concerned with minor and local disputes, manor courts or market courts, where proceedings were even less formal. One of these has survived to the present day: the tribunal at Valencia, which deals with the administration of the ancient irrigation systems drawing water from the river Turia which flows through the city and which since Roman times has provided water for the fruit and vegetable farms in the countryside around. Since at least the thirteenth century, the representatives of eight districts served by the canals have met each Thursday at 10 a.m. before the north door of the cathedral. Against this Gothic backdrop, the disputes are tried in oral proceedings, in which sentence is pronounced immediately; only the decisions are recorded, just as in a medieval manor court.

Institutional survivals such as the Valencia tribunal are rare in continental Europe: they are more frequent in the north, where the Icelandic Althing, originally a general assembly of the heads of families which was first constituted in about 930, is the oldest surviving democratic assembly in the world. The site of the meeting, at Thingvellir, thirty miles east of Reykjavik, remains an open plain ringed by distant hills; the speaker recited one third of the laws each year, encoded in verse, from a cliff above the valley. The thirteen shires were represented by three leaders and one in nine of all the inhabitants. But although the Althing has existed continuously to the present day, its power declined in the thirteenth century, and it became an effective body again only in the late nineteenth century. Likewise, the jury system in English and American law goes back to Norman, if not Norse roots. At a lesser level, a host of English medieval government procedures and titles survive, from the annual testing of the British coinage for purity, the trial of the pyx, to the British name for what any other nation would call the ministry of finance, the exchequer, which originates in the chequered cloth used for counting purposes in the twelfth-century treasury.

The surviving traces of medieval medicine overlap very considerably with functions which we now regard as the province of the state: the care of the sick is not specifically distinguished from the care of the aged and the poor, and the same word, hospital or hospice, was used for an institution which might care for any of these, or indeed for pilgrims and travellers. Hospital means no more than a place where guests are received. The Knights Hospitallers, or order of St John of Jerusalem, earned their name because their order had grown up around a hospice for sick pilgrims at Jerusalem, probably founded around 1080. It was not the only hospice in the city, but was apparently unique in caring for the sick. In an ordinary monastery, the hospice would be the guest-quarters, while the name for the rooms occupied by sick monks was the infirmary. So when we come to look at surviving medieval 'hospitals', such as those at Angers, Siena, Winchester and Beaune, we are talking about a wide-ranging institution rather than the modern specialist establishment for the care of the sick. There were about 750 such establishments in England alone, and they were designed for 'care rather than cure'. Their origins went back to the traditional charitable duty of welcoming travellers, and only later did they concentrate on the sick and the homeless. Bishops still vow at their consecration to shelter 'the poor, the stranger and all in want', and the 'strangers' and the 'infirm people' were often linked in medieval foundation deeds. The most important surviving hospitals are all in towns, where the number of strangers and sick people was too great for the monasteries and other ecclesiastical institutions to cope. The hospital of Saint-Jean at Angers founded by Henry II in the mid twelfth century is now a museum, the main hall of which is the old public ward, with three aisles and 'Angevin' vaulting. It must have been a cheerless place despite its architectural grandeur. As in all such establishments there is a chapel attached. Even today, a quarter of a million people in England alone are still cared for in almshouses founded in the Middle Ages.

At **Siena**, the hospital of Santa Maria della Scala began as a shelter for pilgrims in the tenth or eleventh century, but became a centre for the treatment of the sick by 1080, and was evidently unusually successful. Only lepers were excluded. It was under the authority of the canons of the cathedral, but rapidly grew in wealth through bequests from grateful citizens until it became an independent body in 1404, by which time it was one of the most important institutions in the town, controlling much property. It offered not only treatment for illness, but undertook many other kinds of welfare work, from arranging apprenticeships for poor men's sons or providing dowries for their daughters to paying for paupers' burials and sheltering the homeless. The extensive buildings in the cathedral square are still used as a hospital; the earliest parts date back to the thirteenth century, but the major part belongs to the period after 1336, when a spacious hall for the treatment of the sick was begun; building work on this and other extensions continued for nearly two hundred years. This hall is still used as a ward; bright frescoes of the mid fifteenth century record the different functions of the medieval hospital. The other wards, which are not open to the public, also contain frescoes, while the crypt of the hospital church is famous as the meeting place of the group of young Sienese mystics who gathered around St Catherine of Siena in the 1370s. St Catherine laid great emphasis on the spiritual value of involvement in secular life, and much of her time was spent caring for the sick and the poor in the hospital, in the very wards which we can still see in use today.

A glimpse of the practical work of a medieval hospital, in this case purely an almshouse, can be seen in the hospital of St Cross at **Winchester**, founded in 1133–6 by Henry of Blois, bishop of Winchester (whom we have met earlier as a connoisseur of classical art) under the aegis of the Knights Hospitaller. The original hall, for feeding a hundred poor men each day, still exists as the brewhouse of the much larger establishment which developed under the patronage of Cardinal Beaufort, uncle of Henry VI, in the early fifteenth century. The early buildings became part of an outer court, with kitchens and stables, while an inner court worthy of an Oxford college was built between the hall and the Norman church, with a magnificent gatehouse, a great hall and refectory, and spacious accommodation for the new inhabitants, who were to be impoverished noblemen and noblewomen, in contrast to the original purpose of the foundation. The master was given a lodging similar to that found in Oxford colleges. This is a lone survivor among medieval English almshouses as far as complete or almost complete building complexes go; most other such foundations, if they survive at all, have been largely rebuilt at a later date. Even the Great Hospital at Norwich, whose spectacular main ward has a roof emblazoned with the eagle of Bohemia in honour of Anne of Bohemia, Richard II's queen, proves to be largely of later construction, and the ward is in fact the old nave of the neighbouring church of St Helen, adapted after the Reformation.

The best of all surviving medieval hospitals is the Hospice at **Beaune**, which owes its origin to private charity at the end of the Middle Ages and is a monument to the wealth of the Burgundian court. It was founded in 1443 by Nicholas Rolin, chancellor of Philip the Good, and endowed with vineyards outside the town; later benefactors have added to these, and the Hospice now owns thirty-two vineyards, the wine from which is among the most sought-after in the world. As a result, it is today wealthy enough to run both a modern hospital and home for the elderly and an orphanage, and also to maintain its superb late-Gothic buildings, including the original pharmacy and kitchens. The Hospice was designed by Jean Rateau and was rightly called 'a lodging for a prince rather than a hospital for the poor'. Its façade is discreet, but within the courtyard the polychrome tile roof, the weather vanes

flaunting the founder's arms, the galleries and gargoyles, the spire
and pinnacles, all give it an exotic appearance on two sides, an
artist's fantasy from the background of a medieval miniature made
real, contrasting with the grey mass of the hall opposite. This courtyard used to be hung with tapestries each November on the occasion
of the auction of the year's vintage from the Hospice lands; this
tradition, begun in 1851, has been discontinued, but the tapestries
can be seen in the museum of the Hospice, magnificent Flemish
work of the early sixteenth century, underlining the Hospice's
wealth at that time. Also in the museum is Rogier van der Weyden's
Last Judgement, specially commissioned for the Hospice by
Nicholas Rolin. This originally stood in the chapel at one end of
the great hall, which, as at Siena, was the main ward, a vast timber-
roofed open space 170 feet by 52 feet. It was in use until 1948.
The chapel, behind an open screen at one end, was restored in
the last century after being destroyed at the Revolution, but van
der Weyden's masterpiece was hidden and thus survived. It contrasts with earlier medieval treatments of the Last Judgement,
which emphasize the mass of souls, both damned and saved, and
the hosts of demons and angels. Paradise and Hell are relegated
to the outer panels of the triptych; in the centre, a dozen figures
represent risen mankind, six saints the whole court of heaven. A
stern yet contemplative Christ, flanked by angels bearing the signs
of the passion, watches over the weighing of souls; St Michael holds
the balances, but looks straight ahead, as if to remind us, the on-
lookers, that we too must face this ordeal. The medieval emphasis
on hierarchies and the predestined order of things, of which the
Last Judgement is the culmination, is in retreat; instead, the artist
seems to foreshadow the fluid world proposed by Renaissance
thinkers, where the individual stands or falls by his own efforts.
It is a fitting image on which to take leave of medieval Europe.

Appendix
Libraries and Museums

Libraries and manuscripts

The very considerable collections of manuscripts which have come
down to us are the main witness to the intellectual, and in many
cases to the artistic, achievements of the Middle Ages. Although
manuscripts are very fragile, they have always been scarce and
valuable, and have therefore been cared for and preserved
accordingly, apart from a period in the sixteenth century when
many lesser manuscripts were destroyed because the printed book
had superseded them. But very few manuscripts survive in their
original homes. Firstly, a very large proportion of the manuscripts
produced in early medieval Europe were written and kept in
monasteries, and over the succeeding centuries there were very
few monasteries which have had a totally undisturbed existence;
indeed, it is hard to name a single monastery with holdings comparable to those of the Greek Orthodox monasteries at Athos,
Patmos or Sinai. The best example is perhaps the Austrian
monastery at Admont, south of Salzburg, where some of the manuscripts written there in the twelfth century, as well as the abbey's
later collection of manuscripts, are still in the abbey library, now
housed in Rococo splendour; only in this century have there been
serious losses, due to the enforced sales of some seventy-seven
manuscripts. Among the books is a catalogue of the manuscripts
drawn up in 1370, with detailed instructions on the care of books
and bindings.

Secondly, private collections of the later Middle Ages – when
many manuscripts were produced commercially by professional
scribes for wealthy individuals – have now almost always changed
hands, even in the case of royal libraries. The concept of a public
library was a Renaissance innovation, and the major state,

university and college collections of today were all formed after 1500. Surprisingly, the best example of a medieval library is in England, where the chained library at Hereford cathedral escaped unscathed at the Reformation. Similar libraries abroad survived until the eighteenth century, only to be swept away by the revolutions of the end of that century. It has been estimated that in France 95 per cent of the books in the country changed ownership between 1789 and 1810. The Hereford collection is a relatively modest one, and it is the survival of the original layout of the library which is interesting. At Verona, on the other hand, the remarkable feature is the continuing presence of a handful of the original manuscripts from the ninth-century library, nine of them produced by the director of the *scriptorium* or writing-room, Pacificus, who organized the writing of 218 manuscripts between 801 and 844.

The major collections of today, from the Vatican Library to the Pierpont Morgan library in New York, are the result of the deliberate acquisition of manuscripts since the Renaissance. The Vatican Library and the Bibliothèque Nationale both have elements of earlier collections in them, notably some survivors from the royal library of Charles V in the latter, but the Bibliothèque de l'Arsenal in Paris, with a wealth of medieval material, is basically the work of an eighteenth-century bibliophile with later additions. The British Museum collection, now the British Library, was created in 1753 by an act of Parliament authorizing the purchase by the Treasury of three existing collections, the most important of which had been formed by Sir Robert Cotton in the early seventeenth century and had been public property since 1702. Four years later, the royal library was added; the nucleus of this went back to Edward IV's books of romances, lavishly produced for him in Flanders.

Other major libraries were formed immediately after a period of upheaval; in England, Archbishop Parker's purchases of monastic manuscripts following the dissolution of the monasteries went to Corpus Christi College, Cambridge, in 1575, among them the gospel-book said to have been sent by Gregory the Great to St Augustine in the early seventh century. On the continent, the secularization of monasteries in Bavaria in 1803 led to the wholesale removal of manuscripts to the Bavarian State Library in Munich, while in France it was the municipal libraries which took charge of the 'secularized' manuscripts.

Manuscripts are both fragile and precious, and although they are the commonest of the objects which have come down to us from the Middle Ages, they are physically the least accessible. Of the British Library's holdings of some 75,000 medieval and modern manuscripts, a mere fifty or so are on display at any one time, and of these only one opening can be shown at a time. The same applies to all other major collections; only in very rare instances, where a manuscript has been disbound and mounted leaf by leaf, can more than two pages be seen at a time. As a result, the master-pieces of illumination, an art-form as impressive in its achievements as Gothic architecture, have to be experienced at second hand, in modern reproductions. Again, only a very few works are available in this form, and these might give the idea that all medieval manu-scripts were astonishing works of art, such as the Book of Kells or the Lindisfarne Gospels from the Celtic world of the eighth century, or the Books of Hours commissioned by Jean duc de Berry, the greatest patron of the arts of his day, in the late fourteenth century. For every such lavish masterpiece, there are thousands of workaday manuscripts, of interest only for the texts they contain. But illuminated manuscripts are a vital and influential part of the world of medieval art; they were often the means by which new ideas and styles were spread throughout Europe, and we can see the interaction of manuscript miniatures and larger art-forms – frescoes, sculpture, and later panel-painting – in numerous examples from the eighth century onwards. Carolingian artists derived their knowledge of the classical art-forms they were trying to re-create from manuscripts, while in the mid twelfth century two magnificent Bibles produced at St Albans and Winchester can be linked with frescoes at Sigena in northern Spain, and in the early fifteenth century the miniaturists who worked for Jean duc de Berry had an international reputation. It is as if all we knew of medieval churches were photographs of the cathedrals; behind the few masterpieces of which we can form some idea there is a whole world of medieval experience which must perforce remain closed to all but scholars. But in a sense this is appropriate; for just as the majesty of the churches was experienced by most medieval people, so the manuscripts have always been the province of a few dedicated students.

Museums and Art Galleries

Compared with the great collections of classical and Renaissance art to be found in museums, medieval art is relatively poorly served. Scorned as mere curiosities by the seventeenth- and eighteenth-century patrons whose purchases often form the basis of modern museums, it was only in the nineteenth century that medieval items were once again appreciated. Even then they never aroused the same enthusiasm as works in the classical tradition. Furthermore, the majority of the masterpieces of medieval art were religious in origin, and despite the Reformation many of them remained in their original places and were unlikely to find their way into collections. The result is that many major museums have a rather miscellaneous assembly of objects in their medieval section, and smaller, specialist museums can often outshine national collections.

At a national level, my choice as the outstanding medieval museum would be the Musée de Cluny in Paris, despite a rather old-fashioned display. Its riches range from spectacular jewellery and metalwork to early stained glass and the famous early Renaissance tapestries of 'The Lady with the Unicorn'. The Schnütgen Museum in Cologne comes a close second; its display is modern and effective, but it is restricted to religious artefacts. Of the larger museums, the Victoria and Albert Museum in London, founded at a time when medieval art was at the peak of its popularity, has a wealth of objects, but they are classified by type rather than period, so that it is impossible to see in close proximity a range of medieval artefacts such as ivories, metalwork and woodwork, because they are in different departments. The British Museum collection is relatively small, and, despite one or two spectacular items, is rather disappointing; the same is true of the Louvre, whose four galleries of medieval French sculpture hardly compete with what is still to be seen *in situ*. In addition there is a gallery of *objets d'art* including the ivory Virgin and Child from the Sainte-Chapelle. There are several cathedral treasuries which can outshine these two major collections in the medieval field. The Imperial Treasury (Schatzkammer) in Vienna has the surviving jewellery of the Holy Roman emperors, including the tenth-century imperial crown which may have been used by Otto I in 962, and the coronation cloak of Roger II of Sicily. It also contains insignia from the fifteenth-century Burgundian Order of the Golden Fleece. In

Spain, the Museo Arqueológico has part of the Visigothic treasure of Guarrazar (see p. 213; the rest is at the Musée de Cluny).

As regards painting, the outstanding pieces are from the late Middle Ages and are to be found mostly in Dutch and Italian museums, though many major museums have a room or two of 'primitives'. The collections at Bruges, Siena and Florence are perhaps the pre-eminent ones: the Musée Gruuthuse at Bruges, the Pinacoteca at Siena and the first rooms of the Uffizi at Florence, to which should be added the early rooms of the Wallraf-Richartz Museum at Cologne. At Barcelona, the Museo de Arte de Cataluña has the unusual feature of incorporating large sections of Roman-esque buildings with fine frescoes, removed for safety from remote rural parishes. This removal of buildings to a museum is also found at The Cloisters, now part of the Metropolitan Museum of Art in New York, and, in the case of a Scandinavian stave-church, at the open-air museum at Skansen near Stockholm. Replicas of the famous buildings of France are to be found in the extraordinary Musée des Monuments Nationaux in the Palais de Chaillot in Paris, founded by Viollet-le-Duc; this collection includes reproductions at full scale of most of the major medieval frescoes in France. A small number of casts of medieval sculpture from throughout Europe can be seen in the Cast Gallery at the Victoria and Albert Museum.

Of the smaller museums, a few are outstanding because of a bene-factor's special interest in the medieval period. The Burrell collection in Glasgow, at last properly housed and fully exhibited, has very important holdings of late medieval arts. In particular, items such as furniture and tapestries are very rarely found in their original settings, in contrast to later periods, particularly the eighteenth century, where we can still see great houses with the contents of whole rooms virtually intact. Furnishings of the period are almost always 'dislocated' objects today; but this is not inappro-priate, for most medieval furniture was designed to be portable and was taken by its owner from place to place as he travelled. Chests and coffers are the most usual survivals, ranging from the 'safes' of twelfth-century church chests of hollowed oak to the richly painted *cassoni* of Italy and southern France. Few tapestries from the four-teenth century and earlier survive; the most spectacular is the Apocalypse tapestry at Angers, woven in Paris in the late fourteenth century. The best collection of medieval textiles is at Las Huelgas

(p. 219 above). But many small museums have one or two outstanding medieval pieces, and to come across such a piece is one of the pleasures of exploring provincial museums.

Finally, four American museums with important medieval collections (in addition to the Metropolitan Museum of Art) deserve a mention: they are the Boston Museum of Fine Arts, the Walters Art Gallery at Baltimore, the Cincinnati Art Museum and the Cleveland Museum of Arts.

Index

374   INDEX

378 INDEX

FOR THE BEST IN PAPERBACKS, LOOK FOR THE 🐧

In every corner of the world, on every subject under the sun, Penguin represents quality and variety – the very best in publishing today.

For complete information about books available from Penguin – including Pelicans, Puffins, Peregrines and Penguin Classics – and how to order them, write to us at the appropriate address below. Please note that for copyright reasons the selection of books varies from country to country.

In the United Kingdom: Please write to *Dept E.P., Penguin Books Ltd, Harmondsworth, Middlesex, UB7 0DA*

If you have any difficulty in obtaining a title, please send your order with the correct money, plus ten per cent for postage and packaging, to *PO Box No 11, West Drayton, Middlesex*

In the United States: Please write to *Dept BA, Penguin, 299 Murray Hill Parkway, East Rutherford, New Jersey 07073*

In Canada: Please write to *Penguin Books Canada Ltd, 2801 John Street, Markham, Ontario L3R 1B4*

In Australia: Please write to the *Marketing Department, Penguin Books Australia Ltd, P.O. Box 257, Ringwood, Victoria 3134*

In New Zealand: Please write to the *Marketing Department, Penguin Books (NZ) Ltd, Private Bag, Takapuna, Auckland 9*

In India: Please write to *Penguin Overseas Ltd, 706 Eros Apartments, 56 Nehru Place, New Delhi, 110019*

In Holland: Please write to *Penguin Books Nederland B.V., Postbus 195, NL-1380AD Weesp, Netherlands*

In Germany: Please write to *Penguin Books Ltd, Friedrichstrasse 10–12, D–6000 Frankfurt Main 1, Federal Republic of Germany*

In Spain: Please write to *Longman Penguin España, Calle San Nicolas 15, E–28013 Madrid, Spain*

In France: Please write to *Penguin Books Ltd, 39 Rue de Montmorency, F-75003, Paris, France*

In Japan: Please write to *Longman Penguin Japan Co Ltd, Yamaguchi Building, 2–12–9 Kanda Jimbocho, Chiyoda-Ku, Tokyo 101, Japan*

FOR THE BEST IN PAPERBACKS, LOOK FOR THE 🐧

A CHOICE OF PENGUINS

The Second World War (6 volumes)   Winston S. Churchill

The definitive history of the cataclysm which swept the world for the second time in thirty years.

1917: The Russian Revolutions and the Origins of Present-Day Communism
Leonard Schapiro

A superb narrative history of one of the greatest episodes in modern history by one of our greatest historians.

Imperial Spain 1496–1716   J. H. Elliot

A brilliant modern study of the sudden rise of a barren and isolated country to be the greatest power on earth, and of its equally sudden decline. 'Outstandingly good' – *Daily Telegraph*

Joan of Arc: The Image of Female Heroism   Marina Warner

'A profound book, about human history in general and the place of women in it' – Christopher Hill

Man and the Natural World: Changing Attitudes in England 1500–1800
Keith Thomas

'A delight to read and a pleasure to own' – Auberon Waugh in the *Sunday Telegraph*

The Making of the English Working Class   E. P. Thompson

Probably the most imaginative – and the most famous – post-war work of English social history.